Scheduling: Algorithms and Applications

Scheduling: Algorithms and Applications

Editor

Frank Werner

MDPI • Basel • Beijing • Wuhan • Barcelona • Belgrade • Manchester • Tokyo • Cluj • Tianjin

Editor
Frank Werner
Otto-von-Guericke University
Magdeburg, Germany

Editorial Office
MDPI
St. Alban-Anlage 66
4052 Basel, Switzerland

This is a reprint of articles from the Special Issue published online in the open access journal *Algorithms* (ISSN 1999-4893) (available at: https://www.mdpi.com/journal/algorithms/special_issues/Scheduling_Algorithms_Applications).

For citation purposes, cite each article independently as indicated on the article page online and as indicated below:

LastName, A.A.; LastName, B.B.; LastName, C.C. Article Title. *Journal Name* **Year**, *Volume Number*, Page Range.

ISBN 978-3-0365-8276-4 (Hbk)
ISBN 978-3-0365-8277-1 (PDF)

Contents

About the Editor

Frank Werner

Frank Werner studied mathematics from 1975 to 1980 and graduated from the Technical University Magdeburg (Germany) with honors. He received a Ph.D. degree (with summa cum laude) in Mathematics in 1984 and defended his habilitation thesis in 1989. From this time on, he worked at the Faculty of Mathematics of the Otto-von-Guericke University Magdeburg in Germany, and since 1998 as an extraordinary professor. In 1992, he received a grant from the Alexander von Humboldt Foundation. He was a manager of several research projects supported by the German Research Society (DFG) and the European Union (INTAS). Since 2019, he has been the Editor-in-Chief of the journal *Algorithms*. He is also an Associate Editor of the *International Journal of Production Research*, of the *Journal of Scheduling*, and the *Journal of Operations Research and Decisions* and a member of the editorial/advisory boards of 15 further international journals. He has been a guest editor of Special Issues in nine international journals, and has served as a member of the program committee of more than 125 international conferences. Frank Werner is an author/editor of 12 books, among them the textbooks *Mathematics of Economics and Business* and *A Refresher Course in Mathematics*. In addition, he has co-edited three proceedings volumes and published more than 300 journal papers, e.g., in the *International Journal of Production Research*, *Computers & Operations Research*, *Journal of Scheduling*, *Applied Mathematical Modelling*, or the *European Journal of Operational Research*. He received Best Paper Awards from the *International Journal of Production Research* (2016) and *IISE Transactions* (2021). His main research subjects are scheduling, discrete optimization, graph theory, and mathematical problems in operations research.

Preface to "Scheduling: Algorithms and Applications"

This is the printed edition of a Special Issue published in the journal *Algorithms*. After the great success of two previous Special Issues published in the same journal in the 2018 and 2020, a third issue was set up in 2021 which again found great resonance. The goal of this issue was to present innovative approaches to solving scheduling problems and finding interesting applications. Potential topics included single-criterion and multi-criteria scheduling problems with additional constraints, such as setup times/costs, precedence constraints, batching/lot sizing, and resource constraints, as well as scheduling algorithms for problems arising in emerging applications, such as healthcare, transport, and energy management.

Since scheduling is an interdisciplinary subject and plays an important role in many fields, this reprint might be interesting not only for applied mathematicians and computer science experts, but also for engineers or economists working in specific areas of optimization or operations research. This reprint presents papers dealing with very different subjects, among them a survey of assembly and production line design and scheduling under uncertainty. Other topics addressed in this reprint include the energy management of power systems, cost scheduling for financial data supply chains, staff scheduling in the construction industry, various assignment problems, single-lane roundabouts, robotic arm-based batching systems with conveyor belts, as well as single-machine and flow-shop scheduling problems, with the hope that readers will find fresh inspiration for future research in this area.

Finally, thanks are given to all who contributed to the success of this issue: authors from 13 countries, many referees from all over the world, and the journal's staff.

Frank Werner
Editor

algorithms

MDPI

Editorial

Special Issue "Scheduling: Algorithms and Applications"

Frank Werner

Faculty of Mathematics, Otto-von-Guericke University Magdeburg, 39106 Magdeburg, Germany; frank.werner@ovgu.de; Tel.: +49-391-675-2025

1. Introduction

This special issue of *Algorithms* is dedicated to recent developments of scheduling algorithms and new applications. After the Special Issue on Algorithms for Scheduling Problems, which had 12 papers (see [1]), and the Special Issue on Exact and Heuristic Scheduling Algorithms, which had 9 papers (see [2]), both of which are also available as printed books, this is the third issue in the field of Scheduling in the journal *Algorithms* since 2018 and underlines the increasing interest of researchers in this subject.

For this issue, high-quality papers were solicited to address both theoretical and practical issues in the wide area of Scheduling. Some topics mentioned in the Call for Papers for this issue were enumerative and approximate scheduling algorithms; meta- and matheuristics; scheduling algorithms for problems in logistics, transport, timetabling, healthcare, and energy management; and scheduling under uncertainty, to name a few.

After a careful refereeing process, 12 papers were selected for this issue. As a rule, all submissions have been reviewed by two or three experts in the corresponding area. The authors of the accepted papers come from 13 countries: Belarus, United Arab Emirates, Colombia, China, Korea, Japan, Indonesia, Czech Republic, Greece, Croatia, Denmark, Morocco, and India. First, the review and then the published papers in increasing order of their publication dates for this special issue are briefly surveyed.

2. Special Issue

The survey paper [3] deals with the design, balancing, and scheduling of assembly and production lines under inaccurate data. This paper discusses 149 references from the recent literature on this interesting research field, in particular 30 surveys and books on assembly and production lines published after 1986, as well as about 100 papers since 1998 for assembly lines and about 30 papers since 2014 dealing with disassembly lines. After first briefly giving deterministic formulations and variants of generalizations of the simple assembly line balancing problem, stochastic, fuzzy, and uncertain formulations of such problems are reviewed. Finally, some unsolved research issues are discussed, and various new settings in this research area are suggested.

The first accepted paper [4] deals with the energy management of a power system with multiple energy sources. The goal is the minimization of the power consumption from all sources, which is needed to satisfy the power demand of the system. The authors present a mathematical model and derive a heuristic approach. Both approaches are tested and analyzed on a ground robot with multiple energy sources.

The second paper [5] studies a multi-criteria permutation flow-shop scheduling problem, where both the processing times and the setup times are of stochastic nature. The authors consider four optimization criteria, namely two quantitative and two qualitative criteria. For this problem, they suggest a hybridized simheuristic approach that combines a GRASP procedure, a Monte Carlo simulation, a Pareto archived evolution strategy, and an analytic hierarchy process. Detailed computational results are presented to test the effects of the processing times and the sequence-dependent setup times.

Citation: Werner, F. Special Issue "Scheduling: Algorithms and Applications". *Algorithms* **2023**, *16*, 268. https://doi.org/10.3390/a16060268

Received: 25 May 2023
Accepted: 26 May 2023
Published: 27 May 2023

In the paper [6], the authors deal with the scheduling of a financial data supply chain in order to evaluate the performance of the efficiency of the banking sector. In particular, the objective is the minimization of different cost types subject to such constraints as the availability of the resources, the customer service level, and the dependency relations of the tasks. This paper develops an iterative dynamic scheduling algorithm to handle the data batching process, which turned out to be effective. In addition, a sensitivity analysis is presented when the parameters of the problems are varied.

The paper [7] considers hybrid mixed-flow workshop scheduling with the goal of minimizing the maximum completion time. Using the Spark platform, they develop a hybrid particle swarm algorithm, which is parallelized. The presented parallel algorithm is particularly effective in the case of large batches and avoids falling into a local optimum.

In the paper [8], a problem from the construction industry in Korea is investigated. In particular, a staff scheduling strategy is suggested, which also considers the irregular absence of employees and a new labor policy by applying linear programming. They derive a deterministic staff schedule and then, via a sensitivity analysis and simulation dealing with the stochastic characteristics of absence, various proactive cases are presented.

The paper [9] investigates a User-PC computing system and presents a static assignment algorithm of uniform jobs to workers in such a system. For finding a lower bound on the makespan, the authors use simultaneous linear equations. Moreover, the paper considers the extension of the algorithm to the case of multiple job types. Computational experiments are made for 651 uniform jobs in 3 applications to run on 6 workers in the testbed system. In the future, they also planned to use this algorithm for a multi-criteria shop scheduling problem.

The paper [10] considers an assignment problem and some modifications which can be converted to routing, distribution, or scheduling problems. For some of the resulting variants, the authors focus on the direct use of mixed-integer programming models within the GAMS environment. Finally, benchmark instances of the permutation flow-shop problem and the travelling salesman problem are applied to present the limits of the applicability of the software. In particular, they show that permutation flow-shop problems with 20 jobs and 10 machines, as well as travelling salesman problems with 100 cities, can be solved within a few minutes using GAMS.

In the paper [11], single machine scheduling problems with time-dependent capacity and the objective to minimize the total aggregated tardiness are considered. The authors formulate linear programming and constraint programming models. In addition, three local search schemes are presented, which are applied in a hybrid approach that takes advantage of the constraint programming part. Detailed computational results confirm that for 48 of the considered instances, new best values have been found by the suggested approach.

The paper [12] deals with a problem related to the design of roundabouts with the goal of reducing the uncertainty in decision making during the final design stage. In particular, they analyze and compare the performance estimations of the roundabout using an analytical and a regression model to give recommendations for possible changes in the geometric parameters of a roundabout. In the experiments, the authors generated 60 single-lane roundabouts with 4 legs, which have different sizes and leg alignments. It turned out that the regression model estimated a higher functionality.

The next paper [13] considers a robotic-arm-based food processing system with multiple conveyors, namely an infeed conveyor and two tray lane conveyors. The core problem consists of fixing which item on an infeed conveyor belt is selected by which robotic arm at which position, and on which tray this item will be located. For this problem, the scheduling part must be solved almost in real time. The authors suggest to decompose the problem into sub-problems formulated as a goal program, where the robotic arms are scheduled only for a single tray. Then, the authors test their approach under a simulation environment.

The last accepted paper [14] considers the flow-shop scheduling problem by minimizing the makespan. For this problem, a hybrid metaheuristic algorithm is presented which combines a genetic algorithm with a so-called spotted hyena optimization algorithm. The algorithm has been tested and compared with other state-of-the-art algorithms on instances of the OR library. It turned out that the new algorithm generates optimal or near-optimal solutions and also outperforms existing algorithms, which is confirmed by the application of several statistical analyses.

Finally, as the editor, it is my pleasure to thank the editorial staff of the journal *Algorithms* for their pleasant cooperation, not only during the preparation of this volume, but also for the previous Special Issues which I handled as editor for the journal. I would also like to thank all referees for their thorough and timely reports on the submitted works, and also the authors for submitting many interesting works from a broad spectrum in the Scheduling field.

Funding: This research received no external funding.

Conflicts of Interest: The author declares no conflict of interest.

References

1. Werner, F.; Burtseva, L.; Sotskov, Y. (Eds.) Special Issue on Algorithms for Scheduling Problems. *Algorithms* **2018**, *11*, 87. [CrossRef]
2. Werner, F.; Burtseva, L.; Sotskov, Y. (Eds.) Special Issue on Exact and Heuristic Scheduling Algorithms. *Algorithms* **2020**, *13*, 9. [CrossRef]
3. Sotskov, Y. Assembly and Production Line Designing, Balancing and Scheduling with Inaccurate Data: A Survey and Perspectives. *Algorithms* **2022**, *16*, 100. [CrossRef]
4. Salah, O.; Shamayleh, A.; Mukhopadhyay, S. Energy Management of a Multi-Source Power System. *Algorithms* **2021**, *14*, 206. [CrossRef]
5. Gonzalez-Neira, E.M.; Montoya-Torres, J.R.; Jimenez, J.-F. A Multicriteria Simheuristic Approach for Solving a Stochastic Permutation Flow Shop Scheduling Problem. *Algorithms* **2021**, *14*, 210. [CrossRef]
6. Sadawi, A.A.; Shamayleh, A.; Ndiaye, M. Efficient Dynamic Cost Scheduling Algorithm for Financial Data Supply Chain. *Algorithms* **2021**, *11*, 211. [CrossRef]
7. Zheng, T.; Wang, J.; Cai, Y. Parallel Hybrid Particle Swarm Algorithm for Workshop Scheduling Based on Spark. *Algorithms* **2021**, *14*, 262. [CrossRef]
8. Park, C.H.; Ko, Y.D. A Practical Staff Scheduling Strategy Considering Various Types of Employment in the Construction Industry. *Algorithms* **2022**, *15*, 321. [CrossRef]
9. Zhou, X.; Funabiki, N.; Htet, H.; Kamoyedji, A.; Anggraini, I.T.; Huo, Y.; Syaifudin, Y.W. A Static Assignment Algorithm of Uniform Jobs to Workers in a User-PC Computing System Using Simultaneous Linear Equations. *Algorithms* **2022**, *15*, 369. [CrossRef]
10. Seda, M. The Assignment Problem and its Relation to Logistics Problems. *Algorithms* **2022**, *15*, 377. [CrossRef]
11. Valouxis, C.; Gogos, C.; Dimitsas, A.; Potikas, P.; Vittas, A. A Hybrid Exact-Local Search Approach for One–Machine Scheduling with Time-Dependent Capacity. *Algorithms* **2022**, *15*, 450. [CrossRef]
12. Ivancev, A.C.; Ahac, M.; Ahac, S.; Dragcevic, V. Comparison of Single-Lane Roundabout Entry Degree of Saturation Estimations from Analytical and Regression Models. *Algorithms* **2023**, *16*, 164. [CrossRef]
13. Nielsen, K.G.; Sung, I.; El Yafrani, M.; Kilic, D.K.; Nielsen, P. A Scheduling Solution for Robotic Arm-Based Batching Systems with Multiple Conveyor Belts. *Algorithms* **2023**, *16*, 172. [CrossRef]
14. Mzili, T.; Mzili, I.; Riffi, M.E.; Dhiman, G. Hybrid Genetic and Spotted Hyena Optimizer for Flow Shop Scheduling Problem. *Algorithms* **2023**, *16*, 265. [CrossRef]

algorithms

MDPI

Review

Assembly and Production Line Designing, Balancing and Scheduling with Inaccurate Data: A Survey and Perspectives

Yuri N. Sotskov

United Institute of Informatics Problems, National Academy of Sciences of Belarus, 6 Surganov Street, 220012 Minsk, Belarus; sotskov48@mail.ru; Tel.: +375-17-249-61-20

Abstract: Assembly lines (conveyors) are traditional means of large-scale and mass-scale productions. An assembly line balancing problem is needed for optimizing the assembly process by configuring and designing an assembly line for the same or similar types of final products. This problem consists of designing the assembly line and distributing the total workload for manufacturing each unit of the fixed product to be assembled among the ordered workstations along the constructed assembly line. The assembly line balancing research is focused mainly on simple assembly line balancing problems, which are restricted by a set of conditions making a considered assembly line ideal for research. A lot of published research has been carried out in order to describe and solve (usually heuristically) more realistic generalized assembly line balancing problems. Assembly line designing, balancing and scheduling problems with not deterministic (stochastic, fuzzy or uncertain) parameters have been investigated in many published research works. This paper is about the design and optimization methods for assembly and disassembly lines. We survey the recent developments for designing, balancing and scheduling assembly (disassembly) lines. New formulations of simple assembly line balancing problems are presented in order to take into account modifications and uncertainties characterized by real assembly productions.

Keywords: survey; assembly line; optimal line balance; scheduling; uncertainty; stability analysis

Citation: Sotskov, Y.N. Assembly and Production Line Designing, Balancing and Scheduling with Inaccurate Data: A Survey and Perspectives. *Algorithms* **2023**, *16*, 100. https://doi.org/10.3390/a16020100

Academic Editor: Dimitris Fotakis

Received: 7 November 2022
Revised: 4 February 2023
Accepted: 5 February 2023
Published: 10 February 2023

1. Introduction

The assembly line (conveyor) is widely used in large-scale and mass production for the assembly of the same or similar types of products. The assembly line provides strategic production of products close in purpose to existing parts and components, with insignificant costs for training of working personnel. Most assembly lines consist of a linearly ordered set: $S = \{S_1, S_2, \ldots, S_m\}$, of the workstations interconnected by a step-by-step moving belt or other moving mechanism. Each workstation, $S_k \in S$, makes a fixed set, $V_k^b \in V = \{1, 2, \ldots, n\}$, of indivisible assembly operations over a planned cycle time, c. An industrial enterprise organizing a conveyor production must first design an assembly line by determining its composition and configuration. During the exploiting of the designed assembly conveyor, the problem of balancing the assembly line to increase its productivity needs be repeatedly solved. Among the optimization problems that arise at various stages of the assembly line lifecycle, the most important is the problem of balancing the assembly line. Such a problem is denoted by the ALBP (assembly line balancing problem) [1]. To solve the ALBP, it is necessary to optimally distribute a set of all given assembly operations, $V = \{1, 2, \ldots, n\}$, between the available workstations, $S = \{S_1, S_2, \ldots, S_m\}$, which are necessary for assembling the final products of the enterprise.

This review discusses the published results on optimal designing, balancing and scheduling assembly and production lines with inaccurate, not deterministic parameters (such as stochastic parameters, fuzzy parameters or uncertain parameters). The main attention is paid to the most studied simple assembly line balancing problems (SALBP for short) and some of their generalizations (GALBP), which allow a scheduler to more fully consider the specifics of a particular conveyor production. We use the generally accepted classification of the problems of balancing assembly lines presented in [1–3] and the monograph [4]. The numerical parameters of assembly lines are specified, and the permissible restrictions and conditions are listed in Section 2. Various assembly line designing, balancing and scheduling problems and methods for optimization of them are presented based on the articles published in the last two and a half decades.

Due to the high importance of the assembly line designing, balancing and scheduling for mass and large-scale series production, large amounts of relevant research papers have been published in operational research (OR) literature. Most such papers were surveyed in [5–10]. In particular, the paper by Boysen et al. [5] surveys the OR literature on assembly line designing, balancing and scheduling that has been published after previous review papers appeared in 2006, 2007 and 2009 [6–9]. The authors of [5] cover essential stages of the decision processes, including different approaches to the ALBP. Their survey is a supplement and continuation of the previous survey papers on the SALBP [6], the GALBP [7] and the classification schemes of the ALBP [3,7,9]. Other survey papers published after 2009 cover some specific aspects of the ALBP. In particular, the paper [10] surveys two-sided assembly lines. The paper [11] surveys the requirements of different real-world applications. The papers [12,13] surveyed the ALBP that were solved using soft computing. The paper [14] surveys genetic algorithms used for solving the ALBP. The paper [15] surveys balancing of multiple and parallel assembly lines. The paper [16] surveys cost- and profit-oriented assembly line balancing problems. The paper [17] surveys rebalancing of the unbalanced assembly lines. Disassembly line balancing problems are surveyed in the paper [18]. The paper [19] surveys the ALBP arising in industry 4.0. A bibliographic analysis of the ALBP through the Web of Science in the period from 1990 to 2017 is presented in [20].

This paper is about the design and optimization algorithms for assembly (disassembly) lines. The survey covers assembly line designing, balancing and scheduling problems with inaccurate parameters (i.e., stochastic, fuzzy or uncertain numerical parameters) and different variations from the deterministic manufactory conditions. This survey may be considered as a continuation of the surveys in [21,22]. We first consider deterministic formulations of the SALBP, ALBP and GALBP with different types of variations from the fixed manufactory conditions. Then, we review the stochastic, fuzzy and uncertain formulations of the SALBP, ALBP and GALBP, along with disassembly line balancing problems under uncertainty. This paper covers about 30 surveys and books on assembly and production lines published since 1986, about 100 research papers since 1998 for assembly lines and about 30 research papers since 2014 for disassembly lines.

The sections are ordered with respect to the increasingly considered problem uncertainties. In Section 2, we determine the scope of this survey and describe the considered problem settings. The deterministic ALBP with possible deviation from normal (deterministic) manufactory conditions are considered in Section 3. The ALBP with stochastic or fuzzy parameters are surveyed in Section 4. Designing and balancing production lines of disassembly of similar obsolete products are considered in Section 5. Section 6 addresses to designing, balancing and scheduling assembly lines with uncertain (interval) parameters. Before concluding in Section 8, in Section 7, some unresolved issues are discussed and several new settings for designing, balancing and scheduling the assembly and production lines are proposed, allowing taking into account fuller economic indicators of assembly and production lines, as well as the uncertainty characteristic of operating conveyors.

2. A Division of Manual Labor, Assembly and Production Lines

In 1776, Smith [23] identified the advantages of the division of manual labor, which made it possible to increase labor productivity as a result of the specialization of workers in the joint manufacture of simple products. A century and a half later, on the basis of assembly conveyors that were used in Chicago's food factories in the United States, Ford [24] combined, in a moving stream, the process of assembling a car by operators who specialized in a limited set of specific assembly operations. In Ford factories, assembly conveyors were used to make car components and to assemble the entire car. Since then, more than a century has passed, and assembly lines are still widely used both for the production of fairly simple products and for the assembly of complex products in large-scale and mass production. Modern assembly lines are specialized production systems designed to assemble similar types of products in rather large quantities. Assembly lines have been used in mass production, ensuring a rhythmic assembly of products with limited operator training costs. Training of workstation operators is carried out in a short time. Workstations of modern assembly lines are often robotic. Industrial robots perform the most complex assembly operations in the absence of people on such types of workstations.

The mathematical statements of the ALBP were first described by Salveson [1], who discussed the various configurations of assembly lines and the optimization problems of assigning (balancing) assembly operations to the workstations. Due to the complexity of the problems of designing and controlling assembly lines, the researchers looked at various constraints that simplified the actual problems of balancing the pipeline. Such simplifications were summarized by Baybars [2], who considered the problem of balancing an assembly line with nine conditions, (1)–(9) (see Section 2.1), simplifying a real assembly problem, called a simple assembly line balancing problem (SALBP). There are many essential differences between the SALBP and the actual assembly lines and production lines. In the OR literature, the approximations of the SALBP to the real conveyor production were based on the easing of certain limitations and conditions of the SALBP. Various generalizations based on the weakening of the conditions of the SALBP are called a general assembly line balancing problem, denoted as GALBP.

2.1. Simple Assembly Line Balancing Problems

Distribution, $V = V_1^b \cup V_2^b \cup \ldots \cup V_m^b$, of the given set of assembly operations, V, between the available workstations, $S = \{S_1, S_2, \ldots, S_m\}$ (i.e., splitting a partially ordered set V of assembly operations on m non-intersecting subsets), is called a line balance, $b = (V_1^b, V_2^b, \ldots, V_m^b)$, of the assembly line, $S = \{S_1, S_2, \ldots, S_m\}$. A line balance is feasible, if a technological order of all assembly operations that is determined by the precedence digraph, $G = (V, A)$, is not violated, where V denotes a set of vertices and A is a set of directed arcs. A search for the optimal assembly line balance, $b = (V_1^b, V_2^b, \ldots, V_m^b)$, is called an assembly line balancing problem (ALBP).

Large financial costs for the design, manufacture, installation and equipment of the assembly line can pay off only with a periodical optimization of the line balance, $b = (V_1^b, V_2^b, \ldots, V_m^b)$, used for the assembly line, $S = \{S_1, S_2, \ldots, S_m\}$. Repeatedly balancing the assembly line increases the productivity of the assembly conveyor, and therefore the efficiency of the entire assembly plant. Balancing the assembly line provides the required performance of the assembly line with minimal (or limited) costs for its assembly operations. The most studied problems of the balancing of the assembly line are the SALBP. As stated in the review in [2] and monograph in [4], the following conditions must be met for the SALBP: (A-1) all input parameters of the ALBP are deterministic, (A-2) each assembly operation is indivisible (its execution cannot be divided between two or more workstations), (A-3) the sequence of indivisible assembly operations is subject to the precedence constraints specified by the digraph $G = (V, A)$ and (A-4) all assembly operations are performed within the cycle time, C, uniquely determined for all workstations of the assembly line.

The ALBP is to distribute assembly operations, $V = \{1, 2, \ldots, n\}$, between the ordered workstations, $S_1, S_2, \ldots, S_m$ (therefore, it is necessary to determine the line balance, $b = (V_1^b, V_2^b, \ldots, V_m^b)$, of the assembly line, $S = \{S_1, S_2, \ldots, S_m\}$), in such a way that the specified criterion is optimized and the specified conditions are not violated. The optimization criterion and conditions of the ALBP are specified in advance. In addition to the above conditions (A-1)–(A-4), the following conditions must be met for a simple assembly line balancing problem: (A-5) All workstations, $S_1, S_2, \ldots, S_m$, are equipped in such a way that each of them can perform any of the assembly operations V. (A-6) The duration of the assembly operation does not depend on the workstation, S_k, to which it is assigned, and this duration does not depend on the workstation, S_{k+1}, following the workstation, S_k, nor does it depend on the previous workstation,S_{k-1}. (A-7) An assembly operation can be performed on any available workstation of the set, $S = \{S_1, S_2, \ldots, S_m\}$. (A-8) The assembly line is serial without duplication of parallel workstations and without taking into accounts the operation of the workpieces' feeding mechanisms. (A-9) The assembly line is designed to produce one type of product during its lifetime (during the whole lifecycle of the assembly line).

2.2. Optimal Design of an Assembly Line and Optimization of the Existing Assembly Line

In the process of designing an assembly line, the ALBP of balancing the assembly line with a predetermined (fixed) cycle time, c, arises. This problem is called SALBP-1 in [2,4]. In addition to the above conditions (A-1)–(A-9), the following condition must be met in the SALBP-1: (A-10) the cycle time, c, is assumed to be constant (fixed) during the whole lifecycle of the assembly line. In the SALBP-1, it is required to assign assembly operations, V, to a linearly ordered set of workstations, $S_1, S_2, \ldots, S_m$, and thus to minimize the number of available workstations in use at a given and fixed cycle time, c. In practice, such a problem is solved at the design stage of the assembly line.

In the process of operating the assembly line, it becomes necessary to solve the SALBP-2 for balancing the assembly line with a fixed set of workstations, which consists in determining the optimal balance of the assembly line at a given number m of the ordered workstations. To solve the SALBP-2, it is required to minimize the possible cycle time, c, when assigning assembly operations, V, on the given set, $S = \{S_1, S_2, \ldots, S_m\}$, of the workstations, i.e., it is necessary to find such an optimal line balance, $b = (V_1^b, V_2^b, \ldots, V_m^b)$, of operations, V, and workstations, $S = \{S_1, S_2, \ldots, S_m\}$, in which the cycle time, c, reaches the minimum possible value. In the SALBP-2, the following condition must be met instead of the condition (A-10): (A-11) a number m, of the workstations, $S = \{S_1, S_2, \ldots, S_m\}$, is given and fixed. The described SALBP-1 and SALBP-2 are two-fold [2].

The OR literature discusses a third more general class of the simple assembly line balancing problems, when neither the number of workstations, m, nor the cycle time, C, is fixed. It is necessary to maximize the efficiency of the assembly line. Such a problem is denoted by SALBP-E [2,4,25]. The efficiency, E, of the assembly line is determined by the following equality:

$$E = t_{sum}/(m \cdot c), \tag{1}$$

where $t_{sum} = \sum_{i=1}^{n} t_i$ denotes the sum of durations, $t_i, i \in V$, of the assembly operations.

2.3. Generalizations of the SALBP and Complexity of These Problems

The OR literature contains investigations of different formulations of the ALBP that result from the weakening of one or more conditions, (A-1)–(A-9). An assembly line can be used to produce several modifications of a product that are divided into batches. Such assembly lines are called multi-model lines. The assembly line can be used to produce two or more modifications of the same product. Different modifications of the product can be mixed in the process of their assembly. Such assembly lines in the OR literature are called mixed-model assembly lines [26–29]. Assembly line configurations can vary. In particular, article [27] discusses a U-shaped assembly line for a mixed-model ALBP. In articles [10,29–33], the SALBP is considered for a two-way assembly line, when workstations are located on both sides of a linear or U-shaped conveyor belt. The assembly line may have parallel workstations that may duplicate one another in the event of a workstation breakdown [34,35]. Other generalizations of the simple assembly line balancing problem can be found in [36,37]. No matter what goal is considered in the problem (minimizing cycle time, C, minimizing the number of workstations or maximizing the efficiency, E), generalized assembly line balancing problems are called general assembly line balancing problems [38]. Thus, the GALBP can denote a generalization of the SALBP-1, the SALBP-2 or the SALBP-E.

It should be noted that «simple» SALBP-1, SALBP-2 and SALBP-E are in fact binary NP-hard even in the simplest possible case, i.e., when $m = 2$ and the given precedence digraph $G = (V, A)$ does not contain any arc, $A = \varnothing$ (it is clear that there is no conveyer with $m = 1$). Thus, one could use the term «ideal» instead of «simple» for the NP-hard SALBP. The proof of the NP-hardness of the SALBP-1, SALBP-2 and SALBP-E follows from the fact that the binary NP-hard scheduling problem, $I2||C_{max}$ (see monographs in [39,40] on scheduling theory), is reduced in a polynomial number of elementary operations to a determined special case of the SALBP, namely: SALBP-1, SALBP-2 and SALBP-E. Hereafter, a three-field notation, $\alpha|\beta|\gamma$, is used to denote a scheduling problem, in which α indicates the type of processing system, β denotes specified restrictions on the set of jobs to be processed and γ denotes the criterion of optimality (see [41]). In particular, in the problem $I2||C_{max}$, it is necessary to construct a schedule with minimum schedule length C_{max} for fulfilling a given set of jobs on two identical machines. The proof of the NP-hardness of the SALBP can be found in the monograph [4].

Before starting the survey section, it would be useful to explain why the remaining Sections 3–7 are mainly devoted to the SALBP. Note that a simple assembly line balancing problem may be rarely met in real-world productions, since the most practical assembly lines violate some or most conditions of (A-1)–(A-11). On the other hand, the most final mathematical results (lemmas and theorems) have been proven only for the SALBP-1, SALBP-2 and SALBP-E. Furthermore, these mathematical results may be used for real assembly and production lines. Due to the limited paper length, the proven mathematical claims are not presented in Sections 3–7 (they are only mentioned in their descriptions). Hopefully, increasing the uncertainty level in the considered ALBP may be useful for constructing a bridge between the ideal SALBP and practical assembly and production lines.

3. Deterministic Problems of Designing and Balancing Assembly Lines with Deviations from Normally Fixed Conditions

If the condition (A-1) for the ALBP is met with a possible change in the other conditions, (A-2)–(A-9), and then such a problem is called a deterministic ALBP. For the deterministic ALBP, the durations of assembly operations, $t_i, i \in V$, are given and do not change during the whole lifecycle of the assembly conveyer. The deterministic ALBP is formulated as follows. A set of assembly operations is specified: $V = \{1, 2, \ldots, n\}$. For each operation, a fixed processing time (duration) is given along with the digraph $G = (V, A)$, which determines the partial strict order on the set V of assembly operations. The deterministic ALBP is to assign assembly operations, V, to the ordered set of workstations $(S_1, S_2, \ldots, S_m)$, such that the precedence relations given in the digraph $G = (V, A)$ are not disturbed and the objective function would take the optimal value. The deterministic SALBP is well-studied, and many exact, approximate and heuristic algorithms have been developed for these problems (see [1–5,10,26–38,42–52]). This section is focused on designing and balancing assembly lines with possible deviations from normal manufacture conditions.

The article [2] presents the exact algorithms for solving the SALBP. In the article [42], the authors divided the published algorithms for solving the ALBP into two groups. The first group includes precise algorithms that guarantee the optimal solution to the ALBP, and the second group includes heuristic algorithms that lead to some acceptable solution to the ALBP, not necessarily optimal. This article contains an overview of heuristic algorithms used for the ALBP, an efficiency comparison of algorithms for solving the ALBP and an overview of the exact and approximate algorithms for solving the multi-model ALBP. The article [43] compared the procedures proposed for solving the SALBP-1. The article [44] presents a hybrid artificial intelligent algorithm, which realizes an artificial immune system in combination with a simulated annealing algorithm. The algorithm aims at enhancing the performance of an artificial immune system via incorporating simulated annealing in order to achieve a global optimum for assembly conveyers with a rather large number of assembly operations. The new algorithm was implemented on a mechanical assembly composed of seven parts joined by connectors. The algorithm was effective in achieving an optimum with a restricted CPU time compared to other artificial intelligent algorithms.

The article [45] describes the application of a differential evolution algorithm to the SALBP. This algorithm is an evolutionary one, similar to a genetic algorithm for global optimization over continuous spaces. The extensive experimental work over public benchmark test instances showed the effectiveness of this algorithm. In most investigated SALBP, smoothing workstation loads were considered. In the work [46], a differential evolution algorithm was developed for minimization of the workload smoothness index in the SALBP-2. The parameters were optimized based on the Taguchi method. To validate the algorithm, the computational experimental results were compared with other published heuristics. The comparison indicated the effectiveness of the new algorithm. An optimization of the numerical parameters has been addressed in order to minimize a workload smoothness index. After presenting a mathematical model, a differential evolution algorithm was developed to minimize the smoothness index. Some advantages were based on a suitable mutation, which ensures the search diversity and enhances the effectiveness based on properties of the objective function. The values of numerical parameters in the developed algorithm have been tuned based on the sizes of the tested instances. A detailed statistical experiment showed that except for one from the medium-sized problems, the levels of other numerical parameters influenced the efficiency of the addressed algorithms for other problems. The computational results indicated supremacy of the algorithm over tested heuristics for small, medium and large instances.

The article [47] is devoted to supply chain designing and conveyer balancing. These problems cover an optimization of manufacturers, assembly conveyers and customer demands. Due to analyzing the characteristics and complexities of the ALBP, the authors of this article decomposed the problem into an upper-level problem and two lower-level problems. The former was used to determine the assignment amount of each assembler. The latter includes the ALBP inside each assembler and the transportation problem between different layers. In order to solve this problem heuristically, a meta-heuristic was developed. The ALBP was exactly solved by a branch-and-bound method. A table method was developed in order to speed up the computations. A transportation problem was solved via mathematical programming. Due to solving the lower-level problems, the cost function of the upper-level problem was evaluated. In order to optimize the upper-level problem, a meta-heuristic was developed. In a population initialization, the specific heuristics were designed. Several numerical tests demonstrated the effectiveness of the proposed algorithms.

The application of industrial robots in mechanical conveyers usually increases the efficiency of industrial productions. Different robot assembly strategies have been used. Fault monitoring and strategy evaluation have attracted the attention of many researchers. The paper [48] reviews the recent research in this field. Respecting the assembly process, this paper separates the research contents into target recognition, searching and fault monitoring. The main characteristics of each published approach were summarized, and evaluations of assembly strategies were proposed with respect to typical metrics. The known benchmarks for supporting a standardized performance evaluation were surveyed. The challenges and potential directions were discussed.

Multi-manned conveyers are usually used in industries to manufacture similar products of large sizes, where several human operators have to be assigned to the ordered workstations for performing a set of different assembly operations simultaneously on the same unit of the product. In the paper [49], it was mentioned that previously published mathematical formulations were able to solve a few small-sized problem instances exactly, while larger cases were solved heuristically by heuristics or meta-heuristics, which do not guarantee the optimality of the obtained solutions. A mixed-integer linear programming formulation is presented with a symmetry constraint, allowing decomposing the original problem into a Benders' decomposition to solve large problem instances. The proposed model was used to minimize the total number of human operators along the assembly conveyer and the number of used workstations as weighted primary and secondary objectives, respectively.

Feasibility cuts and symmetry break constraints were based on Benders' cuts and several numerical parameters, which were applied as constraints for reducing the solution search space via eliminating infeasible allocation sets. Computational tests conducted on the datasets showed that this mathematical model outperforms published formulations both in the solution quality and CPU time for the tested small-sized problem instances. In particular, the proposed algorithm yielded 117 optimal solutions out of 131 tested problem instances.

In the article [50], a main focus is placed on assembly conveyers, where workstations were used for assembling large and bulk products, such as complex trucks, aircrafts, buses and tool machines. The high number of assembly operations performed on the concrete workstation, the several workers simultaneously involved in the process and the long operation durations make the considered assembly conveyer different from most assembly conveyers studied in the OR literature. A conveyer balancing model was addressed to the total cost minimization provided that human operators have different skills. The proposed algorithm was applied to a real industrial case.

Flexibility in assembly conveyers can be achieved due to the use of assembly robots. The robotic ALBP is determined for a robotic assembly line, where a set of similar or different assembly robots may be included in the assembly conveyer. An assembly robot may need different assembly times to perform an assembly operation, because of different specializations. The solution to such an ALBP includes attempts for optimally assigning the robots to the ordered workstations and balancing the distribution of work between the workstations. It is necessary to maximize the production rate of the assembly conveyer. In the paper [51], a genetic algorithm was developed in order to find a heuristic solution to the considered problem. Different heuristic procedures were used for adapting the genetic algorithm to the ALBP. The assigning robots with different capabilities to the workstations were investigated based on a recursive assignment procedure and a consecutive assignment one. The genetic algorithm was improved by a local optimization (hill climbing) of the workpiece. The conducted computational tests on randomly generated instances showed that the assignment procedure achieves a better solution quality (an average cycle time), while other computational tests determine a better combination of parameters for the genetic algorithm. A comparison of the genetic algorithm with a truncated branch-and-bound method for the ALBP demonstrated that the genetic algorithm provided closed results faster than the exact branch-and-bound method. Workload smoothing on assembly conveyers that aims to evenly assign assembly operations to different workstations may support workforce planning and resource optimization. In the paper [52], the authors studied smoothing conveyers and developed an algorithm to heuristically solve a large-sized problem. To find a good heuristic solution, this algorithm uses a set of known rules for assigning assembly operations based on a probabilistic procedure for closing workstations. A computational experiment was conducted for selecting the best-performing priority rules and for tuning the probabilistic procedure. The efficiency of the proposed algorithm was experimentally tested on the computer.

Since the industrial robots are utilized in U-shaped assembly lines to replace human operators, the focus of such assembly lines is not only on productivity, but also on the carbon and noise emissions. In the paper [53], a multi-objective mixed-integer non-linear programming is proposed to minimize carbon emissions, noise emissions and cycle time, concurrently. In the proposed approach, quantifying a carbon emission and a noise emission was achieved via presentations connected with processing times of assembly operations and industrial robots. Existing constraints of the precedence relations were readjusted into an integrated formula to remove worthless equations and to improve the computational efficiency. A hybrid Pareto grey wolf optimization was used to heuristically solve these multi-objective problems. The algorithm included a code to initialize the wolves and designed two searching procedures to update the position of the wolves. Two crossover operators were designed to enhance the communication between the low-grade wolves. The algorithm was compared with five other multi-objective algorithms and the computational results indicated that the proposed algorithm outperforms the compared algorithms in the evaluation metrics of the convergence, maximum spread and hyper-volume ratio. The developed algorithm can achieve the trade-off in reducing carbon and noise emissions and minimizing the cycle time.

In the paper [54], a learning effect was studied in the ALBP. In many realistic settings, the produced workers (or machines) continuously develop by repeating the same or similar activities. The production time of the product shortens if it is processed later. It was shown that polynomial solutions can be obtained for both SALBP and U-shaped ALBP with a learning effect. In a mass manufacturing, neither human operators nor industrial robots alone can efficiently perform all assembly operations. Therefore, a human–robot collaborative conveyer shows great potential to ensure flexibility with the high reliability of robot assistance. It is usually challenging to achieve a harmonious coexistence between humans and industrial robots to efficiently complete the assembly operations. In this regard, the paper [55] provides a formalization of the human–robot coexistence and introduces a key issue in a collaborative conveyer. An assembly graph was used for representing the assembly operation of the complex products. The human network based on self-attention can achieve a higher accuracy. Combined with the robustness of a soft actor-critic, the collaborative system improves the ability of the robot in the dynamic conveyer. The effectiveness of the developed algorithm was verified through an experimental analysis. The computational results indicated that the accuracy of the proposed recognition was 91%. It was proven that the reinforcement learning method was feasible to provide an adaptive decision for industrial robots in human–machine collaboration. The convergence speed of the reward function proved the feasibility of the algorithm for adaptive decision-making in a human–robot collaborative environment.

3.1. Preventive Maintenance and Worker Assignment Problems

The article [56] addresses the mixed-model ALBP, considering preventive maintenance scenarios. A mixed-integer mathematical programming was developed in order to optimize a cycle time and assembly operation alteration. A cooperative algorithm was proposed to simplify a large-sized ALBP due to the divide-and-conquer procedure. An archive was generated to save the obtained complete solutions with better performances, evaluating the fitness of solutions. A mixed-model variable decoding procedure was designed to speed-up the decoding process of the proposed algorithm. An inter-population crossover operator was designed. Four objective-oriented neighbor search operators were proposed to promote the convergence performance of the proposed algorithm. Experimental computational results demonstrated that the algorithm allows obtaining the Pareto solutions for small-sized instances of the mixed-model ALBP. This algorithm outperformed other ones. The obtained Pareto front was close to the true Pareto front.

In the article [57], paced and un-paced assembly lines were compared via simulation on the computer. Human operators can speed-up their processing times when it is needed either to feed other workers downstream or to unblock upstream workers. In the study [57], it was found that un-paced assembly lines were superior to paced assembly lines for some real-world settings, e.g., in the mixed-model production environments with a long assembly line length. The benefit of such assembly lines has been overestimated in previously published studies because of simplifying assumptions, such as disregarding the state-dependent behavior or worker fatigue. With an inhomogeneous workforce, the assembly line efficiency was more sensitive to worker placement. In the un-paced assembly lines, an inexperienced human operator should be placed in the middle of the assembly line; while in paced assembly lines, an inexperienced worker should be placed at the first workstation of the assembly line. Assembly operators capable of speeding up should be placed in the middle of the assembly line in both tested types of assembly lines.

In the article [58], the preventive maintenance in the assembly line balancing problem is investigated for improving the production efficiency and smoothness. For such a two-objective problem, a heuristic rule based on the tacit knowledge and gene expression programming was developed to obtain a good heuristic solution rather quickly. A grey wolf optimizer was developed in order to achieve a Pareto front solution. The neighbor operators prevent the developed algorithm from trapping into local optima. The conducted computational experiments demonstrated that the heuristic rule used outperformed other published rules. A real-world case study was conducted in order to validate the proposed heuristic rule and the developed meta-heuristic rule.

In the assembly lines, it is reasonable to assume that assembly operation durations are the same for each human operator. In sheltered work centers for disabled workers, this assumption is not valid. Some human operators may execute some assembly operations considerably slower than others capable of executing them. Worker heterogeneity leads to problems, called an assembly line worker assignment and line balancing problem. For a fixed set of workers, this problem is to maximize the production rate of an assembly conveyer by assigning human operators to available workstations and assembly operations to workers, while satisfying precedence constraints between the given assembly operations. In the article [59], a heuristic algorithm and an exact algorithm to solve this problem are introduced. A mixed-integer programming formulation for this problem was also presented. The proposed heuristic algorithm is based on a beam search. The exact algorithm was a branch-and-bound method, which used reduction rules and obtained lower bounds for exact solutions. Computational tests on a set of instances showed that these algorithms were effective and improved compared to other published algorithms.

In a real assembly line, variable production situations, such as customer demand changes, the product structure variations and workstation failures, may affect the existing feasible balance of the assembly line, resulting in the need for the rebalancing of the optimal assembly line. In the desired rebalancing of the assembly conveyer, it is usually assumed in the OR literature that the duration of an assembly operation does not depend on the human operator performing it. However, in many practical cases, the time each operator requires to execute an assembly operation may vary due to several reasons (such as the worker experience, skill and disability of some individuals). In the study in [60], the assembly line worker assignment and rebalancing assembly line problem, which considers that assembly operation durations vary in terms of workers, was introduced in order to fill this gap. The considered problem consists of the re-assignment of assembly operations and workers to non-disrupted workstations after disruptions occur due to breakdowns or shutdowns of workstations to minimize variability in terms of assembly line cycle time and workstation assignments of assembly operations relative to the initial assembly line balance. The objectives of this paper are to describe the problem properties, develop a mixed-integer linear programming model and propose an artificial bee colony algorithm to heuristically solve this problem. The numerical experiments have been designed and conducted using 120 instances. The computational experiments indicated that both developed algorithms managed to obtain optimal assembly line balances for small-sized instances. For large-sized instances, the proposed algorithms showed a higher performance in terms of solution value and CPU time.

3.2. Changing Customer Demand and Optimization of Operation Sequences

The assembly sequence and path planning problem involves finding a proper sequence of parts to be assembled into a finished product and to shorten assembly paths for each such part. This problem combines assembly sequence planning and assembly path planning, which are both NP-hard problems and are therefore intractable for a large problem size. In most published results on this problem, it was assumed that path planning was monotone (i.e., each part was moved only once) and each part was completely rigid. Such simplifications are limiting assumptions. Indeed, most assembled complex products such as ships, aircraft and automobiles are composed of rigid and flexible parts. The required generation of an assembly sequence and a path plan for most real-world complex products requires an intermediate placement of parts to be taken into account. The article [61] presents an algorithm for solving both monotone and non-monotone problems for rigid and flexible parts. This algorithm uses an assembly matrix for describing different relations between all pairs of parts and the amounts of compressive stresses needed for assembling flexible parts and obtains a tentative assembly sequence using a greedy algorithm. Short assembly paths are iteratively computed from the initial one to the goal configurations of the parts using a sample path planner. In case of a failure, if the part is flexible, it is determined whether the part can still be assembled by undergoing deformation. To evaluate the developed algorithm, two products were designed, and the problem was solved via four combinations of the proposed algorithms. The means and standard deviations of five criteria were calculated. The computational results showed that the greedy heuristic algorithm outperformed other algorithms with at most a 4.6% average gap in path length and a 2.1% average gap in the CPU time compared to the best solution.

The diversification of customer demand poses a great challenge for many manufacturing enterprises and the scheduling problems of material handling affects the efficiency of assembly conveyers. In the article [62], a scheduling algorithm and a static kitting strategy were proposed in order to solve scheduling problems of the material handling for automotive mixed-model assembly lines based on the integrated super-markets. An integer programming was established with the objective to minimize the number of logistic workers. An improved kitting strategy was presented to solve the problem heuristically and a model based on the graph theory was constructed to transform the considered scheduling problem to another known one. The algorithm was developed to solve the scheduling problem. Computational experiments for the proposed algorithms were carried out in order to compare the proposed algorithms with published ones. The feasibility and effectiveness of the proposed algorithms were verified by the obtained computational results.

In the article [63], an assembly plan was investigated as one of the assembly stages to minimize the cost of a manufacturer and to ensure the safety of an assembly part. The problem of assembly sequence planning is how to reduce the deviation from the real manufacturing conditions. The authors of this paper have investigated an approach to automatically generate the assembly sequences for the industrial field. A physically based assembly representation model includes the predetermined basic assembly information (precedence relations between parts or subassemblies, geometric constraints, different assembly types) and the dynamic real-time properties (the center position of gravity, the force strength of the part). This model considered that the influences on optimum sequences by assembly operations will be modified by the feedback from an interactive virtual environment. The authors of the article [63] selected the safety, efficiency and complexity as the optimization objectives. A hybrid search approach may be used to find the optimum assembly sequence, which will be integrated into an interactive assembly virtual environment. The user can adjust the assembly sequences with obvious good objectives via interaction to improve the performance of the search algorithm. A human–machine cooperation algorithm was proposed, by which a human operator can play a pivotal role instead of pure computing. Numerical experiments were performed to validate the performance of the physical approach to generate an assembly sequence, which showed the efficiency and operability to guide the assembly work.

In the article [64], eight multi-objective ant colony optimization algorithms have been developed and compared for solving ten benchmark instances of the SALBP. Experiments on the computer showed that the commonly used heuristic functions deteriorate the performance of the developed algorithms in a limited CPU time scenario. Even neglecting such costs, the developed algorithms achieved a better performance without heuristics. The developed algorithms were ranked according to three multi-objective indicators and the calculated differences between the top four of them were reviewed using statistical tests. The four best-performing algorithms were favorably compared with the other algorithms designed for industrial optimizations.

A supplier selection problem is a strategic decision-making activity for building a competitive advantage in assembly production. Quality suppliers can understand a firm's operational goals and provide high-quality components. Achieving efficient production requires a good plan. A superior competitive strategy should consider the suppliers' availability and the plant's ability. In the article [65], production line planning was applied to address specific problems associated with a supplier selection by constructing a multi-objective optimization model. The proposed model includes both assembly sequence planning and assembly line balancing. A hybrid algorithm was proposed to heuristically solve the above problems. The proposed algorithm combines a guided search and a multi-objective particle swarm optimization, as well as a particle swarm optimization. A real case of a computer assembly plant was used to verify the algorithm's performance. The computational results showed that the proposed algorithm identifies non-dominated solutions and obtains high Pareto-optimal solution ratios.

Mixed-model assembly lines are widely used in industries where a high variety of products are required in addition to low cost and high responsiveness. When a certain product mix is demanded and different variants require different assembly times on the available workstations, the sequence of variants on the line highly affects the assembly line performance. Although assembly operations are often manual, most sequencing algorithms assume deterministic times for these operations, rendering the obtained results unreliable. The max-plus algebra is a mathematical tool that can model discrete event systems in linear equations analogous to traditional state space dynamic equations. Modeling mixed-model assembly lines with max-plus equations would enable comparing sequences over ranges of values of assembly times, thus increasing the robustness, stability and reliability of the obtained results. In the article [66], mixed-model assembly lines with both closed and open workstations were modeled using the max-plus algebra. The produced models were used to compare possible sequences and to analyze various performance measures of the assembly lines while varying some system parameters. Two examples were presented to demonstrate analyses that can be performed using the proposed model. In the first example, three possible assembly operation sequences were compared and regions of optimality for each sequence were determined. In the second example, the effect of changing the launching rate of work units on the assembly line performance was studied.

The proliferation of just-in-sequence deliveries has raised the vulnerability of assemblies to costly production stoppages or rework due to missing components. Through a real-time supply chain monitoring system, these supply issues can be detected early and affected orders can be removed from planned assembly sequences in time to avoid production disturbances. Using a simulation analysis, the authors of [67] explored the impact of unreliable just-in-sequence deliveries and the mitigation potential of transparent supply chains that allow a rule-based order re-sequencing on a mixed-model assembly line. The obtained results indicated that rework due to unreliable just-in-sequence deliveries can be eliminated and the trade-off between a schedule's uncertainty and optimality can be balanced, making the rule feasible for the considered problem.

Summarizing results published in the papers [1–5,10,26–38,42–67], one can conclude that the deterministic ALBP are convenient for research, and a lot of analytical results have been proven and derived for them. However, for real assembly and production lines, it is not always possible to determine the exact values of the durations of the given assembly operations. Actual operation durations may change during the use of the assembly line for a number of reasons. Among such reasons, one can note a change in the qualifications of the operator, his (her) motivation or fatigue, a change in the composition or purpose of the final products, a possible change in the quality of component materials and assembly parts, as well as characteristics of the operator's workplace.

4. Assembly Line Balancing Problems with Stochastic or Fuzzy Parameters

Assembly (production) line balancing is an important problem for increasing the efficiency of the production processes. However, in practice, a wide range of disruptions can interrupt the current workload balance. A lot of researchers have explored the operation assignment plan for the assembly line balancing problem with the assumption that the assembly processes are smooth with no disruptions. Based on the indicated reason, other researchers and most practitioners have investigated the impacts of disruptions and explored the assembly operation re-assignments for the assembly and production line re-balancing, with the assumption that the re-balancing decisions have been made. It should also be noted that there is limited OR literature exploring online adjustments (layout adjustments and production rate adjustments) for assembly and production lines in a dynamic environment. This is based on real-time monitoring of assembly processes (this is impossible to perform in the past tense). Furthermore, it is usually difficult to incorporate uncertainty factors into the balancing process because of the randomness and non-linearity of most uncertain factors.

Note that Industry 4.0 peaked the information barriers between different branches of assembly and production lines, since smart, interconnected products, which are enabled by advanced information and communication technology, can intelligently interact, and often communicate with each other and collect production processes and produce additional information. Smart control of the assembly and production lines becomes possible with the large amounts of real-time production data in the era of Industry 4.0. However, currently, there is little OR literature considering this new context of the assembly and production lines. Taking into account possible changes in the duration of assembly operations, other formulations of the ALBP are also considered in the OR literature, namely the stochastic ALBP [68–72] and the ALBP with fuzzy data [26,33]. The durations of assembly operations in such fuzzy ALBP belong to fuzzy sets.

The level of uncertainty in the ALBP with fuzzy data is higher than in the similar ALBP with stochastic data. Nevertheless, surveys of both ALBP are presented in the same section since a probability distribution has to be known for each random variable in the stochastic problem, and a specific membership function has to be known for each fuzzy number in the fuzzy problem. Due to this circumstance, mathematical approaches to the stochastic ALBP and those to the fuzzy ALBP have more similarity than those for the uncertain ALBP surveyed in Sections 8 and 9.

4.1. Stochastic Assembly and Production Line Balancing Problems

In the stochastic ALBP, the durations of assembly operations are random variables with a known law of distribution of their probabilities (usually, the normal law of distribution of a random variable with known mathematical expectation and variance is used). The stochastic ALBP can be formulated as follows. The set, $V = \{1, 2, \ldots, n\}$, of assembly operations is given, and the duration of each assembly operation is a random variable for which the probability distribution law is specified before solving the ALBP. The precedence digraph $G = (V, A)$ is given, which determines the partial strict order on the set V of the given assembly operations. The problem is to assign assembly operations, V, to the ordered workstations, $S_1, S_2, \ldots, S_m$, in such a way that the precedence relations determined by the digraph $G = (V, A)$ are not disturbed, and the mathematical expectation of the objective function would take the optimal (respectively, minimum or maximum) value for the desired balance, $b = (V_1^b, V_2^b, \ldots, V_m^b)$, of the assembly line.

As for the deterministic version of the assembly line balancing problem, for the stochastic ALBP, there is a finite but sufficiently large number of feasible solutions (line balances) at large values of m and n. In the article [3], the algorithms for solving stochastic problems of balancing the assembly line were divided into the following three classes: (1) modifications of algorithms developed for the deterministic ALBP [68,72], (2) study of the specific properties of the stochastic ALBP on the basis of computer modeling, with a subsequent comparison of the obtained results of solving the stochastic version and the deterministic version of the ALBP [69], and (3) algorithms developed specifically for the stochastic ALBP [70,71].

Articles [68–72] are devoted to the generalizations of the SALBP as a result of restriction of the condition (A-1). It was assumed that the durations of assembly operations are random variables with laws of probability distributions, which are known before solving the problem. Instead of a deterministic criterion, a corresponding stochastic criterion has to be optimized. Namely, in the stochastic SALBP-1, the mathematical expectation, Em, of the number of the used workstations, m, has to be minimized for the fixed cycle time, c. In the stochastic SALBP-2, the expected value of the cycle time, c, has to be minimized for the given number, m, of the used workstations.

The Industry 4.0 concept aims to bring more flexibility and agility to the assembly and production shop floor. The sequencing and scheduling problems are important issues of Industry 4.0. In fact, a good (or optimal, which is better) schedule has to guarantee a high performance level, which allows a scheduler to take into consideration possible changes and machine perturbations occurring in the production workshop. In [73], the different approaches aim to find stochastic, fuzzy, robust or stable schedules capable of optimizing corresponding single or several criteria, considering possible machine perturbations and variations of assembly operation durations. With the new requirements of the modern production workshop and the high importance of a decision-making process when implementing the constructed schedule, it is essential to extend the scheduling problem with inaccurate data to be adaptable to the needs of a decision-maker in evaluating with respect to properties of the stochastic, fuzzy, robust or stable schedules.

In the paper [74], it is considered a robust scheduling problem. Based on a decision-making framework, a robust specification was developed to evaluate the possible schedule perturbations. The robust measure was based on the service level with a robustness metric. It is defined as a framework gathering several relevant tasks of robustness. Instead of simply trying to evaluate and maximize a single robustness measure, authors of [74] showed that the robust scheduling problem can be enriched. The robust schedule is a multi-faceted issue, which can be used in order to study different points of view, such as stability, sensitivity and the level of service. It is important since the main objective is to support a decision-maker to be able to preserve the different points of view in a robust schedule. It was also illustrated how these robust scheduling problems can be effectively utilized by a decision-maker in solving a real-world scheduling problem with inaccurate data.

Mixed-model assembly lines are usually operated with inaccurate data, such as stochastic product sequences. Balancing such assembly lines can be challenging as their estimation can be difficult to determine in the case when asynchronous pace and buffers have to be taken into account. Several works have addressed problem versions with a target throughput, while a few authors have studied a version of throughput maximizations of the mixed-model ALBP. The paper [75] addresses the ALBP with a fixed number of workstations and a buffer between each pair of the connected workstations. A so-called make-to-order environment was studied and modeled as a stochastic sequence of products with a known rate of the demands. A cycle time simulator was conducted, and a heuristic algorithm was proposed to exploit the cycle time simulator for assessing the cycle time of an assembly line and to provide good line balances. The heuristic algorithm was applied to a dataset with several buffer layouts. The calculated solutions were compared to those of the OR literature. The comparisons showed that the obtained line balances outperform the benchmark ones. The line balance quality difference was greater for tested instances with more buffers, which highlights the capacity to conveniently exploit buffers in the mixed-model assembly lines.

Two-sided assembly lines are used in the factories producing large-sized products. In most OR literature, the assembly operation durations are assumed as deterministic, while these assembly operations may have varying durations in many practical applications, which cause the reduction of performance quality or the infeasibility of the schedule. The ignorance of the specific constraints, including a positional constraint, zoning constraint and synchronism constraint, may result in the invalidation of the constructed schedule. In the paper [76], in order to solve such a stochastic two-sided ALBP with multiple constraints, a hybrid teaching learning-based optimization algorithm is proposed, which allows combining a teaching learning-based optimization for a global search and a neighborhood search with seven neighborhood operators for a local search. A priority-based decoding algorithm was developed in order to ensure that the selected assembly operations satisfy most of the constraints identified by the priority rules and to reduce the idle times related to a sequence dependence among assembly operations. Experimental results on benchmark instances demonstrated the efficiency and universality of the developed decoding algorithm and the comparison among other algorithms showed its effectiveness.

The quality of the balance of the mixed-model assembly line is related to the determined production sequence of assembly operations. Two problems are incompatible in time since balancing is realized simultaneously with planning the assembly line, while assembly operation sequencing is an operational problem closely related to possible market demand fluctuations. In the paper [77], an exact procedure to solve the integrated assembly line balancing problem and assembly operation sequencing problem showed that the demands are stochastic. The searched optimal line balance is required to be flexible in order to cope with possible demand scenarios. A paced assembly line was considered, and the utility work was used as recourse for workstation border violations. A Benders' decomposition algorithm was developed along with different inequalities and a preprocessing stage as a solution algorithm. Three datasets were proposed and used for testing the developed algorithm and treating uncertainty in the mixed-model assembly line. The integration of the strategic ALBP with the operational sequencing one was used in robust assembly lines.

Most of the research papers related to different assembly lines are concentrated on the ALBP, provided that the precedence relations among the given assembly operations are not violated and the objective function is optimized in the desired line balance. The multi-objective ALBP with stochastic assembly operation durations is an important practical topic of the traditional ALBP involving conflicting criteria, such as minimizing the cycle time, variation of workload or the processing cost under uncertain manufacturing conditions. The paper [78] proposes a hybrid multi-objective evolutionary algorithm for heuristically solving such an ALBP, with stochastic assembly operation durations to minimize the cycle time and the processing cost with the given fixed set of the workstations. The special fitness function was adopted, and a hybrid selection was designed to improve the convergence of the solution process. The computational experiments with tested instances showed that the developed multi-objective evolutionary algorithm could display a better convergence distribution performance than other published algorithms.

The paper [79] includes a multi-objective genetic algorithm for heuristically solving a mixed-model ALBP, simultaneously considering the cycle time and number of available workstations. A mixed-model assembly line is capable of producing different types of products to respond to uncertain market demands, while minimizing capital costs of designing a multiple assembly line. According to the stochastic environment of the considered assembly productions, a mixed-model assembly line was put forth in the make-to-order environment. A multi-objective genetic algorithm was developed for solving the corresponding ALBP and a decision-maker was provided with the subsequent replies to pick one of them based on the specific situation. A computational comparison on the computer was carried out between six multi-objective evolutionary algorithms in order to determine the best algorithm to heuristically solve the specified ALBP.

Possible variations of the assembly operation durations in the manufacturing assembly line can result in a longer processing time to complete assembly operations than a given cycle time. This may lead to the assembly line stoppage and to loss of the production time. In practical assembly production, a portion of the cycle time is often allocated as a predefined fixed-size buffer time, which is determined based on experience for accounting uncertain variations of the durations of assembly operations for a paced assembly line without storage-buffers between workstations. The size of the required buffer time in each available workstation depends on the variation levels of the durations of the assembly operations and the desired conservatism level for preventing a cycle time violation. There are uncertainties in other added activity times in available workstations, which are called inter-operation times. Although many studies on designing a stochastic manufacturing assembly line focused on minimizing the cost incurred when the cycle time is exceeded due to assembly operation duration variations, they mostly disregarded the inter-operation times. Therefore, it is worth studying the simultaneous effect of the manufacturing time uncertainty and that of the conservatism level on the cycle time. The paper [80] proposes the algorithm for a robust manufacturing assembly line design that incorporates the conservatism level and uncertainties in the assembly operation and inter-operation times. This interpretation of the non-productive times in available workstations was presented by introducing the concept of the fractal buffer time to manage the effect of manufacturing uncertainties. To overcome the problem of excessive robustness, a robust algorithm with conservatism-level flexibility was used, focusing on the cycle time in a bottleneck workstation. The effect of the uncertainties and conservatism levels on the cycle time was analyzed through several numerical instances. Computational results of the study can be used for improving a manufacturing system in which uncertainties in assembly operations and inter-operation times may significantly degrade its productivity.

Human learning algorithms were developed in many research fields, including the ALBP. Despite the plethora of real contributions and different algorithms used for solving the optimization problems, the autonomous learning phenomenon (the time-dependent or position-dependent reduction of the assembly operation durations due to possible process repetitions) should be explored using a stochastic model, which has been disregarded. In the paper [81], a cost-based stochastic balancing property was coupled with a time-learning curve in order to investigate the role of learning in the rebalancing of the existing assembly conveyers with repetitive assembly operations. A real case study was conducted to demonstrate the applicability of the new algorithms.

The paper [82] presents a mixed-model assembly operation sequencing problem with stochastic operation durations in a multi-workstation assembly line. A mixed-integer nonlinear programming was developed to minimize a weighted sum of the expected total workstation overload and workstation idleness, which was converted into a mixed-integer linear programming to optimally solve small-sized instances of the sequencing problem. Due to the proven NP-hardness of the considered sequencing problem [82], a simulated annealing algorithm was developed. This algorithm employs a learning procedure to select an appropriate heuristic through a search process. Several numerical results were presented on the tested and benchmark instances taken from the OR literature. The computational results of the statistical analysis indicated that the developed algorithm was quite competitive in comparison with the published software packages. The developed algorithm was superior to other published simulated annealing algorithms. These computational results highlight the advantages of the mixed-model sequencing in comparison with deterministic algorithms used for the mixed-model sequencing problems. Assembly lines of determining the optimal order of the available workstations in the U-shaped assembly lines with stochastic durations of the assembly operations were studied in the paper [82], as well.

The ALBP is highly important for efficient and cost-effective assembly production of similar products. Different uncertain events might cause a variation in the assembly operation duration. Due to these variations, there remains a possibility that the completion time of the assembly operations might exceed the predetermined cycle time. To hedge against such an issue, a single-model ALBP with the uncertain operation durations and multiple objective functions was studied in [83]. This research aimed to minimize the cycle time in addition to maximizing the probability that completion times of the operations on the workstations will not exceed the predetermined cycle time and will minimize the smoothness index. A Pareto-based artificial bee colony algorithm was proposed to obtain a Pareto solution for the multiple objective functions. The proposed algorithm introduced extra steps, as follows: sorting of food sources, a niche technique and preserving some elitists in the traditional artificial bee colony algorithm to obtain a Pareto solution. The main parameters of the developed algorithm were tuned using the Taguchi method. Computational experiments were conducted to solve the standard ALBP, which were taken from the OR library. The performance of the developed Pareto-based artificial bee colony algorithm was compared with a multi-objective algorithm, NSGA II. Computational results showed that the proposed algorithm outperforms the NSGA II algorithm in both Pareto solution quality and CPU time.

In [84], a workforce assignment is studied in the assembly line with several workstations and executing final parts of different types. The objective is to minimize the number of human operators over the assembly conveyer. Due to the complex market environment, possible changes in product demands have an influence on production balancing and scheduling. The uncertain demands were investigated in [84]. An ambiguity set was applied to portray the demand uncertainty. A chance-constrained programming was developed. Two probability-distribution-free algorithms were chosen: approximations based on Markov inequality and a mixed-integer second-order conic program, to approximate the chance constraints of the tested problems. Computational experiments were conducted to compare the performances of the two proposed algorithms.

The model assembly conveyer is an industrial arrangement of the available workstations, needed equipment and assembly operators for continuous flow of workpieces in mass production operations. The reliability of the assembly production has been investigated by taking into account operation duration uncertainties. The paper [85] provides a reliability metric which encompasses two types of operation duration uncertainties. A multi-objective mathematical model was developed to maximize the reliability and efficiency of the conveyers. Neighborhood search methods with two restart mechanisms were devised to solve the problem, and then they were compared. The computational results showed some managerial implications for the production planners. The methodology proposed in [85] can be applied to many assembly industries when some historical data of uncertain inputs are available, while some others are not. In [86], chance-constrained binary programming for the stochastic straight- and U-shaped line balancing problems were proposed and investigated. The proposed algorithms were used for solving several instances, which are available from the OR literature. The obtained computational results were described and compared. A goal programming algorithm was also developed for increasing the assembly line reliability, which is needed to investigate the stochastic ALBP.

In the real assembly lines, production planning and inventory control are often subject to different types of uncertainty. The paper [87] is devoted to a control problem for a single-level multi-component inventory, which arises in the assembly line replenishment under stochastic component procurement lead times. In order to follow the common assumption of the MRP software tool, the discrete distributions of random component lead times were investigated. The latter was expressed as the number of the tested time periods. Since the finished product was assembled using several component types simultaneously, the assembly process was stopped if a single type of component was delayed. The assembly stoppage forced by a component delay or stock-out was penalized by a backlogging cost. The considered objective aimed to minimize the total cost composed of holding and backlogging costs. To solve this problem, a joint chance-constrained algorithm was developed based on an equivalent linear reformulation. The practical advantages of the developed approach were estimated in its release from backlogging costs, which are difficult to quantify in the real-world industrial assembly productions.

Summarizing the results of [68–87], one can conclude that the stochastic SALBP turned out to be more complex than the deterministic SALBP. However, stochastic problems do not quite correspond to some real assembly conveyor productions, where it is not possible to obtain sufficient information to determine the probability distribution of a random duration, x_i, of each assembly operation, $i \in V$. Even if the probability distributions of random durations are determined in advance (before solving the problem), these distributions may be very useful when there are a large number of implementations of the fixed line balance under unchanging assembly production conditions. However, in a specific implementation of the assembly process, the given probability distributions may be of little use. In particular, in an unsuccessful case for the fixed balance, $b = (V_1^b, V_2^b, \ldots, V_m^b)$, conditions, this line balance sheet may not only be worse than the factually optimal line balance, but even unacceptable for the worst case for assembly line conditions.

The question also arises whether it is possible to determine the law of probability distribution of random assembly operation durations. Such a law can be determined on the basis of reliable statistics. In other words, it is necessary to conduct a sufficiently large number of full-scale tests (or computational experiments on the computer), which themselves can be expensive, and it will take a lot of time to conduct the needed computational experiments. It is also necessary to analyze the obtained statistics, and only after that is it possible to draw a more or less plausible conclusion about the law of the probability distribution of the random assembly operation durations. The resulting law will reflect the future actual (sometimes unique) probability distribution of random durations of assembly operations only with a certain (possibly gross) approximation level. It is almost impossible to exactly determine the law of probability distribution of random operation durations. How, then, is it possible to obtain reliable statistics if a sufficiently large number of full-scale (computer) tests cannot be carried out due to a lack of time (which is limited in modern market competition) or due to limited resources of the enterprise? Even reliable statistics may not be of great importance for a particular implementation of the assembly production and for several successive implementations of the assembly process, if the production conditions are different from the production conditions for obtaining statistics and, accordingly, the distribution of probabilities of random assembly operation durations, in fact, may be violated in practice.

4.2. Assembly and Production Line Balancing Problems with Fuzzy Parameters

The input data for many practical ALBP are uncertain or questionable, and so only some limits can be set on the original data. The data questionability can be represented by fuzzy numbers to reduce possible errors associated with input data. The duration of assembly operations in such an ALBP can be represented as fuzzy numbers. Such problems are called fuzzy ALBP and can be formulated as follows. Let the set of assembly operations, $V = \{1, 2, \ldots, n\}$, be given. The duration of each operation is presented by a fuzzy number. The precedence digraph $G = (V, A)$ is given, which determines the partial strict order on the set V. The problem is to assign a set of operations, V, to the ordered workstations, $S_1, S_2, \ldots, S_m$, in such a way that the precedence constraints are not disturbed and the objective function would take an optimal fuzzy value [26,33,88,89].

The articles [88,89] provide approximate solutions to the ALBP with fuzzy durations of the assembly operations. A genetic algorithm was developed to minimize the maximum total duration of the assembly operations assigned to each workstation. Genetic operators suitable for solving the fuzzy ALBP were considered. The article [88] provides a heuristic solution to the ALBP with fuzzy durations of the assembly operations. In [26], a mixed-model assembly line is designed to assemble several types of the final product. The optimal sequence of product models was determined to minimize the number of assembly conveyor stops required to move from assembling one product model to assembling another model of the same product. When the operating conditions of the assembly line change or the requirements for the product model change, it is important to determine the assembly sequence of all models of the product, for which the stops of the assembly conveyor would be minimal and there would be no frequent need to rebalance the assembly line. Three objective functions conflicting with each other were considered. To solve the fuzzy ALBP, a mathematical programming method with a fuzzy goal was developed.

The mixed-model assembly lines are highly adopted in the automobile industry and so the part feeding process becomes critical. In [90], the dynamic part feeding scheduling problem was studied for optimization of the throughput of the mixed-model assembly lines, along with the total delivery distance of the automatic guide vehicles. A process considering the feeding operation generation, the loading, sequencing and dispatching problems was analyzed, determining appropriate models and algorithms. To heuristically solve these problems, the research [90] contains a hybrid fuzzy–neural dynamic scheduling algorithm, which integrates the self-organizing maps with a fuzzy algorithm and a knowledge base. This algorithm was adapted to the pre-cluster status of the mixed-model assembly line in order to optimize the initial clustering centers. After that, the algorithm was availed to guide the clusters in a way to improve the clustering performance. The computational experiments were conducted in order to evaluate the scheduling performance in the dynamic manufacturing environment and verify the algorithm's superiority over the benchmark ones. The developed algorithm allows a decision-maker to select a rational scheduling scheme based on the decision impacts in the productivity, feeding costs and the real-time status of the assembly conveyers.

The paper [91] presents the results of the investigation of a single-model SALBP with fuzzy assembly operation durations. This problem is referred to as a fuzzy SALBP-E, consisting of finding the best combination of the number of workstations and the cycle time as well as a respective assembly line balance, such that the determined measure of efficiency of the single-model assembly line is maximized. A fuzzy SALBP-E is an extension of the deterministic SALBP-E under fuzziness of input data. The formal definition of the considered problem was given with the assembly operation durations presented by triangular fuzzy membership functions. The considered problem is known to be NP-hard, and therefore a meta-heuristic based on the genetic algorithm was developed for its heuristic solution. The performance of the proposed algorithm was studied and discussed over several benchmark instances. The computational results demonstrated a satisfactory performance for the developed algorithm in terms of solution CPU time and quality.

The research of the paper [92] addresses both the straight ALBP and the U-shaped ALBP. It is written in this paper that many attempts in the OR literature were made to study the deterministic ALBP and the attention was not given to those with inaccurate data. In [92], a bi-objective fuzzy mixed-integer linear programming was developed, with triangular fuzzy numbers being employed in order to represent uncertainty and vagueness, which are associated with the assembly operation durations arising in the real assembly productions. In the proposed algorithm, two objectives (minimizing the number of available workstations and minimizing the cycle time) were considered with respect to the set of usual constraints presented in Section 2.1. An appropriate strategy was proposed, where two-phase interactive fuzzy programming was used as an algorithm for finding a compromise solution. The validity of the proposed algorithm was evaluated though numerical tests. An experimental comparison study was conducted over several test problems in order to assess the performance of the proposed algorithm. The computational result demonstrated that the interactive fuzzy algorithm can not only be applied to the fuzzy ALBP but was also capable to handle different practical models. The proposed model and algorithm may constitute a framework aiming to assist a decision-maker to deal with inaccurate data in the ALBP.

Due to the main role of the efficient assembly and production lines in modern manufacturing systems, the research of the paper [93] was devoted to both straight and U-shaped assembly line balancing problems. The considered ALBP includes conflicting objective functions that should be optimized subject to a set of constraints. This paper endeavors to develop a fuzzy linear programming algorithm. Having dealt with the inaccurate nature of the real assembly production, triangular fuzzy numbers were employed in order to represent fuzzy input data with possible vagueness associated with the assembly operation durations. The developed algorithm can be regarded as a background of fuzzy programming for further practical development in the ALBP. To heuristically solve the fuzzy ALBP, a multi-objective genetic algorithm was developed. Having respected several important characteristics of the fuzzy straight ALBP and fuzzy U-shaped ALBP, the algorithm includes an initial generation, encoding and decoding schemes and a genetic algorithm. The developed algorithm was evaluated based on several benchmark instances and compared with the exact algorithm. The presented computational results demonstrated the efficiency of the developed algorithm over other ones suggested in the OR literature.

Sequencing and balancing manual mixed-model assembly lines is challenging in assembly production due to the high complexity and uncertainty of human operators' activities. The control of a predetermined cycle time and the sequencing of assembly production can mitigate large losses due to non-optimal line balancing in the case of open-workstation production, where the human operators can work ahead of a normal schedule and try to reduce a backlog. The objective considered in [94] was to provide a cycle time control algorithm, which can provide the efficiency of the assembly line production in the situations based on an appropriate mixed-sequencing strategy. To handle the uncertainty of human operators' activity durations, a fuzzy mixed-model-based solution has been developed. As the production process was modular, the fuzzy sets represented the uncertainty of the activity durations related to processing the modules. Both optimistic estimates and pessimistic estimates of the completion of activities were extracted from the fuzzy model and incorporated into a predictive control algorithm to ensure the constrained optimization of the predetermined cycle time. The applicability of the proposed algorithm was demonstrated using a wire-harness manufacturing process with a paced assembly conveyor. The developed algorithm can handle continuous assembly conveyors as well. The computational results confirmed that the developed algorithm is applicable in the cases where a production line of the supply chain is not well-balanced, and the activity durations are uncertain.

The paper [95] is devoted to both multi-objective straight assembly line balancing problems and U-shaped ALBP with fuzzy operation duration. Four objectives were considered (minimizing numbers of workstations, maximizing fuzzy assembly line efficiency, minimizing the fuzzy idleness percentage and minimizing the fuzzy smoothness index). Two problems were formulated, including uncertainties, variability and imprecision that usually occur in a real-world production. The durations of assembly operations were determined by triangular fuzzy numbers. To heuristically solve this fuzzy problem, a hybrid multi-objective genetic algorithm has been developed. A one-fifth success rule was deployed for selection and mutation operators to improve this genetic algorithm. The results in the genetic algorithm application were controlled in convergence and diversity by means of controlling the selective pressure rate. A fuzzy controller to the selective pressure was employed for the genetic algorithm toward its better implementation. The Taguchi design of the computational experiments was used for the parameter control and calibration. The numerical examples were presented to compare the performance of the proposed algorithm with the existing ones. The computational results showed a better performance of the proposed algorithm. Similar ALBP, modified algorithms and closed results are presented in the paper [96].

Balancing the workloads of available workstations is a key point in the efficiency of the assembly line. An initial line balance can be broken by the changing processing abilities of machines because of their degradation, and therefore re-balancing of the assembly line is inevitable. The impacts of unexpected events on assembly line re-balancing are usually ignored in the OR literature. Using the advanced sensor technologies and Internet of Things, the machine degradation can be continuously monitored, so condition-based maintenance can be implemented to improve the health state of the machine. Using the technology of robotic process automation, workflows of the assembly process can be smoothed, workstations can work autonomously and a higher level of process automation can be achieved. Real-time information of the processing abilities of machines will bring about opportunities for automated workload balance via an adaptive decision. In [97], a fuzzy control system was developed to make real-time decisions to balance the workloads based on the processing abilities of the workstations, given the policy of condition-based maintenance. Fuzzy controllers were used to decide whether to re-balance the assembly line and how to adjust the production rate of each workstation. The conducted numerical experiments showed that the buffer level of the assembly line with the fuzzy control system was lower than that of the assembly line without a control system (the buffer level of the assembly line with another control system was the lowest). The product demands can be satisfied by assembly lines, except the one with another control system since there were too many production losses sacrificed for the low buffer level. The stability analysis of the control performance to the numerical parameter settings was conducted. The effectiveness of the developed fuzzy control was demonstrated. The intelligent automation can improve the performance of the assembly process by the proposed fuzzy control system since real-time information of the assembly line can be used for the adaptive decision-making.

In [98], a fuzzy control system was developed to analyze real-time information of the assembly line with two types of fuzzy controllers. The first type of a fuzzy controller was used to determine whether the assembly line should be re-balanced to satisfy the changed product demands. The second type of fuzzy controller was used to adjust the production rate of each workstation in time, to eliminate blockage and starvation. Hence, the utilization of available workstations increased. Compared with the three assembly lines without the fuzzy control system, the assembly line with the fuzzy control system performed better in terms of the blockage ratio, the starvation ratio and the buffer level. With the improvement of information transparency, the performance of assembly line production was better. The research findings shed light on the smart control of the assembly line production and provide insights into the impacts of Industry 4.0 on the ALBP.

Summarizing the above results published in the papers [26,33,88–98], one can conclude that a fuzzy ALBP is a harder problem than a deterministic or stochastic ALBP with the same problem size. The fuzzy ALBP need complex algorithms to obtain either a good heuristic solution or an exact fuzzy solution. Since fuzzy algorithms are time-consuming, finding a fuzzy optimal solution in a reasonable CPU time is possible only for a fuzzy ALBP with small or moderate sizes.

5. Designing and Balancing Production Lines of Disassembly of Obsolete Products

Due to the rapid development of modern technologies and changes in the consumer market, many products have begun to quickly become obsolete and are subject to destruction. Considering this, it is necessary to disassemble products with an expired period of use and then restore such products. A disassembly of obsolete products is required for their subsequent processing and restoration. In recent years, many specialized production disassembly lines have been created, which are effective for processing obsolete products. Improving the efficiency of the production line is associated with a solution of the DLBP (disassembly line balancing problem), which is aimed at optimizing the disassembly of products in such a way that the total disassembly time spent on each available workstation would be approximately the same for all available workstations and approach the time of the specified cycle of the production line [25,31]. Disassembly operations at workplaces in the disassembly shop are required to ensure the removal of valuable components from the disassembled product and reduce the undesirable environmental impact of everything that remains after the disassembly of the obsolete product. In contrast to the assembly production, which is more stable due to the deterministic durations of many assembly operations, the disassembly of obsolete products often has inaccurate parameters and so the DLBP are usually uncertain.

Obsolete product disassembly may include a separation of the reusable pieces. It is often possible to operate remanufacturing processes on several of the pieces while others may be sold to suppliers [99]. In a robotic disassembly line, the robot may complete repetitive operations with rather continual efficiency. Since most industrial robots cannot handle complex disassembly operations, a human–robot involvement in the disassembly process was proposed to flexibly and efficiently disassemble the obsolete products, with less damage to the environment, a lower operation cost, less energy consumption and a minimal cycle time. The robotic disassembly line balancing problem (RDLBP) is determined as disassembly processes collaboratively carried out by humans and robots or the disassembly performed by robots autonomously. Such a problem has two main avenues of research published in the OR literature, as follows: robotic disassembly line balancing and robotic disassembly sequence planning. The review paper [100] is devoted to the RDLBP and is organized based on the above subjects. The RDLBP is an optimization problem, where the objective is to find an optimal sequence for disassembling the obsolete products. Similar problems may include disassembly sequencing, disassembly sequence optimization, disassembly planning and human–robot collaborative disassembly problems. Disassembly sequence planning may involve three steps, as follows: to decide whether the disassembly mode should be complete or partial, to construct a disassembly model by preventing the generation of unfeasible disassembly sequences and to employ a selected planning algorithm according to the disassembly objective and the used optimization models and techniques. The articles [25,31,101,102] investigated the disassembly line balancing, which may consist of the aggregate machines, mechanisms and devices located in accordance with the sequence of operations of the technological process of disassembling the obsolete product and transport devices that move the disassembled product. The duration of disassembly operations cannot be accurately determined but a few studies are published on the DLBP with inaccurate durations of disassembly operations.

The timely recovery and disassembly of waste electronic and electrical equipment obtained a higher economic benefit and can reduce the impact of hazardous substances on the environment. The parallel disassembly line can disassemble different types of waste electronic and electrical equipment and improve the disassembly efficiency. A parallel disassembly line balancing model with stochastic disassembly times is studied in [102]. The evaluation index of the disassembly line includes a number of workstations, workload smoothness and disassembly profits. A genetic simulated annealing algorithm was proposed to optimize a disassembly line balance. The decoding and encoding strategies were proposed based on characteristics of a partial disassembly and parallel layout. Two-point mapping crossovers and single-point insertion mutations were designed to ensure that the disassembly sequence meets the given precedence and disassembly constraints. The simulated annealing algorithm was applied to the results obtained by the genetic operation. The proposed algorithms obtain better solutions than a tabu search for stochastic parallel DLBP. The proposed algorithm has a better performance than the CPLEX solvers, genetic algorithms and simulated annealing algorithms for parallel DLBP. Parallel disassembly lines for waste refrigerators and televisions were constructed. The performance of the proposed multi-objective algorithm was superior to those of five other multi-objective algorithms. The computational results showed that the proposed model and algorithms have better practical application ability.

To reduce disassembly costs for enterprises and improve the disassembly efficiency of waste products, the paper [103] investigated a partial sequence-dependent DLBP and established a multi-objective model to minimize the number of used workstations, the total disassembly operation duration, the idle balance index and the number of used disassembly tools. A Pareto-discrete hummingbird algorithm was proposed to address a partial sequence-dependent disassembly line balancing problem. This algorithm includes two stages, as follows: a self-searching stage and an information-interacting stage. With these stages, the exploration and exploitation abilities of the Pareto-discrete hummingbird algorithm may be balanced. The effectiveness and superiority of the Pareto-discrete hummingbird algorithm were verified by comparing it with other algorithms for two instances of the DLBP. The mathematical model and Pareto-discrete hummingbird algorithm were applied to the optimization of a partial sequence-dependent disassembly line of waste laptops. The optimization results showed that the partial disassembly can make the disassembly line smoother and the utilization efficiency of workstations higher than full disassembly. The Pareto-discrete hummingbird algorithm was superior in solving the partial sequence-dependent DLBP.

Studies in production engineering focused on disassembly and assembly planning for improving the profitability of remanufacturing. The presentation of assembly and disassembly sequences by analyzing geometrical and technical precedence constraints is an essential necessity of assembly and disassembly planning. A specific and/or graph is used to represent a product's feasible assembly and disassembly sequences, including alternative subassemblies and parallel operations. A lot of researchers have studied the automatic extraction of geometrical precedence constraints by collision analysis within 3D models. Since most of the published approaches focused on collision analysis to identify precedence relations, the generation of and/or graphs for complex products from collision analysis results remain inefficient for many industrial cases. In [98], a computer-aided design interface from previous studies is used to extract liaison and moving wedge information from 3D models. A top-down approach and a bottom-up approach for generating complete and/or graphs from the extracted data were introduced. These approaches for computing performances were analyzed on the several test cases and the developed computer-aided design models. The bottom-up approach performed better for the tested samples. It has been found that the amount of moving wedge constraints has a strong effect on the computing performance. It is an indicator to estimate the complexity of products under examination. The exponential behavior of the needed computing resources can be estimated beforehand. For complex products, graph simplifications or alternative graph representations with less information richness were considered. The obtained computational results contribute to automated assembly and disassembly sequence planning from complex products and increasing remanufacturing profitability.

In [104], a multi-period integrated decision-making model is investigated for the heavy-duty equipment maintenance, involving disassembly, inspection and assembly, with uncertain numbers of replaced parts within a fixed-time horizon. There are large numbers of subway cars exported from other countries and the maintenance is difficult to be conducted in Hong Kong due to the limited space, machinery and technical support teams. Thus, efficient maintenance planning is required to ensure the quality of transportation services. To resolve this problem, a deterministic mixed-integer optimization model was developed to achieve integrated optimization of disassembly and assembly. The model minimizes the total operation cost, consisting of a purchasing cost and a repair cost subject to capacity constraints. A real-life case study from mass transit railway in Hong Kong is presented to verify the proposed model.

The aim of the paper [105] is to reverse an assembly line using a mobile platform equipped with a manipulator. Reversibility means that the assembly line is able to perform disassembly as well. For this purpose, a (dis)assembly line balancing and a synchronized hybrid Petri nets model were used to model and control a (dis)assembly line, with a fixed number of workstations, served by a wheeled mobile robot equipped with a robotic manipulator. The model is of a hybrid type, where the (dis)assembly line is a discrete part while the wheeled mobile robot with a robotic manipulator is a continuous part. The model operates in synchronized mode with signals from several sensors. Disassembly starts after the assembly process and after the assembled piece fails the quality test in order to recover the parts. The wheeled mobile robot with a robotic manipulator was used only during disassembly, to transport the parts from the disassembling locations to the storage locations. Using these models, a real-time control structure has been designed and implemented, allowing automated assembly and disassembly, where the latter was assisted by a mobile platform equipped with a manipulator. The paper [106] aims to study a specific type of disassembly line with multi-robotic workstations, where multiple industrial robots perform different disassembly operations on the obsolete products of different models. The industrial robots on the disassembly line were differently skilled and had non-identical disassembly operation durations along with energy consumption. Considering the given conditions of the returned products, a task-based operation digraph and a subassemblies-based and/or graph were used to represent the precedence constraints of the disassembly operation sequence. A mixed-integer mathematical programming was developed for the considered problem, with three conflicting objectives of minimizing the cycle time, the peak-total energy consumption and the cost of hazardous tasks. Successfully solving practical disassembly line balance problems is usually subject to a great number of uncertainties in the real-life problems. The uncertainties in disassembly operation durations were solved by stochastic, fuzzy and interval programming algorithms. Computational results of the conducted experiments on problem instances were presented.

The disassembly line is one of the most important tools to handle large quantities of waste electronic and electrical equipment. The DLBP is to assign disassembly operations to each available workstation reasonably while satisfying various given constraints, which is one of the challenging topics. Considering the uncertainty, environmental protection and economic benefits of disassembly, the paper [107] established a stochastic partial DLBP that comprehensively evaluates the number of used workstations, workload smoothness, energy consumption and disassembly profit. To obtain feasible solutions with a high quality, a multi-objective discrete flower pollination algorithm was developed. This algorithm establishes heuristic rules, discrete operations and multi-objective algorithms combined with the characteristics of the partial DLBP. The effectiveness and application ability of the proposed model and algorithms were verified by a disassembly example of a waste printer. Various disassembly schemes were obtained, which can provide guidance for a decision-maker to construct disassembly lines.

End-of-life products with large sizes are suitable for disassembly operations on the two-sided disassembly line. The destructive disassembly is required in the disassembly process. The negative impacts caused by destructive disassembly during the disassembly process are usually ignored in the OR literature. In the paper [108], a probability-based operation destructive disassembly model was constructed in the two-sided DLBP, and the negative impact on the total disassembly cost, workload smoothness index and the impact of destructive disassembly operations on other adjacent but unconnected operations were determined. A mixed-integer programming was used to minimize the above objective functions. A multi-objective restart genetic algorithm was developed, which combines the genetic operations and flatworm regeneration processes with an embedded restart mechanism. The effectiveness of the model and the efficiency of the developed algorithm were verified by disassembling mobile phones, laptops, printers and engines on the two-sided disassembly line. Through the application of car disassembly, it was shown that the developed algorithm can assist a decision-maker to choose the preferred disassembly schemes.

The RDLBP is one of the central problems in designing disassembly lines. This problem is used to find the disassembly operations to be optimally assigned to each available workstation for a given obsolete product [109]. There are two classes for disassembly line balancing problems. The first one is based on the variety of obsolete products, including single-model, mixed-model and multi-model disassembly lines. Only one type of obsolete product can be disassembled on a single-model disassembly line, while more than one type of obsolete product could be disassembled simultaneously on a mixed-model disassembly line. Thus, a mixed-model line is more flexible to the product type change and this advantage may reduce disassembly line building and costs. In a multi-model disassembly line, several obsolete products in separate batches are disassembled, though rarely performed. The second class is the classification based on the types of lines, including straight lines, U-shaped lines and those with parallel layouts.

The paper [48] provides a review of robotic publications (225 papers) utilizing optimization techniques from 2005 until 2021. In this review, most developments in robotic problems are cited. A robotic manufacturing system usually includes an industrial robot as a material handling device, a co-worker with human or autonomous robots and other relevant systems. Due to the lack of a deep analysis and complete listing of the robotic articles which apply optimization techniques, this paper aims to report an extensive archive of robotic papers on a structured classification for robotic problems, including robotic cell, robotic disassembly and robotic assembly. Descriptive statistics were provided, including the number of publications and the authorship analysis, and future trends towards the robotic studies were introduced. The review in [48] shows that heuristic or meta-heuristic algorithms are the most frequently used tools to solve the robotic application problems. This review stimulates theoretical and applied studies of industrial robots in order to establish a foundation for robotic problems arising in the industry.

The application of robots in mechanical assembly may increase the efficiency of the industrial production. With the requirements of flexible manufacturing, it has become a research hotspot for accomplishing diversified assembly operations safely and efficiently in unstructured environments. Several advanced robot assembly strategies have been proposed. Fault monitoring and strategy performance evaluation have attracted the attention of researchers and practitioners. To promote the development of robotic assembly, the authors of the paper [110] analyzed the research in this field. According to the assembly process, they separate the research contents into target recognition and searching, compliant strategies for fine insertion motion and fault monitoring. The characteristics of each model and most methods were summarized. A performance evaluation for assembly strategies was proposed with typical metrics. The authors surveyed the benchmarks to provide support for standardized performance evaluation. The challenges and potential directions for future research were discussed. The paper [110] presented the state-of-the-art robotic assembly approaches used in recent years based on the assembly action procedure, including target search, fine motion strategies, along with fault diagnosis and strategy performance evaluation.

A disassembly process is often characterized by a high level of uncertainty due to the quality and types of the end-of-life products. The paper [111] presents an approach for designing disassembly lines with the objective to maximize the disassembly line profit. Disassembly operation durations were assumed to be random variables with probability distributions known before solving the problem. The and/or graph was used to model the precedence relationships among disassembly operations, subassemblies and the disassembly alternatives. A Monte Carlo sampling-based solution algorithm was developed to deal with uncertainties. The obtained results of the conducted computational experiments on the test problems were presented and discussed.

The aim of [112] was to reverse an assembly line using a mobile platform equipped with a manipulator. By reversibility, the authors of this paper mean that the assembly line is able to perform disassembly as well. For this purpose, an assembly/disassembly line balancing and a synchronized hybrid Petri net model are used to model and control an assembly/disassembly line, with a fixed number of workstations, served by a wheeled mobile robot equipped with the robotic manipulator. The synchronized hybrid Petri net model is a hybrid type, where the assembly/disassembly line balancing is a discrete part, and the wheeled mobile robot with the robotic manipulator is a continuous part. The model operates in synchronized mode with signals from sensors. Disassembly starts after the assembly process and after the assembled piece fails the quality test, in order to recover these parts. The wheeled mobile robot with the robotic manipulator is used during disassembly, to transport the parts from the disassembling locations to the storage locations. Using these models and a Lab-View platform, a real-time control structure has been designed and implemented, allowing automated assembly and disassembly, where the latter is assisted by a mobile platform equipped with the robotic manipulator.

Disassembly of end-of-life products is a main step in remanufacturing and recycling. Disassembly sequence planning is the process that finds the optimal sequence of components being removed. An element of disassembly sequence planning is a suitable mathematical representation that describes the interference of components in the product. Most studies on disassembly sequence planning have tended to focus on the interference that is fixed. The interference may be uncertain due to complex end-of-life conditions such as deformation, corrosion and rust. To deal with uncertain interference, the paper [113] proposes an interference probability matrix as a mathematical representation that uses probability to indicate uncertainty in the interference. A multi-threshold planning scheme is established to generate optimal disassembly sequences. Three cases are presented to demonstrate the use of the proposed approach. The performance of four multi-objective optimization algorithms that can be adopted in the planning scheme is tested.

Since the disassembly of end-of-life products is affected by many dynamic and uncertain factors, many mathematical models and algorithms were established for uncertain DLBP. With more extended objectives, constraints and different algorithms of disassembly, inconsistent models relating to product representations and types of disassembly lines have become the main barriers for the transfer of research to disassembly practice. In [114], an overview of recent models to summarize the input data, parameters, decision variables, constraints and objectives of the DLBP was presented. After discussing the adaptation and extensibility of the published models for different environments, a unified encoding scheme was designed to apply typical multi-objective evolutionary algorithms on the DLBP, with extensive decision variables and seven significant objectives. Algorithm comparison on four typical cases was carried out based on commonly used products to verify the optimization process for the integrated version of existing models and demonstrate the overall performance of the typical multi-objective evolutionary algorithms on the DLBP. Experimental results can be a baseline for further algorithm design and practical algorithm selection on the DLBP scenarios.

6. Designing, Balancing and Scheduling Assembly Lines with Uncertain Parameters

The uncertainty may be modeled by specifying a set of scenarios containing possible vectors of the ALBP parameters which may occur. No additional information for the given scenario set, such as a probability distribution or membership function, is provided. To choose a line balance, the robust or stable optimization framework may be applied (see [73]). In Section 6.1, the goal is to find a line balance with the best worst-case performance over the given set of possible scenarios. This performance can be measured by a min-max regret criterion based on regret theory.

6.1. A Robust Approach to the ALBP with Uncertain Parameters

A design for a disassembly line is the essential procedure in determining the disassembly and recyclability of the end-of-life products. An efficient procedure aims to provide the disassembling and recycling. The recent trends of disassembling and recycling include environmental and social sustainability. Due to a shortage of energy and deterioration of the ecological environment, the sustainable production is an active research topic to use the economic benefits as the evaluation standard of a design scheme and environmental characteristics. The paper [115] provides an approach for designing a disassembly line based on sustainability. A hybrid multi-attribute decision-making algorithm integrating the regret theory and the entropy weighting procedure was developed. To implement the proposed algorithm, several criterions were used (disassembly energy consumption, disassembly accessibility, fastener ratio, toxic material proportion, material recovery rate, disassembly expense, waste emissions, production and use noise). To better describe the fuzziness of human thinking and to avoid a loss of information and distortion during information aggregation phases, the evaluation information given by experts was presented by the interval linguistic intuition of fuzzy numbers. The weighted vector of the index structure was determined by the entropy weighting procedure under a fuzzy environment. The regret theory was employed to obtain a final order of alternatives via considering and guaranteeing the risk attitude and the regret attitude of experts. To show the applicability of the developed algorithm, a case study including four kinds of refrigerator schemes was conducted to validate the proposed algorithm. A comparison with other algorithms along with a sensitivity and stability analysis of experiments was executed to verify the effectiveness and reliability of the developed algorithm. The computational experimental results showed that disassembly accessibility, the fastener ratio, waste emissions and disassembly energy consumption have a large impact on the scheme selection based on sustainability. The proposed algorithm outperforms other tested ones. The chosen scheme was a winner in majority of the sensitivity and stability analyses.

Robotic disassembly sequence planning is a research area that looks at the sequence of actions in the disassembly intending to achieve autonomous disassembly with high efficiency and low cost in remanufacturing and recycling applications. Key information being factored in disassembly sequence planning is the interference condition of a product (a mathematical representation of the spatial location of components in the assembly in the form of a matrix). An observed challenge is that the interference condition can be uncertain due to variations in the end-of-life conditions. Therefore, there is a lack of tools available in disassembly sequence planning under uncertain interference. To address this challenge, in [116], a disassembly sequence planning algorithm is proposed that can cope with uncertain interference conditions enabled by the fuzzification of disassembly sequence planning. This algorithm is a fuzzy and dynamic modeling one, in combination with an iterative re-planning strategy. The fuzzification of disassembly sequence planning offers the capability for the disassembly sequence to adapt to failures and self-evolve online. Three disassembly products were used to demonstrate the properties of this algorithm.

In [21], the case of the ALBP-1 is considered, in which assembly operation durations are worker-dependent and uncertain, and being expressed as segments (closed intervals) of possible duration values. The main goal is to find an assignment of assembly operations and workers to a minimal number of used workstations such that the resulting productivity level is in respect to a desired robust measure. Two mixed-integer programming settings were proposed for this uncertain ALBP-1 and explain how these settings can be adapted to handle the special case, where one must integrate a particular set of workers in the assembly line. A construction heuristic was developed that yields high-quality solutions in a fraction of the CPU time needed to solve the uncertain ALBP-1 to optimality in the robust sense. Computational results showed the benefits of solving this robust optimization problem instead of its deterministic counterpart.

The problem of placing the inventory over a network, which is used for assembling a final product, is a challenging issue in supply chain designs because the manufacturer wants to reduce inventory over the supply chain. The process of designing a supply chain and placing inventory, to offer a higher service level at the lowest possible cost, is not an easy choice for a decision-maker. In the paper [117], the authors used the supply chain representation, where a supply chain was divided into supplying, manufacturing and delivering stages. The main problem was to select a resource option in order to perform each above stage based on the selected options and to place an amount of inventory at each stage in order to offer satisfactory customer service with a low total supply chain cost. A resource option represents suppliers, manufacturing plants (production lines) and transport modes in the supplying, manufacturing or delivering stage. The assembly algorithm based on an ant colony optimization was developed to minimize the total supply chain cost and the lead time of the products to ensure all product deliveries without delays.

The concerns of most companies related to economic savings, optimal utilization of resources along with increasing environmental protection regulations prompt the manufacturer to be focused on recycling the products that are at the end of their life. In [118], a job-shop scheduling problem is considered with reverse flows under uncertainty. Since most parameters of the model (e.g., operation durations) were tainted with uncertainty in real-world applications, a robust programming was used. Due to the complexity of solving the job-shop scheduling problem, an exact algorithm for small-sized instances and simulated annealing with a discrete harmony search for large-sized instances were developed. The model performance was evaluated by comparing the computational results available from the OR literature. The performance of the proposed meta-heuristic algorithms was evaluated by comparing the obtained schedules with the exact algorithm for small-sized instances and with three meta-heuristics (the discrete particle swarm optimization, the invasive weed optimization and the greedy algorithm) for medium-sized and large-sized instances. The satisfying results showed that the presented model and proposed algorithms ensure a good solution quality within a reasonable CPU time for the tested instances.

Assembly operation duration variations in a manufacturing production line can result in a longer duration to complete operations than a predetermined cycle time, leading to a production line stoppage and loss of production time. In practice, a portion of the predetermined cycle time may be allocated as a predefined fixed-size buffer time, which is determined based on the experience, to account for such uncertain duration variations for a paced assembly line without storage-buffers between workstations. The size of the required buffer time in each workstation depends on the variation levels of operation durations and the desired conservatism level for preventing cycle time violations. Moreover, there are uncertainties in other nonviable activity durations in the workstations, which are known as inter-task times. Although many studies on the stochastic manufacturing assembly line design focused on minimizing the cost incurred when the predetermined cycle time is exceeded due to operation duration variations, they mostly disregarded the inter-task times. It is worth studying the common effect of the manufacturing duration uncertainty level and that of the conservatism level on the predetermined cycle time. The paper [74] proposes an algorithm for a robust manufacturing assembly line design that incorporates the conservatism level and uncertainties in the assembly operation and inter-task times. This interpretation of the non-productive times in the workstations is presented by introducing the concept of the α-fractal buffer time to manage the effect of manufacturing operation duration uncertainties. To overcome the above problem of an excessive robustness, a moderate robust approach with conservatism-level flexibility has been used, focusing on the predetermined cycle time in the bottleneck workstation. The effect of the uncertainties and conservatism levels on the predetermined cycle time was analyzed through several numerical examples. The obtained computational results can be used for improving the manufacturing production line, in which uncertainties in assembly operation and inter-task times may considerably degrade the productivity.

Balancing U-shaped assembly lines under uncertainty is addressed in [119] by formulating a robust optimization problem and developing an optimization model and heuristic algorithm. U-shaped assembly layouts were shown to be more efficient than conventional straight lines. A great majority of studies on U-shaped assembly lines assume deterministic environments and ignore uncertainty in the assembly operation durations. In [119], the robust optimization was used for U-shaped assembly planning. It was assumed that the assembly operation durations are not fixed and can vary from time to time. A robust optimization that considers worst-case scenarios was employed. To avoid over-pessimism, the authors of this paper assumed that only a subset of assembly operation times may take their worst-case values. To heuristically solve such an uncertain problem, an iterative heuristic algorithm has been developed. The efficiency of the developed algorithm was evaluated with computational tests. In [120], an algorithm for robust scheduling on parallel unrelated (or uniform) machines is proposed [40,41]. The proposed algorithm is based on the combination of a robust model and discrete event models, which are iteratively called one after another in order to converge towards a robust schedule, with the required robustness determined by a decision-maker. Computer experiments in a small instance (10 jobs and 2 unrelated machines) and in a large instance (30 jobs and 6 uniform machines) showed that the proposed algorithm permits to quickly converge to a robust optimal schedule, even if the probability distribution of the random job durations is not symmetrical. The proposed algorithm achieved a better rate of convergence than those of the OR literature's algorithms.

Digital material structure is a lattice composed by discrete elements, which are connected to create assemblies that can exhibit the high-performance mechanical characteristics. The paper [121] presents the development and robustness of the processing system, which is called the gantry autonomous robotic integrator. This integrator is designed to automatically assemble these digital material structures. The relative positioning tolerance of the connecting elements and algorithms increasing the reliability of the automated assembly of these structures have been specified in this paper. A compact end-effectors design was presented, which showed a high precision and adjustability. The calibration procedures for building a plate were determined. The bolting reliability for the end-effectors was analyzed in order to identify tolerance requirements and establish performance benchmarks for component feed workstations. Two external cases for testing the bolting reliability of the end-effectors were explored.

Human operators are often faced with accelerating job demands, such as elevated cognitive complexities. An objective measure of a mental workload is in high demand, as indicated in theory and practice. The article [122] explored the wearability and external validity of pupillometry, a measure of mental workload, estimated robustly and validated in laboratory settings and deployable in work settings, demanding human operator mobility. In an ecologically valid work environment, participants performed two manual assembly operations (one of low complexity and another of high complexity) while wearing eye-tracking glasses for pupil size measurement. The obtained results revealed that the device was perceived as fairly wearable in terms of physical and mental comfort. In terms of validity, no significant differences in mean pupil size were found between the assemblies, even though the subjective mental workload significantly differed. Exploratory analyses on the pupil size when attending to the assembly instructions were inconclusive. It is suggested that current laboratory-based procedures might not be adequate yet for mobile pupillometry. These findings invite a more nuanced view on the current validity of laboratory-validated physiological measures of mental workload when applied in real-life problem settings.

Industry 4.0 reflects a new stage for production workshops. This concept aims to bring flexibility and agility to the production workshop. The scheduling problem is an important issue. A schedule has to guarantee a high level, able to take into consideration several possible changes and duration perturbations occurring in the workshop. The algorithms proposed in [123] aim to find a robust optimal schedule capable of optimizing both the usual scheduling theory criterion and robust criterion, considering a possible operation duration perturbation. With these requirements of the workshop and the importance of decision-making when implementing the constructed schedule in the uncertain environment, it is essential to extend the robust scheduling problem to be adaptable to the needs of a decision-maker in evaluating robust properties. In [123], a robust scheduling framework was proposed based on a robustness specification. The paper demonstrates the use of this framework in a decision-making context.

Mass customization requires a frequent product changeover that leads to the need of manufacturing systems endowed with the flexibility and reconfiguration capabilities in order to be robust to possible changes in the production scenarios. Manufacturing companies face a risk when making strategic decisions on the system resources. This risk can be mitigated by exploiting performance evaluation models (such as analytical ones and a discrete event simulation) that may be adopted to estimate the performance of suitable system configurations. Decision-support tools for optimizing production system configurations can be loosely coupled with performance evaluation models. Hence, such models undermine the actual optimization of the production system, even more if production requirements may evolve in the future. The paper [124] presents a methodology for supporting the optimization of a manufacturing system configuration and reconfiguration subject to evolving production requirements. The proposed analytical methodology integrates a stochastic analytical model for a performance evaluation of manufacturing production lines into a mixed-integer programming based on the original problem linearization. The advantage of using the proposed methodology was shown on a production line configuration problem, where buffer capacity and machine capability have to be jointly optimized in order to minimize total costs and satisfy the target performance.

The approach described in [125] attempts to integrate agility aspects used in the APRS project, which was developed at the National Institute of Standards and Technology. The main idea for the APRS project was to develop the measurement science in the form of an integrated agility framework, enabling manufacturers to assess and assure the agility performance of the used robot systems. This includes robot agility performance metrics, several information models, test algorithms and some protocols. A model for a planning domain definition language was presented, which is used within the APRS project. It was an attempt to standardize artificial intelligence planning languages. The described model has been defined in the XMLS language and in the Web ontology language for kit building applications. Kit building is a process that brings parts that will be used in assembly operations together in a kit, and then moves the kit to the area where the parts are used in the final assembly. The paper [125] presented a tool that was capable of automatically and dynamically generating files from the model in order to generate a plan from scratch. The ability of the tool to update a problem file from a relational database for re-planning to recover from failures was also presented.

A frequently changing order stream and product variety require specific robust planning and control, along with a flexible system structure to fulfill the higher customer service level and to keep the total production costs at a reasonable restricted level. In [126], combined production planning and capacity control algorithms for assembly lines were proposed, aiming at balancing the workload of the operators and decreasing the production costs on a considered time horizon. Instead of using an ideal cycle time and manufacturing control rules, the proposed planning and control algorithms were based on adaptive calculations, which were taken from the continuously updated historical production data. The manufacturing execution data were applied for building regression models, predicting the capacity requirements of the possible production scenarios. The historical production data were used as a direct input of discrete-event simulations in order to determine the proper control policies of operator allocations for the possible scenarios. In order to calculate a reliable feasible production plan, the regression models and control policies were integrated in the mathematical programming model for minimizing the total production costs.

The final assembly of the vehicles is frequently designed as a mixed-model assembly line, which effectively produces at a fixed ratio of possible variants. Market forecasts indicate a volatile future demand for the different types of vehicles, including the electrified ones. The resulting uncertainty of the demand affects the ALBP. In [127], a planning algorithm is presented to provide a decision support for the ALBP with an inherent variant flexibility while maintaining the feasibility robustness. In the first step, a worst-case scenario analysis of the uncertain production program was conducted. As a result, assembly operation duration buffers were derived from the expected fluctuations in the model mix. The ALBP was solved by the proposed algorithm, which focused on the trade-off. It aims to distribute the different durations of assembly operations in such a way that the aggregated possible fluctuation of the assembly steps assigned to a workstation was minimized. The number of workstations was to be kept to a minimum. By presenting the resolution options of the trade-off, it was possible to show which options for an action were open to a decision-maker. The combined approach of scenario analyses and the line balancing optimization was developed. The proposed algorithm was applied to the use case in the automotive industry.

The paper [128] addresses production optimization in the case of uncertain parameters. A standard framework for solving such type of problems was depicted in a three-step algorithm. The first two steps were analyzed in [128]. These steps consist of off-line characterization of the problem and the calculation of solutions with the desired performance. A generic algorithm to implement these off-line steps was developed. This approach relies on the calculation of robust off-line solutions. A generic framework of robustness was determined. Five standard optimization problems were derived and related to the stability and sensitivity analysis. The generic approach was applied to a multi-purpose machines problem. The paper [129] addresses the ALBP with the uncertain operation durations. Special machines are used, where the assembly operation duration can be any real number between the given lower and upper bounds. These special machines can compress the durations of assembly operations. This action may lead to a higher cost due to cumulative wear, erosion, fatigue, etc. The cost was described in terms of operation durations via a linear function. A bi-criteria non-linear integer programming was developed, which comprises two inconsistent objective functions (minimizing the predetermined cycle time and minimizing the specific machine total costs). In order to sustain the considered objectives concurrently, the authors of [129] applied the linear programming algorithm for making a combined dimensionless objective. A genetic algorithm was described to heuristically solve the ALBP. Design of experiments was used to tune various parameters of the proposed genetic algorithm.

Assembly lines are manufacturing systems in which a product is assembled progressively in workstations by different workers or machines, each executing a subset of the needed assembly operations. In [130], it is considered the case in which operation execution times are worker-dependent and uncertain, being expressed as intervals of possible values. The goal is to find an assignment of operations and workers to a minimal number of workstations such that the resulting productivity level respects a desired robust measure. Two mixed-integer programming formulations for this problem are proposed. It is shown how these formulations can be adapted to handle the special case in which one must integrate a particular set of workers in the assembly line. A fast construction heuristic is presented that yields high-quality solutions in just a fraction of the time needed to solve the problem to optimality. Computational results showed the benefits of solving the robust optimization problem instead of its deterministic counterpart.

6.2. Stability Analysis of Assembly and Production Lines

The paper [131] deals with the optimization problem, which arises when a new simple assembly line has to be designed subject to a fixed number of the workstations, a predetermined cycle time constraint and the precedence constraints determined on a set of assembly operations. The studied ALBP consists in assigning a set of assembly operations to workstations so as to find the robust assembly line, which can withstand operation duration uncertainty in the robust sense. The assembly line robustness was measured by an indicator called a stability factor. The studied ALBP was proven to be strongly NP-hard, upper bounds were derived on the stability factor and the relation of the stability factor with the stability indicator, called a stability radius, was investigated. A mixed-integer linear programming was proposed for maximizing the stability factor. An alternative formulation was derived when uncertainty originates in the used workstations only. Computational results were reported on a collection of ALBP instances derived from benchmark data used in the OR literature for the deterministic SALBP.

The paper [132] is devoted to study optimization problems arising if a transfer line has to be designed subject to a limited number of available workstations, a cycle time constraint and predetermined precedence relations on the set of assembly operations. The considered problem consists in assigning a set of operations to blocks and the determined blocks to workstations in order to construct a robust transfer line configuration under operation duration uncertainty. The robustness of a transfer line configuration is measured by the stability radius, determined as the maximal amplitude of deviations from the nominal value of the durations of uncertain operations that do not violate the solution feasibility. In order to consider different hypotheses on operation duration uncertainty, the stability radius was based on the Manhattan norm or the Chebyshev norm. The considered problem was proven to be strongly NP-hard. A mixed-integer linear programming was proposed for addressing these problems. In order to accelerate the search for an optimal transfer line, two heuristic algorithms and several reduction rules were derived for the mixed-integer linear programming. Computational results were reported on a collection of instances derived from benchmark data used in the OR literature for the deterministic transfer line balancing problems.

The paper [133] is devoted to the SALBP, which arises when a paced simple assembly line has to be designed for the limited number of workstations, predetermined cycle time and precedence constraints given on a set of the assembly operations. The studied problem consists in assigning a set of assembly operations to available workstations in such a way that the constructed line configuration (a feasible solution) will be robust under the operation duration variability. The solution robustness was measured via the stability radius, which is equal to the maximal amplitude of deviations of assembly operation durations that do not violate the solution feasibility. In this paper, the concept of the stability radius was considered for the Manhattan and Chebyshev norms. For each of these norms, the SALBP was proven to be strongly NP-hard, and a mixed-integer linear programming was developed for addressing these uncertain problems. To accelerate the search for optimal solutions, an upper bound on the stability radius was proven and integrated into the corresponding mixed-integer linear programming. Computational results were reported on uncertain instances derived from benchmark data used for the deterministic SALBP.

In [38], the GALBP was studied, where several workplaces were associated with each available workstation. The sets of assembly operations assigned to the workstation have to be partitioned into blocks. Each assembly operation block regroups all assembly operations to be performed at the same workplace of the workstation. The product items visit workplaces sequentially. The blocks are preceded in a sequential way. The assembly operations grouped into one block are executed simultaneously, and therefore the execution of all operations of the block takes the duration of the longest operation in this block. Such a parallel execution of the assembly operations from the block modifies the manner to take into account the assembly conveyer cycle time. The precedence relations and exclusion constraints exist for available workstations and workplaces. The considered GALBP objective is to assign all given assembly operations to the available workstations and workplaces in order to minimize the assembly line cost, which is estimated as a weighted sum of the number of used workstations and workplaces. The main goal of the article [38] is to propose a stability measure for feasible solutions of the GALBP regarding possible variations of the durations of a certain subset of assembly operations. A heuristic algorithm, providing a compromise between the above objective function and the used stability radius measure, was developed and evaluated on the modified benchmark set of the deterministic instances.

The paper [134] addresses the ALBP, where assembly operation durations are not known before solving the problem but there are the given segments of their possible real values. The objective is to assign the assembly operations to available workstations to minimize the number of workstations while respecting the precedence constraints and the predetermined cycle time of the conveyer. A robust optimization model was developed to hedge against the worst-case scenario of the assembly operation durations. To find a robustly optimal line balance, a breadth-first search algorithm was proposed and evaluated on benchmark problem instances. The computational results obtained were analyzed and some practical recommendations were presented. The SALBP is considered in [135] for describing a special case of the above problem with the infinitely large stability radius of the fixed optimal line balance. For the general case of the SALBP, the lower bounds and upper bounds on the stability radius of the fixed optimal line balance were obtained in the case of an independent perturbation of the numerical assembly line parameters.

The paper [136] deals with a study of the uncertain SALBP-1 with durations of the assembly operations, $t_i, i \in V$, such that segments, $[l_i, u_i]$, of possible durations are only known in advance. When implementing an assembly line balance, the duration, $t_i, i \in V$, of the assembly operation may be equal to any real value enclosed between the lower bound, $l_i \geq 0$, and the upper bound, $u_i \geq l_i$, including these boundaries. A special case of such an uncertain ALBP has been studied, when the lower limit of the allowable segment of possible durations of assembly operations is zero: $l_i = 0$, and the upper limit of the allowable segment is not limited: $u_i = \infty$. The actual duration of the assembly operation, $t_i, i \in V$, must belong to the semi-interval, $[0, \infty)$. In the considered SALBP-1, it is assumed that the set V includes the following two types of assembly operations: A subset $\widetilde{V}$ of the set V contains all assembly operations for which it is impossible to determine exact values of the duration of their execution (such assembly operations include manual operations, that is, operations performed manually without a special automation). The duration of each of the other assembly operations is precisely determined in advance and does not change during the pipeline lifecycle. To analyze the stability of the optimal line balance, the radius, $\rho_{b_1}(t)$, of its stability (called a stability radius) is used. If the stability radius of the optimal line balance, b_1, is strictly positive, then any joint and independent changes in the durations of manual operations, $t_i, i \in \widetilde{V}$, within a ball with the radius, $\rho_{b_1}(t)$, in $\widetilde{n} = \left|\widetilde{V}\right|$-dimensional real space with the Chebyshev norm, must maintain the optimality of the line balance, b_1. If the stability radius of the optimal line balance is zero, then there will be arbitrarily small changes in the durations of the manual operations, which can deprive the optimality of the line balance, b_1. The paper [136] contains the criterion for the stability of the optimal line balance for the SALBP-1 and the formula for calculating the stability radius of the optimal line balance for a general case of the SALBP-1.

In [137], the uncertain SALBP-2 is considered. The assembly operation set is partitioned into two subsets, manual and automated. The durations of the manual operations are variable and those of the automated operations are fixed during the whole period of using the assembly line. A stability analysis is conducted for this uncertain problem. First, a sufficient and necessary condition for the optimal line balance is derived to have an infinitely large stability radius. Second, formulas and an algorithm for calculating the stability radii for the optimal line balances are derived. Third, computational results for the stability analysis of the benchmark instances are reported. Managerial implications of the stability results are outlined for choosing the most stable line balances, which save their optimality despite the variations of the assembly operation durations, and for identifying the right time for the re-balancing of the assembly line.

The book chapter [138] is devoted to the stability analysis of the SALBP-2. For an optimal line balance, its stability is investigated with respect to simultaneous independent variations of the processing times of the assembly operations. Necessary and sufficient conditions when optimality of a line balance is stable with respect to sufficiently small variations of operation times were proven. It was shown how to calculate lower and upper bounds on the stability radius, i.e., the maximal value of simultaneous independent variations of the processing times, keeping the optimality of the line balance at hand. The algorithm was developed for selecting the set of all stable line balances (for each stable line balance, the stability radius is strictly positive).

The article [139] is devoted to the uncertain SALBP-2. In this problem, it is assumed that the given set of operations includes two types of assembly operations: manual and automated. For the assembly line, it is necessary to minimize the cycle time for processing a partially ordered set of operations on the linearly ordered workstations. The number of workstations and the initial processing times of the assembly operations are given. However, for a set of the manual operations, it is impossible to fix the processing times for the whole lifecycle of the assembly line. On the other hand, for each automated operation, the processing time is fixed. The stability of an optimal line balance of the assembly line with respect to independent variations of the processing times of the manual operations is investigated. It is shown how to calculate the stability radius of the optimal line balance, i.e., the maximal value of simultaneous independent variations of the processing times of the manual operations, keeping the optimality of this line balance. The criterion for the stability of the optimal line balance for the SALBP-2 is proven. Published results on the stability radius of an optimal line balance for a dual SALBP-1 were also surveyed, which minimized the number of workstations for the fixed cycle time.

For the simple assembly line, it is required to minimize the number of workstations for processing a partially ordered set of the operations within a fixed cycle time (SALBP-1). A dual assembly line balancing problem SALBP-2 is to minimize the cycle time, provided that the number of the workstations is fixed. An initial vector of the processing times of the assembly operations is given for both problems, SALBP-1 and SALBP-2. For a subset of the manual operations, the processing times may vary since operators may have different skills, levels of fatigue, experience and motivation. For each automated operation, the processing time cannot vary. In [140], the stability of an optimal line balance for the assembly line is investigated with respect to variations of the processing times of the manual operations (a line balance is stable, if it is optimal for any sufficiently small variation of the processing times). The enumerative algorithms are developed for constructing feasible and stable optimal line balances for the problems SALBP-1 and SALBP-2. Computational results for the stability of the assembly line balances showed that there are a lot of unstable optimal line balances for the tested benchmark assembly lines. The simulation for the benchmark assembly line showed that the stable optimal line balance considerably outperforms the unstable ones. The complexity analysis of the assembly line balancing problems with different partial orders given on the operation set has been developed.

The SALBP-E with interval durations of the manual assembly operations was investigated in [141]. The authors consider the SALBP-E, in which each assembly operation of the partially ordered set of assembly operations needs to be assigned to one workstation of the set of available workstations used for processing the assembly operations. The objective of the SALBP-E is to minimize the product of the number of workstations used in the considered line balance and the cycle time of this line balance among all admissible line balances. This objective is equivalent to maximization of the efficiency, E, which is determined by Equality (1). A feasible line balance is a partition of assembly operations into at least two available workstations, without violating the set of given precedence relations among the assembly operations. It is assumed that during the long lifespan of this existing assembly line, the duration of each manual operation may deviate from an initially estimated real value, while the real duration of each automated operation is deterministic during the lifespan of the assembly line. Sufficient and necessary conditions have been proven for the optimal line balance to be stable (i.e., the stability radius of the optimal line balance is strictly positive). It was shown that the stability radius of an optimal line balance could be infinitely large. Sufficient and necessary conditions were proven for the existence of an infinite optimal line balance. Several lower and upper bounds for a finite stability radius were proven. The formula was proven for obtaining the stability radius of an optimal line balance existing for the SALBP-E.

The book chapter [142] presents a survey of sequencing and scheduling problems with inaccurate data, which can be solved by a stability method. It was assumed that the job processing times (and other given numerical parameters) may take any real values from the given closed intervals. For different possible types of sequencing and scheduling problems, the known mathematical models were discussed along with proven mathematical results and developed algorithms, which are based on the stability analysis of the optimal solutions (i.e., optimal operation sequences or optimal semi-active schedules) with respect to possible variations of input data. The stability method combines a stability analysis, a multi-stage scheduling framework (i.e., off-line planning stages and online scheduling stages) and the solution concept of a minimal dominant set of the semi-active schedules [39,40] (e.g., job or operation sequences), that optimally covers all possible scenarios in the sense that for any feasible scenario, such a dominant set contains at least one optimal solution (optimal operation sequence or optimal semi-active schedule). The mathematical results discussed in this book chapter have been obtained in the period from 1988 to 2013.

The paper [143] is devoted to the calculation of the stability radius of an optimal semi-active schedule for a general shop scheduling problem, where the objective is to minimize the mean (total) flow time. The stability radius denotes the largest quantity of independent variations of the durations of the operations, such that an optimal semi-active schedule of the considered general shop scheduling problem remains optimal. The authors of this paper derived formulas for calculating the stability radius and necessary and sufficient conditions when the stability radius is equal to zero. Computational results on the calculation of the stability radius for randomly generated job-shop scheduling problems were also discussed.

The paper [144] addresses the calculation of the stability radius of the semi-active schedule for a job-shop scheduling problem, when the objectives are to minimize either mean or maximal flow times. The proposed approach may be regarded as a posteriori analysis, in which an optimal semi-active schedule has already been constructed and the main question is to determine such possible changes in the durations of operations so as to not destroy the optimality of the semi-active schedule. The stability radius of the optimal semi-active schedule denotes the largest quantity of independent and simultaneous variations of the durations of the operations, such that an optimal semi-active schedule of the job-shop scheduling problem remains optimal. In scheduling theory [39–41], mainly deterministic problems have been considered, and the durations of jobs and operations are supposed to be provided in advance. Such deterministic scheduling problems do not very often arise in practice. Even if the operation (or job) durations are known before applying a scheduling algorithm, OR workers are forced to consider possible changes and errors within the practical realization of the constructed schedule, e.g., due to additionally arrived jobs, machine breakdowns and the precision of equipment, which are used to calculate the operation durations (or job durations) and so on. In other words, usually in practice, a semi-active schedule has to be realized under uncertain conditions. The influence of errors and changes of the operation durations on the optimality of a semi-active schedule is investigated in [144]. The extensive numerical experiments with randomly generated job-shop scheduling problems were performed and discussed. The developed software provides the possibility of comparing the values of the stability radii, the numbers of optimal semi-active schedules for two criteria: minimization of maximal job completion times and minimization of the sum of job completion times. How large the stability radius was for the tested randomly generated problems was investigated.

6.3. A Stability Approach to Job-Shop Scheduling Problems with Uncertain Parameters

In [142–144], the stability radius of the optimal semi-active schedule for shop scheduling problems was investigated. The developed algorithms can be used to solve a set of uncertain scheduling problems arising in optimization of the assembly and disassembly lines. The authors of these articles present the necessary and sufficient conditions for the existence of a zero-stability radius of the optimal semi-active schedule, as well as formulas for calculating the stability radii in a general case.

The uncertain scheduling problem, $Im||C_{max}$, is studied in [145]. A set of jobs has to be processed on identical machines. Every job may be processed on any available machine without preemptions. The criterion is to minimize the makespan (the completion time of the last job in the schedule). During the realization of a schedule, durations of some jobs may deviate from the initial values estimated before scheduling. Other jobs have fixed durations that are known before scheduling and do not change in the realization of any feasible semi-active schedule. For this uncertain scheduling problem, $Im||C_{max}$, which is NP-hard even for the simplest deterministic case with $m = 2$, a stability analysis of the optimal semi-active schedule was conducted. The necessary and sufficient conditions for an optimal semi-active schedule were proven to be unstable with respect to infinitely small variations of the non-fixed job durations (in this case, the stability radius of the unstable semi-active schedule is equal to zero). It was shown that the stability radius of an optimal semi-active schedule could be infinitely large. The necessary and sufficient conditions for an infinitely large stability radius were proven. Several lower and upper bounds on the stability radius have been established. A formula was proven, and the algorithm was developed for calculating the exact stability radius in a general case of the uncertain problem, $Im||C_{max}$.

In [146], a two-machine shop scheduling problem was studied, provided that only lower and upper bounds on processing times of the jobs are known before scheduling. An exact value of the job processing time remains unknown until completion of this job. The objective is to minimize the makespan (schedule length). The authors of this paper address the issue of how to best execute a semi-active schedule if the job processing time may take any real value from the given segment. Scheduling decisions consist of two phases: an off-line phase and an online phase. Using available information on the lower bounds and upper bounds for each job processing time that are available in the off-line phase, a scheduler can determine a minimal dominant set of semi-active schedules (DS for short) based on sufficient conditions for a schedule domination. The DS optimally covers all possible scenarios of the uncertain job processing times in the sense that, for each scenario, there is at least one semi-active schedule in the DS which is optimal. The DS enables a scheduler to quickly make an online scheduling decision whenever additional information on completing some jobs is available. A scheduler can choose a semi-active schedule, which is optimal for the most scenarios. An algorithm for testing a set of conditions for schedule dominance was developed. The developed algorithm is polynomial in the number of jobs. Computational experiments have shown the effectiveness of the algorithms. If there were no more than 600 jobs, then all 1000 tested instances in each tested series were solved in 1 s. A problem instance with 10,000 jobs was solved in 0.4 s on average. The most problem instances from nine tested problem classes were optimally solved. If the maximum relative error of the job processing time was not greater than 20%, then more than 80% of the tested instances were optimally solved. If the maximum relative error was equal to 50%, then 45%

of the tested instances from the nine problem classes were optimally solved despite the processing time uncertainty.

The paper [147] addresses the issue of how to best execute a schedule in a two-phase scheduling decision framework by considering a two-machine flow-shop scheduling problem, in which the uncertain duration of a job on a machine may take any real value between the lower and upper bounds. The scheduling objective is to minimize the makespan. There are two phases in the proposed scheduling process: the off-line phase (the schedule planning phase) and the online phase (the schedule execution phase). The available information of the lower and upper bounds for uncertain job duration is available at the beginning of the off-line phase, while the local information on the realization (the actual value) of the uncertain duration is available once the corresponding operation of the job on the machine is completed. In the off-line phase, a scheduler prepares a minimal dominant set (DS) of semi-active schedules, which is derived based on a set of sufficient conditions for a semi-active schedule domination that was developed in [146,147]. This dominant set of schedules enables a scheduler to quickly make an online scheduling decision whenever additional local information on the realization of uncertain job durations is available. This DS of schedules optimally covers all feasible realizations of the uncertain job durations. The proposed algorithm enables a scheduler to best execute a semi-active schedule and may end up executing the optimal schedule in instances according to the extensive computational experiments, which was based on randomly generated data up to 1000 jobs. The algorithm for testing the set of sufficient conditions of schedule domination was not only theoretically appealing (polynomial in the number of jobs) but also empirically fast, as the computational experiments indicated.

In [148], a scheduling problem is investigated, provided that input data are uncertain (the duration of a job can take any real value from the closed interval). The criterion is to minimize the total weighted completion time for the jobs. As a solution concept to such an uncertain scheduling problem with uncertain job durations, it is reasonable to consider a minimal dominant set (DS) of job permutations containing an optimal one for each possible realization of the job durations. To find an optimal or approximate permutation to be realized, the authors look for a job permutation with the largest stability box, being a subset of the stability region. A branch-and-bound algorithm was developed for constructing a job permutation with the largest stability box. If several permutations have the same volume of the stability box, one of them was selected due to simple heuristics. The efficiency of the constructed job permutations (how close they are to the optimal permutation) and the efficiency of the developed software, i.e., average CPU time used for an instance, were demonstrated on a wide set of randomly generated instances.

The book chapter [149] addresses a two-stage, minimum-length scheduling problem with n jobs to be processed on two specified machines, where the job processing times are uncertain (only lower and upper bounds for the random processing times are provided before scheduling). For such an uncertain scheduling problem, usually, there is not a single semi-active schedule that remains optimal for all possible realizations of the job processing times. Therefore, it is required to look for a minimal set of semi-active schedules that is dominant. Such a minimal dominant set (DS) of schedules may be represented by a dominance circuit-free digraph. Some useful properties of such a digraph are investigated. To the uncertain scheduling problem under consideration, the stability method is applied, combining a stability analysis, a multi-stage decision framework and the solution concept of a minimal dominant set of semi-active schedules.

7. New Settings of Simple Assembly Line Balancing Problems and Unresolved Issues

As determined by Smith [5], advantages of the division of manual labor can be considered not only as a specialization of human operators, to perform a variety of assembly operations assigned to them, but also as the need to remove workplaces on the assembly line from one another. The need for such a division of manual labor arises in connection with the spread of coronavirus infection (COVID-19) when the financial costs of preventing, treating and coping with the consequences of the disease for workers who have had COVID-19 have become comparable to other costs of an inefficient use of the assembly line. The necessary removal of workstations from one another can be achieved as a result of changing (increasing or, conversely, reducing) the number of actually used workstations (it is assumed that such a workstation is used by one human operator).

Depending on the specific conditions of assembly production and the market's needs for the products to be harvested, an enterprise can either reduce the number of workplaces actually used (i.e., some workplaces will temporarily not be used) or create new workplaces if there is space for this in the assembly shop. Such changes in the composition and location of the assembly line will increase the distance between the human operators of the assembly plant.

One can find other reasons for the need to modernize the composition and configuration of the assembly line during the exploitation of the assembly plant. For example, during the holiday period (in summertime), there is a periodic need to replace qualified assembly line operators with seasonal workers, which may lead to an increase in the duration of some assembly operations. In this case, the required value of the cycle time of the assembly line can be provided, for example, by increasing the number of workstations and the subsequent solution of the SALBP-2 with an increased number of workstations. The division of SALBP into three classes: SALBP-1, SALBP-2 and SALBP-E, proposed in [2], does not provide for the re-designing or optimal modernization of the assembly line during its exploitation. In the most complex simple assembly line balancing problem, SALBP-E, special cases of which are both problems SALBP-1 and SALBP-2, the efficiency of the assembly line is determined by the equality: $E = t_{sum}/(m \cdot c)$, see (1), which does not allow for differentiating the financial costs of commissioning new workstations and the financial losses associated with an increase in the cycle time of the assembly line.

Next, we introduce new settings of simply assembly line balancing problems.

7.1. Maximization of the Effectiveness of Assembly Line Modifications

Due to a significant change in the conditions of assembly production, it may be necessary to solve the following optimization problem, which we denote SALBP-E_α^β. Suppose there is a set, $S = \{S_1, S_2, \dots, S_m\}$, of workstations that can be used in assembly production. The duration, $t_i, i \in V$, of the assembly operations and the partial strict order of their execution, defined by the digraph $G = (V, A)$, are also specified. The average costs $\alpha \geq 0$, for using one workstation from the selected workstation subset of the set, $S = \{S_1, S_2, \dots, S_m\}$, of the workstations available at the enterprise. This cost, $\alpha \geq 0$, includes depreciation of one workstation, energy costs, creation and exploiting of a new workstation, and commissioning of a previously reserved workstation.

The average cost $\beta \geq 0$ of assembling one product on the assembly conveyor is usually known before solving the problem. In the SALBP-E_α^β, it is necessary to find an optimal line balance, $b = (V_1^b, V_2^b, \dots, V_m^b)$, of assembly operations, V, and the cardinality, m, of a subset of workstations used on the assembly conveyor. Using the optimal line balance is required to minimize the following weighted costs:

$$E_\alpha^\beta = \alpha \cdot m + \beta \cdot c \tag{2}$$

for the exploitation of the assembly conveyor and the assembly of the final products of the assembly conveyor. Recall that the SALBP-E proposed in [2] requires maximizing the efficiency of the assembly line, which is determined by the Equality (1).

If the relative costs of the exploitation of the assembly line and the production of assembly products are considered and the equality $\alpha + \beta = 1$ is assumed, then the problem SALBP-E_α^β turns into the problem SALBP-1 with the equality $\beta = 0$, and into the problem SALBP-2 with the equality $\alpha = 0$. If the absolute cost of the exploitation of the assembly line and the production of assembly products are considered, then the objective function of the SALBP-E_α^β takes the form:

$$E_\alpha^\beta = \alpha \cdot \left(\sum_{i=1}^{m} E_i + \sum_{j=m+1}^{m+k} E_j \right) + \beta \cdot c, \tag{3}$$

in the case of increasing the set of workstations of the assembly line by including $k \geq 1$ new workstations in the assembly production.

The objective function of the SALBP-E_α^β is of the form:

$$E_\alpha^\beta = \alpha \cdot \left(\sum_{i=1}^{m} E_i - \sum_{j=k}^{m} E_j \right) + \beta \cdot c \tag{4}$$

if it is needed to reduce the set of workstations of the existing assembly line by excluding $(m - k + 1)$ workstations from the assembly production.

In the Formula (4), the value of E_i determines the total cost of the exploitation of a workstation S_i from a set of the workstations, $S = \{S_1, S_2, \ldots, S_m\}$, used on an operating assembly line. The Formula (3) defines the values of E_i for all the workstations, $S_i \in S$. For workstations of the set, $\{S_{m+1}, S_{m+1}, \ldots, S_{m+k}\}$, the value of $E_j, j \in \{m+1, m+2, \ldots, m+k\}$, in addition to the total cost of operating a workstation S_j includes the cost of creating a workstation, if it is a new workstation, and the cost of putting it into operation, if the workstation S_j was previously reserved.

If the set of workstations in use is increased to a set, $S^+ = \{S_1, S_2, \ldots, S_m, S_{m+1}, \ldots, S_{m+k}\}$, it is necessary to renumber all the workstations in use so that when the workstations are indexed again, the inequality, $u < v$, implies that the workstation S_u precedes the workstation S_v in the modified assembly line, $S^+ = \{\ldots, S_u, \ldots, S_v \ldots\}$.

Similarly, one should renumber the workstations of the set, $S^- = \{S_1, S_2, \ldots, S_{k-1}\}$, which is obtained after removing the set of $(m - k + 1)$ workstations from the original set of workstations, $S = \{S_{i_1}, S_{i_2}, \ldots, S_{i_m}\}$, of the existing assembly conveyor. Note that to simplify the symbols in the Equality (4), a new numbering of workstations that remained in the assembly line reduced on $(m - k + 1)$ workstations was used. The numbering of workstations used in (4) may not correspond to the previous indexing of workstations of the set S, which is consistent with the linear order of the workstations on the assembly line, $S = \{S_{i_1}, S_{i_2}, \ldots, S_{i_m}\}$.

The above problem, SALBP-E_α^β, and its variants, with various objective Functions (2)–(4), are intended for frequent modifications of existing assembly lines, which have become popular due to the accelerated development of technologies and frequent changes in the consumer market, which necessitates the assembly of new product models instead of obsolete assembly products.

7.2. Assembly Line Balancing Problems with Uncertain (Interval) Durations of Assembly Operations

The ALBP with interval durations of assembly operations are not sufficiently investigated in the OR literature. In the articles [136–140], for the problems SALBP-1 and SALBP-2, an analysis of the stability of the optimal line balances of the assembly line was carried out. In the future research, it is planned to study the uncertain problems SALBP-1, SALBP-2, SALBP-E and SALBP-E_α^β, provided that only lower bounds $l_i \geq 0$ and upper bounds $l_i \geq u_i$ with $u_i < \infty$ are known for possible durations of the assembly operations.

To solve the uncertain problems SALBP-1, SALBP-2, SALBP-E and SALBP-E_α^β with interval durations of the assembly operations, one can apply a stable method, similar to the use of this method for solving different scheduling problems with uncertain (interval) durations of the jobs and operations [146–149]. This method is based on the stability analysis of the optimal line balance to interval variations in the durations of assembly operations and uses the following concept of the minimum dominant set. The set of line balances, B, is called the minimum dominant set (DS) for the SALBP, with interval durations of the assembly operation, if for any possible set of operation durations, the set B contains at least one optimal line balance $b \in B$, and the set B has the minimum cardinality among all the dominant sets existing for the SALBP.

8. Conclusions

The simple assembly line balancing problems are fundamental versions of the general ALBP, which has attracted the attention of practitioners and researchers of OR. With respect to the objective functions, the SALBP was classified into SALBP-1, SALBP-2 and SALBP-E. These deterministic problems are not always applicable for real assembly and production lines, since in practice the durations of the assembly operations and other parameters may depend on many factors and are not constant values throughout the lifecycle of the assembly and production lines.

This survey covered most of the papers dealing with the assembly and disassembly line design and balancing under uncertainty. Deterministic models for assembly lines have also been discussed, provided that they are subject to some deviations from normally fixed manufacture conditions. The survey showed that for non-deterministic assembly line design and balancing, most of the referenced papers modeled the assembly operation durations as independent with known probability distributions. Most frequently, such optimization problems have been addressed by heuristic and meta-heuristic approaches. Since the design of assembly and production lines is a strategic problem of high importance, defining the optimal line balances over a large planning horizon, more effort needs to be devoted to the development of efficient exact methods. In the case of the disassembly lines, more attention needs to be paid to the high uncertainty of end-of-life product quantity and quality, as well as to the environmental impact of such lines.

This review focused on assembly and production lines with stochastic, fuzzy and uncertain parameters. We surveyed both the progress in academic knowledge and the current needs of the practitioners. Reviewing the previous studies and studying the needs of the industry led us to propose new settings for the SALBP and highlight the research areas that are worth further investigation. To reduce the financial costs associated with the modification of the existing assembly line, a new formulation, SALBP-E_{α}^{β}, of the SALBP, balancing the assembly line with three variants of the objective Functions (2)–(4), was proposed for further research. These problems, SALBP-E_{α}^{β}, with various objective functions, are intended for frequent modifications of existing assembly lines and production lines due to the accelerated development of technologies and frequent changes in the consumer market, which necessitates the assembly of new product models instead of obsolete assembly products.

Funding: The research was funded by Belarusian Republican Foundation for Fundamental Research, grant number Φ21-010 and grant number Φ23PH-017.

Data Availability Statement: Not applicable.

Conflicts of Interest: The author declares no conflict of interest.

References

1. Salveson, M.E. The assembly line balancing problem. *J. Ind. Eng.* **1955**, *6*, 18–25. [CrossRef]
2. Baybars, I. A survey of exact algorithms for the simple assembly line balancing problem. *Manag. Sci.* **1986**, *32*, 909–932. [CrossRef]
3. Boysen, N.; Fliedner, M.; Scholl, A. A classification of assembly line balancing problems. *Eur. J. Oper. Res.* **2007**, *183*, 674–693. [CrossRef]
4. Scholl, A. *Balancing and Sequencing of Assembly Line*, 2nd ed.; Physical-Verlag: Heidelberg, Germany, 1999.
5. Boysen, N.; Schulze, P.; Scholl, A. Assembly line balancing: What happened in the last fifteen years? *Eur. J. Oper. Res.* **2022**, *301*, 797–814. [CrossRef]
6. Scholl, A.; Becker, C. State-of-the-art exact and heuristic solution procedures for simple assembly line balancing. *Eur. J. Oper. Res.* **2006**, *168*, 666–693. [CrossRef]

7. Becker, C.; Scholl, A. A survey on problems and methods in generalized assembly line balancing. *Eur. J. Oper. Res.* **2006**, *168*, 694–715. [CrossRef]
8. Boysen, N.; Fliedner, M.; Scholl, A. Sequencing mixed-model assembly lines: Survey, classification and model critique. *Eur. J. Oper. Res.* **2009**, *192*, 349–373. [CrossRef]
9. Battaïa, O.; Dolgui, A. Taxonomy of line balancing problems and their solution approaches. *Int. J. Prod. Econ.* **2013**, *142*, 259–277. [CrossRef]
10. Make, M.R.A.; Rashid, M.F.F.A.; Razali, M.M. A review of two-sided assembly line balancing problem. *Int. J. Adv. Manuf. Technol.* **2017**, *89*, 1743–1763. [CrossRef]
11. Boysen, N.; Fliedner, M.; Scholl, A. Assembly line balancing: Which model to use when? *Int. J. Prod. Econ.* **2008**, *111*, 509–528. [CrossRef]
12. Fathi, M.; Ghobakhloo, M. A technical comment on "a review on assembly sequence planning and assembly line balancing optimization using soft computing approaches". *Int. J. Advan. Manuf. Then.* **2014**, *71*, 2033–2042. [CrossRef]
13. Rashid, M.F.F.; Hutabarat, W.; Tiwari, A. A review on assembly sequence planning and assembly line balancing optimisation using soft computing approaches. *Int. J. Adv. Manuf. Technol.* **2012**, *59*, 335–349. [CrossRef]
14. Tasan, S.O.; Tunali, S. A review of the current applications of genetic algorithms in assembly line balancing. *J. Intel. Manuf.* **2008**, *19*, 49–69. [CrossRef]
15. Lusa, A. A survey of the literature on the multiple or parallel assembly line balancing problem. *Eur. J. Indust. Eng.* **2008**, *2*, 50–72. [CrossRef]
16. Hazır, Ö.; Delorme, X.; Dolgui, A. A review of cost and profit oriented line design and balancing problems and solution approaches. *Ann. Rev. Cont.* **2015**, *40*, 14–24. [CrossRef]
17. Hudson, S.; McNamara, T.; Shaaban, S. Unbalanced lines: Where are we now? *Int. J. Prod. Res.* **2014**, *53*, 1895–1911. [CrossRef]
18. Özceylan, E.; Kalayci, C.B.; Güngör, A.; Gupta, S.M. Disassembly line balancing problem: A review of the state of the art and future directions. *Int. J. Prod. Res.* **2019**, *57*, 4805–4827. [CrossRef]
19. Dolgui, A.; Sgarbossa, F.; Simonetto, M. Design and management of assembly systems 4.0: Systematic literature review and research agenda. *Int. J. Prod. Res.* **2021**, *60*, 184–210. [CrossRef]
20. Eghtesadifard, M.; Khalifeh, M.; Khorram, M. A systematic review of research themes and hot topics in assembly line balancing through the web of science within 1990–2017. *Comput. Indust. Eng.* **2020**, *139*, 106182. [CrossRef]
21. Hazır, Ö.; Dolgui, A. Assembly line balancing under uncertainty: Robust optimization models and exact solution method. *Comput. Indust. Eng.* **2013**, *65*, 261–267. [CrossRef]
22. Boysen, N.; Scholl, A.; Wopperer, N. Resequencing of mixed-model assembly lines: Survey and research agenda. *Eur. J. Oper. Res.* **2012**, *216*, 594–604. [CrossRef]
23. Smith, A. *The Glasgow Edition of the Works and Correspondence of Adam Smith: An Inquiry into the Nature and Causes of the Wealth of Nations*; Campbell, R.H., Skinner, A.S., Eds.; Oxford University Press: Oxford, UK, 1776/1979.
24. Ford, H. *My Life and Work*; Open Road Media: New York, NY, USA, 1923/2015.
25. Kucukkoc, I.; Li, Z.; Li, Y. Type-E disassembly line balancing problem with multi-manned workstations. *Optim. Eng.* **2020**, *21*, 611–630. [CrossRef]
26. Rabbani, M.; Radmehr, F.; Manavizadeh, N. Considering the conveyer stoppages in sequencing mixed-model assembly lines by a new fuzzy programming approach. *Int. J. Adv. Manuf. Technol.* **2010**, *10*, 170–180. [CrossRef]
27. Sparling, D.; Miltenburg, J. The mixed-model U-line balancing problem. *Int. J. Oper. Res.* **1998**, *36*, 485–501. [CrossRef]
28. Thomopoulos, N.T. Line balancing—Sequencing for mixed model assembly. *Manag. Sci.* **1967**, *14*, 59–75. [CrossRef]
29. Dar-El, E.M. Mixed-model assembly line sequencing problems. *Omega* **1978**, *6*, 317–323. [CrossRef]
30. Ege, Y.; Azizoglu, M.; Ozdemirel, N. Assembly line balancing with station paralleling. *Comput. Ind. Eng.* **2009**, *57*, 1218–1225. [CrossRef]
31. Kucukkoc, I. Balancing of two-sided disassembly lines: Problem definition, MILP model and genetic algorithm approach. *Comput. Oper. Res.* **2020**, *124*, 105064. [CrossRef]
32. Li, Z.; Kucukkoc, I.; Zhang, Z. Branch, bound and remember algorithm for two sided assembly line balancing problem. *Eur. J. Oper. Res.* **2020**, *284*, 896–905. [CrossRef]
33. Ozcan, U.; Toklu, B. Multiple—Criteria decision-making in two-sided assembly line balancing: A goal programming and a fuzzy goal programming models. *Comput. Oper. Res.* **2009**, *36*, 1955–1965. [CrossRef]
34. Tonge, F.M. *A Heuristic Program for Assembly Line Balancing*; Prentice-Hall: Englewood Cliffs, NJ, USA, 1961.
35. Pinto, P.A.; Dannenbring, D.G.; Khumawala, B.M. A branch and bound algorithm for assembly line balancing with paralleling. *Int. J. Prod. Res.* **1975**, *13*, 183–196. [CrossRef]
36. Mansoor, E.M. Assembly line balancing—An improvement on the ranked positional weight technique. *J. Ind. Eng.* **1964**, *15*, 73–78.
37. Freeman, D.R. A general line balancing model. In Proceedings of the 19th Annual Conference AIIE, Tampa, FL, USA, 9–11 May 1968; pp. 230–235.
38. Gurevsky, E.; Battaïa, O.; Dolgui, A. Stability measure for a generalized assembly line balancing problem. *Discret. Appl. Math.* **2013**, *161*, 377–394. [CrossRef]

39. Tanaev, V.S.; Sotskov, Y.N.; Strusevich, V.A. *Scheduling Theory: Multi-Stage Systems;* Kluwer Academic Publishers: Dordrecht, The Netherlands, 1994.
40. Brucker, P. *Scheduling Algorithms*; Springer: Berlin/Heidelberg, Germany, 1995.
41. Graham, R.E.; Lawler, E.L.; Lenstra, J.K.; Rinnooy Kan, A.H.G. Optimization and approximation in deterministic sequencing and scheduling: A survey. *Ann. Discret. Math.* **1979**, *5*, 287–326.
42. Erel, E.; Sarin, S.C. A survey of the assembly line balancing procedures. *Prod. Planning Control.* **1998**, *9*, 414–434. [CrossRef]
43. Scholl, A.; Klein, R. Balancing assembly lines effectively—A computational comparison. *Eur. J. Oper. Res.* **1999**, *144*, 50–58. [CrossRef]
44. Bala Muralia, G.; Deepakb, B.B.V.L.; Raju Bahubalendrunic, M.V.A.; Biswald, B.B. Optimal assembly sequence planning using hybridized immune simulated annealing technique. *Mater. Today Proc.* **2017**, *4*, 8313–8322. [CrossRef]
45. Nearchou, A.C. A differential evolution algorithm for simple assembly line balancing. In Proceedings of the IFAC 16th Triennial World Congrs, Prague, Czech Republic, 4–8 July 2005; pp. 247–252.
46. Mozdgir, A.; Mahdavi, I.; Badeleh, I.S.; Solimanpur, M. Using the Taguchi method to optimize the differential evolution algorithm parameters for minimizing the workload smoothness index in simple assembly line balancing. *Math. Comput. Model.* **2013**, *57*, 137–151. [CrossRef]
47. Michels, A.S.; Lopes, T.C.; Sikora, C.G.S.; Magatão, L. A Benders' decomposition algorithm with combinatorial cuts for the multi-manned assembly line balancing problem. *Eur. J. Oper. Res.* **2019**, *278*, 796–808. [CrossRef]
48. Jiang, Y.; Huang, Z.; Yang, B.; Yang, W. A review of robotic assembly strategies for the full operation procedure: Planning, execution and evaluation. *Robot. Comput. Integr. Manuf.* **2022**, *78*, 102366. [CrossRef]
49. Sun, B.S.; Wang, L. A decomposition-based matheuristic for supply chain network design with assembly line balancing. *Comput. Ind. Eng.* **2019**, *131*, 408–417. [CrossRef]
50. Martignago, M.; Battaia, O.; Battini, D. Workforce management in manual assembly lines of large products: A case study. *IFAC-PapersOnLine* **2017**, *50*, 6906–6911. [CrossRef]
51. Levitin, G.; Rubinovitz, J.; Shnits, B. A genetic algorithm for robotic assembly line balancing. *Eur. J. Oper. Res.* **2006**, *168*, 811–825. [CrossRef]
52. Hazır, Ö.; Agi, M.A.N.; Guérin, J. A fast and effective heuristic for smoothing workloads on assembly lines: Algorithm design and experimental analysis. *Comput. Oper. Res.* **2020**, *115*, 104857. [CrossRef]
53. Zhang, Z.; Tang, Q.; Zhang, L. Mathematical model and grey wolf optimization for low-carbon and low-noise U-shaped robotic assembly line balancing problem. *J. Cleaner. Prod.* **2019**, *215*, 744–756. [CrossRef]
54. Toksar, M.D.; Isleyen, S.K.; Guner, E.; Baykoc, O.F. Simple and U-type assembly line balancing problems with a learning effect. *Appl. Math. Model.* **2008**, *32*, 2954–2961. [CrossRef]
55. Zhang, R.; Lv, J.; Li, J.; Bao, J.; Zheng, P.; Peng, T. A graph-based reinforcement learning-enabled approach for adaptive human-robot collaborative assembly operations. *J. Manuf. Syst.* **2022**, *63*, 491–503. [CrossRef]
56. Meng, K.; Tang, Q.; Cheng, L.; Zhang, Z.; Yu, C. Solving multi-objective model of assembly line balancing considering preventive maintenance scenarios using heuristic and grey wolf optimizer algorithm. *Eng. Appl. Artif. Intel.* **2021**, *127*, 109341. [CrossRef]
57. Öner-Közen, M.; Minner, S.; Steinthaler, F. Efficiency of paced and unpaced assembly lines under consideration of worker variability—A simulation study. *Comput. Ind. Eng.* **2017**, *111*, 516–526. [CrossRef]
58. Hoedt, S.; Claeys, A.; Schamp, M.; Van Landeghem, H.; Cottyn, J. Countering the forgetting effect in mixed-model manual assembly. *IFAC-PapersOnLine* **2018**, *51*, 856–861. [CrossRef]
59. Borba, L.; Ritt, M. A heuristic and a branch-and-bound algorithm for the assembly line worker assignment and balancing problem. *Comput. Oper. Res.* **2014**, *45*, 87–96. [CrossRef]
60. Karas, A.; Ozcelik, F. Assembly line worker assignment and rebalancing problem: A mathematical model and an artificial bee colony algorithm. *Comput. Indust. Eng.* **2021**, *156*, 107195. [CrossRef]
61. Masehian, E.; Ghandi, S. Assembly sequence and path planning for monotone and nonmonotone assemblies with rigid and flexible parts. *Robot. Comput.-Integr. Manuf.* **2021**, *72*, 102180. [CrossRef]
62. Zhou, B.; He, Z. A material handling scheduling method for mixed-model automotive assembly lines based on an improved static kitting strategy. *Comput. Indust. Eng.* **2020**, *140*, 106268. [CrossRef]
63. Lu, H.; Zhen, H.; Mi, W.; Huang, Y. A physically based approach with human–machine cooperation concept to generate assembly sequences. *Comput. Indust. Eng.* **2015**, *89*, 213–225. [CrossRef]
64. Rade-Vilela, J.R.; Chica, M.; Cordon, O.; Damas, S. A comparative study of multi-objective ant colony optimization algorithms for the time and space assembly line balancing problem. *Appl. Soft. Comput.* **2013**, *13*, 4370–4382. [CrossRef]
65. Che, Z.H. A multi-objective optimization algorithm for solving the supplier selection problem with assembly sequence planning and assembly line balancing. *Comput. Indust. Eng.* **2017**, *105*, 247–259. [CrossRef]
66. Seleim, A.; ElMaraghy, H. Parametric analysis of mixed-model assembly lines using max-plus algebra. *CIRP J. Manuf. Sci. Technol.* **2014**, *7*, 305–314. [CrossRef]
67. Heinecke, G.; Lamparter, S.; Lepratti, R.; Kunz, A. Advanced supply chain information for rule-based sequence adaptations on a mixed-model assembly line with unreliable just-in-sequence deliveries. In Proceedings of the 7th IFAC Conference on Manufacturing Modeling, Management, and Control, Saint Petersburg, Russia, 19–21 June 2013; pp. 1902–1907.
68. Kottas, J.F.; Lau, H.S. A cost oriented approach to stochastic line balancing. *AIIE Trans.* **1973**, *5*, 164–171. [CrossRef]

69. Reeve, N.R.; Thomas, W.H. Balancing stochastic assembly lines. *AIIE Trans.* **1973**, *5*, 223–229. [CrossRef]
70. Silverman, F.N.; Carter, J.C. A cost- based methodology for stochastic line balancing with intermittent line stoppages. *Manag. Sci.* **1986**, *32*, 455–463. [CrossRef]
71. Shin, D. An efficient heuristic for solving stochastic assembly line balancing problem. *Comput. Ind. Eng.* **1990**, *18*, 285–295. [CrossRef]
72. Shin, D.; Min, H. Uniform assembly line balancing with stochastic task limes in just-in-time manufacturing. *Int. J. Oper. Prod. Manag.* **1991**, *11*, 23–34. [CrossRef]
73. Sotskov, Y.N.; Werner, F. (Eds.) *Sequencing and Scheduling with Inaccurate Data*; Nova Science Publishers: Hauppauge, NY, USA, 2014.
74. Himmiche, S.; Aubry, A.; Marange, P.; Petin, J.-F. A framework for robust scheduling under stochastic perturbations. *IFAC-PapersOnLine* **2021**, *54*, 1168–1173. [CrossRef]
75. Lopes, T.C.; Michels, A.S.; Lüders, R.; Magatão, L. A simheuristic approach for throughput maximization of asynchronous buffered stochastic mixed-model assembly lines. *Comput. Oper. Res.* **2020**, *115*, 104863. [CrossRef]
76. Tang, Q.; Li, Z.; Zhang, L.P.; Zhang, C. Balancing stochastic two-sided assembly line with multiple constraints using hybrid teaching-learning-based optimization algorithm. *Comput. Oper. Res.* **2017**, *82*, 102–113. [CrossRef]
77. Gustavo, C.; Sikora, S. Benders' decomposition for the balancing of assembly lines with stochastic demand. *Eur. J. Oper. Res.* **2021**, *292*, 108–124.
78. Zhanga, W.; Xua, W.; Genb, M. Hybrid multiobjective evolutionary algorithm for assembly line balancing problem with stochastic processing time. *Procedia Comput. Sci.* **2014**, *36*, 287–292. [CrossRef]
79. Manavizadeh, N.; Rabbani, M.; Moshtaghi, D.; Jolai, F. Mixed-model assembly line balancing in the make-to-order and stochastic environment using multi-objective evolutionary algorithms. *Expert Syst. Appl.* **2012**, *39*, 12026–12031. [CrossRef]
80. Nazariana, E.; Kob, J. Robust manufacturing line design with controlled moderate robustness in bottleneck buffer time to manage stochastic inter-task times. *J. Manuf. Syst.* **2013**, *32*, 382–391. [CrossRef]
81. Lolli, F.; Balugani, E.; Gamberini, R.; Rimini, B. Assembly line balancing with learning effects. *IFAC-PapersOnLine* **2017**, *50*, 5706–5711. [CrossRef]
82. Mosadegh, H.; Fatemi Ghomi, S.M.T.; Süer, G.A. Stochastic mixed-model assembly line sequencing problem: Mathematical modeling and Q-learning based simulated annealing hyper-heuristics. *Eur. J. Oper. Res.* **2020**, *282*, 530–544. [CrossRef]
83. Saif, U.; Guan, Z.; Liu, W.; Zhana, C.; Wang, B. Pareto based artificial bee colony algorithm for multi objective single model assembly line balancing with uncertain task times. *Comput. Indust. Eng.* **2014**, *76*, 1–15. [CrossRef]
84. Liu, M.; Liu, R.; Yang, X. Workforce assignment in assembly line considering uncertain demand. *IFAC-PapersOnLine* **2019**, *52*, 223–228. [CrossRef]
85. Li, Y.; Peng, R.; Kucukkoc, I.; Tang, X.; Wei, F. System reliability optimization for an assembly line under uncertain random environment. *Comput. Indust. Eng.* **2020**, *146*, 106540. [CrossRef]
86. Agpak, K.; Gökçen, H. A chance-constrained approach to stochastic line balancing problem. *Eur. J. Oper. Res.* **2007**, *180*, 1098–1115. [CrossRef]
87. Borodin, V.; Dolgui, A.; Hnaien, F.; Labadie, N. Component replenishment planning for a single-level assembly system under random lead times: A chance constrained programming approach. *Int. J. Prod. Econ.* **2016**, *181*, 79–86. [CrossRef]
88. Gen, M.; Tsujimura, Y.; Kubot, E. Solving fuzzy assembly-line balancing problem with genetic algorithms. *Comput. Eng.* **1995**, *29*, 543–547.
89. Gen, M.; Tsujimura, Y.; Li, Y. Fuzzy assembly line balancing using genetic algorithms. *Comput. Eng.* **1995**, *31*, 631–634. [CrossRef]
90. Zhou, B.; Zhao, Z. A hybrid fuzzy-neural-based dynamic scheduling method for part feeding of mixed-model assembly lines. *Comput. Ind. Eng.* **2022**, *163*, 107794. [CrossRef]
91. Zacharia, P.T.; Nearchou, A.C. A meta-heuristic algorithm for the fuzzy assembly line balancing type-E problem. *Comput. Oper. Res.* **2013**, *40*, 3033–3044. [CrossRef]
92. Babazadeh, H.; Alavidoost, M.H.; Zarandi, M.H.F.; Sayyari, S.T. An enhanced NSGA-II algorithm for fuzzy bi-objective assembly line balancing problems. *Comput. Indust. Eng.* **2018**, *123*, 189–208. [CrossRef]
93. Alavidoost, M.H.; Babazadeh, H.; Sayyari, S.T. An interactive fuzzy programming approach for bi-objective straight and U-shaped assembly line balancing problem. *Appl. Soft Comput.* **2016**, *40*, 221–235. [CrossRef]
94. Ruppert, T.; Dorgo, G.; Abonyi, J. Fuzzy activity time-based model predictive control of open-station assembly lines. *J. Manuf. Syst.* **2020**, *54*, 12–23. [CrossRef]
95. Alavidoost, M.H.; Tarimoradi, M.; Zarandi, M.H.F. Fuzzy adaptive genetic algorithm for multi-objective assembly line balancing problems. *Appl. Soft Comput.* **2015**, *34*, 655–677. [CrossRef]
96. Alavidoost, M.H.; Zarandi, M.F.; Tarimoradi, M.; Nemati, Y. Modified genetic algorithm for simple straight and U-shaped assembly line balancing with fuzzy processing times. *J. Intel. Manuf.* **2016**, *28*, 313–336. [CrossRef]
97. Huo, J.; Lee, C.K.M. Intelligent workload balance control of the assembly process considering condition-based maintenance. *Advan. Eng. Inform.* **2021**, *49*, 101341. [CrossRef]
98. Huo, J.; Chan, F.T.S.; Lee, C.K.M.; Strandhagen, J.O.; Niu, B. Smart control of the assembly process with a fuzzy control system in the context of Industry 4.0. *Advan. Eng. Inform.* **2020**, *43*, 101031. [CrossRef]
99. Li, K.; Liu, Q.; Xu, W.; Liu, J.; Zhou, Z.; Feng, H. Sequence planning considering human fatigue for human–robot collaboration in disassembly. *Procedia CIRP* **2019**, *83*, 95–104. [CrossRef]

100. Zhou, Z.; Liu, J.; Pham, D.T.; Xu, W.; Ramirez, F.J.; Ji, C.; Liu, Q. Disassembly sequence planning: Recent developments and future trends. *Proc. Inst. Mech. Eng. B* **2019**, *233*, 1450–1471. [CrossRef]
101. Fang, Y.; Ming, H.; Li, M.; Liu, Q.; Pham, D.T. Multi-objective evolutionary simulated annealing optimisation for mixed-model multi-robotic disassembly line balancing with interval processing time. *Int. J. Prod. Res.* **2020**, *58*, 846–862. [CrossRef]
102. Yin, T.; Zhang, Z.; Jiang, J. A Pareto-discrete hummingbird algorithm for partial sequence-dependent disassembly line balancing problem considering tool requirements. *J. Manuf. Syst.* **2021**, *60*, 406–428. [CrossRef]
103. Munker, S.; Schmitt, R.H. CAD-based and/or graph generation algorithms in (dis)assembly sequence planning of complex products. *Procedia CIRP* **2022**, *106*, 144–149. [CrossRef]
104. Wang, K.; Li, X.; Gao, L.; Li, P.; Gupta, S.M. A genetic simulated annealing algorithm for parallel partial disassembly line balancing problem. *Appl. Soft Comput.* **2021**, *107*, 107404. [CrossRef]
105. Liu, J.; Wang, S. Balancing disassembly line in product recovery to promote the coordinated development of economy and environment. *Sustainability* **2017**, *9*, 309. [CrossRef]
106. Ren, Y.; Yu, D.; Zhang, C.; Tian, G.; Meng, L.; Zhou, X. An improved gravitational search algorithm for profit-oriented partial disassembly line balancing problem. *Int. J. Prod. Res.* **2017**, *55*, 7302–7316. [CrossRef]
107. Kang, K.; Zhong, R.Y.; Nassehi, A. Integrated disassembly and assembly model for heavy duty equipment maintenance. *Procedia CIRP* **2020**, *93*, 995–1000. [CrossRef]
108. Liang, J.; Guo, S.; Du, B.; Liu, W.; Zhang, Y. Restart genetic flatworm algorithm for two-sided disassembly line balancing problem considering negative impact of destructive disassembly. *J. Clean. Prod.* **2022**, *355*, 131708. [CrossRef]
109. Vaisi, B. A review of optimization models and applications in robotic manufacturing systems: Industry 4.0 and beyond. *Decis. Anal. J.* **2022**, *2*, 100031. [CrossRef]
110. Stief, P.; Dantan, J.-Y.; Etienne, A.; Siadat, A. A new methodology to analyze the functional and physical architecture of existing products for an assembly oriented product family identification. *Procedia CIRP* **2019**, *83*, 71–76. [CrossRef]
111. Kaipu, W.; Xinyu, L.; Liang, G.; Garg, A. Partial disassembly line balancing for energy consumption and profit under uncertainty. *Robot. Comput. Integ. Manuf.* **2019**, *59*, 235–251.
112. Minca, E.; Filipescu, A.; Voda, A. Modelling and control of an assembly/disassembly mechatronics line served by mobile robot with manipulator. *Control. Eng. Pract.* **2014**, *31*, 50–62. [CrossRef]
113. Laili, Y.; Feia, W.; Wang, Y.; Pham, D.T.; Zhang, L. Interference probability matrix for disassembly sequence planning under uncertain interference. *J. Manuf. Syst.* **2021**, *60*, 214–225. [CrossRef]
114. Laili, Y.; Li, Y.; Fang, Y.; Pham, D.T.; Zhang, L. Model review and algorithm comparison on multi-objective disassembly line balancing. *J. Manuf. Syst.* **2020**, *56*, 484–500. [CrossRef]
115. Wang, W.; Tiana, G.; Zhang, T.; Jabarullah, N.H.; Li, F.; Fathollahi-Fard, A.M.; Wang, D.; Li, Z. Scheme selection of design for disassembly (DFD) based on sustainability: A novel hybrid of interval 2-tuple linguistic intuitionist fuzzy numbers and regret theory. *J. Clean. Prod.* **2021**, *281*, 124724. [CrossRef]
116. Fei, Y.; James, P.; Zhang, L.; Yuanjun, L.; Yongjing, W. A self-evolving system for robotic disassembly sequence planning under uncertain interference conditions. *Robot. Comp. Integ. Manuf.* **2022**, *78*, 102392.
117. Moncayo-Martınez, L.A.; Zhang, D.Z. Optimising safety stock placement and lead time in an assembly supply chain using bi-objective MAX–MIN ant system. *Int. J. Prod. Econ.* **2013**, *145*, 18–28. [CrossRef]
118. Dehghan-Sanej, K.; Eghbali-Zarch, M.; Tavakkoli-Moghaddam, R.; Sajadi, S.M.; Sadjadi, S.J. Solving a new robust reverse job shop scheduling problem by meta-heuristic algorithms. *Eng. Appl. Artif. Intel.* **2021**, *101*, 104207. [CrossRef]
119. Hazır, Ö.; Dolgui, A. A decomposition based solution algorithm for U-type assembly line balancing with interval data. *Comput. Oper. Res.* **2015**, *59*, 126–131. [CrossRef]
120. Aubry, A.; Marangé, P.; Lemoine, D.; Himmiche, S.; Norre, S. Hybridization of mixed-integer linear program and discrete event systems for robust scheduling on parallel machines. *IFIP Advan. Inform. Comm. Techn.* **2021**, *630*, 73–80.
121. Formoso, O.; Trinh, G.; Hu, S.; Cheung, K. Development and robustness characterization of a digital material assembly system. *Procedia Manuf.* **2018**, *26*, 1003–1013. [CrossRef]
122. Van Acker, B.B.; Bombeke, K.; Durnez, W.; Parmentier, D.D.; Mateus, J.C.; Biondi, A.; Saldien, J.; Vlerick, P. Mobile pupillometry in manual assembly: A pilot study exploring the wearability and external validity of a renowned mental workload lab measure. *Int. J. Industr. Ergonom.* **2020**, *75*, 102891. [CrossRef]
123. Magnanini, M.C.; Terkaj, W.; Tolio, T. Robust optimization of manufacturing systems flexibility. *Procedia CIRP* **2021**, *96*, 63–68. [CrossRef]
124. Gyulai, D.; Kadar, B.; Monosotori, L. Robust production planning and capacity control for flexible assembly lines. *IFAC-PapersOnLine* **2015**, *48*, 2312–2317. [CrossRef]
125. Kootbally, Z.; Schlenoff, C.; Lawler, C.; Kramer, T.; Gupta, S.K. Towards robust assembly with knowledge representation for the planning domain definition language (PDDL) Robot. *Comput. Integr. Manuf.* **2015**, *33*, 42–55. [CrossRef]
126. Breckle, T.; Manns, M.; Kiefer, J. Assembly system design using interval-based customer demand. *J. Manuf. Syst.* **2021**, *60*, 239–251. [CrossRef]
127. Fisel, J.; Exner, Y.; Stricker, N.; Lanza, G. Variant flexibility in assembly line balancing under the premise of feasibility robustness. *Procedia CIRP* **2018**, *72*, 774–779. [CrossRef]

128. Aubry, A.; Rossi, A.; Jacomino, M. A generic off-line approach for dealing with uncertainty in production systems optimization. In Proceedings of the 13th IFAC Symposium on Information Control Problems in Manufacturing, Moscow, Russia, 3–5 June 2009; pp. 1481–1486.
129. Hamta, N.; Fatemi Ghomi, S.M.T.; Jolai, F.; Bahalke, U. Bi-criteria assembly line balancing by considering flexible operation times. *Appl. Math. Model.* **2011**, *35*, 5592–5608. [CrossRef]
130. Moreira, M.C.O.; Cordeau, J.-F.; Costa, A.M.; Laporte, G. Robust assembly line balancing with heterogeneous workers. *Comput. Ind. Eng.* **2015**, *88*, 254–263. [CrossRef]
131. Gurevsky, E.; Rasamimanana, A.; Pirogov, A.; Dolgui, A.; Rossi, A. Stability factor for robust balancing of simple assembly lines under uncertainty. *Discr. Appl. Math.* **2022**, *318*, 113–132. [CrossRef]
132. Pirogov, A.; Gurevsky, E.; Rossi, A.; Dolgui, A. Robust balancing of transfer lines with blocks of uncertain parallel tasks under fixed cycle time and space restrictions. *Eur. J. Oper. Res.* **2021**, *290*, 946–955. [CrossRef]
133. Rossi, A.; Gurevsky, E.; Battaia, O.; Dolgui, A. Maximizing the robustness for simple assembly lines with fixed cycle time and limited number of workstations. *Discret. Appl. Math.* **2016**, *208*, 123–136. [CrossRef]
134. Gurevsky, E.; Battaia, O.; Dolgui, A. Robust balancing of straight assembly lines with interval task times. *J. Oper. Res. Soc.* **2013**, *64*, 1607–1613. [CrossRef]
135. Kuzmin, K.G.; Haritonova, V.R. Estimating the stability radius of an optimal solution to the simple assembly line balancing problem. *J. Appl. Indust. Math.* **2019**, *13*, 250–260. [CrossRef]
136. Sotskov, Y.N.; Dolgui, A.; Portmann, M.-C. Stability analysis of optimal balance for assembly line with fixed cycle time. *Eur. J. Oper. Res.* **2006**, *168*, 783–797. [CrossRef]
137. Lai, T.-C.; Sotskov, Y.N.; Dolgui, A.; Zatsiupa, A. Stability radii of optimal assembly line balances with a fixed workstation set. *Int. J. Prod. Econ.* **2016**, *162*, 356–371. [CrossRef]
138. Sotskov, Y.N.; Dolgui, A.; Sotskova, N.; Werner, F. Stability of optimal line balance with given station set. In *Supply Chain Optimization, Applied Optimization*; Springer: New York, NY, USA, 2005; Volume 94, pp. 135–149.
139. Sotskov, Y.N.; Werner, F.; Zatsiupa, A. Calculation of the stability radius of an optimal line balance. In Proceedings of the 14th IFAC Symposium on Information Control Problems in Manufacturing, Bucharest, Romania, 23–25 May 2012; pp. 192–197.
140. Sotskov, Y.N.; Dolgui, A.; Lai, T.-C.; Zatsiupa, A. Enumerations and stability analysis of feasible and optimal line balances for simple assembly lines. *Comput. Indust. Eng.* **2015**, *90*, 241–258. [CrossRef]
141. Lai, T.-C.; Sotskov, Y.N.; Dolgui, A. The stability radius of an optimal line balance with maximum efficiency for a simple assembly line. *Eur. J. Oper. Res.* **2019**, *274*, 466–481. [CrossRef]
142. Sotskov, Y.N.; Werner, F. (Eds.) A stability approach in sequencing and scheduling. In *Sequencing and Scheduling with Inaccurate Data*; Nova Science Publishers: Hauppauge, NY, USA, 2014; pp. 283–344.
143. Brasel, H.; Sotskov, Y.N.; Werner, F. Stability of a schedule minimizing mean flow time. *Math. Comput. Model.* **1996**, *24*, 39–53. [CrossRef]
144. Sotskov, Y.N.; Sotskova, N.; Werner, F. Stability of an optimal schedule in a job shop. *Omega-Int. J. Manag. Sci.* **1997**, *25*, 397–414. [CrossRef]
145. Sotskov, Y.N. Stability of a schedule minimising the makespan for processing jobs on identical machines. *Int. J. Prod. Res.. in press*. [CrossRef]
146. Sotskov, Y.N.; Matsveichuk, N.M.; Hatsura, V.D. Two-machine job-shop scheduling problem to minimize the makespan with uncertain job durations. *Algorithms* **2020**, *13*, 4. [CrossRef]
147. Matsveichuk, N.M.; Sotskov, Y.N.; Egorova, N.G.; Lai, T.-C. Schedule execution for two-machine flow-shop with interval processing times. *Math. Comput. Model.* **2009**, *49*, 991–1011. [CrossRef]
148. Sotskov, Y.N.; Egorova, N.G.; Werner, F. Minimizing total weighted completion time with uncertain data: A stability approach. *Autom. Remote Control.* **2010**, *71*, 2038–2057. [CrossRef]
149. Matsveichuk, N.M.; Sotskov, Y.N. A stability approach to two-stage scheduling problem with uncertain processing times. In *Sequencing and Scheduling with Inaccurate Data*; Sotskov, Y.N., Werner, F., Eds.; Nova Science Publishers: Hauppauge, NY, USA, 2014; pp. 377–408.

algorithms

MDPI

Article

Energy Management of a Multi-Source Power System

Omar Salah [1], Abdulrahim Shamayleh [1,2,*] and Shayok Mukhopadhyay [3,*]

1 Engineering Systems Management Program, American University of Sharjah, Sharjah 26666, United Arab Emirates; b00049968@alumni.aus.edu
2 Department of Industrial Engineering, American University of Sharjah, Sharjah 26666, United Arab Emirates
3 Department of Electrical Engineering, American University of Sharjah, Sharjah 26666, United Arab Emirates
* Correspondence: ashamayleh@aus.edu (A.S.); smukhopadhyay@aus.edu (S.M.)

Abstract: This work focuses on energy management for a system operated by multiple energy sources which include batteries, super capacitors, a hydrogen fuel cell, and a photovoltaic cell. The overall objective is to minimize the power consumption from all sources needed to satisfy the system's power demand by optimizing the switching between the different energy sources. A dynamic mathematical model representing the energy sources is developed taking into account the different constraints on the system, i.e., primarily the state-of-charge of the battery and the super capacitors. In addition to the model, a heuristic approach is developed and compared with the mathematical model. Both approaches were tested on a multi-energy source ground robot as a prototype. The novelty of this work is that the scheduling of an energy system consisting of four different types of sources is compared by performing analysis via dynamic programming, and a heuristic approach. The results generated using both methods are analyzed and compared to a standard mode of operation. The comparison validated that the proposed approaches minimize the average power consumption across all sources. The dynamic modeling approach performs well in terms of optimization and provided a superior switching sequence, while the heuristic approach offers the definite advantages in terms of ease of implementation and simple computation requirements. Additionally, the switching sequence provided by the dynamic approach was able to meet the power demand for all simulations performed and showed that the average power consumption across all sources is minimized.

Keywords: batteries; photovoltaic cell; fuel cell; super capacitor; state-of-charge; energy management

Citation: Salah, O.; Shamayleh, A.; Mukhopadhyay, S. Energy Management of a Multi-Source Power System. *Algorithms* **2021**, *14*, 206. https://doi.org/10.3390/a14070206

Academic Editor: Frank Werner

Received: 5 May 2021
Accepted: 6 July 2021
Published: 7 July 2021

1. Introduction

To limit the effects of pollution due to the use of fossil fuels, there is a move toward renewable and sustainable energy sources. This has potential to ensure a better future for our environment. Currently, the transportation industry is responsible for consuming the most significant amount of fossil fuels, where "two-thirds of the oil used around the world currently goes to power vehicles, of which half goes to passenger cars and light trucks" [1]. Therefore, developments in this industry that could result in a reduction in the consumption of fossil fuels would have a significant impact on our environment and society. Consequently, companies and governments are eager to find new methods to generate energy that pave the way toward a clean and efficient transportation system [2].

Research into developing efficient drones and electric vehicles has significantly increased in recent times. There is research on integrating multiple energy sources such as batteries, fuel cells, photovoltaic cells, and super capacitors, onboard such vehicles. Electric vehicles containing only a single source of power can face limitations on the maximum distance they can travel before having to recharge [3]. This is especially important to consider when one wishes to build a robust and reasonably failure resistant power system for a vehicle. The integration of multiple renewable and sustainable sources, along with traditional energy sources, has the potential to improve robustness to failures of individual types of power sources. This was in fact the motivation of the researchers in [4] in developing a fuel-cell battery hybrid propulsion system for a small utility vehicle. According to the authors, the fuel economy was apparently improved by a factor of three. Further, it is important to note that, the integration of multiple types of energy sources is not only important for electric vehicles. But, this is also of definite importance when considering islanded micro grid systems, where the objective is to have a variety of types of energy systems available to meet demand specifically in the absence of a main power grid [5]. Currently even traditional power grids are incorporating multiple different renewable energy sources and batteries [6]. The main principle in energy management of such systems with many different energy sources, is efficiently matching the demand and supply of power in the system. The main challenge faced is determining in what proportion each of the available sources is used to ensure that enough power is available to meet the demand in the system. The process is tedious because of the different characteristics of the various sources integrated into a multi-source power system. The behavior of the power sources must be taken into account to achieve efficient management of the sources.

Drones are ubiquitous, and future drones/flight systems could benefit from multiple onboard energy sources. Drones are used by delivery companies [7,8], as well as by photographers. They are also being used in the medical field to deliver automated external defibrillators to out-of-hospital cardiac arrest patients [9]. Most commercial drones are equipped only with a single lithium-ion battery that allows a maximum flight time of about thirty minutes, mostly less [10]. Presently, researchers are attempting to incorporate multiple renewable and sustainable energy sources in drones [11]. While successful integration of multiple energy sources for long duration flight remains to be researched, as reported in the works above, there are many avenues where utilizing multiple energy sources improves efficiency. This also extends the duration of usage of such a multi-source power system compared to one that uses a single source of a specific type.

Thus, this work is concerned with optimizing the energy management of a system that contains four different types of power sources. The objective is to optimize the scheduling of the switching sequence of the sources to minimize the power dissipation in the system and ensure meeting the power demand. The problem can be approached as a resource-constrained scheduling problem of multiple sources, and is subject to several constraints, mainly the state of charge of the battery and super capacitor [10]. The novelty of this work is that the scheduling of an energy system consisting of four different types of sources is compared by performing analysis via dynamic programming, and a heuristic approach. While the dynamic programming approach performs well in terms of optimization, yet the heuristic based method has definite advantages in terms of ease of implementation and simple computation requirements.

This remainder of this paper is organized as follows: Section 2 presents a review of the literature pertaining to the problem at hand. The methodology, which includes the energy management model, Analytic Hierarchy Process (AHP), and heuristics, is presented in Section 3. Section 4 presents the results and discussion of the demonstration example and the experimental work. Lastly, concluding remarks along with suggestions for future work are presented in Section 5.

2. Literature Review

In this section, we review previous work related to scheduling approaches, battery modeling, fuel cell modeling, super capacitor modeling, usage of power electronics, and control strategies.

2.1. Scheduling Approaches

Researchers have proposed different approaches to optimize the usage of multiple energy sources. One of the approaches is predictive modeling. Torreglosa et al. [12] used predictive control to manage the energy generated from a fuel cell, battery, and super capacitor operated tramway in Spain. The predictive control collected data to generate a sequence of operations of the three sources. Xie et al. [13] compared a stochastic predictive control model of a hybrid electric bus to the traditional dynamic programming with no prediction. The electric bus has two sources of energy; the battery and an engine that uses petrol. The stochastic predictive control model uses Markov Chain Monte Carlo methods to predict the future velocities of the bus. The forecasted velocities are then input into a dynamic programming algorithm to provide the optimal control sequence to minimize the energy consumption of the bus while taking into consideration the state of charge of the battery.

Hu et al. [2] used convex programming on a hybrid bus, integrating a fuel cell and battery, to optimize the power management and sizing of the sources. Hadj-Said et al. [14] also used convex programming for the energy management of an electric powertrain. The researchers used a convex model of the powertrain to minimize the fuel consumption of the vehicle. They compared the model results to traditional dynamic programming. Convex programming provided an optimal solution close to that of dynamic programming. However, convex programming provided one advantage of requiring a lower computation time compared to dynamic programming.

Another method for scheduling sources in electric vehicles is real-time programming. Trovão et al. [15] developed an optimal real-time energy management architecture for electric vehicles using two different sources. The system restricts its search for the optimal solution to the high level categorization considering the capabilities of the available sources to preserve the battery's state of charge by trying to rely heavily on the super capacitors to meet the demands of the vehicle. At the middle level, the energy management system is used to ensure that the power supply is uninterrupted and minimizes the difference in the power demanded and power supplied. Trovão et al. [16] also studied another real-time energy management approach using a fuzzy logic approach on a three-wheeled vehicle. In this approach, a super capacitor was combined with a battery on an electric vehicle. The battery is responsible for supplying the average power demand of the vehicle, while the super capacitor provided the rest of the required energy. They found that there was a 3% reduction in energy consumption by the vehicle, and the battery current RMS value was reduced by 12%.

Zhou et al. [17] proposed an online energy management strategy that combines both an online and offline approach test on hybrid vehicles consisting of a fuel cell and battery. The online energy management is based on the time series prediction model nonlinear autoregressive neural network. After the data is collected, offline optimization-based strategies are used to optimize the use of the sources in the next time window. Additionally, Chen et al. [18] implemented online energy management on a hybrid electric vehicle to reduce energy consumption. The online energy management strategy is divided into two layers. The first layer is used to determine whether the battery alone or the battery and engine will supply the energy demand of the vehicle. The second layer of the strategy is used for the power allocation between the battery and engine when both sources are being used based on a sequence generated by dynamic programming. Under specific driving conditions, the researchers were able to reduce energy consumption by up to 5.77%. Qin et al. [19] employed neuro-dynamic programming (NDP) method to simultaneously optimize fuel economy and battery state-of-charge (SOC). Mathur et al. [20] developed a robust online scheduling framework that utilizes stochastic optimization within a model-based feedback scheme to tackle the uncertainties in electricity prices, electric power demands, water inflows and plant model parameters.

Park et al. [21] used a greedy heuristic to assign batteries and chargers of drones to services with a temporal order. The objective was to find the optimal charging schedule and task dispatching. The researchers divide the batteries and services into categories depending on the required energy to complete tasks and the battery capacity of the drones. They also used integer linear programming to schedule the charging of batteries and dispatching of drones to complete their tasks. They took into account the battery's maximum and minimum states of charge to protect the battery's life and not degrade the battery. Also, Umetani et al. [22] used a linear programming based heuristic algorithm for charging and discharging scheduling the electric vehicles. The algorithm consists of two steps:

solving the linear programming problem and rounding the optimal solution to obtain feasible integer solutions. The heuristic algorithm was able to reduce the peak load of the vehicle while also handling the uncertain demands of the electric vehicle with minimal computation time. Zhen et al. [23] designed a fuzzy mixed integer programming method to support the planning of energy systems management and air pollution mitigation control under multiple uncertainties. Vaccari et al. [24] developed an optimization tool for a general hybrid renewable energy system to generate an operating plan to meet electrical and thermal load requirements with possibly minimum operating costs plan over a specified time horizon.

2.2. Modeling of Power Sources

There are two crucial factors for batteries which are power dissipation and runtime. Chen and Rincon-Mora [25] presented an accurate and efficient battery model that could help researchers predict and optimize the battery's runtime as well as the overall system performance. The model accounts for various dynamic characteristics of the battery, including open-circuit voltage, current, temperature, and many more. While testing their model, the researchers observed less than 0.4% runtime error and a mere 30 mV error in the voltage. While designing hybrid systems, consisting of fuel cells along with batteries and super capacitors, the battery is selected based on its energy requirements to reduce its size and weight. This does not take into account the deep discharges of the battery, which have a significant effect on the battery's lifetime. Therefore, Schaltz et al. [26] and Lami et al. [27] argued that the lifetime of the battery must be considered alongside the energy and power requirements of the battery.

Another aspect of the system that must be modeled and managed is the fuel cell. This is required to minimize the hydrogen consumption to ensure the appropriate runtime. Bernard et al. [28] investigated the effects of the sizing and modeling of the fuel cells in a powertrain powered by fuel cell and energy storage systems. They examined different combinations of fuel cell models alongside energy storage systems to determine which combination results in the least hydrogen consumption to increase the runtime of the powertrain. Pukrushpan [29] stated that the efficiency of fuel cells depends on understanding, predicting, and controlling the distinctive performance of fuel cell systems. He provided a number of modeling and control techniques that can be used to ensure quick and stable dynamic system behavior. Also, he discussed various limitations of the controlling techniques and ways to measure the performance of the fuel cell system.

Lastly, super capacitors are being used more frequently in hybrid vehicles because of their ability to provide a quick burst of current needed during acceleration [8]. Spyker and Nelms [30] explained how to model a super capacitors. Amjadi and Williamson [31] added that a super capacitor can be used to supply the excess instantaneous power needed by a hybrid system. By doing so, the battery's lifetime can be protected and the dynamic stress on the battery is reduced with the help of the super capacitor.

3. Methodology

The methodology includes two parts. First, a dynamic mathematical model representing the energy sources is developed taking into account the different constraints on the system. In the second part, a heuristic approach is developed and compared with the mathematical model.

3.1. Mathematical Model

The decision problem is to determine the optimal switching sequence between the multiple energy sources with the objective of supplying the needed power for a system and minimizing the power dissipation of the energy sources. The basics of some details related to models for batteries, fuel cells, and supercapacitors, used at the level necessary for this work can be found in [5,29,30]. For simplification of the overall model, it is assumed that the power profile of a photovoltaic cell is available beforehand.

3.1.1. Assumptions and Notation

The mathematical model presented in this paper is developed under the following assumptions:

1. The initial state-o-charge of the battery is 100%.
2. The initial state-of-charge of the super capacitor is 100%.
3. The hydrogen tank of the fuel cell is full.
4. The batteries can only be charged by the photovoltaic cell.
5. The super capacitor can be charged from either the batteries or the photovoltaic cell.

The following notation will be used throughout the paper.

3.1.2. Model Formulation

Objective Function

$$Min \sum_{k=1}^{N}\left(\sum_{j=1}^{2} w_{B_j} P_k^{B_j}\left(1-ch_k^{B_j}\right)\right)+\left(w_C P_k^C\left(1-ch_k^C\right)\right)+\left(w_{PV} P_k^{PV}\right)+\left(w_{FC} P_k^{FC}\right) \quad (1)$$

The objective function (1) is of minimization type based on weights assigned to the different power sources that are utilized by the system. The model will use the sources with lowest weight as the preferred source to meet the needed power while the sources with highest weight will be used as needed to ensure that the duration of usage of the system is extended by considering the demand and its nature. The weights are based on four criteria which are cost of using the source, the ease of charging the source, the duration in which the source is able to supply power, and the discharge speed of the source. The first term in the objective function is for the battery, the second term is for the super capacitor, the third is for the photovoltaic cell, and the last term is for the fuel cell. If the batteries or the super capacitor are being charged, the power used to charge these sources will not be considered in the objective function. For instance, if the first battery is being charged from the photovoltaic cell, the power consumed by the battery and supplied by the photovoltaic cell will not be considered in the objective function. Therefore, the power provided by the batteries and super capacitor is multiplied by a factor, $\left(1-ch_k^{B_j}\right)$ and $\left(1-ch_k^C\right)$, made equal to zero when one of these sources is being charged, as shown in the objective function above. All of these sources do not behave in the same manner; each has its own unique characteristics and running costs. A weighting system will be used to account for these differences, developed using an analytic hierarchy process (AHP) presented in Section 3.2. The power supplied by each of the sources will be multiplied by the assigned weight to it; $w_{B_j}, w_C, w_{PV}, w_{FC}$ as shown in the objective function. As an example, we are considering the weights to be $/W (watt of power), but they can have any monetary/appropriate unit as necessary.

Constraints

All of the below equations are essentially constraints to be obeyed while minimizing (1).

Battery Model

The state-of-charge (*SOC*) of the battery is calculated continuously as the system is running using the following Equation (2). The current through the battery is calculated using Equation (3). The battery is operated at rated conditions, providing the maximum continuous current the system is designed for, and for which a specific battery is selected.

$$SOC_k^{B_j} = \Delta t \frac{-1}{C_C} I_k^{B_j}\left(S_k^{B_j} - ch_k^{B_j}\right) + SOC_k^{B_j}((k-1)) \ \forall k \quad (2)$$

$$I_k^{B_j} = I_{Brated} \ \forall k \quad (3)$$

It is assumed that the battery voltage remains constant. The assumption of a constant voltage is valid because a voltage regulator is usually present along with such a battery based supply system. Therefore, the power provided by the battery is calculated using Equation (4).

$$P_k^{B_j} = V_k^{B_j} I_k^{B_j} \left(S_k^{B_j} + ch_k^{B_j}\right) \ \forall k \tag{4}$$

Constraint (5) ensures that both batteries are either charging, idle, or supplying at each time step k. Constraint (6) ensures that only one of the batteries is charging at time step k. Constraint (7) ensures that the state of charge of the batteries stays between 30% and 100% to protect the lifetime of the battery.

$$S_k^{B_j} + ch_k^{B_j} \leq 1 \ \forall k \tag{5}$$

$$\sum_{j=1}^{2} ch_k^{B_j} \leq 1 \ \forall k \tag{6}$$

$$30\% \leq SOC_k^{B_j} \leq 100\% \ \forall k \tag{7}$$

Super Capacitor Model

The time constant of the super capacitor is calculated using Equation (8). When the super capacitor is charging, the voltage is calculated using Equation (9).

$$\tau = \mathrm{RC} \tag{8}$$

$$V_k^C = V_s\left(1 - e^{\frac{-\mathrm{k}\Delta \mathrm{t}}{\tau}}\right) ch_k^C \ \forall k \tag{9}$$

When the super capacitor is supplying the system, the voltage is calculated using Equation (10).

$$V_k^C = V_{k-1}^C \, e^{\frac{-\mathrm{k}\Delta \mathrm{t}}{\tau}} S_k^C \ \forall k \tag{10}$$

If the capacitor is left idle, the voltage remains the same as shown in Equation (11).

$$V_k^C = V_{k-1}^C\left(1 - \left(S_k^C + ch_k^C\right)\right) \forall k \tag{11}$$

The current of the super capacitor is calculated using the following Equation (12).

$$I_k^C = \frac{C \cdot Vs}{\tau} \cdot e^{\frac{-\mathrm{k}\Delta \mathrm{t}}{\tau}} \cdot ch_k^C + \frac{C \cdot Vc((k-1)\Delta t)}{\tau} \cdot e^{\frac{-\mathrm{k}\Delta \mathrm{t}}{\tau}} S_k^C \quad \forall k \tag{12}$$

The power provided by the super capacitor is calculated using Equation (13) and the state-of-charge (SOC) of the super capacitor is calculated continuously as the system runs using Equation (14).

$$P_k^C = I_k^C V_k^C \left(S_k^C + ch_k^C \right) \ \forall k \tag{13}$$

$$SOC_k^C = \frac{V_k^C}{V_{Crated}} \ \forall k \tag{14}$$

The sizing of the super capacitor is based on the rush of current needed during spikes in the energy demand. As an example for the case of considering a drone needing to suddenly navigate to a higher altitude compared to its present altitude, a spike in the drone's demand can occur due to a sudden increase in the drone's traveling altitude. Therefore, the size of the super capacitor needed can be found as follows:

The energy E needed to raise an object of mass m to a height h is:

$$E = mgh \tag{15}$$

where g is the gravitational acceleration.

By definition, 1 joule is equal to 1 volt multiplied by 1 coulomb. Therefore:

$$E = QV \tag{16}$$

where Q is the charge of the super capacitor in coulombs and V is the voltage in volts.

Additionally, the charge of the capacitor is dependent on the capacitance and voltage:

$$Q = CV \tag{17}$$

where C is the capacitance in Farads.

Therefore, by using Equations (15)–(17) the following Equation (18) can be used to determine the size of the super capacitor need. Considering the example of drone flight, a safety factor could also be considered to ensure that the super capacitor can handle any spikes in demand resulting from turbulences encountered during the flight,

$$C = \frac{mgh}{V^2} \tag{18}$$

Constraints (19) ensures that the super capacitor is either charging, supplying, or unused at each time step k.

$$S_k^C + ch_k^C \leq 1 \ \forall k \tag{19}$$

Please note that the capacitor sizing is not constrained to the type of problem, i.e., if the problem is not of drone flight, but of supplying power to an islanded micro grid; then instead of considering the height h in (15), one can simply calculate the energy needed to supply such a spike in demand. Then equating such a spike to the stored energy in a supercapacitor, can trivially give the size of the capacitor necessary.

Photovoltaic Cell Model

The power profile of the photovoltaic cell, $PV(k)$, is uploaded into the system via a controller and its output is determined using Equation (20). The photovoltaic cell can either be supplying the demand of the system or charging one of the batteries.

$$P_k^{PV} = S_k^{PV} PV(k)\left(1 - \left[ch_k^{B_1} + ch_k^{B_2} + ch_k^C\right]\right) \forall k \tag{20}$$

Fuel Cell Model

$$I = \frac{I_{st}}{A_{fc}} \tag{21}$$

where I is the current density, I_{st} is the stack current, and A_{fc} is active cell area of the fuel cell.

Activation losses:

$$V_{act} = a \ln \frac{I}{I_o} \tag{22}$$

where a and I_o are both constants determined experimentally.

Ohmic losses:

$$V_{ohm} = IR_{ohm} \tag{23}$$

$$R_{ohm} = \frac{T_m}{\sigma_m} \tag{24}$$

where T_m is the thickness of the membrane and σ_m is the conductivity of the membrane.

$$\sigma_m = B_1 e^{\left(B_2\left(\frac{1}{303} - \frac{1}{T_{fc}}\right)\right)} \ \mathrm{S/m} \tag{25}$$

where T_{fc} is the operating temperature of the fuel cell.

$$B_1 = B_{11}\lambda_m - B_{12} \tag{26}$$

where B_{11}, B_{12}, and B_2 are constants determined experimentally.

Concentration losses:

$$V_{conc} = I(C_2\frac{I}{I_{max}})^{C_3} \tag{27}$$

where C_2, C_3, I_{max} are constants determined experimentally.

$$V_k^{FC} = E_k - V_k^{act} - V_k^{ohm} - V_k^{conc} \ \forall k \tag{28}$$

where E is the open circuit voltage. Taking into account all the losses involved in the fuel cell, the output voltage can be found using Equation (29) where n is the number of cells in the fuel cell.

$$V_{FCc_{total}} = nV_k^{FC} \ \forall k \tag{29}$$

The power provided by the fuel cell will be calculated using Equation (30).

$$P_k^{FC} = I_k^{FC} V_k^{FC_{total}} S_k^{FC} \ \forall k \tag{30}$$

Constraints (31) and (32) ensure that both batteries are only charged from the photovoltaic cell at time step k.

$$ch_k^{B_1} \le S_k^{PV} \ \forall k \tag{31}$$

$$ch_k^{B_2} \le S_k^{PV} \ \forall k \tag{32}$$

Constraint (33) ensures that the super capacitor can only be charged from the photovoltaic cell at time step k.

$$ch_k^{C} \le S_k^{PV} \ \forall k \tag{33}$$

Constraint (34) ensures that enough power is supplied to meet the demand of the system at all times.

$$P_k^{B_1}\left(1 - ch_k^{B_1}\right) + P_k^{B_2}\left(1 - ch_k^{B_2}\right) + P_k^{C}\left(1 - ch_k^{C}\right) + P_k^{PV} + P_k^{FC}) \ge P_k^{demand} \ \forall k \tag{34}$$

Constraint (35) ensures the super capacitor cannot be charged if any of the batteries is being charged.

$$ch_k^{C} + \sum_{j=1}^{2} ch_k^{B_j} \le 1 \ \forall k \tag{35}$$

3.2. Analytic Hierarchy Process (AHP)

The Analytic hierarchy process is a tool used for making complex decisions reducing them into a sequence of pairwise comparisons to help include both subjective and objective features of a decision. It is important to note that the best option of the alternatives is not one that is the most superior alternative at all criteria, rather it is the one that accomplishes the most appropriate trade-off between the set of criteria.

An AHP will be used to calculate the weights used in the objective function. The criteria by which the sources will be evaluated on are the cost of using the source, the ease of charging the source, the duration in which the source is able to supply power, and the discharge speed of the source. For each criterion, a score is assigned to each of the alternatives according to the decision maker's pairwise comparisons of the alternatives regarding that specific criterion. The higher the score of the alternative, the more important that alternative is with regards to that specific criterion. The scores used in the pairwise comparisons of the alternatives are shown in Table 1.

Table 1. AHP table of relative score [32].

The Verbal Judgment of Preference	Numerical Rating
Extremely important	9
Very strong to extremely important	8
Very strongly important	7
Strongly to very strongly important	6
Strongly important	5
Moderately to strongly important	4
Moderately important	3
Equally to moderately important	2
Equally important	1

AHP also provides a weight for each of the evaluation criteria considered using the decision maker's pairwise comparisons of the criteria. The more important the a criterion is to the decision makers, the higher the weight assigned to that criteria. The AHP then combines each of the alternative's scores with the weights of each criterion, to determine a global score for the alternatives. The global score for the alternatives is a weighted sum of the scores given to the alternative about each of the criteria [32].

3.2.1. Cost of Usage

Table 2 shows the relative scores of the cost of usage for the different power sources. The cost of usage criteria refers to the cost incurred by the system each time the source is used to supply the demand of the system. The scores were allocated by conducting a pair wise comparison between the different sources. For example, the fuel cell will be less costly to use than the battery. Some of the costs a source could experience are the degradation that occurs to the source each time it is used, or it could be the fuel used by the source, for instance, the hydrogen used by fuel cells. Therefore, the cost of usage of the sources is as follows from most feasible to least feasible cost [33]:

$$\text{Photovoltaic cell} \longrightarrow \text{Super capacitor} \longrightarrow \text{Fuel Cell} \longrightarrow \text{Battery}$$

Table 2. Cost of usage relative scores.

Source	Battery	Fuel Cell	SC	PV	Average
Battery	1	1/3	1/6	1/8	0.05
Fuel cell	3	1	1/4	1/6	0.10
SC	6	4	1	1/3	0.28
PV	8	6	3	1	0.57

3.2.2. Ease of Charge

Table 3 shows the relative scores for the different power sources. The ease of charge criteria refers to how easily a source can be charged. Some of the aspects considered were the duration needed to charge the source, and by how many other sources can a source can be charged by, for example, the super capacitor can be charged by the batteries or the PV panel, but the batteries can only be charged by the PV panel. Therefore, the ease of charge of the sources is as follows from highest to lowest [34,35]:

$$\text{Super capacitor} \longrightarrow \text{Battery} \longrightarrow \text{Fuel Cell} \longrightarrow \text{Photovoltaic cell}$$

Table 3. Ease of charge relative scores.

Source	Battery	Fuel Cell	SC	PV	Average
Battery	1	4	1/2	8	0.32
Fuel cell	1/4	1	1/5	7	0.14
SC	2	5	1	9	0.50
PV	1/8	1/7	1/9	1	0.04

3.2.3. Duration

Table 4 shows the duration relative scores for the different power sources. The duration criteria refer to how long the source can supply power to help meet the demand of the system before needing to be charged. Therefore, the duration of the sources from the highest duration to the lowest is as follows [35]:

$$\text{Battery} \longrightarrow \text{Fuel cell} \longrightarrow \text{Photovoltaic cell} \longrightarrow \text{Super capacitor}$$

Table 4. Duration relative scores.

Source	Battery	Fuel Cell	SC	PV	Average
Battery	1	3	8	6	0.55
Fuel cell	1/3	1	7	5	0.30
SC	1/8	1/7	1	1/3	0.05
PV	1/6	15	3	1	0.10

3.2.4. Discharge Speed

Table 5 shows the discharge speed relative scores for the different power sources. The discharge speed criteria refer to how quickly the source can react and discharge to meet the demand of the system once given the command. Therefore, the discharge speed of the sources from the highest to the lowest is as follows [8,33,34]:

$$\text{Super capacitor} \longrightarrow \text{Battery} \longrightarrow \text{Fuel Cell} \longrightarrow \text{Photovoltaic cell}$$

Table 5. Discharge speed relative scores.

Source	Battery	Fuel Cell	SC	PV	Average
Battery	1	3	1/7	5	0.19
Fuel cell	1/3	1	1/8	2	0.08
SC	7	8	1	9	0.68
PV	1/5	1/2	1/9	1	0.05

3.2.5. Criteria

Table 6 shows the relative criteria scores. The importance of each of the criteria will depend on the demand profile of the system. For instance, if the demand profile contains many spikes, then the discharge speed criteria will be given greater weight. This is done to make sure that the system can react in an adequate time to the spikes in demand.

Table 6. Criteria relative scores.

Criteria	Cost of Usage	Ease of Charge	Duration	Discharge Speed	Average
Cost of usage	1	2	1/5	1/3	0.11
Ease of charge	1/2	1	1/7	1/5	0.06
Duration	5	7	1	3	0.56
Discharge speed	3	5	1/3	1	0.27

Finally, the ratings of each of the alternatives are then multiplied by the weights of the sub-criteria and combined to get local ratings concerning each of the criteria. The local ratings are then multiplied by the weights of the criteria and combined to get overall ratings of the alternatives shown in Table 7. For example, the battery weight is found by multiplying $(0.05 \times 0.11) + (0.32 \times 0.06) + (0.55 \times 0.56) + (0.19 \times 0.27) = 0.39$

Table 7. Weights assigned to each of the sources.

Source	Weight
Battery	0.39
Fuel cell	0.21
SC	0.27
PV	0.13

3.3. Heuristic Approach

The developed mathematical model requires a long time to compute the optimal solution; therefore, a heuristic approach was developed to solve the problem under study. The developed heuristic identifies the smallest combination of sources needed to meet the demand of the system. The heuristic algorithm used, assuming two batteries, is shown in Figure 1 and detailed steps are as Algorithm 1:

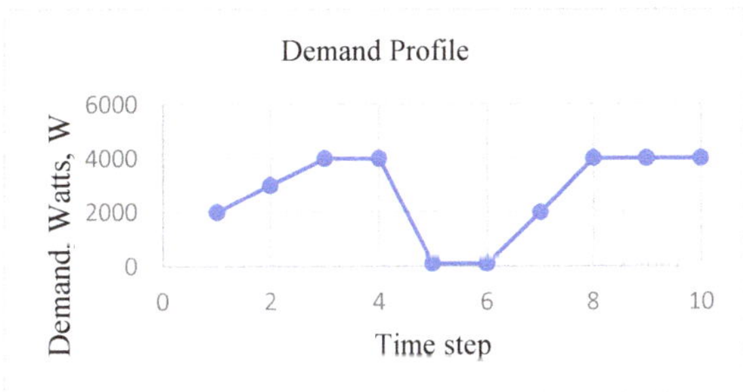

Figure 1. Demand profile.

The heuristic starts with checking if the demand for power is greater than 200 W. The value of 200 W was chosen because the fuel cell provides 210 W of power at rated conditions. If the power demand is less than or equal to 200 W, the system will move into a charging mode. The system will turn on the fuel cell to meet the demand of the drone and check if there is an output from the photovoltaic cell. If the photovoltaic cell is providing an output, the system will check whether or not the super capacitor is fully charged. If the super capacitor is not fully charged, the photovoltaic cell will charge it. Next, the system will check if the batteries are fully charged; if not, they will be charged by the photovoltaic cell individually. On the other hand, if the photovoltaic cell does not provide an output, the system will take no action and move to the next time instant.

If the power demand is greater than 200 W, the system will move to supply mode. First, the system will check if there is a spike in demand. A spike in demand is considered when the demand increases by 30% from a one-time instance to the next. This is done so that the system can discharge the super capacitor during spikes in demand due to the super capacitor's rapid discharge speed [36]. If there is a spike in power demand and the super capacitor is charged, the system will discharge the super capacitor along with other sources to meet the demand of the system.

Algorithm 1. Energy management Heuristic.

for k = 1:10
  if ($P_k^{demand} > 200$)
      if $P_k^{demand} < P_k^{FC}$
    $S_k^{FC} = 1;$
    else if $P_k^{demand} < P_k^{FC} + P_k^{PV}$
    $S_k^{FC} = 1;$
    $S_k^{PV} = 1;.$
    else if $SOC_k^{B_1} > 47$
      if $P_k^{demand} < P_k^{FC} + P_k^{PV} + P_k^{B_1}$
    $S_k^{FC} = 1;$
    $S_k^{PV} = 1;$
    $S_k^{B_1} = 1;$
      else if $SOC_k^{B_2} > 47.$
    $S_k^{FC} = 1;$
    $S_k^{PV} = 1;$
    $S_k^{B_1} = 1;$
    $S_k^{B_2} = 1;$
     else if $SOC_k^{C} = 100$
    $S_k^{FC} = 1;$
    $S_k^{PV} = 1;.$
    $S_k^{B_1} = 1;$
    $S_k^{C} = 1;$
     end
    else if $SOC_k^{B_2} > 47.$
    $S_k^{FC} = 1;$
    $S_k^{PV} = 1;$
    $S_k^{B_2} = 1;$
     else if $SOC_k^{C} = 100$
    $S_k^{FC} = 1;$
    $S_k^{PV} = 1;$
    $S_k^{B_2} = 1;$
    $S_k^{C} = 1;$
     end
end
     if $P_k^{demand} \leq 200$
    $S_k^{FC} = 1;$
      if $SOC_k^{C} < 99$
     $S_k^{PV} = 1;$
$ch_k^{C} = 1;$
else if $SOC_k^{B_1} < 100$
$S_k^{PV} - 1;$
$ch_k^{B_1} = 1;$
else if $SOC_k^{B_2} < 100$
$S_k^{PV} = 1;$
$ch_k^{B_2} = 1;$
      end
end for
return $S_k^{FC}, S_k^{PV}, S_k^{B_1}, S_k^{B_2}, S_k^{C}, ch_k^{C}, ch_k^{B_1}, ch_k^{B_2}$

On the other hand, if there is no spike in demand, the system will not discharge the super capacitor. Next, the system will check if there is an output from the photovoltaic cell to make use of the photovoltaic cell while it provides an output. Assuming that the photovoltaic cell is providing an output, the system will check which combination of sources along with the photovoltaic cell will be able to meet the demand of the system. For instance, if the photovoltaic cell and fuel cell are not enough to meet the demand, the system will first check the state-of-charge of the first battery. If the state-of-charge of the battery is between 47% and 100%, the system will use the fuel cell, photovoltaic cell, and battery to meet the demand of the drone. If the state-of-charge of the first battery is less than 47%, the system will move to check the state-of-charge of the second battery and so on. The range of 47% to 100% was chosen because at the ratings used for simulation (Supercapacitor ratings: 24 V, 200 A, time constant 0.36; Battery ratings: 22.4 V, 165 A; Fuel Cell ratings: 21 V, 10 A; Photovoltaic Cell power rating: 120 W), using a battery for one-time instance reduces the state-of-charge of the battery by 17%, based on the rated power demand considered in this example. If the rated power requirement of the application at hand changes, then this 47% number used for the SOC will have to be changed in the heuristic approach accordingly. Further, the age/health of the battery can also be used to arrive at an appropriate threshold for the SOC to be checked other than 47%-and this is left for future work. Therefore to keep the state-of-charge of the battery greater than or equal to 30%, a lower bound of 47% was chosen for the range. On the occasion that there is no output from the photovoltaic cell, the system will check the remaining sources to meet the demand of the system. Moreover, the heuristic approach could generate a solution in a matter of seconds on Matlab, while the dynamic algorithm used on Lingo sometimes required hours depending on the instance size and model complexity. Please also note that to be able to visualize all the possible switching scenarios in a reasonably short time frame, the battery Ah capacity was reduced the simulation so as not to have to wait for a very long time for energy source switching behavior to be noticed.

4. Demonstration Example and Results

In this section, the results and analysis are presented for generating an optimal switching sequence between the energy sources for a system using the dynamic model and heuristic approaches. To demonstrate that the methodologies developed are not limited to any particular application, the results are demonstrated on two types of applications: (i) simulated power profiles which may be realized in drone flight (ii) experimental verification on a multi-source ground vehicle (robot). In case of the simulated results, three different demonstration scenarios were conducted that simulate the system, a drone in this case. The executed scenarios include object pickup, altitude maintenance, and multiple object pickup. The first scenario will be presented next and the other two are presented in Appendices A and B. Similarly, in case of the experimental results, both approaches were used for experimental verification on a ground robot. Lingo modeling software was used to obtain an optimal solution to the dynamic model, and Matlab was used to obtain the solutions for the heuristic approach and the standard mode of operation. The considered standard mode of operation represents using each source separately until the source is completely depleted, starting with the first battery, followed by the second battery, super capacitor, fuel cell, and finally, the photovoltaic cell. The simulations were conducted for ten-time steps where the step size is five seconds. Only ten time steps were considered due to the large computing power needed to conduct simulations for the full length of a drone's flight. The object pickup scenario and the experimental work are presented next. The other two simulation scenarios, altitude maintenance and multiple object pickup, are presented in Appendices A and B, respectively.

4.1. Object Pickup Scenario–Simulated For Drone Flight

The following simulation represents the situation where a drone must travel to a specific location to pick up an object and return the object to the drone's base. During this simulation, ideal conditions are considered where the drone does not face any disturbances or turbulence during its flight. The assumed demand profile for this simulation is shown in Figure 1. Initially, the drone starts traveling to the location where the object is located. At time step 4, the drone reaches the object's location and descends to pick up the desired object. After the drone picks up the object, it continues its flight to return to its base.

Figures 2–4 display the system voltages, current, and state-of-charge, respectively, for both the dynamic and heuristic approaches. The switching sequence generated by the dynamic approach chose not to use the super capacitor. As for the current, as the super capacitor was not used by the dynamic approach, the current remains 0 while the currents of the batteries vary as they are being used. However, in the heuristic approach, both batteries and the super capacitor were used; therefore, their currents vary accordingly.

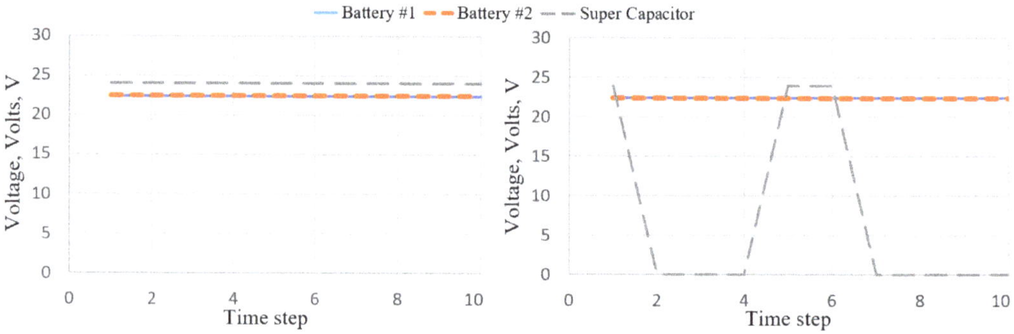

(**a**) Dynamic approach (**b**) Heuristic approach

Figure 2. System voltage.

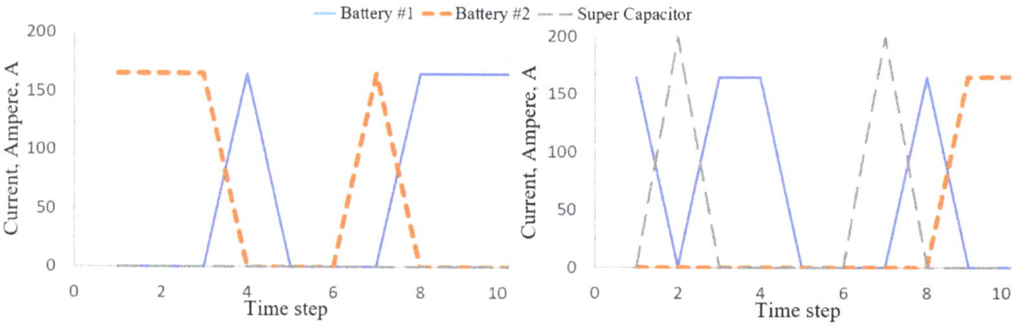

(**a**) Dynamic approach (**b**) Heuristic approach

Figure 3. System currents.

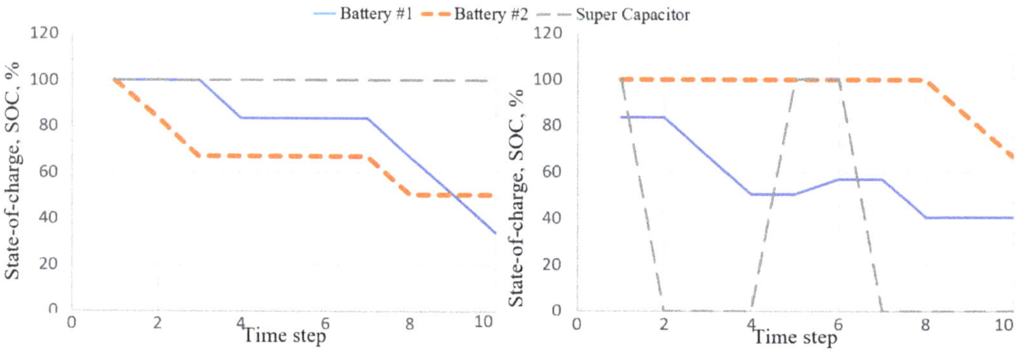

(**a**) Dynamic approach (**b**) Heuristic approach

Figure 4. System state-of-charge.

In the object pickup simulation, both the switching sequences of the dynamic approach and heuristic approach were able to meet the demand of the drone, but that of the standard approach did not. After both batteries and the super capacitor were completely depleted, the standard approach was unable to meet the demand of the drone in the 10th time instance. However, although both the switching sequences of the dynamic approach and heuristic approach met the demand, the dynamic approach provided a sequence of switching superior to that of the heuristic approach. The obtained objective function value of the dynamic approach was 9% lower with a value of 6536.2, while the heuristic approach was 7123.3. However, the switching sequences of the heuristic approach had a lower average power consumption of 3361.2 W compared to the dynamic approach's 3720 W. This was due to the switching sequence of the dynamic approach resulting in significant power consumption in time steps 6 and 7. From Figure 4, the following can also be seen. The dynamic approach resulted in battery 1 having a SOC level of around 35% and battery 2 with a SOC level of around 50% after 10 s. While the SOC level of the supercapacitor was unchanged and remained at 100% throughout the time period. It is worth noting is that none of the batteries enter charging. In contrast, the heuristic approach seems to favor using the supercapacitor as a result of which the supercapacitor is completely discharged, re-charged, and discharged to SOC level zero again within the ten second time period. Battery 1 ends at a SOC level of 40%, and battery 2 ends at a SOC level of around 70%. The differences in behavior can be attributed to the optimization of the objective function value as mentioned above. The power used to meet the demand of the drone during each time step is shown in Figure 5. Figure 6 shows as additional examples the switching sequence and the sources used to meet demand shown in Figure 6a,b at each time step.

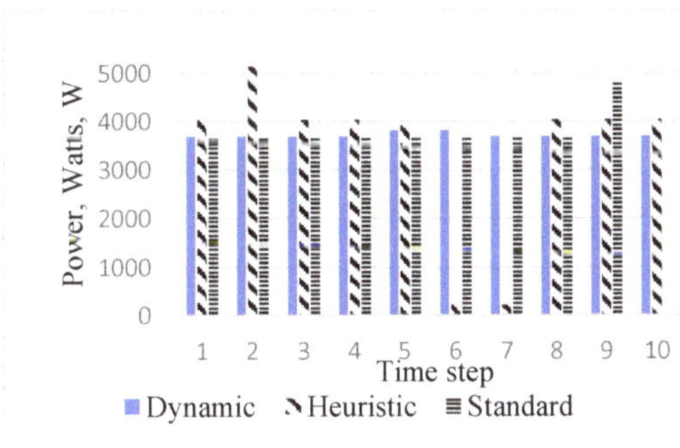

Figure 5. Power consumption comparison.

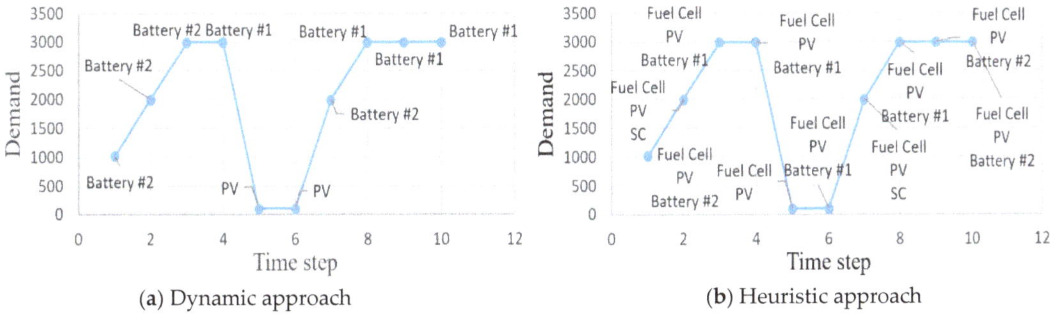

Figure 6. Switching sequence and sources used to meet demand.

4.2. Experimental Work—On a Multi-Energy Source Ground Robot

The following experiment was conducted on a ground robot shown in Figure 7. The ground robot contains three sources: batteries, super capacitor, and fuel cell. The robot was run in remote-control mode while conducting the tests. The robot was controlled by the remote controller to move around a lab bench in a rectangular path. The demand profile for all tests is shown in Figure 8.

Figure 7. Ground Robot and power sources.

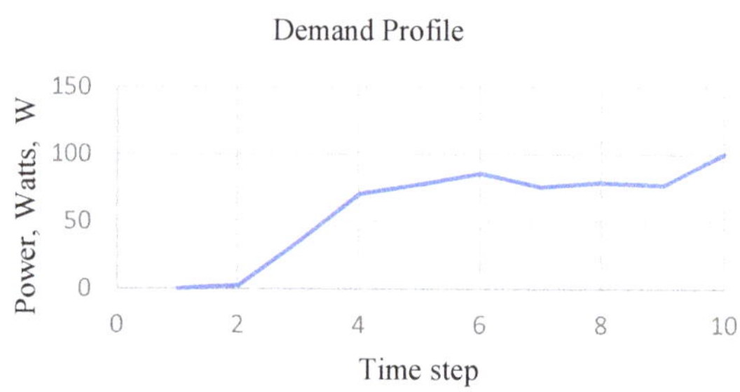

Figure 8. Demand profile for experimental work.

For experimental work, a multi-energy source ground robot was preferred over a drone because of several factors: i.e., (i) limitations related to drone flight height and seeking clearances for flight paths at certain heights, (ii) even if an accurate flight power demand profile was obtained by flying a drone in good weather conditions, the actual flight power demand profile obtained when trying to verify results–cannot be guaranteed because the weather may change and sudden wind gusts may introduce power demand, not accounted for when solving for the dynamic programming solution, and (iii) it is also possible that the wind disturbances introduce differences in the demand profiles when performing an experiment with the heuristic approach, and entirely different power demand profile disturbances occur because of wind gusts when testing the dynamic approach. So, to make a comparison between the proposed approaches, which is free from random power surges due to weather effects, a ground robot with multiple energy sources was favored. Also, it is worth noting that when considering a drone, the demand profile can be easily calculated from first principles, as seen in Equation (15). But when considering a ground robot we have to actually run the robot around a path and acquire a demand curve. This is the procedure followed to get the curve in Figure 8, and therefore it is different from the curve in Figure 1. Please note that the developed approaches are not profile-specific, and can compute a switching sequence for a given demand profile.

The demand profile was uploaded to both the dynamic and heuristic algorithm to obtain a switching sequence. The ground robot has a controller which supplies a given amount of current to the motors if it is given a reference current. The two motors on the robot chassis (one for controlling left side wheel speeds, and one for controlling right side wheel speeds) rotate clockwise or anticlockwise depending on the current received. Based on the direction of the rotation of the motors and the speed of rotation, the robot can be made to move in straight lines, curves, or in circles. This is extremely common in robotics literature and hence the details of the driving process (called differential drive) are not included here. However, there is not necessarily a controller that controls where the current comes from. The switching sequences generated by the dynamic and heuristic approaches tell this same lower level controller what sources to use to supply the required current; to satisfy the demand and still reduce the average power consumption across the sources. The switching sequences were then uploaded to the main controller of the ground robot, an Arduino microcontroller that controls the switches attached to the sources. After the switching sequence was uploaded, the ground robot performed a lap along the rectangular path. The power consumption across all sources after the ground robot completed a lap with the uploaded switching sequences was then compared with the standard mode of operation. For a ground robot, the standard mode of operation assumes no scheduling; however the needed power is first supplied by the battery until it's completely depleted then moving to the other available sources.

Figures 9–11 display the system voltages, current, and state-of-charge, respectively, for the standard mode, the dynamic approach, and the heuristic approach. The standard mode of operation did not involve the super capacitor in meeting the demand of the ground robot. However, the dynamic programming approach and heuristic approach did. As for the current, the use of the super capacitor by the dynamic programming approach and heuristic approach is apparent in Figure 10. The state-of-charge of the battery decreases most in the standard mode of operation, reaching 99.2%.

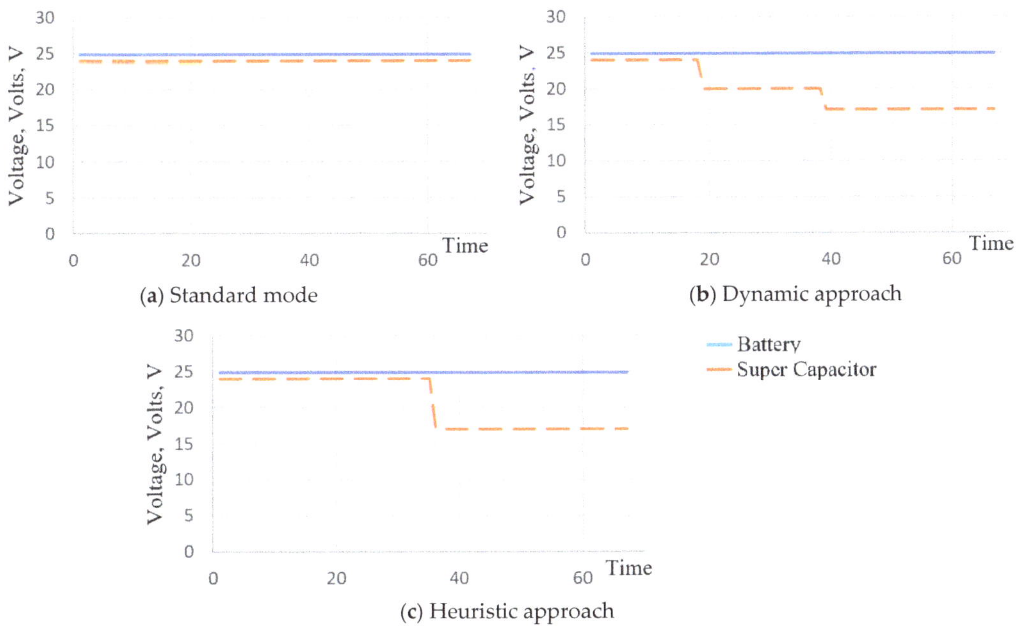

Figure 9. System voltage.

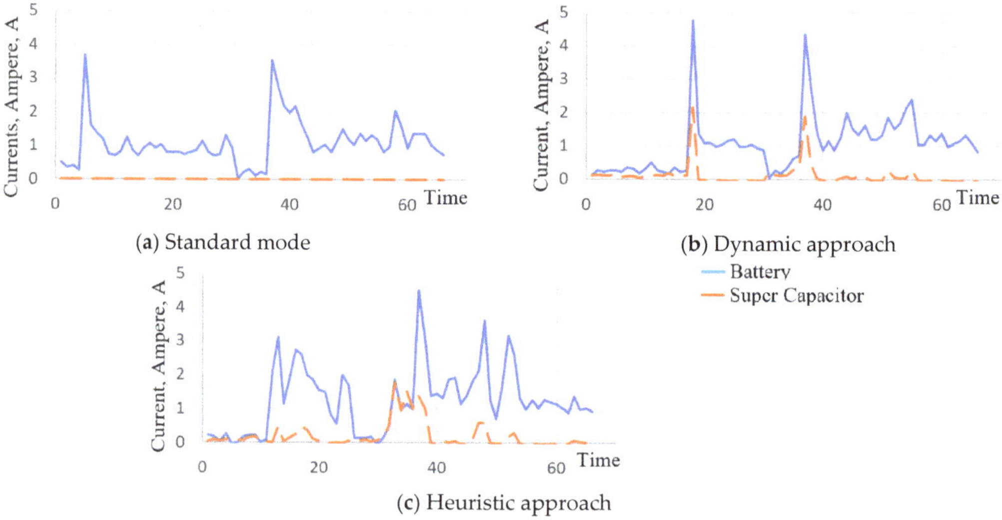

Figure 10. System current.

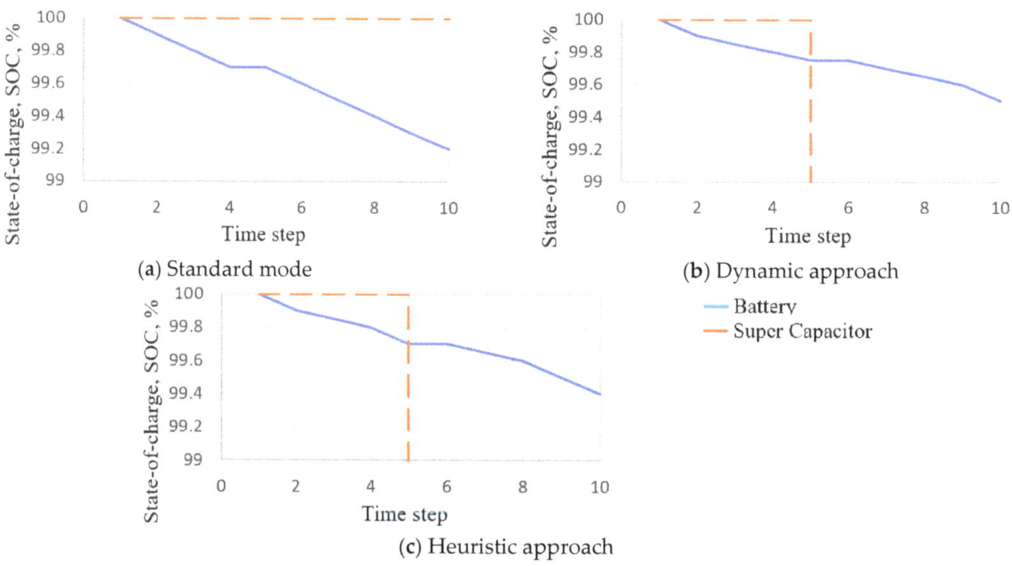

Figure 11. System State-of-Charge.

The standard mode of operation of the ground robot relied solely on the battery to meet the demand. On the other hand, the switching sequence of the dynamic approach chose to use the battery and super capacitor to meet the demand, while the switching sequence of the heuristic approach chose all three sources. Although not visible in the current plots in Figure 10c, it can be seen from the algorithm of the heuristic approach proposed that the fuel cell is chosen by the heuristic approach at all times. Additionally, the current plots for the fuel cell are not shown because the fuel cell unit functions as a base load unit. This is because the fuel cell cannot be turned on/off very quick and has a hydrogen pressure regulator attached to its hydrogen input lines, which maintains a certain amount of gas flow, so the terminal voltage of the fuel cell remains constant, and the fuel cell supplies a certain amount of power. Thus in the heuristic approach, the fuel cell is used as a based load handling device, and the current for the fuel cell is not shown because depending on the overall circuit impedances, and depending on which other source is active, the fuel cell will supply the remainder of the load, and it is not subjected to rapid starts/stops in operation. The switching sequence of the standard mode of operation resulted in the highest average power consumption from the sources, 33.3 W. However, the dynamic approach generated a switching sequence that resulted in a 5.5% decrease in the average power consumption compared to the standard mode of operation due to the voltage dynamics of the sources. Similarly, the switching sequence of the heuristic approach was able to reduce the average power consumption by 2.5%, which is shown in Figure 12. Furthermore, the run time of the ground robot should increase since the system is less dependent on only one source to satisfy the demand.

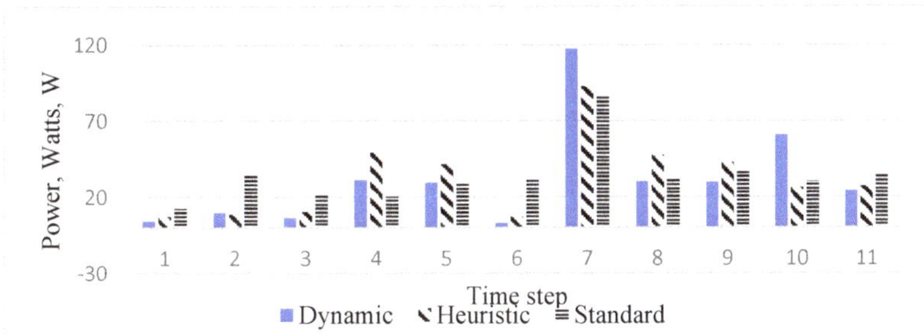

Figure 12. Power consumption comparison.

5. Conclusions

This paper is concerned with multi source power systems consisting of batteries, super capacitors, a hydrogen fuel cell, and a photovoltaic cell. The usage of each of the sources is controlled by turning connected switches on or off as needed to supply the needed power demand of the system. A mathematical model was developed for the efficient energy management of the integrated sources, generating an optimal switching sequence between the sources. Two methods have been developed to solve for the optimal switching sequence.

The first method uses a dynamic mathematical model solved using Lingo to minimize the running cost of the system by generating a switching sequence. The second method uses a heuristic approach, where a set of rules were used to generate the switching sequence. The heuristic algorithm was primarily tested on Matlab. The switching sequences generated by the dynamic approach resulted in power consumption that was on average 9% lower than those of the heuristic approach. However, the main advantage introduced by the heuristic algorithm was the short computational time needed to generate the switching sequence between the sources. The developed approaches were implemented offline before running the system, but can be implemented online. To be implemented online, the algorithms would require readings of the system's behavior and demand to generate the optimal switching sequence.

Additionally, both approaches were tested in simulations of a drone flight scenario, and also experimentally tested on a multi-energy source ground robot. The developed dynamic model was capable of generating a switching sequence that minimized the power dissipation of the energy sources for the illustrative simulation examples of a drone, while the standard mode of operation was failed to provide the needed power. Also, the model was able to prolong the simulated flight time of the drone by charging the batteries and the super capacitor as needed depending on the demand profile. The switching sequences generated by the heuristic algorithm were also able to prolong the flight time in the simulation tests related to the drone, and minimize the power dissipation of the energy sources; but not as well as those of the dynamic modeling approach.

Both the dynamic modeling, and heuristic approaches, when tested on a multi-energy source ground robot, were able to generate switching sequences that minimize the power dissipation by reducing the average power consumption across the sources due to the voltage dynamics of the different sources. However, the dynamic approach's switching sequence resulted in the most significant reduction in the average power consumption; 5.5% lower average power consumption compared to the standard mode of operation of the robot. The switching sequence of the heuristic approach was also able to reduce the average power consumption by 2.5% compared to the standard mode of operation.

The limitations faced in this work include the length of the simulations conducted. Due to the large computing power required by the dynamic model based approach, the simulations were conducted for only fifty seconds. However, with access to more computing power, better switching sequences could be generated that provide a further reduction in the running cost of the system. Additionally, future work could include the real-time management of the sources integrated into the system, alongside continuous readings of the behavior of the system while it is being used. By implementing the real-time management of the sources, the system could become more responsive to fluctuations in demand.

Author Contributions: O.S.: Conceptualization, methodology, programming and writing the original draft. A.S. and S.M.: Conceptualization, methodology, and finalizing the manuscript. All authors have read and agreed to the published version of the manuscript.

Funding: The authors received no specific funding for this work.

Institutional Review Board Statement: Not applicable.

Informed Consent Statement: Not applicable. This article does not contain any studies with human participants or animals performed by any of the authors.

Data Availability Statement: The data presented in this study are available on request from the corresponding author.

Conflicts of Interest: The authors have no conflict of interest to declare.

Abbreviations

k	Time step
Δt	Step size (seconds), using this and k we get time t = kΔt seconds
N	Number of time steps
j	Battery index ∀ j{1,2}
τ	Time constant of the super capacitor
w	Power source relative weight
B_j	Battery number j
C	Super capacitor
PV	Photovoltaic cell
FC	Fuel cell
$S_k^{B_j}$	A binary variable that equals 1, if battery j is supplying the demand of the system at time step k, 0 otherwise
$ch_k^{B_j}$	A binary variable that equals 1, if battery j is being charged from the system time step k, 0 otherwise
S_k^C	A binary variable that equals 1, if the super capacitor is supplying the demand of the system at time step k, 0 otherwise
ch_k^C	A binary variable that equals 1, if the super capacitor is being charged from the system at time step k, 0 otherwise
S_k^{PV}	A binary variable that equals 1, if the photovoltaic cell is supplying the demand of the system at time step k, 0 otherwise

S_k^{FC}	A binary variable that equals 1, if the fuel cell is supplying the demand of the system at time step k, 0 otherwise
$SOC_k^{B_j}$	State of charge of the battery j at time step k
SOC_k^C	State of charge of the super capacitor at time step k
$V_k^{B_j}$	Voltage of the battery j at time step k
$I_k^{B_j}$	Current of the battery j at time step k
$P_k^{B_j}$	Power supplied by the battery j at time step k
V_k^C	Voltage of the super capacitor at time step k
I_k^C	Current of the super capacitor at time step k
P_k^C	Power supplied by the super capacitor at time step k
P_k^{PV}	Power supplied by the photovoltaic cell at time step k
V_k^{FC}	Voltage of the fuel cell at time step k
I_k^{FC}	Current of the fuel cell at time step k
P_k^{FC}	Power supplied by the fuel cell at time step k
P_k^{demand}	Power demanded by the system at time step k

Appendix A. Illustrative Example: Altitude Maintenance

The following simulation represents the situation where a drone must maintain a certain height above the ground for a short period of time. During its flight, the drone faces turbulence causing fluctuations in the demand profile. The demand profile of this simulation is shown in Figure A1; the drone starts ascending to the required height, thus causing an increase in the energy of the drone. At time step 3, the drone reaches the required height and tries to maintain it for five time steps. However, the drone faces significant turbulence causing fluctuations in the height it maintains, which is represented in the demand profile. Finally, the drone begins to descend back to its base.

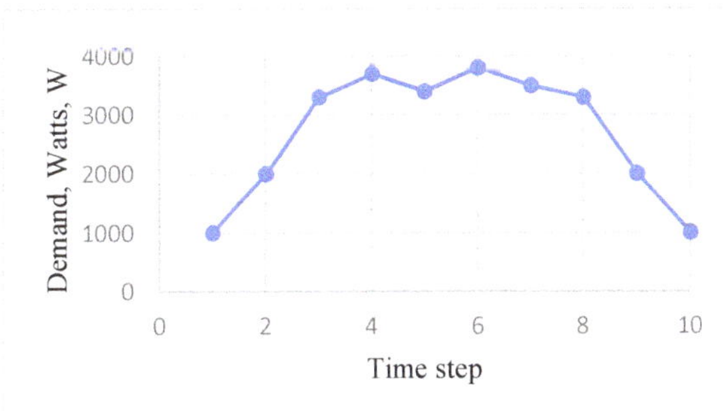

Figure A1. Demand profile.

Figures A2–A4 display the system voltages, current, and state-of-charge, respectively, for both the dynamic and heuristic approaches.

In the altitude maintenance simulation, both the switching sequences of both the dynamic and heuristic approaches were able to meet the demand of the drone, but that of the standard approach did not. While the drone was attempting to maintain the required altitude, the demand was higher than the power that the sources could provide separately. Therefore, resulting in the standard approach's inability to meet the demand of the drone. Additionally, in this simulation, the dynamic approach performed better than the heuristic approach. The dynamic approach provided a sequence of switching between the sources that resulted in an objective function value of 8301.2, while the heuristic approach was 8501.3. Additionally, the average power consumption obtained using the dynamic approach was 3827.4 W, while the heuristic approached resulted in 4136.4 W. The power used to meet the demand of the drone during each time step is shown in Figure A5. The switching sequence and sources used to meet demand are shown in Figure A6

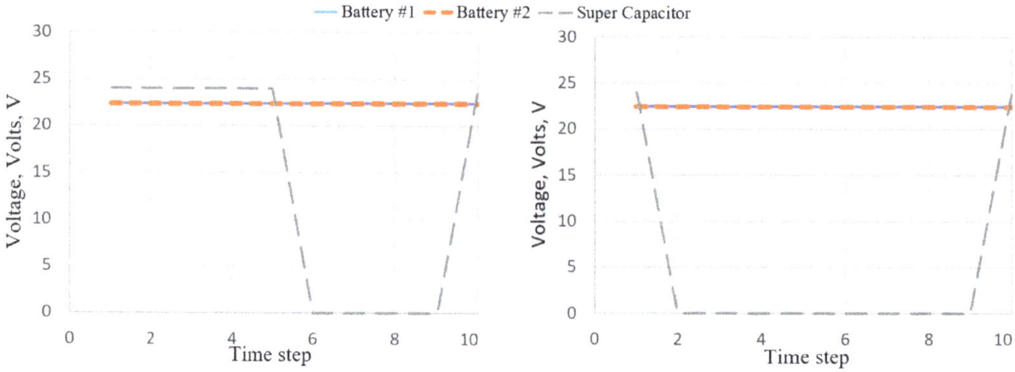

(**a**) Dynamic approach (**b**) Heuristic approach

Figure A2. System voltage for simulation 2.

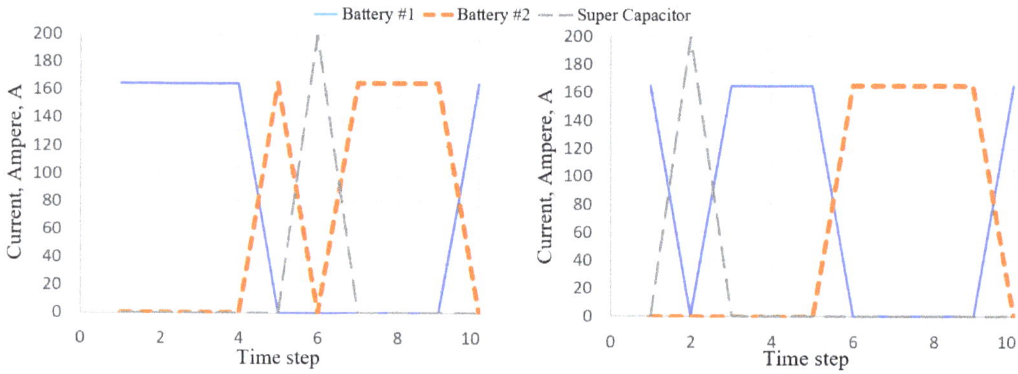

(**a**) Dynamic approach (**b**) Heuristic approach

Figure A3. System currents.

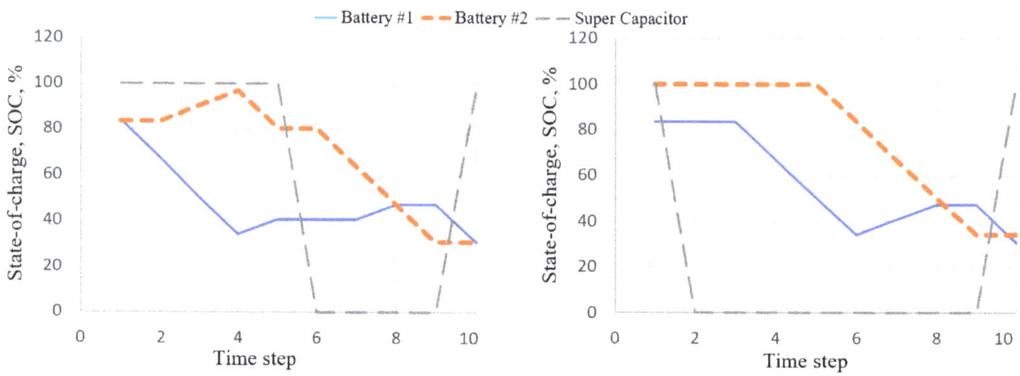

(**a**) Dynamic approach (**b**) Heuristic approach

Figure A4. System state-of-charges.

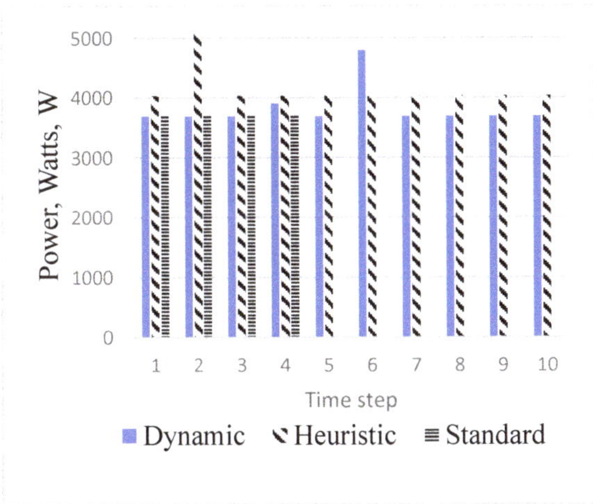

Figure A5. Power consumption comparison for simulation 2.

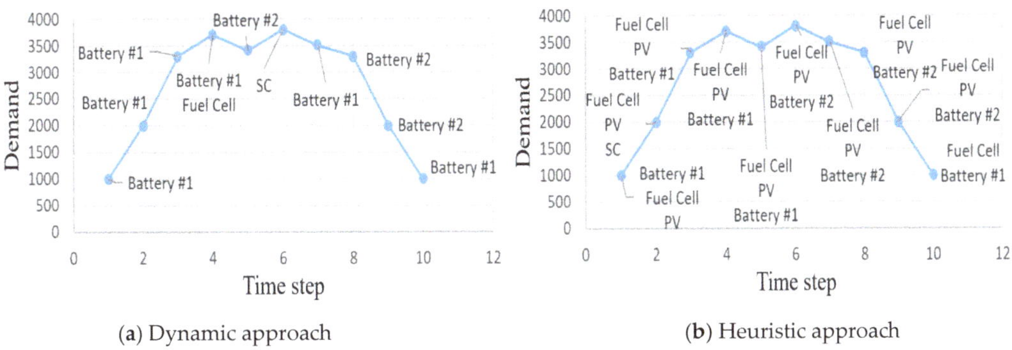

Figure A6. Switching sequence and sources used to meet demand.

Appendix B. Illustrative Example-Multiple Object Pickup

The following simulation represents a drone conducting multiple pickups of objects located in close proximity to each other. The demand profile of this simulation is shown in Figure A7. The weights assigned to the sources in the objective function have to be updated to account for the multiple spikes of demand during the drone's flight. As shown in the demand profile, the drone starts traveling to the location of the first object is located. At time step 2, the drone reaches the object's location and descends to pick up the object. After the drone picks up the object, it proceeds to proceed to pick up the next object until all four objects are obtained. The demand increases as the drone picks up each object, as the load carried by the drone increases.

Figures A8–A10 display the system voltage, current, and state-of-charge, respectively, for both the dynamic and heuristic approaches. In this simulation, the switching sequence generated by the dynamic approach chose to mainly use the super capacitor to meet the demand of the drone, as did the heuristic approach. It can be noted that the super capacitor's current varies in a similar manner to that of the drone's demand as the super capacitor was mainly used by both the dynamic and heuristic approaches. As for the state-of-charge, since the batteries were not used in this example, the state-of-charge of the batteries remains 100% while the super capacitor is charged and discharged multiple times to meet the demand.

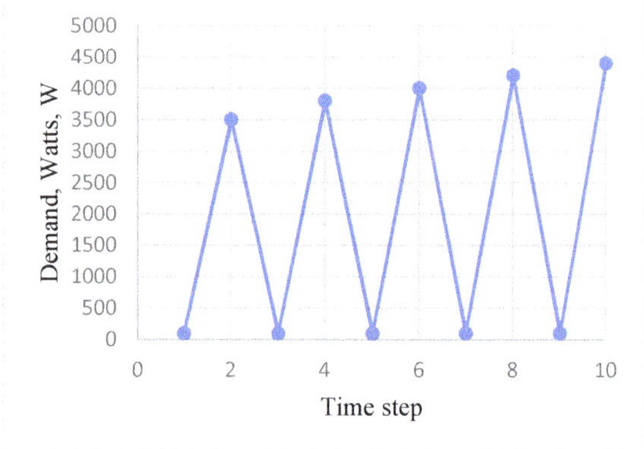

Figure A7. Demand Profile for simulation 3.

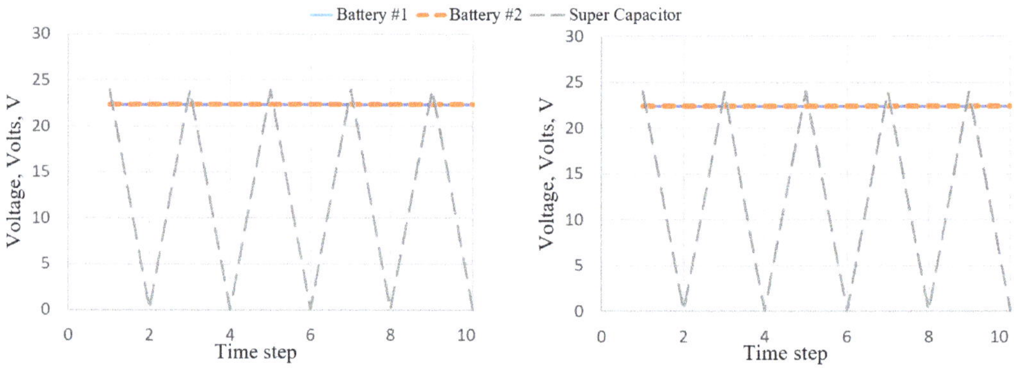

(**a**) Dynamic approach (**b**) Heuristic approach

Figure A8. System voltage.

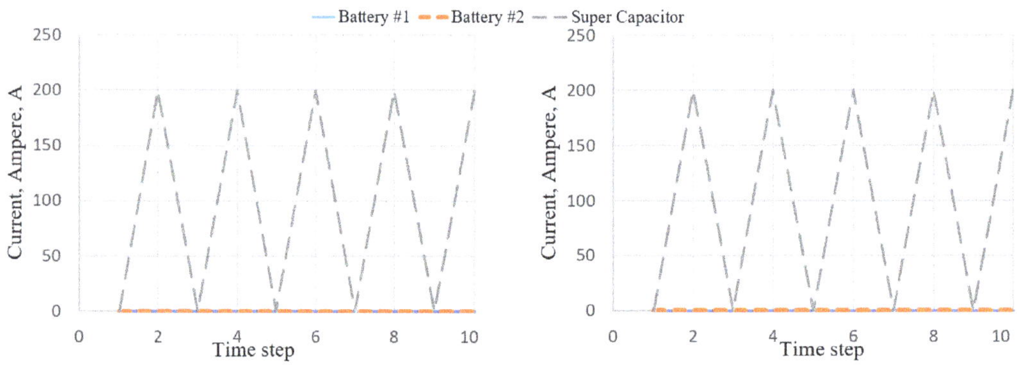

(**a**) Dynamic approach (**b**) Heuristic approach

Figure A9. System currents.

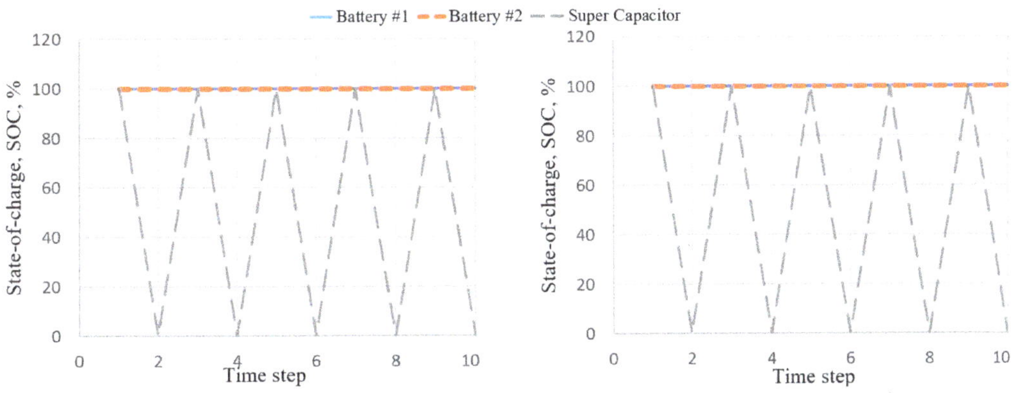

(a) Dynamic approach

(b) Heuristic approach

Figure A10. System state-of-charges.

In the multiple object pickup simulation, both the switching sequences of the dynamic and heuristic approach were able to meet the demand of the drone, but that of the standard approach did not. The switching sequences of the standard approach were unable to meet the demand of the drone due to the multiple spikes in demand. During spikes in demand, the use of the super capacitor is preferred due to its rapid discharge rate making it best-equipped to handle spikes. The switching sequences of the dynamic and heuristic approaches both utilized the super capacitor to meet the spikes in demand of the drone.

Additionally, in both approaches, the super capacitor was charged when the demand was low so that it could be used during the next spike in demand. However, although both the methods performed similarly, the dynamic approach chose to use the photovoltaic cell in the first time step rather than the fuel cell to meet the demand. Therefore, resulting in an objective function value of 3499.2 and average power consumption of 2496 W for the switching sequence of the dynamic approach. On the other hand, the switching sequence of the heuristic approach resulted in an objective function value of 3517.5 and average power consumption of 2505 W. Therefore, resulting in slightly lower power consumption, which is shown in Figure A11. The switching sequence and sources used to meet demand are shown in Figure A12.

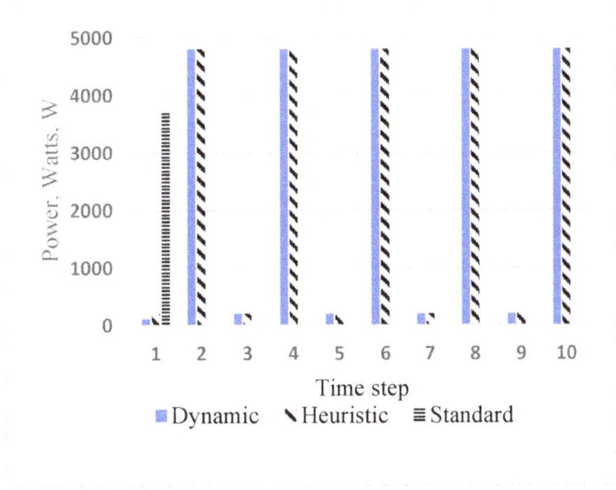

Figure A11. Power consumption comparison.

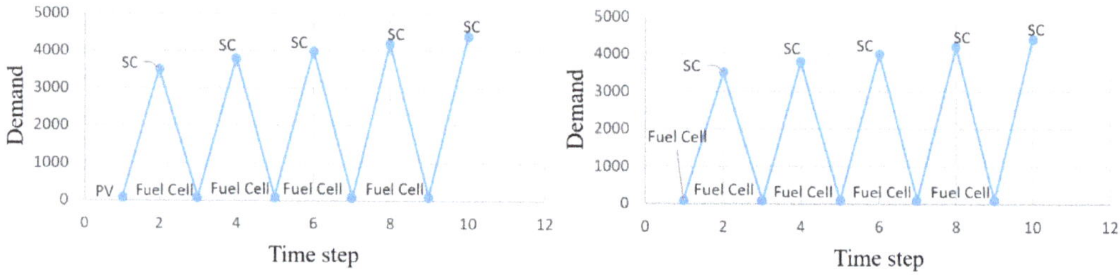

(**a**) Dynamic approach (**b**) Heuristic approach

Figure A12. Switching sequence and sources used to meet demand.

References

1. Malikopoulos, A.A. Supervisory Power Management Control Algorithms for Hybrid Electric Vehicles: A Survey. *IEEE Trans. Intell. Transp. Syst.* **2014**, *15*, 1869–1885. [CrossRef]
2. Hu, X.; Murgovski, N.; Johannesson, L.M.; Egardt, B. Optimal Dimensioning and Power Management of a Fuel Cell/Battery Hybrid Bus via Convex Programming. *IEEE/ASME Trans. Mechatronics* **2015**, *20*, 457–468. [CrossRef]
3. Naamane, A.; M'Sirdi, N.K. Improving Multiple Source Power Management Using State Flow Approach. *Blockchain Technol. Innov. Bus. Process.* **2013**, *22*, 779–785. [CrossRef]
4. Keller, S.; Christmann, K.; Gonzalez, M.S.-A.; Heuer, A. A Modular Fuel Cell Battery Hybrid Propulsion System for Powering Small Utility Vehicles. In Proceedings of the 2017 IEEE Vehicle Power and Propulsion Conference (VPPC), Belfort, France, 14–17 December 2017; pp. 1–4.
5. Chen, X.; Shi, M.; Zhou, J.; Chen, Y.; Zuo, W.; Wen, J.; He, H. Distributed Cooperative Control of Multiple Hybrid Energy Storage Systems in a DC Microgrid Using Consensus Protocol. *IEEE Trans. Ind. Electron.* **2019**, *67*, 1968–1979. [CrossRef]
6. Suárez- Suarez-Velazquez, G.; Mejia-Ruiz, G.E.; Garcia-Vite, P.M. Control and Grid Connection of Fuel Cell Power System. In Proceedings of the 2020 IEEE International Autumn Meeting on Power, Electronics and Computing (ROPEC), Ixtapa, México, 4–6 November 2020; pp. 1–5.
7. Ferrandez, S.M.; Harbison, T.; Weber, T.; Sturges, R.; Rich, R. Optimization of a truck-drone in tandem delivery network using k-means and genetic algorithm. *J. Ind. Eng. Manag.* **2016**, *9*, 374–388. [CrossRef]
8. Masjosthusmann, C.; Kohler, U.; Decius, N.; Buker, U. A vehicle energy management system for a Battery Electric Vehicle. In Proceedings of the 2012 IEEE Vehicle Power and Propulsion Conference (VPPC), Seoul, Korea, 9–12 October 2012; pp. 339–344.
9. Boutilier, J.J.; Brooks, S.C.; Janmohamed, A.; Byers, A.; Buick, J.; Zhan, C.; Schoellig, A.; Cheskes, S.; Morrison, L.J.; Chan, T.C.Y. Optimizing a Drone Network to Deliver Automated External Defibrillators. *Circulation* **2017**, *135*, 2454–2465. [CrossRef] [PubMed]
10. Lee, J. Optimization of a modular drone delivery system. In Proceedings of the 2017 Annual IEEE International Systems Conference (SysCon), Montreal, QC, Canada, 24–27 April 2017; pp. 1–8.
11. Banerjee, A.; Roychoudhury, A. Future of Mobile Software for Smartphones and Drones: Energy and Performance. In Proceedings of the 2017 IEEE/ACM 4th International Conference on Mobile Software Engineering and Systems (MOBILESoft), Buenos Aires, Argentina, 22–23 May 2017; pp. 1–12.
12. Torreglosa, J.; Garcia, P.; Fernandez, L.; Jurado, F. Predictive Control for the Energy Management of a Fuel-Cell–Battery–Supercapacitor Tramway. *IEEE Trans. Ind. Inform.* **2014**, *10*, 276–285. [CrossRef]
13. Xie, S.; Peng, J.; He, H. Plug-In Hybrid Electric Bus Energy Management Based on Stochastic Model Predictive Control. *Energy Procedia* **2017**, *105*, 2672–2677. [CrossRef]
14. Hadj-Said, S.; Colin, G.; Ketfi-Cherif, A.; Chamaillard, Y. Convex Optimization for Energy Management of Parallel Hybrid Electric Vehicles. *IFAC-PapersOnLine* **2016**, *49*, 271–276. [CrossRef]
15. Trovao, J.; Santos, V.; Antunes, C.; Pereirinha, P.; Jorge, H. A Real-Time Energy Management Architecture for Multisource Electric Vehicles. *IEEE Trans. Ind. Electron.* **2015**, *62*, 3223–3233. [CrossRef]
16. Trovao, J.P.F.; Roux, M.-A.; Menard, E.; Dubois, M.R. Energy- and Power-Split Management of Dual Energy Storage System for a Three-Wheel Electric Vehicle. *IEEE Trans. Veh. Technol.* **2017**, *66*, 5540–5550. [CrossRef]
17. Zhou, D.; Gao, F.; Ravey, A.; Al-Durra, A.; Simoes, M.G. Online energy management strategy of fuel cell hybrid electric vehicles based on time series prediction. In Proceedings of the 2017 IEEE Transportation Electrification Conference and Expo (ITEC), Chicago, IL, USA, 22–24 June 2017; pp. 113–118.
18. Chen, Z.; Liu, W.; Yang, Y.; Chen, W. Online Energy Management of Plug-In Hybrid Electric Vehicles for Prolongation of All-Electric Range Based on Dynamic Programming. *Math. Probl. Eng.* **2015**, *2015*, 1–11. [CrossRef]
19. Qin, F.; Li, W.; Hu, Y.; Xu, G. An Online Energy Management Control for Hybrid Electric Vehicles Based on Neuro-Dynamic Programming. *Algorithms* **2018**, *11*, 33. [CrossRef]

20. Mathur, P.; Swartz, C.L.; Zyngier, D.; Welt, F. Robust online scheduling for optimal short-term operation of cascaded hydropower systems under uncertainty. *J. Process. Control.* **2021**, *98*, 52–65. [CrossRef]
21. Park, S.; Zhang, L.; Chakraborty, S. Battery assignment and scheduling for drone delivery businesses. In Proceedings of the 2017 IEEE/ACM International Symposium on Low Power Electronics and Design (ISLPED), Taipei, Taiwan, 24–26 July 2017; pp. 1–6.
22. Umetani, S.; Fukushima, Y.; Morita, H. A linear programming based heuristic algorithm for charge and discharge scheduling of electric vehicles in a building energy management system. *Omega* **2017**, *67*, 115–122. [CrossRef]
23. Zhen, J.; Huang, G.; Li, W.; Wu, C.; Liu, Z. An optimization model design for energy systems planning andmanagement under considering air pollution control in TangshanCity, China. *J. Process. Control* **2016**, *47*, 58–77. [CrossRef]
24. Vaccari, M.; Mancuso, G.; Riccardi, J.; Cantù, M.; Pannocchia, G. A Sequential Linear Programming algorithm for economicoptimization of Hybrid Renewable Energy Systems. *J. Process. Control* **2019**, *74*, 189–201. [CrossRef]
25. Chen, M.; Rincon-Mora, G. Accurate Electrical Battery Model Capable of Predicting Runtime and I–V Performance. *IEEE Trans. Energy Convers.* **2006**, *21*, 504–511. [CrossRef]
26. Schaltz, E.; Khaligh, A.; Rasmussen, P.O. Influence of Battery/Ultracapacitor Energy-Storage Sizing on Battery Lifetime in a Fuel Cell Hybrid Electric Vehicle. *IEEE Trans. Veh. Technol.* **2009**, *58*, 3882–3891. [CrossRef]
27. Lami, M.; Shamayleh, A.; Mukhopadhyay, S. Minimizing the state of health degradation of Li-ion batteries onboard low earth orbit satellites. *Soft Comput.* **2019**, *24*, 4131–4147. [CrossRef]
28. Bernard, J.; Delprat, S.; Buchi, F.; Guerra, T.M. Fuel-Cell Hybrid Powertrain: Toward Minimization of Hydrogen Consumption. *IEEE Trans. Veh. Technol.* **2009**, *58*, 3168–3176. [CrossRef]
29. Pukrushpan, J. *Modeling and Control of Fuel Cell Systems and Fuel Processors*; University of Michigan: Ann Arbor, MI, USA, 2003.
30. Spyker, R.; Nelms, R. Classical equivalent circuit parameters for a double-layer capacitor. *IEEE Trans. Aerosp. Electron. Syst.* **2000**, *36*, 829–836. [CrossRef]
31. Amjadi, Z.; Williamson, S.S. Power-Electronics-Based Solutions for Plug-in Hybrid Electric Vehicle Energy Storage and Management Systems. *IEEE Trans. Ind. Electron.* **2010**, *57*, 608–616. [CrossRef]
32. Saaty, T. *The Analytic Hierarchy Process*; McGraw-Hill: New York, NY, USA, 1980.
33. Eaves, S.; Eaves, J. A cost comparison of fuel-cell and battery electric vehicles. *J. Power Sources* **2004**, *130*, 208–212. [CrossRef]
34. Kunze, J.; Paschos, O.; Stimming, U. Fuel Cell Comparison to Alternate Technologies. *Fuel Cells* **2012**, *1*, 77–95. [CrossRef]
35. Berckmans, G.; Messagie, M.; Smekens, J.; Omar, N.; Vanhaverbeke, L.; Van Mierlo, J. Cost Projection of State of the Art Lithium-Ion Batteries for Electric Vehicles Up to 2030. *Energies* **2017**, *10*, 1314. [CrossRef]
36. Camara, M.B.; Dakyo, B.; Gualous, H. Polynomial Control Method of DC/DC Converters for DC-Bus Voltage and Currents Management—Battery and Supercapacitors. *IEEE Trans. Power Electron.* **2012**, *27*, 1455–1467. [CrossRef]

algorithms

MDPI

Article

A Multicriteria Simheuristic Approach for Solving a Stochastic Permutation Flow Shop Scheduling Problem

Eliana Maria Gonzalez-Neira [1,*,†], Jairo R. Montoya-Torres [2] and Jose-Fernando Jimenez [1]

1 Departamento de Ingeniería Industrial, Facultad de Ingeniería, Pontificia Universidad Javeriana, Bogotá 110231, Colombia; j-jimenez@javeriana.edu.co
2 Facultad de Ingeniería, Universidad de La Sabana, Chía 140013, Colombia; jairo.montoya@unisabana.edu.co
* Correspondence: eliana.gonzalez@javeriana.edu.co
† Current address: Carrera 7 No 40-62, Bogotá 110231, Colombia.

Abstract: This paper proposes a hybridized simheuristic approach that couples a greedy randomized adaptive search procedure (GRASP), a Monte Carlo simulation, a Pareto archived evolution strategy (PAES), and an analytic hierarchy process (AHP), in order to solve a multicriteria stochastic permutation flow shop problem with stochastic processing times and stochastic sequence-dependent setup times. For the decisional criteria, the proposed approach considers four objective functions, including two quantitative and two qualitative criteria. While the expected value and the standard deviation of the earliness/tardiness of jobs are included in the quantitative criteria to address a robust solution in a just-in-time environment, this approach also includes a qualitative assessment of the product and customer importance in order to appraise a weighted priority for each job. An experimental design was carried out in several study instances of the flow shop problem to test the effects of the processing times and sequence-dependent setup times, obtained through lognormal and uniform probability distributions with three levels of coefficients of variation, settled as 0.3, 0.4, and 0.5. The results show that both probability distributions and coefficients of variation have a significant effect on the four decision criteria selected. In addition, the analytical hierarchical process makes it possible to choose the best sequence exhibited by the Pareto frontier that adjusts more adequately to the decision-makers' objectives.

Keywords: permutation flow shop; simheuristic; multicriteria; PAES, GRASP, AHP

Citation: Gonzalez-Neira, E.M.; Montoya-Torres, J.R.; Jimenez, J.-F. A Multicriteria Simheuristic Approach for Solving a Stochastic Permutation Flow Shop Scheduling Problem. *Algorithms* **2021**, *14*, 210. https://doi.org/10.3390/a14070210

Academic Editor: Frank Werner

Received: 27 June 2021
Accepted: 13 July 2021
Published: 14 July 2021

1. Introduction

The flow shop problem (FSP) is a largely studied scheduling problem, as it models a wide set of industrial manufacturing environments [1], such as in the chemical, food-processing, automobile, and assembly industries. The purpose of solving the stated problem lies in determining the best processing sequence from n production jobs to process on m machines placed in series, aiming to optimize one or several KPIs such as the flowtime, makespan, earliness, or tardiness. A permutation flow shop scheduling problem (PFSP), which is an extension case of the FSP, considers only permutation schedules, i.e., the processing sequence of the jobs is the same for all m machines. The PFSP is considered an NP-complete problem for three or more machines [2] and an NP-hard problem for one or more machines when minimizing tardiness [3]. Furthermore, this problem augments the complexity when the uncertainty is considered for its resolution. From several approaches, a preliminary approach for tackling the stochastic permutation flow shop problems is elaborating a systematic procedure that includes uncertainties within the scheduling problems [4]. In fact, the scheduling problem and the associated complexity could be as important for designing a proper systematic technique to solve these problems [4].

After analyzing the literature on the FSP and PFSP, four aspects should be highlighted. At first, a set of approaches in the literature considers a single performance indicator as the objective function. The most common approaches are related to the makespan, due date, or just-in-time characteristics. The makespan or the expected makespan indicator, which is an absolute performance indicator, focuses on minimizing the lapsed time from the start to the end of the execution [5,6]. The due date indicator, which is a relative performance indicator, compares the objective function regarding the expected processing completion. The just-in-time indicator, which is an accuracy performance indicator, indicates the positive or negative deviation occurring from an expected completion time. Certainly, the use of each performance indicator depends on the aim from the scheduling perspective.

Second, another set of approaches is focused on single-objective problems rather than multicriteria problems. Certainly, even industrial problems must solve various objectives simultaneously [7], and researchers have focused on optimizing a single objective function rather than multiple ones. This issue can be addressed by considering earliness and tardiness objectives jointly in a JIT environment.

Third, most studies consider only quantitative decision criteria. However, researchers have recently become interested in qualitative criteria as this approach might reduce the gap between the theoretical concept of problems and the execution. Some examples are Chang and Lo [8] and Chang et al. [9]. These authors studied a multicriteria job shop, whereas the customers' strategic importance was considered as a qualitative criterion. While Chang and Lo [8] proposed a hybridized genetic algorithm, tabu search, analytic hierarchy process, and fuzzy theory to solve the problem, Chang et al. [9] proposed a hybridization of an ant colony algorithm and an analytic hierarchy process for solving the FSP. Another approach minimized the expected costs of tardiness as a quantitative criterion and strategic customer importance as a qualitative criterion in a stochastic hybrid FSP [10]. The authors employed a GRASP metaheuristic and a Monte Carlo simulation method with a stochastic multicriteria acceptability analysis to handle both qualitative and quantitative criteria.

Finally, some research approaches consider scheduling under uncertain conditions, and these are generally divided into two approaches: the stochastic approach, in which parameters are modeled with probability distributions (PDs) aiming to minimize the expected value of a selected metric, and the robust approach (RA), in which uncertain parameters are modeled with intervals and the schedule obtained is more stable and less variable. Nonetheless, previous studies have not dealt with a combination of stochastic and robust approaches for solving the flow shop problem. Companies can collect production data in a short time, yielding enough data to accurately estimate the probability distribution of uncertain parameters. Then, we believe that the latter approach leverages the robust schedule as it can be more easily adjusted than other schedules in which uncertainties are modeled with intervals.

One of the recent approaches to solve stochastic combinatorial optimization problems is simheuristics. These hybridize a metaheuristic approach with a simulation to obtain solutions for stochastic problems. Simheuristics have been successfully used in vehicle routing problems [11–13], inventory routing problems [14], facility location problems [15], and scheduling problems [16–19].

In this sense, this paper attempts to contribute to the literature by proposing a systematic technique for solving the stochastic permutation flow shop problem (SPFSP) considering stochastic processing times and sequence-dependent setup times to optimize multiple criteria. To the best of our knowledge, no previous study has included the simultaneous analysis of a JIT environment with stochastic parameters, quantitative metrics, and qualitative metrics for obtaining robust solutions. Therefore, the current research proposes a multicriteria simheuristic approach to solve an SPFSP, including both quantitative and qualitative objectives, providing robust solutions. On the one hand, for quantitative objectives, the proposed approach addresses the expected earliness/tardiness (E[E/T]) and the standard deviation of earliness/tardiness (SD(E/T)), for estimating the JIT metrics and obtaining several robust schedules. On the other hand, as qualitative metrics, this research considers the expected customer importance of jobs (E[CI]) and the expected product importance (E[PI]), favoring the job priority for the company. Then, this paper considers both customer and product importance as a company might be more interested in delivering high-profitability products regardless of the customer or, conversely, it might be more interested in delivering frequently with high-spending customers rather than sporadic ones. This paper is an extension of a previous conference work [20] that only considered one qualitative criterion and solved a partial set of benchmark instances. This work includes one more qualitative criterion (the maximization of the accomplishment of product importance) and executes more computational experiments by evaluating 180 instances proposed by [21] and analyzing the behavior of Pareto frontiers with more coefficients of variation of processing times and sequence-dependent setup times.

The remainder of this paper is organized as follows. Section 2 presents a literature review of the single-objective stochastic FSP (SFSP), robust FSP, and multi-objective SFSP. Section 3 describes the proposed solution for the SPFSP under qualitative and quantitative decision criteria. Section 4 provides the results of the computational experiments that validate the proposed approach. Finally, conclusions and recommendations for future work are presented in Section 5.

2. Literature Review

The deterministic FSP is one of the most frequently studied problems in the scheduling literature, but the stochastic version has been addressed less often. The FSP under the conditions of uncertainty has received more attention recently because it is closer to real manufacturing environments. Nevertheless, there are fewer FSP studies under uncertain conditions than there are deterministic FSP studies. For the literature reviews, deterministic FSPs and its solution methods have more than ten literature reviews, including Yenisey and Yagmahan [7], Pan and Ruiz [22], Arora and Agarwal [23], Nagano and Miyata [24], Rossit et al. [25], and Fernandez-Viagas et al. [26]. Meanwhile, their stochastic and uncertain counterparts have had only two literature reviews in the past 18 years, Gourgand et al. [5] and González-Neira et al. [27]. Studies of the FSP with uncertainty generally use one of three approaches to deal with uncertain parameters: the stochastic approach, the robustness approach, and the fuzzy approach. The most frequently used approach is stochastic, with the uncertain parameters modeled using probability distributions. Examples of this approach can be found in Framinan and Perez-Gonzalez [28], Lin and Chen [29], and Qin et al. [30]. For the robustness approach, there is no need for acknowledging the distribution of the data of uncertain parameters due to this being modeled with intervals or datasets. Examples of this approach can be found in Fazayeli et al. [31] and Ying [32]. For the fuzzy approach, uncertain parameters are modeled using fuzzy numbers, as in Behnamian and Fatemi Ghomi [33] and Huang et al. [34].

The aim of this paper is to obtain robust schedules for the stochastic permutation flow shop problem (SPFSP), considering both quantitative and qualitative objective criteria. Then, the literature review in this paper is organized into four subsections: Section 2.1 presents the literature review for single-objective SFSPs. Section 2.2 presents an overview of studies using the robust FSP with a single objective. Section 2.3 examines current approaches for a multi-objective FSP under uncertain conditions, including robust, stochastic, and fuzzy approaches. Section 2.4 presents a review of qualitative production criteria.

2.1. Single-Objective SFSP

Since the 1950s, the deterministic FSP has received considerable attention, but the SFSP has been less studied because it is more difficult to solve than the deterministic version. Nevertheless, with the advances in computation, the SFSP has been studied more in the last few years. Therefore, we present in chronological order the most important studies on the SFSP since its beginnings.

From the early days of this topic until the 2010s, the following approaches have been found. Makino [35] presented an optimal solution for the expected makespan in an SFSP with two jobs and general distributions for two machines, as well as with three machines, considering the exponential and Erlang distributions of the processing times.

Talwar [36] proposed a rule to optimally sequence n jobs and two machines with exponentially distributed processing times, and this was proved optimal by Cunningham and Dutta [37]. Alcaide et al. [38] developed a dynamic procedure for considering stochastic machine breakdowns in an SFSP. This procedure can obtain an optimal solution for the initial stochastic problem when the associated without-breakdowns stochastic partial problems are solved optimally. Gourgand et al. [39] proposed simulated annealing with a Markovian model to solve the SPFSP with stochastic processing times and limited buffers. Wang et al. [40] presented a genetic ordinal optimization approach that hybridizes ordinal optimization, optimal computing budget allocation, and a genetic algorithm with uniformly distributed processing times. Kalczynski and Kamburowski [41] developed a new rule that enables optimal solutions when processing times are Weibull distributed. This rule includes Johnson's and Talwar's rules as special cases. Portougal and Trietsch [42] proposed a heuristic called API that consists of two steps: (1) the ordering of jobs with expected processing times through Johnson's rule and (2) applying all possible interchanges of two jobs in the sequence.

Then, in the early 2010s, Baker and Trietsch [43] compared Talwar's, Johnson's, and the API rules, testing different types of probability distributions. The authors concluded that for a high coefficient of variation, Talwar's and Johnson's rules yield better results, but when the coefficients of variation are low, Johnson's rule alone provides good results. Baker and Altheimer [44] compared three heuristic procedures adapted from rules that performed well in deterministic counterparts. The procedures used were CDS/Johnson, CDS/Talwar, and NEH. The authors found that NEH had the best results. Elyasi and Salmasi [45] solved the SFSP considering normally distributed processing times and variances proportional to their means, as well as gamma distributed processing times with the same scale parameter for all jobs. The authors aimed to minimize the expected tardy jobs by using chance constraint programming. Elyasi and Salmasi [46] proposed a dynamic method to solve the SFSP in which the stochastic parameters were the due dates of jobs, in order to minimize the expected tardy jobs. Juan et al. [18] developed a simheuristic that involves an iterated local search metaheuristic considering stochastic processing times distributed lognormally. Framinan and Perez-Gonzalez [28] compared well-known heuristics through a simulation procedure with a variable number of iterations and different probability distributions. The procedures compared were stochastic NEH, stochastic CDS/Talwar, deterministic NEH, deterministic CDS/Talwar, and deterministic NEH using CDS/Talwar as the initial solution. These authors found that stochastic NEH obtained the best results.

Finally, in the late 2010s and the beginning of the 2020s, Gonzalez-Neira et al. [47] minimized the expected makespan in a distributed assembly PFSP with stochastic processing times through a GRASP simheuristic, evaluating the robustness of the problem as well. González-Neira et al. [48] compared thirteen dispatching rules through a simulation procedure with variable iterations for ten different objective functions (five expected values and five standard deviations of the makespan, flowtime, tardiness, maximum tardiness, and tardy jobs) under lognormal, uniform, and exponential distributions of processing times. Hatami et al. [17] addressed a parallel SFSP where products had components produced in different parallel flow shops. The authors developed a simheuristic that embeds an iterated local search algorithm to minimize the expected makespan and makespan percentiles. Marichelvam and Geetha [49] considered uncertain processing times and machine breakdowns to minimize the makespan. To solve the problem, a hybridization of a firefly algorithm and a variable neighborhood algorithm was designed, demonstrating promising results with extensive computational experiments. Villarinho et al. [50] proposed a simheuristic that integrates a biased randomized heuristic into a variable neighborhood descent with Monte Carlo simulation to maximize the expected payoff in an SFSP that considers stochastic processing times.

2.2. Robust FSP

Such as the studies on the SFSP, few studies have addressed the robustness for the FSP. Table 1 presents the main characteristics of previous studies in this field. As the table shows, most of them studied the makespan as a single objective, and only three works addressed multiple objectives. These three studies included only one parameter under uncertainty conditions. While Liu et al. [51] studied stochastic machine breakdowns, dynamic job arrivals, and unexpected job availability, Liao and Fu [52] and Goli et al. [53] considered uncertain processing times. It is important to note that none of these works simultaneously studied stochastic sequence-dependent setup times and stochastic processing times while considering robustness.

2.3. Multi-Objective FSP under Uncertainty Conditions

Few works have examined uncertainties simultaneously with multi-objective decisions in comparison with a single objective. Table 2 presents the main characteristics of the studies performed in this area. Makespan, tardiness, and flowtime are the most analyzed measures, and earliness is not widely studied. In addition, stochastic setup times are not considered.

Table 1. Modeling approaches for the stochastic flow shop problem (SFSP) that address robustness.

Reference	Objective Function(s)	Problem Characteristics	Solution Approach	Remarks
Azadeh et al. [54]	Makespan.	Normally distributed processing times.	Genetic algorithm.	Considered that jobs have different expected completion times or different expected due dates.
Liu et al. [55]	Makespan.	Processing times with a normal probability distribution.	Improved genetic algorithm with a new generation scheme, which can preserve the good characteristics of the parents in the new generations. Robustness is achieved by maximizing Prob(Cmax < expected completion time)	No recommendations given.
Kasperski et al. [56]	Makespan.	Two-machine PFSP. Processing times modeled through scenario sets.	2-approximation algorithm.	The 2-approximation algorithm may be improved to find results better than the 2 worst-cases' ratio for the unbounded min–max version.
Gören and Pierreval [57]	Makespan.	Machine breakdowns generated by a generic probability distribution.	The multimodal optimization approach generates different schedules, and the most robust solution is selected depending on the negative effects of machine breakdowns.	High flexibility given to the decision-maker for dealing with additional concerns. The inclusion of preference aggregation methods with social choice theory is recommended.
Rahmani and Heydari [58]	Makespan.	Dynamic arrivals. Processing times under a uniform distribution.	Proactive–reactive approach. Proactive robust method and reactive phase that incorporates dynamic arrivals that minimize the deterministic makespan.	No recommendations given.
Ying [32]	Makespan.	Two-machine flow shop. Interval processing times.	Simulated annealing and iterated greedy algorithm implemented independently.	The iterated greedy algorithm achieved better results in small instances, and simulated annealing performed better in large instances.
Fazayeli et al. [31]	Makespan.	β-robustness criterion.	Simulation-optimization algorithm that incorporates genetic and simulated annealing algorithms.	No recommendations given.
Shahnaghi et al. [59]	Makespan.	Interval processing times/ interval setup times.	Particle swarm optimization hybridized with the Bertsimas and Ben-Tal robust models.	The Bertsimas model performed better than the Ben-Tal model for large instances. Implemented these models for other scheduling problems.
Liu et al. [51]	Flowtime and dissatisfaction of managers, operators, and customers.	Uncertain machine breakdown.	Proactive–reactive approach that hybridizes a non-dominated sorting genetic algorithm, a multi-objective evolutionary algorithm, and a multi-objective memetic algorithm.	The robustness measure is determined by the expected flowtime and its stability by the dissatisfaction of managers, operators, and customers.
Gholami-Zanjani et al. [60]	Weighted mean completion time.	Interval setup times and processing times.	Ben-Tal and robust optimization and fuzzy optimization.	Comparison of robust, fuzzy, and deterministic solutions, obtaining that the robust method gives better solutions regarding variability.
Ćwik and Józefczyk [61]	Makespan.	Interval processing times.	Minimax regret criterion hybridized with a new proposed greedy algorithm.	The greedy algorithm outperforms the middle and evolutionary interval approaches (OSP).
Liao and Fu [52]	Makespan and tardiness.	Interval processing times	Min–max regret criterion hybridized with a meta-heuristic.	According to the authors, this manuscript compensated the lack of the consideration of tardiness.
Goli et al. [53]	Weighted completion times and costs of outsourcing.	Interval processing times.	Robust mixed-integer linear programming model.	The authors evaluated the model against a nonlinear programming model, demonstrating the effectiveness of their development.

Table 2. Modeling approaches for the multi-objective stochastic flow shop problem (MO-SFSP).

Reference	Objective Function(s)	Problem Characteristics	Solution Approach	Remarks
Forst [62]	Total weighted tardiness and total weighted flowtime.	Stochastic processing times and common due dates.	Theorem.	Optimal solutions can be obtained by sequencing the jobs in increasing stochastic order of their processing times. Study other measures as the expected tardy jobs of expected variation in flowtimes.
CELANO et al. [63]	Makespan and maximum tardiness.	Fuzzy processing times and fuzzy due dates.	Genetic algorithm.	No recommendations given.
Temiz and Erol [64]	Fuzzy makespan, fuzzy maximum tardiness, and fuzzy total flowtime.	Fuzzy processing times and fuzzy due dates.	Genetic algorithm.	The algorithm produces efficient solutions for medium- and large-sized problems in a reasonable amount of time.
Qiang Zhou and Xunxue Cui [65]	Flow time and delay time of jobs.	Stochastic processing times and stochastic machine breakdowns.	Hybrid multi-objective genetic algorithm.	No recommendations given.
Azadeh et al. [66]	Makespan and mean completion time.	Stochastic processing times, stochastic machine breakdowns, and stochastic setup times.	Artificial neural network.	The advantage of the proposed solution approach is the reduction in the number of simulations runs and, consequently, a reduced run time. Furthermore, this is the first study that introduced an intelligent and flexible algorithm for handling the stochastic two-machine FS problem.
Liefooghe et al. [67]	Makespan and total tardiness.	Stochastic processing times.	Evolutionary algorithm.	The authors demonstrated that an uncertainty-handling strategy is a key issue to obtain good-quality solutions and that the algorithm's performance is strongly related to the level of uncertainty about the environment.
Rahmani et al. [68]	Fuzzy makespan, flowtime, and total tardiness.	Stochastic processing times and stochastic release times.	Chance constrained.	The genetic algorithm was allowed to solve large instances with relatively good solutions in a reasonable computational time.
Mou et al. [69]	Hamming distance, adjustment of total completion times, and adjustments of processing times.	Inverse permutation flow shop scheduling problem and stochastic processing times.	Hybrid multi-objective evolutionary algorithm with the NEH-based insertion method.	The algorithm presents better results than a nondominated sorting genetic algorithm. The study can be extended by adding other measures.
Fu et al. [70]	Expected makespan and expected tardiness.	Stochastic processing times with deteriorating and learning effects.	Multi-objective discrete fireworks algorithm.	The algorithm presents good results in comparison with the MILP model for small instances.
González-Neira et al. [16]	Expected tardiness and standard deviation of tardiness.	Stochastic processing times.	Simheuristic that hybridizes the Pareto archive evolution strategy with tabu search.	The algorithm presents good results for the deterministic case and obtains the Pareto frontier of expected tardiness and standard deviation of tardiness.
Faraji Amiri and Behnamian [71]	Makespan and energy consumption.	Stochastic processing times.	Mathematical formulation and scenario-based estimation of the distribution algorithm.	The algorithm obtains the Pareto frontier of the makespan and energy consumption and presents good results in comparison to another algorithm.

2.4. Qualitative Criteria

Within organizations, main processes have their own objectives, which are often in conflict. For instance, the objectives of marketing involve maximizing service levels and sales; procurement seeks the prioritization of products and order replenishment; and production and manufacturing aim to maximize throughput and minimize costs. That is why it is important to use an approach that takes into account all of these objectives simultaneously [72]. In this context, production should consider marketing criteria (often qualitative) in the decision-making process in order to improve customer service and reduce conflicts between marketing and production [73]. Among the marketing objectives, production planning is affected by the product importance and customer importance. Georgakopoulos and Mihiotis [74] analyzed these two aspects in a distribution network design. Considering the product importance, aspects such as turnover, profit rate, image, and discount policies must be considered in order to categorize the product. With regard to customer importance, aspects such as turnover, image, and customer requirements must be considered in order to categorize the customer. For instance, González-Neira et al. [10] included the customer importance in a hybrid FSP through the integral analysis method García Cáceres et al. [75] based on stochastic multicriteria acceptability analysis Lahdelma et al. [76].

The academic literature includes very few studies on scheduling problems that considered qualitative decision criteria. As stated above, Chang and Lo [8] and Chang et al. [9] proposed a multicriteria objective function that included qualitative aspects such as marketing considerations, the strategic importance of customers, and order profit/risk in a job shop environment with fuzzy parameters. Chang and Lo [8] proposed a GA/TS approach hybridized with AHP, while Chang et al. [9] examined an ant colony optimization with an AHP process to solve job shop problems. In our opinion, some possible reasons for the few studies on this research topic are the lack of objectivity while measuring these metrics and the difficulty of having unbiased indicators.

3. Proposed Approach

This paper proposes a simheuristic technique that integrates Monte Carlo simulation into a GRASP metaheuristic hybridized with the Pareto archived evolution strategy (PAES) technique for optimizing multiple objectives. Interested readers may consult Resende and Ribeiro [77] for the GRASP metaheuristic and Knowles and Corne [78] for the PAES technique. In addition, an AHP methodology is integrated with the simheuristic to assess the Pareto solutions under different weight arrays for the selected criteria. The algorithm is named multicriteria simheuristic with GRASP (MC-SIM-GRASP). A GRASP metaheuristic for optimization purposes was selected due to it having the advantage of constructing its own initial solution and the no memory characteristic, which makes it useful for scheduling problems. PAES was selected because it has the advantage of avoiding favoring a search direction in the local search and exploring different solutions across the Pareto front.

3.1. MC-SIM-GRASP: Construction Phase

The purpose of the construction phase in GRASP and in the proposed algorithm is to construct a solution by the sequential aggregation of jobs to the solution from a set of possible jobs ranked through a greedy or fitness function. Even though the studied problem is a multicriteria objective, a pure strategy was selected for the construction phase, meaning that a unique objective function guides the entire construction [79]. Then, for this phase, an earliest due date (EDD) rule was selected to deal with the earliness/tardiness objective as a single greedy function. However, considering the other functions, a respective penalization was included for the customer and product importance functions regarding each job, each depending on customer importance or product importance, in comparison with the position of the job in the sequence. Table 3 shows the penalization for the customer importance criterion for an example of 10 jobs with five levels of customer importance. These penalization scores are based on the following criteria: A job that is not belated has a score of zero. If a job is delayed, the penalization is greater if the customer importance is high and lower if the customer importance is low. Then, the job penalization increases if the job is taking the place of a job that has greater importance. The case study for this paper defines five levels of customer importance, where Level 1 corresponds to the most important customers and Level 5 to the least important. For the instances tested in this research, the customer importance for each job was randomly assigned using the probabilities indicated in Table 4. Naturally, this scale for customer importance and the probability of the importance level were established here for testing purposes. In real scenarios, the assignment of customer importance will not be probabilistic, but rather deterministic according to the views of the decision-maker. A similar procedure was conducted to assign a product importance for each job and the corresponding penalization.

Table 3. Job sequence position penalization depending on customer importance.

	Job ID	**5**	**4**	**10**	**1**	**3**	**7**	**2**	**6**	**9**	**8**
	Customer Importance	**1**	**2**	**2**	**2**	**3**	**3**	**4**	**4**	**4**	**5**
Job position in sequence	1	1	5	5	5	7	7	7	7	7	5
	2	6	1	1	1	4	4	5	5	5	4
	3	6	1	1	1	4	4	5	5	5	4
	4	6	1	1	1	4	4	5	5	5	4
	5	11	5	5	5	1	1	3	3	3	3
	6	11	5	5	5	1	1	3	3	3	3
	7	16	9	9	9	4	4	1	1	1	2
	8	16	9	9	9	4	4	1	1	1	2
	9	16	9	9	9	4	4	1	1	1	2
	10	21	13	13	13	7	7	3	3	3	1

Table 4. Customer importance probability.

Customer Importance	1	2	3	4	5
Probability of Occurrence	8%	12%	20%	28%	32%

The main contribution of the construction phase of the proposed approach is the alternation of three different greedy functions at each iteration of GRASP. For instance, the first iteration begins the construction phase with an EDD rule criterion; the second iteration continues using the customer importance; and the third iteration continues using the product importance. These iterations are repeated in the same order until the solution/schedule is completed. It is important to note that the EDD rule criterion is used to guide the constructions for both the earliness/tardiness mean and standard deviation objectives at the same time. Inside each step of construction, the restricted candidate list (RCL) is defined as the subset of jobs with the best value of 10% of the total range of the greedy function values obtained. A job is then randomly selected from the RCL to form part of the solution. The method continues iteratively until all jobs have been scheduled, included in the solution. After the sequence is completed, a Monte Carlo simulation is performed with as many runs as needed to obtain confidence intervals of at least 1% for the four objective functions (expected earliness/tardiness, standard deviation of earliness/tardiness, customer importance, and product importance). In the first iteration of the construction phase, this solution is included in the nondominated solutions (NDS) archive, which is initially empty. In the remaining iterations, this solution is evaluated using PAES to determine whether it is considered within the set of NDS. Figure 1 presents the flow diagram of the construction phase of the proposed approach.

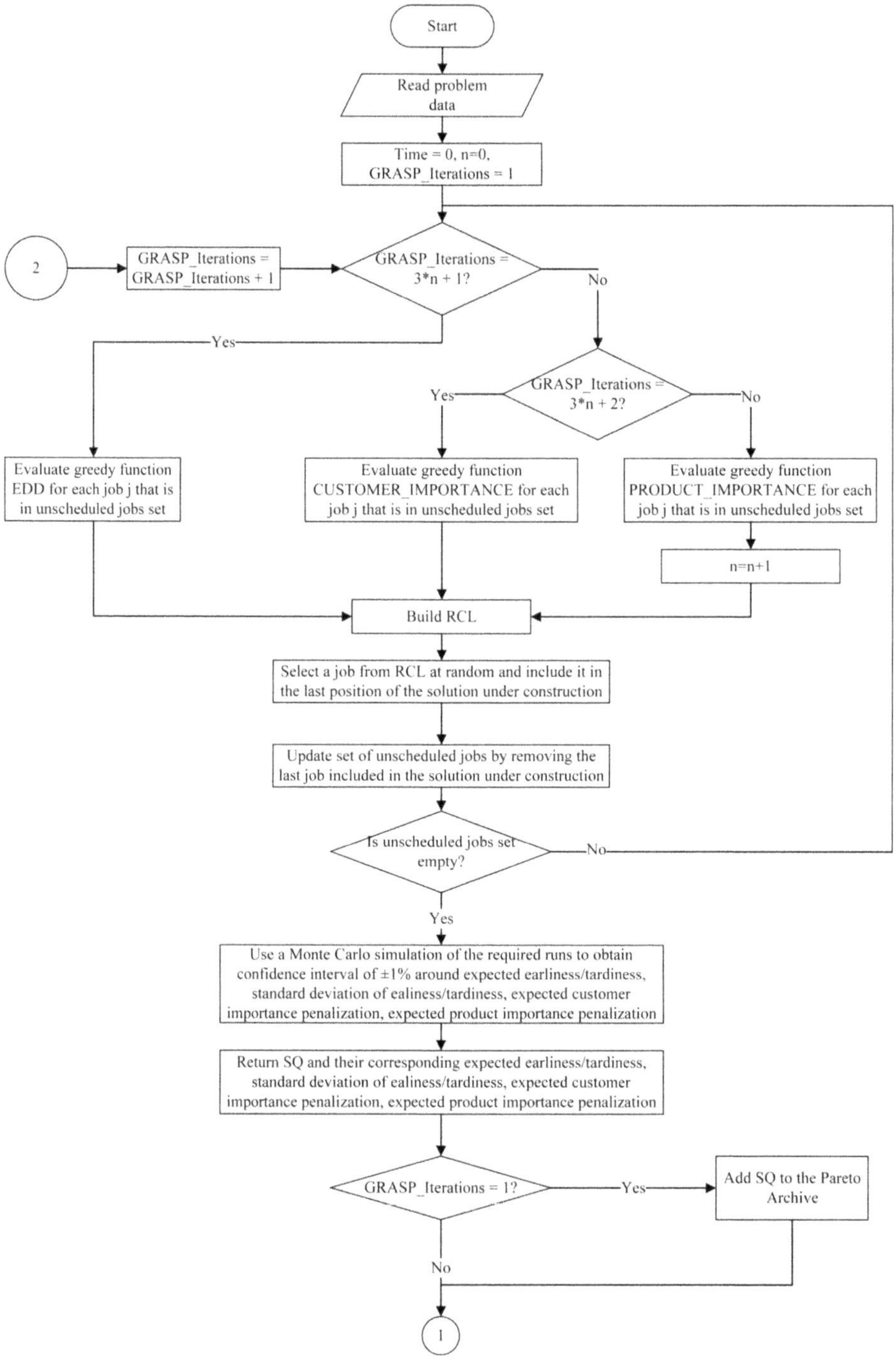

Figure 1. Flowchart of the GRASP construction phase.

3.2. MC-SIM-GRASP: Local Search Phase

The purpose of the local search phase in GRASP and in the proposed algorithm is to execute consecutive iterative improvements of the solution obtained from the construction phase to obtain a better solution. In this paper, the local search phase consists of 2-opt interchanges between jobs. Each time an interchange is performed, a Monte Carlo simulation is executed to estimate the four objective functions with a confidence interval accuracy of at least ±1% for each value and a confidence of 95%. The solution is then evaluated to decide whether it should be placed in the NDS archive. If so, the other solutions already saved in the NDS archive are evaluated to determine whether they should remain in the NDS archive. If the solution does not belong in the NDS archive, it is discarded. This procedure is conducted according to the PAES proposed by Knowles and Corne [78]. A MC-SIM-GRASP iteration ends when no interchanges can enter into the NDS archive, and a new iteration is begun, maintaining the actual NDS archive. The simheuristic stop time is established as the number of jobs × number of machines × 1.0 second. Figure 2 presents the flowchart of the local search phase.

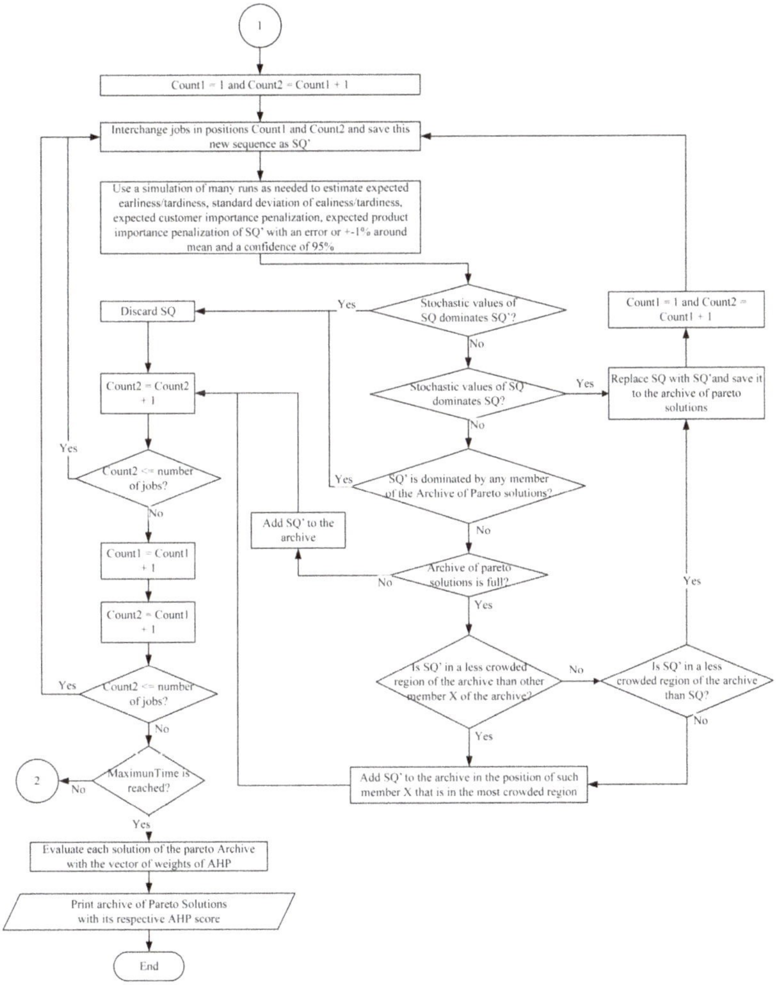

Figure 2. Flowchart of the GRASP local search phase.

3.3. NDS Archive Solution Selection Using the AHP Methodology

After the MC-SIM-GRASP has finished, the entire Pareto sequence is scored using the AHP methodology. As is shown in Table 5, eight vectors are used for the criteria weights for the four objectives. First, a 4×4 pairwise comparison matrix is created for scoring each ith objective function versus the jth objective, on a scale from 1 to 9, as indicated in the AHP technique. An example of the obtainment of a criteria weight vector is shown in Table 6. Then, eight different comparisons are performed to obtain the eight mentioned different vectors of the criteria weights. Considering the usage of each weight vector, the Pareto frontier solution that presents the best AHP score can be selected. In order to compute the matrix of option scores, for each pair of sequences s_1 and s_2, we divided the expected earliness/tardiness of s_1 by the expected earliness/tardiness of s_2, so if the division is greater than 1, the earliness/tardiness of s_1 is worse than the earliness/tardiness of s_2, and vice versa. Similar divisions are performed for the other two objective functions (standard deviation of earliness/tardiness and customer importance).

Table 5. Criteria weights for Pareto solutions.

	Weights Vector							
Objective Function	**1**	**2**	**3**	**4**	**5**	**6**	**7**	**8**
E[E/T]	57.64%	25.56%	5.07%	5.07%	11.72%	11.72%	25.56%	57.64%
SD(E/T)	25.56%	57.64%	57.64%	25.56%	5.07%	5.07%	11.72%	11.72%
CI	11.72%	11.72%	25.56%	57.64%	57.64%	25.56%	5.07%	5.07%
PI	5.07%	5.07%	11.72%	11.72%	25.56%	57.64%	57.64%	25.56%

Table 6. Example of AHP scores and the resultant priority vector.

	E[E/T]	**SD(E/T)**	**CI**	**PI**	**Resulting Weight Vector**
E[E/T]	1	1/3	3	5	**25.56%**
SD(E/T)	3	1	5	9	**57.64%**
CI	1/3	1/5	1	3	**11.72%**
PI	1/5	1/9	1/3	1	**5.07%**

4. Computational Experiments and Statistical Analysis

For experimentation purposes, a set of 180 benchmark instances proposed by Ciavotta et al. [21] were selected to evaluate the effects of different probability distributions (PDs) and coefficients of variation (CVs) of the processing and setup times in the objective functions. Specifically, the 180 instances were 10 instances for each combination of 20, 50, and 100 jobs with 5, 10, and 20 machines and a size of sequence-dependent setup times of 50% and 125%. Two PDs, lognormal, uniform, and three CVs, 0.3, 0.4, and 0.5, were selected to model both the stochastic processing and setup times. This corresponds to 6480 NDS archives. The proposed method was implemented in Java and run on an Intel Core i7-4770 with a 3.4 GHz processor and 8GB of RAM. The stopping criterion for MC-SIM-GRASP was established as $numberOfJobs \cdot numberOfMachines \cdot 1.0$ s. The best-qualified solution of each NDS archive was selected by using the AHP method. This results in a total of 51,840 solutions, each of which has an AHP score and a value for the four objective functions. Four ANOVAs were conducted to jointly analyze the effect of the eight factors on the four selected objective functions (E[E/T], SD[E/T], E[CI], and E[PI]). The factors selected for the experimental design are: probability distribution of processing times (PDPT), coefficient of variation of processing times (CVPT), probability distribution of setup times (PDST), coefficient of variation of setup times (CVST), the vectors of criteria weights of the AHP (WV), number of jobs, number of machines, and generation size of the standard deviation of sequence-dependent setup times (SDST). The factors and their levels are presented in Table 7.

Table 7. Factors of the experimental design and their corresponding levels.

Factor	Levels
PD of processing times (PDPT)	lognormal [lgn] and uniform [unf]
CV of processing times (CVPT)	0.3, 0.4 and 0.5
PD of setup times (PDST)	lognormal [lgn] and uniform [unf]
CV of setup times (CVST)	0.3, 0.4, and 0.5
vectors of criteria weights of AHP (WV)	1, 2, 3, 4, 5, 6, 7, and 8
number of jobs	20, 50, and 100
number of machines	5, 10, and 20
generation size of SDST	SSD50, and SSD125

The results showed that all main effects are statistically significant on the four objective functions except PDPT for E[CI] and E[PI] and the PDST and CVST for E[PI]. Nevertheless, some double and triple interactions that include the PDPT, PDST, and CVST have a significant effect on E[CI] and E[PI]. In fact, for at least one of the four objective functions, the double interaction effects are also significant (see Table 8). This shows that the WV discriminates among the Pareto solutions, helping the decision-maker select a solution from the Pareto frontier. We identified in addition that as the CVPT and CVST increase, the expected value of earliness (E[E/T]) and the standard deviation of earliness tardiness indicator (SD[E/T]) augment as well. The same occurs with E[CI], but not to the same degree. Additionally, the measures tend to be greater for the lognormal distribution than for the uniform distribution. This shows the importance of accurately fitting the PD to obtain adjusted robust measures.

Figures 3 and 4 show the main effect plots of the factors WV, PDST, PDPT, CVST, and CVPT on E[E/T] and SD[E/T], respectively. The axes of the main effect plots are the levels of each factor. It can be seen that for different weight vectors, the objectives E[E/T] and SD[E/T] imply that the AHP is capable of selecting a different solution of the Pareto frontier according to the preferences given by the decision-maker in the AHP method. In the case of the probability distributions (the PDST and PDPT factors), the lognormal distribution presents a slightly greater E [E/T] and SD[E/T] in comparison with the uniform distribution, which gives the idea that despite using the same expected values of the processing and setup times under the same coefficient of variation, the solutions vary with the change of the distribution used. Additionally, as expected, as the coefficient of variation of the setup and the processing times increase (the CVST and CVPT factors) the objectives E[E/T] and SD[E/T] also increment, indicating a higher variability in the obtained solutions of the Pareto frontier. These aspects led us to highlight the importance of including uncertainty in the optimization problem when it is really present, and the value of making an accurate distribution fitting to make adequate decisions.

Table 8. *p*-values and R^2_{adj} of the ANOVAs for each objective function.

Source	E[E/T]	SD(E/T)	E[CI]	E[PI]
WV	0.0000	0.0000	0.0000	0.0000
PDST	0.0000	0.0000	0.0000	0.1750
PDPT	0.0000	0.0000	0.0530	0.1920
SizeSDST	0.0000	0.0000	0.0000	0.0000
CVST	0.0000	0.0000	0.0160	0.1620
CVPT	0.0000	0.0000	0.0030	0.0460
Jobs	0.0000	0.0000	0.0000	0.0000
Machines	0.0000	0.0000	0.0000	0.0000
WV*PDST	0.0000	0.0000	0.0000	0.0000
WV*PDPT	0.0030	0.9150	0.0210	0.9510
WV*SizeSDST	0.0040	0.0000	0.0000	0.0000
WV*CVST	0.0580	0.0040	0.0000	0.9440
WV*CVPT	0.0000	0.0000	0.0000	0.6190
WV*Jobs	0.0000	0.0000	0.0000	0.0000
WV*Machines	0.0000	0.0010	0.0060	0.0010
PDST*PDPT	0.5290	0.0470	0.4400	0.8040
PDST*SizeSDST	0.0000	0.0000	0.0000	0.9560
PDST*CVST	0.0310	0.0000	0.0010	0.3280
PDST*CVPT	0.1570	0.0000	0.0050	0.0070
PDST*Jobs	0.0000	0.0000	0.0000	0.6420
PDST*Machines	0.9610	0.0000	0.0600	0.3650
PDPT*SizeSDST	0.4970	0.0000	0.2970	0.9380
PDPT*CVST	0.0100	0.3370	0.0000	0.0000
PDPT*CVPT	0.0070	0.0000	0.0150	0.3610
PDPT*Jobs	0.0000	0.0000	0.0390	0.2530
PDPT*Machines	0.1500	0.0000	0.5470	0.0000
SizeSDST*CVST	0.0000	0.0000	0.0000	0.0110
SizeSDST*CVPT	0.0000	0.0000	0.0010	0.0000
SizeSDST*Jobs	0.0000	0.0000	0.0000	0.0000
SizeSDST*Machines	0.0000	0.0090	0.0000	0.0000
CVST*CVPT	0.0340	0.0000	0.0470	0.0000
CVST*Jobs	0.0000	0.0000	0.0040	0.0000
CVST*Machines	0.0000	0.1730	0.2650	0.7880
CVPT*Jobs	0.0000	0.0000	0.0000	0.0780
CVPT*Machines	0.0000	0.2110	0.0000	0.0230
R^2_{aj}	99.82%	77.30%	89.76%	92.01%

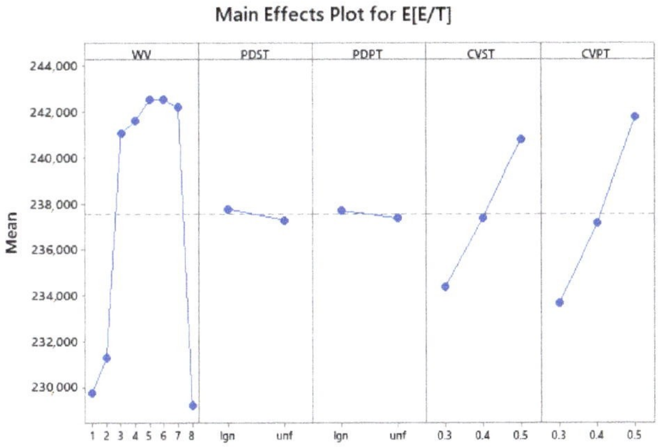

Figure 3. Main effects plots for E[E/T].

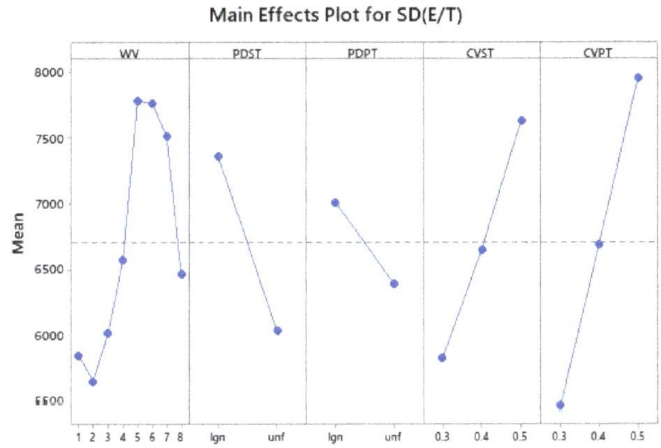

Figure 4. Main effects plots for S(E/T).

Figures 5 and 6 present the interaction plots between factors CVST and CVPT for the E[CI] and E[PI] objectives, respectively. The axes of the plots are the levels of the coefficients of variation. These plots confirm that for both qualitative objectives, there exists an interaction effect between the coefficients of variation of the processing times (CVPT) and the coefficients of variation of the setup times (CVST), which means that the best solution selected with the AHP method, in terms of the qualitative criteria, varies depending on the variability of the processing and setup times. This leads again to the relevance of including uncertainties in the optimization process and the execution of an accurate distribution fitting.

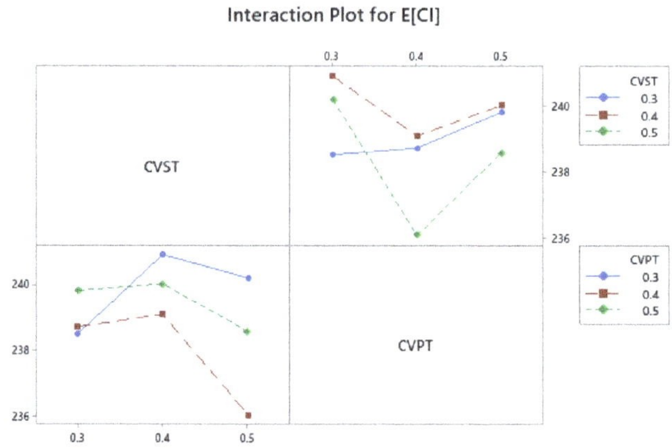

Figure 5. Interaction plots of the CVST-CVPT for E[E/T].

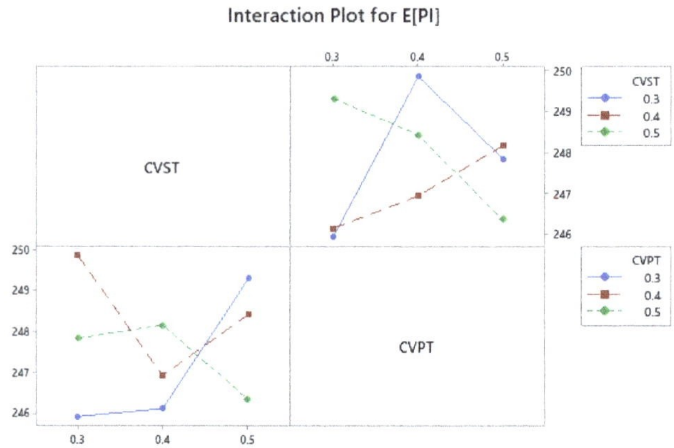

Figure 6. Interaction plots of the CVST-CVPT for S(E/T).

To conduct the experimental design and validate the validity and objectivity, the assumptions of homoscedasticity, normality, and independence were tested. Because the homoscedasticity and normality tests were not fulfilled, we performed a Friedman test to corroborate the ANOVA results. Tables 9 and 10 present the detailed Friedman tests for E[E/T] and SD[E/T] in terms of the factors PDPT, CVPT, PDST, and CVST. To the best of our knowledge, this is the only work that has studied these four objective functions in an SPFSP. We present three indicators for the multi-objective problems proposed by Ebrahimi et al. [80] and Karimi et al. [81], which can be used for future comparisons. For this work, these indicators were adjusted for the four objective functions analyzed:

- Number of Pareto solutions (NPS), which means the number of nondominated points for each instance;
- Mean ideal distance (MID), which is a measure of the closeness between Pareto solutions and an ideal point (0,0,0,0). The quality of a Pareto frontier is higher as the value of MID decreases. Equation (1) shows the function for this indicator;
- Spread of the nondominance solution (SNS), which is an indicator of the diversity of Pareto points. The Pareto frontier presents more diversity as the value of SNS increases. Equation (3) shows the function of this indicator.

$$MID = \frac{\sum_{i=1}^{NPS} c_i}{NPS} \quad (1)$$

where:

$$c_i = \sqrt{E[E/T]_i^2 + SD[E/T]_i^2 + E[CI]_i^2 + E[PI]_i^2} \quad (2)$$

$$SNS = \sqrt{\frac{\sum_{i=1}^{NPS} (MID - c_i)^2}{NPS}} \quad (3)$$

Table 9. Friedman test for E[E/T] versus the factors PDPT, CVPT, PDST, and CVST.

Factor	Levels of Factor	N	Expected Median	Sum of Ranks	Overall Median	DF	p-Value
PDPT	Lgn	25,920	132,275	39,378	132,234	1	0
	Unf	25,920	132,194	38,382			
CVPT	0.3	17,280	129,225	27,574	131,165	2	0
	0.4	17,280	130,886	33,622			
	0.5	17,280	133,385	42,484			
PDST	Lgn	25,920	132,331	39,465	132,301	1	0
	Unf	25,920	132,271	38,295			
CVST	0.3	17,280	130,486	29,026	131,757	2	0
	0.4	17,280	131,744	34,544			
	0.5	17,280	133,040	40,110			

Table 10. Friedman test for SD(E/T) versus the factors PDPT, PDST, CVPT, and CVST.

Factor	Levels of Factor	N	Expected Median	Sum of Ranks	Overall Median	DF	p-Value
PDPT	Lgn	25,920	5243.6	44,156	5090.4	1	0
	Unf	25,920	4937.2	33,604			
CVPT	0.3	17,280	4450.2	22,359	5093	2	0
	0.4	17,280	5059.4	34,166			
	0.5	17,280	5769.4	47,155			
PDST	Lgn	25,920	5247	43,715	2112.9	1	0
	Unf	25,920	4978.8	34,045			
CVST	0.3	17,280	4954.2	25,591	5296.1	2	0
	0.4	17,280	5265.5	34,108			
	0.5	17,280	5668.6	43,981			

Tables 11–13 show the averages of the NPS, MID, and SNS for each instance size, each combination of the PDPT with CVPT, and each combination of the PDST with CVST, respectively. In Table 11, it can be seen that the MID and SNS increase as the number of jobs or machines increases, and due to the increment of the jobs or machines, the expected and standard deviation of tardiness present a crescent behavior. Moreover, the NPS also tends to augment, giving more possible solutions to chose in scenarios with higher variability.

Table 11. Performance results of the proposed approach.

Number of Jobs	Machines	NPS	MID	SNS
20	5	182.59	18,412.20	915.68
	10	169.80	19,660.78	1386.57
	20	183.03	23,370.81	2142.31
Total 20		**178.47**	**20,481.26**	**1481.52**
50	5	262.71	123,904.5	2784.69
	10	254.54	138,695.12	2920.58
	20	247.28	153,472.48	3480.98
Total 50		**254.84**	**138,690.7**	**3062.08**
100	5	210.46	500,238.28	7475.30
	10	227.30	550,636.3	7165.95
	20	250.03	601,917.09	7166.19
Total 100		**229.26**	**550,930.55**	**7269.15**

Table 12 shows the minimum difference in the MID and SNS between the lognormal and uniform distributions for the processing times, under the same coefficient of variation. Nevertheless, as the coefficient of variation of the processing times increases, independently of the probability distribution, the MID and SNS augment. That means that the quality of the Pareto frontier is worse as the coefficient of variation of the processing times increases. This suggests that production managers should encourage a continuous improvement of the production processes to reduce the variability of the process insofar as that is possible. Moreover, it is interesting to see that the NPS decreases as the coefficient of variation of the processing times increments, showing that high variability scenarios present fewer possible solutions to choose for the decision-maker.

Table 12. Performance multi-objective metrics for the PDPT and CVPT.

PDPT	CVPT	NPS	MID	SNS
lgn	0.3	273.64	232,650.34	3884.93
	0.4	194.92	236,692.91	3928.33
	0.5	144.34	241,086.47	4045.65
Total lgn		**204.3**	**236,809.91**	**3952.97**
unf	0.3	297.71	232,730.09	3925.04
	0.4	225.32	236,299.54	3862.35
	0.5	189.23	240,745.7	3979.21
Total unf		**237.42**	**236,591.77**	**3922.20**

The measures presented in Table 13 show a large difference in the SNS between the lognormal and uniform distributions of the sequence-dependent setup times, under the same coefficient of variation of the setup times, which is a different behavior than that presented for the coefficient of variation of the processing times. Moreover, the NPS also presents high differences between the uniform and lognormal distributions of the setup times, whereas for the coefficient of variation of the processing times, the NPS values were very close. This allowed us to conclude that each input parameter can cause different performances of the solutions, and thus, the AHP selects the corresponding solution of the Pareto frontier to fulfill the decision-maker's expectations.

Table 13. Performance multi-objective metrics for the PDST and CVST.

PDST	CVST	NPS	MID	SNS
lgn	0.3	115.69	233,355.91	4183.21
	0.4	81.23	236,692.94	4223.27
	0.5	66.40	240,032.78	4283.50
Total lgn		**87.78**	**236,693.88**	**4229.99**
unf	0.3	413.55	233,671.64	3625.21
	0.4	357.49	236,430.32	3607.72
	0.5	290.78	240,021.45	3702.59
Total unf		**353.94**	**236,707.8**	**3645.18**

5. Conclusions and Recommendations

This paper presented a multicriteria simheuristic that hybridizes a GRASP, a PAES algorithm, and a Monte Carlo simulation (MC-SIM-GRASP) to solve a multi-objective stochastic permutation flow shop scheduling problem (SPFSP). The approach obtains a set of nondominated solutions for four objectives: for expected earliness/tardiness, standard deviation of earliness/tardiness, expected customer importance, and expected product importance in an SPFSP. It was used an analytical hierarchical process (AHP) to select the desired solution for the decision-maker from the set of solutions from the Pareto frontier. The purpose of this method was to ease the selection of a solution and include a qualitative criterion for the objective of the decision-making. This paper analyzed the effect of eight factors in the behavior of the four objective functions selected. To this end, four ANOVAs were carried out with seven factors: type of probability distribution (PD) of stochastic processing times, coefficient of variation (CV) of stochastic processing times, PD of sequence-dependent setup times, CV of sequence-dependent setup times, the vector weights of criteria in the AHP methodology, the number of jobs, and the number of machines. The outcomes showed that all factors had significant effects on the four objective functions. The results obtained in this paper support the importance of including uncertainty, modeled with adequate PDs, to obtain robust solutions. Additionally, a set of multi-objective metrics (number of Pareto solutions, means' ideal distance, and spread of the nondominance solution) was calculated for future comparisons, as this problem has not been solved in the literature before. Future work may analyze other PDs and CVs. It would be useful to analyze a case in which the processing time PD of each job has a different CV, which is generally true in real cases. Finally, other qualitative criteria should be incorporated in the analysis.

Author Contributions: Conceptualization, E.M.G.-N.; methodology, E.M.G.-N.; programming, E.M.G.-N.; formal analysis, E.M.G.-N.; writing—original draft, E.M.G.-N. and J.-F.J.; writing—review and editing, J.-F.J. and J.-F.J.; supervision, J.R.M.-T. All authors read and agreed to the published version of the manuscript.

Funding: This research received no external funding.

Institutional Review Board Statement: Not applicable.

Informed Consent Statement: Not applicable.

Data Availability Statement: The benchmark instances evaluated in this paper were taken from Ciavotta et al. [21], and the results obtained for the analysis are available in https://livejaverianaedu-my.sharepoint.com/:x:/g/personal/eliana_gonzalez_javeriana_edu_co/EdOPPW3UqvtLsAmLusoECKwBZXGoMPwwfHQFQCCkbh1-Qg?e=54af92 (acessed on 27 June 2021).

Conflicts of Interest: The authors declare no conflict of interest.

References

1. Pinedo, M.L. *Scheduling*, 5th ed.; Springer International Publishing: Cham, Switzerland, 2016; pp. 1–670. [CrossRef]
2. Ruiz, R.; Maroto, C. A comprehensive review and evaluation of permutation flowshop heuristics. *Eur. J. Oper. Res.* **2005**, *165*, 479–494. [CrossRef]
3. Du, J.; Leung, J.Y.T. Minimizing Total Tardiness on One Machine Is NP-Hard. *Math. Oper. Res.* **1990**, *15*, 483–495. [CrossRef]
4. Li, Z.; Ierapetritou, M. Process scheduling under uncertainty: Review and challenges. *Comput. Chem. Eng.* **2008**, *32*, 715–727. [CrossRef]
5. Gourgand, M.; Grangeon, N.; Norre, S. A review of the static stochastic flow-shop scheduling problem. *J. Decis. Syst.* **2000**, *9*, 1–31. [CrossRef]
6. Vallada, E.; Ruiz, R.; Framinan, J.M. New hard benchmark for flowshop scheduling problems minimising makespan. *Eur. J. Oper. Res.* **2015**, *240*, 666–677. [CrossRef]
7. Yenisey, M.M.; Yagmahan, B. Multi-objective permutation flow shop scheduling problem: Literature review, classification and current trends. *Omega* **2014**, *45*, 119–135. [CrossRef]
8. Chang, P.T.; Lo, Y.T. Modelling of job-shop scheduling with multiple quantitative and qualitative objectives and a GA/TS mixture approach. *Int. J. Comput. Integr. Manuf.* **2001**, *14*, 367–384. [CrossRef]
9. Chang, P.T.; Lin, K.P.; Pai, P.F.; Zhong, C.Z.; Lin, C.H.; Hung, L.T. Ant colony optimization system for a multi-quantitative and qualitative objective job-shop parallel-machine-scheduling problem. *Int. J. Prod. Res.* **2008**, *46*, 5719–5759. [CrossRef]
10. González-Neira, E.M.; García-Cáceres, R.G.; Caballero-Villalobos, J.P.; Molina-Sánchez, L.P.; Montoya-Torres, J.R. Stochastic flexible flow shop scheduling problem under quantitative and qualitative decision criteria. *Comput. Ind. Eng.* **2016**, *101*, 128–144. [CrossRef]
11. Gonzalez-Martin, S.; Juan, A.A.; Riera, D.; Elizondo, M.G.; Ramos, J.J. A simheuristic algorithm for solving the arc routing problem with stochastic demands. *J. Simul.* **2018**, *12*, 53–66. [CrossRef]
12. Latorre-Biel, J.I.; Ferone, D.; Juan, A.A.; Faulin, J. Combining simheuristics with Petri nets for solving the stochastic vehicle routing problem with correlated demands. *Expert Syst. Appl.* **2021**, *168*, 114240. [CrossRef]
13. Quintero-Araujo, C.L.; Guimarans, D.; Juan, A.A. A simheuristic algorithm for the capacitated location routing problem with stochastic demands. *J. Simul.* **2019**, 1–18. [CrossRef]
14. Juan, A.A.; Grasman, S.E.; Caceres-Cruz, J.; Bektaş, T. A simheuristic algorithm for the Single-Period Stochastic Inventory-Routing Problem with stock-outs. *Simul. Model. Pract. Theory* **2014**, *46*, 40–52. [CrossRef]
15. de Armas, J.; Juan, A.A.; Marquès, J.M.; Pedroso, J.P. Solving the deterministic and stochastic uncapacitated facility location problem: From a heuristic to a simheuristic. *J. Oper. Res. Soc.* **2017**, *68*, 1161–1176. [CrossRef]
16. González-Neira, E.M.; Urrego-Torres, A.M.; Cruz-Riveros, A.M.; Henao-García, C.; Montoya-Torres, J.R.; Molina-Sánchez, L.P.; Jiménez, J.F. Robust solutions in multi-objective stochastic permutation flow shop problem. *Comput. Ind. Eng.* **2019**, *137*, 106026. [CrossRef]
17. Hatami, S.; Calvet, L.; Fernández-Viagas, V.; Framiñán, J.M.; Juan, A.A. A simheuristic algorithm to set up starting times in the stochastic parallel flowshop problem. *Simul. Model. Pract. Theory* **2018**, *86*, 55–71. [CrossRef]
18. Juan, A.A.; Barrios, B.B.; Vallada, E.; Riera, D.; Jorba, J. A simheuristic algorithm for solving the permutation flow shop problem with stochastic processing times. *Simul. Model. Pract. Theory* **2014**, *46*, 101–117. [CrossRef]
19. Mokhtari, H.; Salmasnia, A. A Monte Carlo simulation based chaotic differential evolution algorithm for scheduling a stochastic parallel processor system. *Expert Syst. Appl.* **2015**, *42*, 7132–7147. [CrossRef]
20. González-Neira, E.M.; Montoya-Torres, J.R. A simheuristic for stochastic permutation flow shop problem considering quantitative and qualitative decision criteria. In *Proceedings of the 16th International Conference on Project Management and Scheduling*; Caramia, M., Bianco, L., Giordani, S., Eds.; TexMat: Rome, Italy, 2018; pp. 104–109.
21. Ciavotta, M.; Minella, G.; Ruiz, R. Multi-objective sequence dependent setup times permutation flowshop: A new algorithm and a comprehensive study. *Eur. J. Oper. Res.* **2013**, *227*, 301–313. [CrossRef]
22. Pan, Q.K.; Ruiz, R. A comprehensive review and evaluation of permutation flowshop heuristics to minimize flowtime. *Comput. Oper. Res.* **2013**, *40*, 117–128. [CrossRef]
23. Arora, D.; Agarwal, G. Meta-heuristic approaches for flowshop scheduling problems: A review. *Int. J. Adv. Oper. Manag.* **2016**, *8*, 1. [CrossRef]
24. Nagano, M.S.; Miyata, H.H. Review and classification of constructive heuristics mechanisms for no-wait flow shop problem. *Int. J. Adv. Manuf. Technol.* **2016**, *86*, 2161–2174. [CrossRef]
25. Rossit, D.A.; Tohmé, F.; Frutos, M. The Non-Permutation Flow-Shop scheduling problem: A literature review. *Omega* **2018**, *77*, 143–153. [CrossRef]
26. Fernandez-Viagas, V.; Ruiz, R.; Framinan, J.M. A new vision of approximate methods for the permutation flowshop to minimise makespan: State-of-the-art and computational evaluation. *Eur. J. Oper. Res.* **2017**, *257*, 707–721. [CrossRef]
27. González-Neira, E.M.; Montoya-Torres, J.R.; Barrera, D. Flow-shop scheduling problem under uncertainties: Review and trends. *Int. J. Ind. Eng. Comput.* **2017**, *8*, 399–426. [CrossRef]
28. Framinan, J.M.; Perez-Gonzalez, P. On heuristic solutions for the stochastic flowshop scheduling problem. *Eur. J. Oper. Res.* **2015**, *246*, 413–420. [CrossRef]

29. Lin, J.T.; Chen, C.M. Simulation optimization approach for hybrid flow shop scheduling problem in semiconductor back-end manufacturing. *Simul. Model. Pract. Theory* **2015**, *51*, 100–114. [CrossRef]
30. Qin, W.; Zhang, J.; Song, D. An improved ant colony algorithm for dynamic hybrid flow shop scheduling with uncertain processing time. *J. Intell. Manuf.* **2018**, *29*, 891–904. [CrossRef]
31. Fazayeli, M.; Aleagha, M.R.; Bashirzadeh, R.; Shafaei, R. A hybrid meta-heuristic algorithm for flowshop robust scheduling under machine breakdown uncertainty. *Int. J. Comput. Integr. Manuf.* **2016**, *29*, 709–719. [CrossRef]
32. Ying, K.C. Scheduling the two-machine flowshop to hedge against processing time uncertainty. *J. Oper. Res. Soc.* **2015**, *66*, 1413–1425. [CrossRef]
33. Behnamian, J.; Fatemi Ghomi, S.M.T. A survey of multi-factory scheduling. *J. Intell. Manuf.* **2016**, *27*, 231–249. [CrossRef]
34. Huang, C.S.; Huang, Y.C.; Lai, P.J. Modified genetic algorithms for solving fuzzy flow shop scheduling problems and their implementation with CUDA. *Expert Syst. Appl.* **2012**, *39*, 4999–5005. [CrossRef]
35. Makino, T. On a scheduling problem. *J. Oper. Res. Soc. Jpn.* **1965**, *8*, 32–44.

Talwar, P.P. A Note on Sequencing Problem with Uncertain Job Time. *J. Oper. Res. Soc. Jpn.* **1967**, *9*, 93–97.

37. Cunningham, A.A.; Dutta, S.K. Scheduling jobs, with exponentially distributed processing times, on two machines of a flow shop. *Nav. Res. Logist. Q.* **1973**, *20*, 69–81. [CrossRef]
38. Alcaide, D.; Rodriguez-Gonzalez, A.; Sicilia, J. An approach to solve the minimum expected makespan flow-shop problem subject to breakdowns. *Eur. J. Oper. Res.* **2002**, *140*, 384–398. [CrossRef]
39. Gourgand, M.; Grangeon, N.; Norre, S. A contribution to the stochastic flow shop scheduling problem. *Eur. J. Oper. Res.* **2003**, *151*, 415–433. [CrossRef]
40. Wang, L.; Zhang, L.; Zheng, D.Z. Ordinal optimisation of genetic control parameters for flow shop scheduling. *Int. J. Adv. Manuf. Technol.* **2005**, *26*, 1414–1420. [CrossRef]
41. Kalczynski, P.J.; Kamburowski, J. A heuristic for minimizing the expected makespan in two-machine flow shops with consistent coefficients of variation. *Eur. J. Oper. Res.* **2006**, *169*, 742–750. [CrossRef]
42. Portougal, V.; Trietsch, D. Johnson's problem with stochastic processing times and optimal service level. *Eur. J. Oper. Res.* **2006**, *169*, 751–760. [CrossRef]
43. Baker, K.R.; Trietsch, D. Three heuristic procedures for the stochastic, two-machine flow shop problem. *J. Sched.* **2011**, *14*, 445–454. [CrossRef]
44. Baker, K.R.; Altheimer, D. Heuristic solution methods for the stochastic flow shop problem. *Eur. J. Oper. Res.* **2012**, *216*, 172–177. [CrossRef]
45. Elyasi, A.; Salmasi, N. Stochastic scheduling with minimizing the number of tardy jobs using chance constrained programming. *Math. Comput. Model.* **2013**, *57*, 1154–1164. [CrossRef]
46. Elyasi, A.; Salmasi, N. Stochastic flow-shop scheduling with minimizing the expected number of tardy jobs. *Int. J. Adv. Manuf. Technol.* **2013**, *66*, 337–346. [CrossRef]
47. Gonzalez-Neira, E.M.; Ferone, D.; Hatami, S.; Juan, A.A. A biased-randomized simheuristic for the distributed assembly permutation flowshop problem with stochastic processing times. *Simul. Model. Pract. Theory* **2017**, *79*, 23–36. [CrossRef]
48. González-Neira, E.M.; Montoya-Torres, J.R.; Caballero-Villalobos, J.P. A comparison of dispatching rules hybridised with Monte Carlo Simulation in stochastic permutation flow shop problem. *J. Simul.* **2019**, *13*, 128–137. [CrossRef]
49. Marichelvam, M.; Geetha, M. A hybrid algorithm to solve the stochastic flow shop scheduling problems with machine break down. *Int. J. Enterp. Netw. Manag.* **2019**, *10*, 162. [CrossRef]
50. Villarinho, P.A.; Panadero, J.; Pessoa, L.S.; Juan, A.A.; Oliveira, F.L.C. A simheuristic algorithm for the stochastic permutation flow-shop problem with delivery dates and cumulative payoffs. *Int. Trans. Oper. Res.* **2021**, *28*, 716–737. [CrossRef]
51. Liu, F.; Wang, S.; Hong, Y.; Yue, X. On the Robust and Stable Flowshop Scheduling Under Stochastic and Dynamic Disruptions. *IEEE Trans. Eng. Manag.* **2017**, *64*, 539–553. [CrossRef]
52. Liao, W.; Fu, Y. Min–max regret criterion-based robust model for the permutation flow-shop scheduling problem. *Eng. Optim.* **2020**, *52*, 687–700. [CrossRef]
53. Goli, A.; Babaee Tirkolaee, E.; Soltani, M. A robust just-in-time flow shop scheduling problem with outsourcing option on subcontractors. *Prod. Manuf. Res.* **2019**, *7*, 294–315. [CrossRef]
54. Azadeh, A.; Moghaddam, M.; Geranmayeh, P.; Naghavi, A. A flexible artificial neural network–fuzzy simulation algorithm for scheduling a flow shop with multiple processors. *Int. J. Adv. Manuf. Technol.* **2010**, *50*, 699–715. [CrossRef]
55. Liu, Q.; Ullah, S.; Zhang, C. An improved genetic algorithm for robust permutation flowshop scheduling. *Int. J. Adv. Manuf. Technol.* **2011**, *56*, 345–354. [CrossRef]
56. Kasperski, A.; Kurpisz, A.; Zieliński, P. Approximating a two-machine flow shop scheduling under discrete scenario uncertainty. *Eur. J. Oper. Res.* **2012**, *217*, 36–43. [CrossRef]
57. Gören, S.; Pierreval, H. Taking advantage of a diverse set of efficient production schedules: A two-step approach for scheduling with side concerns. *Comput. Oper. Res.* **2013**, *40*, 1979–1990. [CrossRef]
58. Rahmani, D.; Heydari, M. Robust and stable flow shop scheduling with unexpected arrivals of new jobs and uncertain processing times. *J. Manuf. Syst.* **2014**, *33*, 84–92. [CrossRef]

59. Shahnaghi, K.; Shahmoradi-Moghadam, H.; Noroozi, A.; Mokhtari, H. A robust modelling and optimisation framework for a batch processing flow shop production system in the presence of uncertainties. *Int. J. Comput. Integr. Manuf.* **2015**, *29*, 1–15. [CrossRef]
60. Gholami-Zanjani, S.M.; Hakimifar, M.; Nazemi, N.; Jolai, F. Robust and Fuzzy Optimisation Models for a Flow shop Scheduling Problem with Sequence Dependent Setup Times: A real case study on a PCB assembly company. *Int. J. Comput. Integr. Manuf.* **2017**, *30*, 552–563. [CrossRef]
61. Ćwik, M.; Józefczyk, J. Heuristic algorithms for the minmax regret flow-shop problem with interval processing times. *Cent. Eur. J. Oper. Res.* **2018**, *26*, 215–238. [CrossRef] [PubMed]
62. Forst, F.G. Bicriterion stochastic scheduling on one or more machines. *Eur. J. Oper. Res.* **1995**, *80*, 404–409. [CrossRef]
63. Celano, G.; Costa, A.; Fichera, S. An Evolutionary Algorithm for Pure Fuzzy Flowshop Scheduling Problems. *Int. J. Uncertain. Fuzziness Knowl. Based Syst.* **2003**, *11*, 655–669. [CrossRef]
64. Temiz, I.; Erol, S. Multiobjective genetic algorithm for fuzzy flowshop scheduling problem. *J. Fac. Eng. Archit. Gazi Univ.* **2007**, *22*, 855–862.
65. Zhou, Q.; Cui, X. Research on multiobjective flow shop scheduling with stochastic processing times and machine breakdowns. In Proceedings of the 2008 IEEE International Conference on Service Operations and Logistics, and Informatics, Beijing, China, 12–15 October 2008; IEEE: New York, NY, USA, 2008; Volume 22, pp. 1718–1724. [CrossRef]
66. Azadeh, A.; Jeihoonian, M.; Shoja, B.M.; Seyedmahmoudi, S. An integrated neural network–simulation algorithm for performance optimisation of the bi-criteria two-stage assembly flow-shop scheduling problem with stochastic activities. *Int. J. Prod. Res.* **2012**, *50*, 7271–7284. [CrossRef]
67. Liefooghe, A.; Basseur, M.; Humeau, J.; Jourdan, L.; Talbi, E.G. On optimizing a bi-objective flowshop scheduling problem in an uncertain environment. *Comput. Math. Appl.* **2012**, *64*, 3747–3762. [CrossRef]
68. Rahmani, D.; Ramezanian, R.; Mehrabad, M.S. Multi-objective flow shop scheduling problem with stochastic parameters: Fuzzy goal programming approach. *Int. J. Oper. Res.* **2014**, *21*, 322–340. [CrossRef]
69. Mou, J.; Li, X.; Gao, L.; Yi, W. An effective L-MONG algorithm for solving multi-objective flow-shop inverse scheduling problems. *J. Intell. Manuf.* **2018**, *29*, 789–807. [CrossRef]
70. Fu, Y.; Wang, H.; Tian, G.; Li, Z.; Hu, H. Two-agent stochastic flow shop deteriorating scheduling via a hybrid multi-objective evolutionary algorithm. *J. Intell. Manuf.* **2019**, *30*, 2257–2272. [CrossRef]
71. Faraji Amiri, M.; Behnamian, J. Multi-objective green flowshop scheduling problem under uncertainty: Estimation of distribution algorithm. *J. Clean. Prod.* **2020**, *251*, 119734. [CrossRef]
72. Rajan, A.J.; Rao, K.S.; Ganesh, K. VEPCE: Decision-making model for vendor evaluation with respect to product prioritisation and customer expectation. *Int. J. Logist. Syst. Manag.* **2007**, *3*, 34. [CrossRef]
73. Brown, J.R.; Ozgur, C.O. Priority class scheduling: Production scheduling for multi-objective environments. *Prod. Plan. Control* **1997**, *8*, 762–770. [CrossRef]
74. Georgakopoulos, A.; Mihiotis, A. Distribution network design: An integer programming approach. *J. Retail. Consum. Serv.* **2004**, *11*, 41–49. [CrossRef]
75. García Cáceres, R.G.; Aráoz Durand, J.A.; Gómez, F.P. Integral analysis method—IAM. *Eur. J. Oper. Res.* **2009**, *192*, 891–903. [CrossRef]
76. Lahdelma, R.; Miettinen, K.; Salminen, P. Ordinal criteria in stochastic multicriteria acceptability analysis (SMAA). *Eur. J. Oper. Res.* **2003**, *147*, 117–127. [CrossRef]
77. Resende, M.G.; Ribeiro, C.C. Greedy Randomized Adaptive Search Procedures: Advances, Hybridizations, and Applications. In *Handbook of Metaheuristics SE-10*; Gendreau, M., Potvin, J.Y., Eds.; Springer: New York, NY, USA, 2010; Volume 146, pp. 283–319. [CrossRef]
78. Knowles, J.D.; Corne, D.W. Approximating the Nondominated Front Using the Pareto Archived Evolution Strategy. *Evol. Comput.* **2000**, *8*, 149–172. [CrossRef] [PubMed]
79. Martí, R.; Campos, V.; Resende, M.G.; Duarte, A. Multiobjective GRASP with Path Relinking. *Eur. J. Oper. Res.* **2015**, *240*, 54–71. [CrossRef]
80. Ebrahimi, M.; Fatemi Ghomi, S.; Karimi, B. Hybrid flow shop scheduling with sequence dependent family setup time and uncertain due dates. *Appl. Math. Model.* **2014**, *38*, 2490–2504. [CrossRef]
81. Karimi, N.; Zandieh, M.; Karamooz, H. Bi-objective group scheduling in hybrid flexible flowshop: A multi-phase approach. *Expert Syst. Appl.* **2010**, *37*, 4024–4032. [CrossRef]

algorithms

MDPI

Article

Efficient Dynamic Cost Scheduling Algorithm for Financial Data Supply Chain

Alia Al Sadawi [1], Abdulrahim Shamayleh [1,2,*] and Malick Ndiaye [1,2]

1 Engineering Systems Management Graduate Program, American University of Sharjah, Sharjah 26666, United Arab Emirates; g00047863@alumni.aus.edu (A.A.S.); mndiaye@aus.edu (M.N.)
2 Industrial Engineering, American University of Sharjah, Sharjah 26666, United Arab Emirates
* Correspondence: ashamayleh@aus.edu

Abstract: The financial data supply chain is vital to the economy, especially for banks. It affects their customer service level, therefore, it is crucial to manage the scheduling of the financial data supply chain to elevate the efficiency of banking sectors' performance. The primary tool used in the data supply chain is data batch processing which requires efficient scheduling. This work investigates the problem of scheduling the processing of tasks with non-identical sizes and different priorities on a set of parallel processors. An iterative dynamic scheduling algorithm (DCSDBP) was developed to address the data batching process. The objective is to minimize different cost types while satisfying constraints such as resources availability, customer service level, and tasks dependency relation. The algorithm proved its effectiveness by allocating tasks with higher priority and weight while taking into consideration customers' Service Level Agreement, time, and different types of costs, which led to a lower total cost of the batching process. The developed algorithm proved effective by testing it on an illustrative network. Also, a sensitivity analysis is conducted by varying the model parameters for networks with different sizes and complexities to study their impact on the total cost and the problem under study.

Keywords: financial data; supply chain management; data batching; scheduling; batching cost; parallel processing; optimization; multi-processing commitment

Citation: Al Sadawi, A.; Shamayleh, A.; Ndiaye, M. Efficient Dynamic Cost Scheduling Algorithm for Financial Data Supply Chain. *Algorithms* **2021**, *14*, 211. https://doi.org/10.3390/a14070211

Academic Editor: Frank Werner

Received: 18 June 2021
Accepted: 12 July 2021
Published: 14 July 2021

1. Introduction

In today's world, economies and commodity markets swing rapidly; personal, organizational, and business networks are becoming more interconnected, instrumented, and intelligent [1]. One of the important aspects of the business world is supply chain management. It works towards satisfying customers' requirements through the efficient use of resources resulting in reducing cost and increasing profit margin for companies [2]. With a highly competitive global market, supply chains have to be more responsive to customers' needs. Supply chain represents all stages of a process; usually, researchers focus on materials that are manufactured to become an end product; however, the supply chain covers a wider range that extends beyond physical assets. For instance, looking at the banking sector, their main supply chain is of financial data that needs to be processed using available resources which are software and hardware processors.

One of the main instruments used in business networks for the management of the financial data supply chain is data batch processing (DBP). It plays a critical role in daily operations carried out in most organizations in different business fields. Data batch processing can be defined as the execution of data files as input batches using the available resources and gather the resulted files as output batches while satisfying files priorities, predecessors constraints, and time constraints [3,4]. The execution is carried out on the mainframe computer that runs at a scheduled time or on an as-needed basis without user interaction and minimal or no interaction with a computer operator [3,4]. The main feature of data batch processing is its ability to handle an enormous amount of data files which makes it attractive and essential to many organizations that are constantly dealing with heavy business activities [5]. It contributes to the major part of the workload on mainframe computers that will often run a large number of business workflows with complex interrelations, requiring careful scheduling and prioritizing to ensure that all batch jobs run in the correct order and meet strict deadlines [3,4,6].

Our research considers the case of processing end-of-day (EOD) operations which include highly important and frequently used activities and services such as: preparing customers' bank statements; credit card processing bills; fraud detection data; merging the day's transactions into master files; sorting data files for optimal processing; providing daily, weekly, monthly, and annual reports; invoices and bank statements; performing periodic payroll calculations; and applying interest to financial accounts [4]. Banks seek to elevate their level of customer service by optimizing their data supply chain scheduling. This supply chain consists of the bank, a service provider that arranges the processing of data, and processors providing company that rents and leases processors and software to service providers. Also, in our research, data supply chains adopt the technique of lot streaming which is a technique that splits a given data job, each consisting of similar files, into tasks to allow overlapping of successive operations in processing systems thereby reducing the processing makespan.

The proposed work addresses the financial data supply chain scheduling problem from an operational perspective by considering the scheduling at an individual job level. The problem can be viewed as a single-stage supply chain scheduling problem where jobs are arranged to be processed by mainframe processors that can be modeled as a series of flow shop machines. Processors are leased and rented from manufacturing and supplying company as needed by a third-party company that performs the data scheduling. Data arrives raw and unprocessed from banks to a service provider which needs to manage scheduling them for processing as per the available resources (software and hardware) in the most efficient way. After processing, jobs must be returned back to banks where they will be charged for the provided service.

In order to address financial data supply chain, this research covers all aspects of data batch processing, being that it is the tool that manages banks' financial data supply chain scheduling. The scheduling aspects of DBP are job priorities, precedence relationships, constraints in addition to cost. It is important to understand that cost consideration in data batch processing is vital due to the extremely high cost of the resources involved. However, previous research has overlooked the cost despite its importance, and the focus was on the effectiveness of the scheduling component of the process. The high cost of software and hardware resources used in the batch process and the patent rights of companies that own the platform made it not only beneficial, but also essential for DBP users to reduce the cost associated with it. Therefore, this research intends to bridge such a gap and provides a comprehensive study that covers the important aspects of data batch processing. Thus, the main contributions of this work can be summarized as follows:

- Consider all types of costs related to the batch process which are the servers and software basic leasing cost, rental cost for additional resources needed in case of overload and extra work, penalty cost of failing to execute the batch process as per the Service Level Agreement (SLA), and the opportunity cost representing the cost of idling a resource for any period of time due to inefficient task allocation.
- Develop an iterative dynamic scheduling algorithm (DCSDBP) to optimize the data batch processing considering the different costs, availability of resources, and customer service level agreement (SLA) along with the rest of the batch process factors such as the clients' priorities, tasks predecessors and time.
- Utilize the created optimization model to address the problem of controlling the availability of resources such as processors and software required to process input batches and balance the usage of current owned resources and the need to rent additional ones while maintaining the lowest possible cost for the whole data batch processing.

The rest of the paper is organized as follows: Section 2, the background related to this work is presented. The data batch algorithm is presented in Section 3. The illustrative example and sensitivity analysis are presented in Sections 4 and 5 respectively. Finally, the conclusions are presented in Section 6.

2. Literature Review

Supply chain management has another perspective when associated with the financial sector. An alternative concept appears that relates to information or data and supply chain known as Financial Information Supply Chain Management. The researchers in [7] emphasized the need to improve financial operating processes in order to optimize financial data supply chain management by reducing processing time, improving efficiency, and decreasing associated costs of equipment and computers.

Other studies reached an aligned outcome such as the case study by [8] to design, develop, and implement an inter-organizational system by the Reserve Bank of Australia (central bank) and other authorities to remodel data reporting by financial institutions in Australia. The research concluded that the complexity of data consumption patterns led to an increased interdependence within the financial information supply chain which requires developing data exchanges and commodity-like IT infrastructures.

Also, a study by [9] stated that multiple governments have implemented Integrated Financial Management Information Systems to improve effectiveness and streamline business processes. Authors determine the need for automated financial operations to improve data supply chain efficiency.

The authors of [7] believe that in order to improve financial performance, we need to utilize a tool from lean manufacturing. They state that although financial operations are not the same as manufacturing operations, they share more similarities than might be acknowledged. These similarities entitle the financial data supply chain to adopt batch processing and scheduling from lean manufacturing.

Batch processing is widely used because of its ability to meet business-critical functions. It is mainly applied when dealing with large, repeated jobs that can be carried out at a prescribed time. The batch process is complex posing a challenge to efficiently allocate the needed resources. In this section, related literature to approaches used in data batching is presented. Also, related work of using data batching in other fields is presented as well.

The scheduling problem was studied by many researchers since it is a critical issue in batch process operation and performance improvement. Page et al. [10] considered eight common heuristics along with the genetic algorithm (GA) evolutionary strategy to dynamically schedule tasks to processors in a heterogeneous distributed system; they found that using multiple heuristics to generate schedules provides more efficient schedules than using each heuristic on its own. Méndez et al. [11] classified and presented the different state-of-the-art optimization methods associated with the batch scheduling problem. Osman et al. [12] proposed a model for data batch scheduling; they presented a dynamic, iterative framework to assign the required tasks to available resources taking into consideration the predecessors, constraints, and priority of each job. Al Sadawi et al. [13] studied the data batch problem with the goal of minimizing costs and satisfying customer service level agreement. Lim and Chao [14] used fuzzy inference systems to model the preferences of users and decide on the priority of each schedule with the goal of providing users with more efficient throughput. Xhafa and Abraham [15] developed heuristic and metaheuristic methods to deal with scheduling in grid technologies which are considered more complicated than scheduling in classical parallel and distributed systems. Aida [16] evaluated multiple job scheduling algorithms performance to investigate the effect of job size characteristics on job scheduling in a parallel computer system. Stoica et al. [17] described a schedule based on the microeconomic paradigm for online scheduling of a set of parallel jobs in a multiprocessor system. The user was granted control over the performances of his jobs by providing him with a saving account containing an amount of money used to run the jobs. Stoica [18] considered the problem of scheduling an online set of jobs on a parallel computer with identical processors by using simulation to compare three microeconomic policies with three variable partitioning policies. Islam et al. [19] demonstrated higher revenue and better performance by using their proposed new scheduling heuristic called Normalized Urgency to prioritize jobs based on their urgency and their processing times.

A study by Damodaran and Vélez-Gallego [20] developed a simulated annealing algorithm to evaluate the performance of batch systems in terms of total completion time with the goal of minimizing the processing time, and Mehta et al. [21] proposed a parallel query scheduling algorithm by dividing the workload into batches and exploiting common operations within queries in a batch, resulting in significant savings compared to single query scheduling techniques. Grigoriev et al. [22] developed a two-phased LP rounding technique that was used to assign resources to jobs and jobs to machines where a maximum number of units of a resource may be used to speed up the jobs, and the available amount of units of that resource must not be exceeded at any time. Also, Bouganim et al. [23] studied execution plans performance of data integration systems where they proposed an execution strategy to reduce the query response time by concurrently executing several query fragments to overlap data delivery delays with the processing of these query fragments. Ngubiri and van Vliet [24] proposed a new approach for parallel job schedulers fairness evaluation where jobs are not expected to have the same performance in a fair set up when they do not have the same resource requirements and arrive when the queue and system have different states. Arpaci-Dusseau and Culler [25] used a proportional-share scheduler as a building-block and showed that extensions to the above scheduler for improving response time can still fairly allocate resources to a mix of sequential, interactive, and parallel jobs in a distributed environment.

From an economic point of view, Ferguson et al. [26] adopted the human economic model and implemented it on resource allocation in a computer network system which resulted in limiting the complexity of resource sharing algorithms by decentralizing the control of resources. Additionally, Kuwabara et al. [27] presented a market-based approach, where resources are allocated to activities through buying and selling of resources between agents and resource allocation in a multi-agent system. Chun and Culler [28] presented a performance analysis of market-based batch schedulers for clusters of workstations using user-centric performance metrics as the basis for system evaluation. Also, Sairamesh et al. [29] proposed a new methodology based on economic models to provide Quality of Service (QoS) guarantees to competing traffic classes in packet networks. Yeo et al. [30] outlined a taxonomy that describes how market-based resource management systems can support utility-driven cluster computing; the taxonomy is used to survey existing market-based resource management systems to better understand how they can be utilized.

Islam et al. [31] designed a framework that provides an admission control mechanism that only accepts jobs whose requested deadlines can be met and, once accepted, guarantees these deadlines. However, the framework is completely blind to the revenue these jobs can fetch for the supercomputer center. They analyzed the impact of job opportunity cost on the overall revenue of the supercomputer center and attempted to minimize it through predictive techniques. Mutz and Wolski [32] presented a novel implementation of the Generalized Vickrey Auction that uses dynamic programming to schedule jobs and computes payments in pseudo-polynomial time. Mutz et al. [33] proposed and evaluated the application of the Expected Externality Mechanism as an approach to solving the problem of efficiently and fairly allocating resources in a number of different computational settings based on economic principles. Tests indicated that the mechanism meets its theoretical predictions in practice and can be implemented in a computationally tractable manner.

Lavanya et al. [34] proposed two task scheduling algorithms for heterogeneous systems. Their offline and online scheduling algorithms aimed at reducing the overall makespan of task allocation in cloud computing environments. The algorithms' simulation proved that they outperformed standard algorithms in terms of makespan and cloud utilization. Minimizing makespan was the objective of the research conducted by Muter [35] which tackled single and parallel batch processing machine scheduling. The author presented a reformulation for parallel batch processing machines and proposed an exact algorithm to solve this problem. Also, Jia et al. [36] developed a mathematical model and a fuzzy ant colony optimization (FACO) algorithm to schedule parallel non-identical size jobs with fuzzy processing times. The batch processing utilized machines with different capacities and aimed at minimizing the makespan. Additionally, Li [37] proposed two fast algorithms and a polynomial time approximation scheme (PTAS) to tackle the problem of scheduling n jobs on m parallel batching machines with inclusive processing set restrictions and non-identical capacities. The research aimed at finding a non-preemptive schedule to minimize makespan.

Another study by Josephson and Ramesh [38] aimed at creating a task scheduling process by examining the various real times scheduling algorithm. The study presented a new algorithm for task scheduling in a multiprocessor environment. The authors used TORSCHE toolbox for developing real-time scheduling in addition to utilizing features of particle swarm optimization. The proposed algorithm succeeded in executing a maximum number of the process in a minimum time. Also, Ying et al. [39] investigated the Distributed No-idle Permutation Flowshop Scheduling Problem (DNIPFSP) with the objective of minimizing the makespan. The authors proposed an Iterated Reference Greedy (IRG) algorithm that was compared with a state-of-the-art iterated greedy (IG) algorithm, as well as the Mixed Integer Linear Programming (MILP) model on two benchmark problems showing promising results.

An energy-efficient flexible job shop scheduling problem (EFJSP) with transportation was the core of research by Li and Lei [40]. The authors developed an imperialist competitive algorithm with feedback to minimize makespan, total tardiness, and total energy consumption. The conducted experiments provided promising computational results, which proved the effectiveness of the proposed algorithm. Furthermore, a study addressing distributed unrelated parallel machines scheduling problem aiming at minimizing makespan in the heterogeneous production network was proposed by Lei et al. [41]. A novel imperialist competitive algorithm with memory was developed by authors and experiments were conducted to test the performance of where the computational results proved the effectiveness of the algorithm. A study aimed at optimizing the trade-off between the total cost of tardiness and batch delivery was conducted by Rahman et al. [42]. To achieve this goal, the authors proposed three new metaheuristic algorithms which are the Differential Evolution with different mutation strategy variation, a Moth Flame Optimization, and Lévy-Flight Moth Flame Optimization algorithm. The algorithms were validated through an industrial case study.

Luo [43] tackled the dynamic flexible job shop scheduling problem under new job insertions. The goal of the research was to minimize the total tardiness; therefore, the authors proposed a deep Q-network (DQN). The developed DQN was trained using deep Q-learning and numerical experiments confirmed the superiority and generality of DQN. Also, Yun et al. [44] suggested a genetic algorithm based energy-efficient design-time task scheduling algorithm for an asymmetric multiprocessor system. The proposed algorithm adaptively applies different generation strategies to solution candidates based on their completion time and energy consumption. Experiments proved that it minimized energy consumption compared to existing methods. Finally, Saraswati et al. [45] aimed at minimizing the total tardiness in batch completion time using the metaheuristic approach of simulated annealing. The programming was done using Python programming. The research case study scheduled batches to parallel independent machines where the results of data processing demonstrated reduced total tardiness.

As concluded from the above survey, none of the articles found in the literature covered all aspects of data batch processing and scheduling. While some researchers concentrated on fulfilling the time constraint, others aimed at scheduling the maximum number of tasks effectively; however, none of the studies found in the literature considered cost during the scheduling process of data batches. This work tackles the significantly effective and widely used data batching process covering all its aspects. It will focus on scheduling a set of required jobs to be processed in a batch using the available resources (i.e., processors) as per the predecessors, job priorities and constraints stated in the SLA while batch job's predecessors and priorities are specified by the client depending on the type of tasks handled. This work represents a major contribution to the literature since it comprises all aspects of the DBP including cost.

3. Data Batch Algorithm

This research tackles the financial data supply chain management for the banking and financial sector which mainly revolves around processing financial-related data using available resources. Those resources are usually software and hardware processors. A major tool used in the management of the financial data supply chain is data batch processing (DBP). Our study covers all aspects of data batch processing—such as job priorities, precedence task relation, and time constraints—in addition to different types of cost. It is vital to emphasize the importance of the cost aspect in data batch processing since the utilized resources' costs are very high. Yet, previous research work has neglected considering DBP cost despite its significance. Therefore, this research is extremely important since it includes different types of DBP costs in addition to all other aspects in a scheduling algorithm.

The DBP which the financial sector relies heavily on has been bounded by the IT systems that drive banking businesses making them in severe need of rapid, efficient and effective processes to be able to focus on their clients holistically. They use DBP widely in their daily operations like processing end-of-day (EOD) jobs which include highly important and frequently used activities and services such as: preparing employees' payroll, interest rate calculations, and customer's bank statements, credit card processing bills, fraud detection data, and many others [4]. Banks usually outsource DBP to a third-party company (service provider) that takes charge of arranging and processing the data and aggregating the output as shown in Figure 1. The service provider company leases processors and software from a provider to perform the batch process for the bank based on a Service Level Agreement (SLA). The service provider usually operates after closing hours so there will be no more data entries or online intervention.

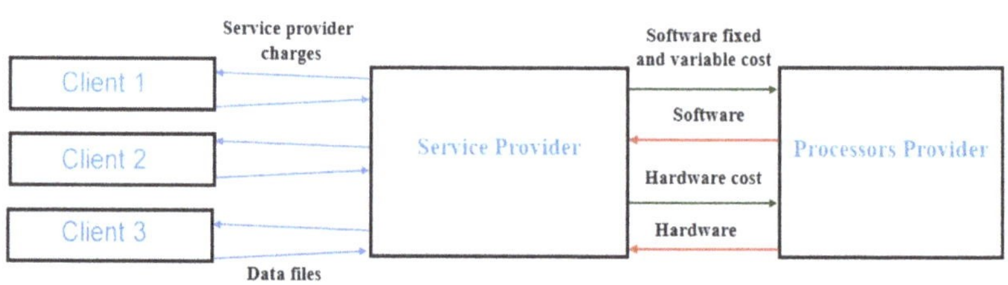

Figure 1. Data batching service network.

DBP begins with scheduling data, gathered in batches by type, to the available processor. The data files are scheduled while taking into consideration job priorities, predecessors and other constraints meaning that jobs will not be processed simultaneously but rather as per their schedule. The objective is to execute the tasks using the available resources to improve utilization, reduce cost and increase their profit while meeting the SLA. Each job consists of one or more executable data files. It is considered the surface layer of batch systems. A job consists of multiple tasks; therefore, the network of tasks is a detailed network view of jobs. In other words, a job is defined as a collection of tasks that are used to perform a computation. The developed dynamic scheduling algorithm considers cost types associated with the data batch scheduling which are: servers and software leasing cost, rental cost for additional resources needed in case of overload and extra work, penalty cost of failing to execute the batch process as per the (SLA), and the opportunity cost representing the cost of idling a resource for any period of time due to inefficient task allocation.

The data batching dynamic algorithm will be presented next. The algorithm will efficiently decide on resources allocation for the service provider to minimize the total operational cost. The service provider will batch process data for its clients one at a time according to a specific service agreement with that client.

3.1. Dynamic Cost Scheduling Algorithm for Data Batch Processing (DCSDBP)

Usually, given the current business practice dealing with such techniques, certain market-based rules govern the implementation of these scheduling processes. Therefore, the following assumptions underpinning the proposed algorithm are applied:

- The service-providing company lease a fixed number of data processors.
- Reserving processors is not allowed at the beginning or during the batch process scheduling. A processor is immediately acquired once a decision is made to rent it.
- The characteristics of data files that will be processed as batches such as size and priorities are specified at the beginning of the scheduling process.
- Hardware and software costs are incurred for processing data.
- The hardware cost is a fixed amount.
- Software cost will have fixed and variable cost amounts; the variable cost is charged based on usage per unit time.
- Additional processors can be rented anytime during the execution; however, costs will be higher, 1.25 times, than the currently leased processors' hardware and software fixed cost. Also, a software variable cost is charged per unit time of usage. These assumptions are derived from practices in the field.
- Additional processors are rented only if there is a chance of not meeting the SLA.
- When an additional processor is acquired, it will be accounted for from the time it is acquired until the end of the batch window.
- Whenever an additional processor is rented at any time unit T, the endorsed fixed hardware and software costs will be calculated from the time of renting until the end of the batch process.
- Each leased or additionally rented processor executes a single task at a time.
- Different tasks can be processed in parallel. Parallel processing can occur only if there is no restriction due to priorities and predecessors relations provided in advance.
- A single data file containing multiple tasks can be multi-processed on multiple processors at the same time if it is allowed by the tasks predefined predecessors relations and the hardware and software resources are available.
- The iteration clock time unit is estimated by the time it takes to process the smallest size unit of the data file.
- The total DBP time is a multiple of the iteration unit time. Files are allocated to processors until a predetermined SLA time is reached. A penalty cost is imposed on each delay unit of time if the SLA is exceeded. The total penalty cost is calculated by multiplying the time delay by the penalty cost per unit time.
- At the beginning of each time unit T, files are allocated and resources are captured. However, at the end of the time period T, all resources are freed and ready for the next time period T.

3.1.1. Indices

i,j	Data file.
k	Leased processor
r	Rented processor.
T	Clock discrete time

3.1.2. Problem Parameters

I	Set of data files.
$I\prime^T$	Subset of the data files that are available for processing at any time T.
n_i	Required processing time for data file i.
SLA	Batch process time as agreed on in the SLA.
K	Set of all leased processors.
R	Set of rented processors.
V^T	Number of rented extra processors that can be acquired at any discrete time T.
l_{ij}^T	Binary parameter equal to 1 if data file j immediately precedes data file i, and 0 otherwise (parameters of precedence/dependency matrix).
α_i^T	Data file weight based on precedence/dependency matrix.
β_i	Data file scheduling priority provided by the client.
l_{ij}^T	Precedence/dependency matrix at each period T.
BW	Available batch process window.
Csf	Leased processor software fixed leasing cost.
Csv	Variable leasing cost per unit time of a processor software.
Ch	Leased processor hardware cost.
$Cesf$	Fixed rental cost per unit time of additional processor software.
$Cesv$	Variable rental cost per unit time of additional processor software.
Ceh	Rental cost per unit time of additional processor hardware.
Cp	Penalty cost per unit time for failing to execute the batch process as per the SLA.
e_i	Number of times file i can be multi processed.
TCp	Delay time total penalty cost.
T_H	Total cost of renting one additional processor at any time unit T.
D^T	Available files total multiprocessing ei at any time T.
T^r	Clock discrete time at which extra processor r is rented.
END	End of batch process.
TBC	Total batch process cost.

3.1.3. Problem Variables

P_k	Binary variable equal to1 if processor *k* is available and 0 otherwise.
W_r	Binary variable equal to1 if processor *r* is available and 0 otherwise.
f_i^T	Binary variable equal to 1 if data file *i* is available for processing at discrete time *T*, and 0 otherwise.
q_i^T	Number of times data file *i* has been processed. It is incremented by one every time data file *i* being processed.
A^T	Binary variable equal to 1 if $T > SLA$, and 0 otherwise.
U^T	Critical path at time *T* for each file *i* included in the subset $I\prime^T$.
ES_i^T	Early start of file *i*.
LS_i^T	Late start of file *i*.
S_i^T	Slack (the difference between early start and late start) of file *i*.
O_i^T	Binary variable equal to1 if $n_i - q_i^T > 0$, and 0 otherwise.

3.1.4. Problem Decision Variables

X_{iK}^T	Binary variable equal to 1 if data file *i* allocated to processor *k*, and 0 otherwise.
Y_{ir}^T	Binary variable equal to 1 if data file *i* is allocated to extra processor *r*, and 0 otherwise.

The DCSDBP algorithm is illustrated in Figure 2 and the step-by-step description of the algorithm is as follows.

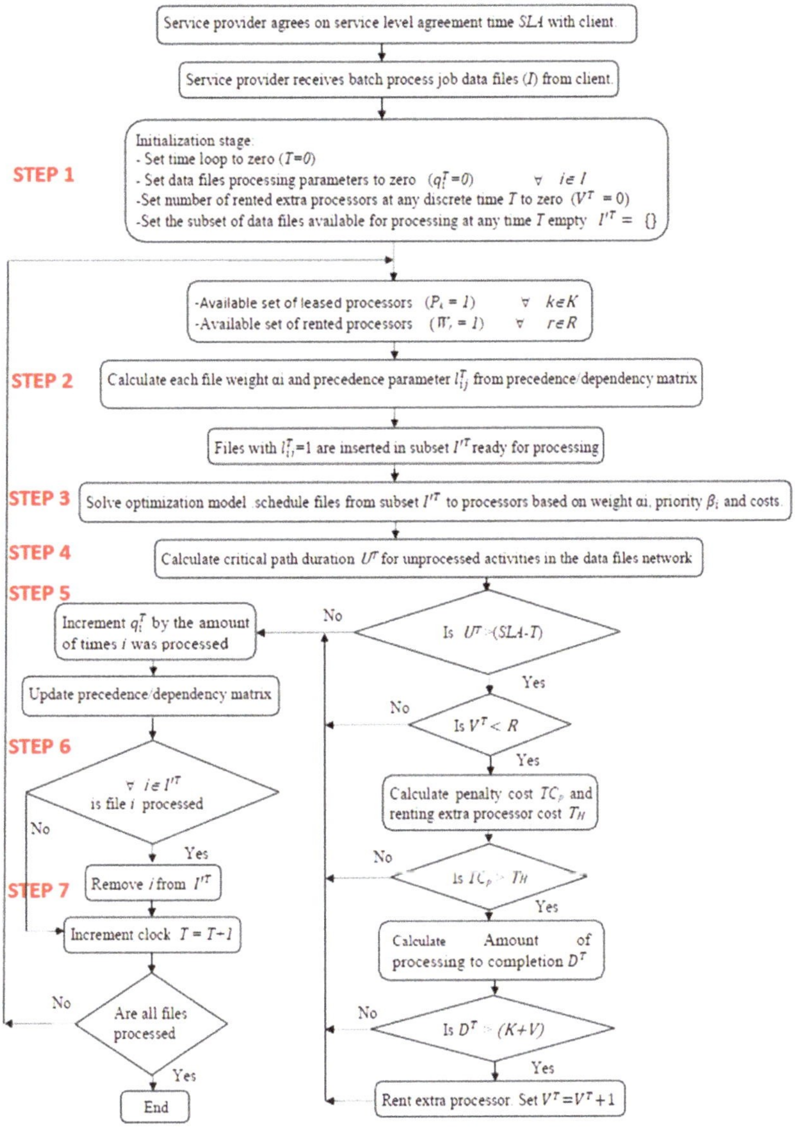

Figure 2. Dynamic Cost Scheduling Algorithm for Data Batch Processing (DCSDBP).

Step 1: Preparatory and Initialization Stage

This step involves preparing the initial data which consists of the subset of data files that are ready for processing and the availability of leased and rented. We also set:

1. The extra processors' utilization parameter to zero indicating that no extra processor is used at the beginning of the allocation process.
2. The data files processing parameters to zero meaning that files are not being processed yet. In addition to that, the time loop is initialized where time is set to zero. At the end of the step, we initialize all data needed to start the iterative algorithm.

$$I'^T = \{\} \tag{1}$$

Set

$$P_k = 1 \; \forall \; k \in K \tag{2}$$

Equation (2) indicates that leased processors are ready since the binary variable P_k is set to 1.

Set

$$Wr = 1 \; \forall \; r \in R \tag{3}$$

Equation (3) indicates that rented processors are ready since the binary variable W_r is set to 1.

Set

$$V^T = 0 \tag{4}$$

Equation (4) indicates that the number of rented extra processors acquired at this time period V^T is zero.

Set

$$q_i^T = 0 \; \forall \; i \in I \tag{5}$$

Equation (5) indicates that a data file i have never been processed since q_i^T is set to zero.

Set

$$T = 0 \tag{6}$$

Equation (6) indicates the beginning of the time loop of the algorithm where the time T is set to zero.

Step 2: Set of Files Available for Processing

We assign parameters and weights to the subset of data files available for processing $I\prime^T$ based on their precedence obtained from the dependency matrix.

If:

$$\sum_{j=1}^{J} l_{ij}^T = 1 \; \forall \; i \tag{7}$$

Then set:

$$f_i^T = 1 \tag{8}$$

$$I\prime^T = I\prime^T + \{i\} \tag{9}$$

$$\alpha_i^T = \sum_{\theta=1}^{I} l_{\theta i}^T \; \forall \; i \tag{10}$$

α_i^T is the weight for each data file. It is calculated using the precedence/dependency matrix by finding the number of files that depend on file i.

This step will indicate the set of data files available for processing which will serve as input for step 3 to start the scheduling of available files on the available processors.

Step 3: Allocation of Files to Processors

In this step, the algorithm allocates files to processors. The model presented in this step will allocate files with the objective function (11) of minimizing data file allocation cost while taking into consideration priority, weight and criticality of each file included in each subset at any time T.

$$\begin{aligned} \text{Min } (\text{Z T}) = & \sum_{i=1}^{I'} \sum_{k=1}^{K} \left(\frac{Csv + \left(\frac{Csf + Ch}{BW}\right)}{\beta_i \; \alpha_i^T}\right) X_{iK}^T + \sum_{k=1}^{K} \left(\frac{Csf+Ch}{BW}\right) \left(1 - \sum_{i=1}^{I'} X_{iK}^T\right) + \sum_{i=1}^{I'} \sum_{v=1}^{V} \left(\frac{Cesv+Cesf+Ceh}{\beta_i \; \alpha_i^T}\right) Y_{ir}^T + \\ & \sum_{v=1}^{V} (Cesf + Ceh) \left(1 - \sum_{i=1}^{I'} Y_{ir}^T\right) + A^T * Cp * (T - SLA) \end{aligned} \tag{11}$$

The first term considers the basic processors leasing cost, weight α_i^T and priority β_i at any time unit T. The second term considers the opportunity cost of not utilizing the leased processors at any time unit T. The third term handles the cost of renting additional processors, weight α_i^T and priority β_i at any time unit T. The fourth term considers the opportunity cost of not utilizing the additionally rented processors at any time *T*. the last term is concerned with the penalty cost of exceeding the *SLA*. The $\beta_i\ \alpha_i^T$ used in terms 1 and 3 ensures that files with higher priority and weight are scheduled first. *BW* is the available time during which processing can take place. It is used in Equation (11) to find what the fixed cost of resources per unit time is.

Subject to:

$$\sum_{k=1}^{K} X_{ik}^T + \sum_{r=1}^{V} Y_{ir}^T \le M_i f_i^T\ \forall\ i \in I\prime^T \text{ where M}i = \min\{e_i, n_i - q_i^T,\ K + V\} \tag{12}$$

The constraint in Equation (12) is concerned with leased and additionally rented processors allocation and their availability to ensure that the total file allocation does not exceed either file multiprocessing *ei* or file required remaining processing n_i or the total number of available basic and extra processors (*K*,*V*) for any file *i* at a certain time *T*.

$$q_i^T \le n_i\ \forall\ i \in I \tag{13}$$

The constraint in Equation (13) ensures that the number of times a file is processed is less or equal to the needed processing time.

$$\sum_{i=1}^{I'} X_{ik}^T \le P_k^T\ \forall\ k \in K \tag{14}$$

The constraint in Equation (14) ensures that exactly one data file is allocated to a single leased processor.

$$\sum_{i=1}^{I'} Y_{ir}^T \le W_r^T\ \forall\ r \in R \tag{15}$$

The constraint in Equation (15) ensures that exactly one data file is allocated to a single additionally rented processor.

$$X_{iK}^T\ 0 \text{ or } 1\ \forall\ i \in I \text{ and } k \in K \tag{16}$$

The constraint in Equation (16) declares that the decision variable X_{ik} is binary, meaning that file *i* either be assigned to a leased processor or not.

$$Y_{ir}^T = 0 \quad \text{or} \quad 1\ \ \forall\ i \in I \text{ and } r \in R \tag{17}$$

The constraint in Equation (17) declares that the decision variable Y_{ir} is binary, meaning that a file *i* either be assigned to an additionally rented processor or not.

Step 4: Update Utilized Extra Processors

At this stage, we check if an additional processor should be rented at this time unit to avoid delay and penalty cost. This step involves calculating the critical path duration for the rest of the unprocessed activities in the data files network at each time unit and compare it to the remaining time until the end of the batch process time that is agreed on in the *SLA*. A trade-off between the cost of renting an additional processor and the penalty cost is made, and according to that, it will be decided whether to rent a new processor or incur a penalty cost. Renting a new processor is subject to the condition that the total number of data files available for processing is higher than the total number of rented basic and extra processors.

Critical path duration

$$\text{Calculate } U^T = \text{duration of the remaining critical path at time } T.ES_i^T = \text{Max}\ \{ES_j^T + (n_i - q_i{}^T)\}\ \forall\ i \text{ and } j\ \in\ I \text{ where } (i \ne j) \text{ and} \alpha_i <= \alpha_j \tag{18}$$

$$ES_i^T = 0 \,\forall\, i = 0 \tag{19}$$

$$LS_i^T = \text{Min}\ \{LS_j^T - (n_i - q_i{}^T)\}\ \forall\, i \text{ and } j \in I \text{ where } (i \neq j) \text{ and} \alpha_i <= \alpha_j \tag{20}$$

$$S_i^T = LS_i^T - ES_i \tag{21}$$

$$U^T = \sum_{i=1}^{I} (n_i - q_i{}^T)\ \forall\, i \in I \text{ and } S_i^T = 0 \tag{22}$$

In the above equations the slack S_i^T for each file i is calculated and the critical path for the network U^T is found for the files with slack equal to zero (S_i^T = 0).

Checking critical path duration against SLA

If

$$U^T \geq SLA-T \tag{23}$$

Then

$$TC_p = C_p * (U^T-(SLA-T)) \tag{24}$$

Else

$$TC_p = 0 \tag{25}$$

The above equations calculate the penalty cost TC_p for all cases of critical path duration against SLA.

Cost of renting extra processor in case there is a delay

If

$$U^T \geq SLA-T \tag{26}$$

Then

$$T_H = (Cesf + Cesh + Cesv) * U^T \tag{27}$$

Else

$$T_H = 0 \tag{28}$$

The above equations calculate the extra processor renting cost T_H in case of a delay.

Amount of processing to completion

$$D^T = (\textstyle\sum_{i=1}^{I'} e_i - q_i^T)\ \forall\, i \in I\prime^T \text{ and } e_i > 1 + (\textstyle\sum_{i=1}^{I'} e_i^T)\ \forall\, i \in I\prime^T \text{ and } e_i = 1 \tag{29}$$

Decision on renting extra processor

If

$$TC_p \geq T_H \text{ and } D^T > (K + V) \tag{30}$$

Then

$$V^T = V^T + 1 \tag{31}$$

$$T^r = T \tag{32}$$

$$V^T \leq R \tag{33}$$

In the above equations, the number of rented extra processor V^T is increased by one if the penalty cost TC_p is greater than the extra processor renting cost T_H.

In this step, we are calculating the maximum completion time using CPM without considering splitting because the decision to multi-process a job is not taken yet. A job multi-processing means it can be split if needed to minimize the completion time of the batch process. CPM is not the only tool in this study to make the decision. Looking at Equations (29) and (31), the decision to rent an additional processor is based on another criterion. D was introduced which, as per Equation (29), ensures that no extra processor shall be rented unless there is an available task ready to be allocated to it. This ensures that no additional processor will be rented unless it will be used.

Step 5: Update the Availability of Files

Each data file processing parameter is incremented by the number of times it was processed. When a file is fully processed, then it is removed from the subset for the following time unit and the rest of the process.

Update f_i^T Matrix:

$$q_i^T = q_i^T + \sum_{k=1}^{K} X_{ik}^T + \sum_{r=1}^{R} Y_{ir}^T \; \forall \, i \in I\prime^T \tag{34}$$

If

$$O_i^T = 1 \tag{35}$$

Then

$$f_i^{T+\Delta} = 1 \tag{36}$$

Else

$$f_i^{T+\Delta} = 0 \tag{37}$$

And

$$l_{ji}^{T+\Delta} = 0 \; \forall \, j \tag{38}$$

If

$$q_i^T = n_i$$

Then

$$\sum_{j=1}^{J} l_{ij}^{T+\Delta} = 0 \; \forall \, i \tag{39}$$

And

$$\sum_{i=1}^{I} l_{ji}^{T+\Delta} = 0 \; \forall \, j \tag{40}$$

This step will update the file availability to determine if any file needs further processing or all files are completed.

Step 6: Check Termination Condition

When all files are processed, then the algorithm shall stop, else the model will go to step 7.

If

$$\sum_{i=1}^{I} q_i^T = \sum_{i=1}^{I} n_i \tag{41}$$

Then

Stop.

If

$$T > SLA \tag{42}$$

Then

$$A^T - 1 \tag{43}$$

Else

$$A^T = 0 \tag{44}$$

Step 7: Update Clock

Increment iteration clock by one time unit until the DCSDBP algorithm allocates all files.

$$T = T{+}1 \tag{45}$$

Go to Step 2

Steps 2 through 7 of the DCSDBP will be repeated until all tasks are allocated to available resources and there are no more jobs waiting in the queue.

The Total batch process cost is updated as follows:

$$
\begin{aligned}
TBC \; &= (C_{sf} + C_h\,) * K + \sum_{T=1}^{END} \sum_{i=1}^{I'^T} \sum_{k=1}^{K} C_{sv} * X_{ik}^T \\
&+ \sum_{T=1}^{BW} \sum_{i=1}^{I'^T} \sum_{k=1}^{K} \frac{(C_{sf}+C_h\,)}{BW} * (1 - X_{ik}^T) \\
&+ \sum_{r=1}^{V} (C_{esf} + C_{eh})(END - T') + \sum_{T=1}^{END} \sum_{i=1}^{I'^T} \sum_{r=1}^{V} C_{esv} * Y_{ir}^T \\
&+ \sum_{r=1}^{V} \sum_{i=1}^{I'^T} \sum_{T=T'}^{END} (C_{esf} + C_{eh})(1 - Y_{ir}^T) + A^{END} * Cp * (T^{END} - SLA)
\end{aligned}
\tag{46}
$$

The total cost and the completion time will be calculated at the end of the DCSDBP algorithm. The total batch process cost (C) = leased processors fixed hardware cost + leased processors fixed software cost+ leased processors variable software cost + leased processors opportunity cost + rented processors variable software cost + rented processors fixed software cost + rented processors hardware cost + rented processors opportunity cost + penalty cost.

4. Illustrative Example

In this section, we present a numerical example to illustrate the proposed DCSDBP algorithm. Consider a network of 15 data files with the precedence relations as shown in Figure 3.

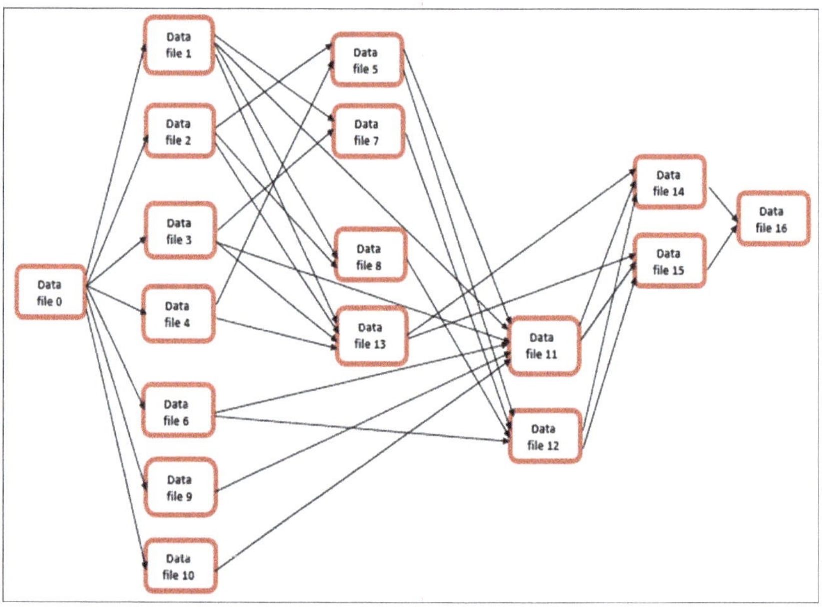

Figure 3. Illustrative example.

The precedence relationships are fixed relationships provided by the client that the service provider must use in processing the files; therefore, there cannot be any deadlocks relation. Table 1 presents the different parameters' values; these values are either given directly such as file's multiprocessing *ei*, processing time *ni* and priority *βi*, or derived from the files precedence relation such as file's weight *αi^T* and precedence parameter *Lij^T*. The following data were also used: there are two available leased processors; maximum number of available processors than can be rented is 5, *SLA* = 18 time units; batch window

BW = 22 time unit; leased processor fixed software cost Csf = \$10; leased processor hardware cost Ch = \$100; leased processor variable software cost per time unit Csv = \$2; rented processor fixed software cost $Cesf$ = \$12.5; rented processor Hardware Cost Ceh = \$125; rented processor variable software cost per time unit $Cesv$ = \$2.5; penalty cost per time unit in case of exceeding the SLA is Cp = \$200.

Table 1. Model parameters at $T = 0$.

File	e_i	n_i	β_i	$\alpha_i^{T=0}$	L_{ij}
0	0	0	1	1	1
1	3	9	2	6	1
2	1	1	3	5	1
3	2	8	2	5	1
4	3	9	4	4	1
5	1	3	2	4	3
6	1	1	5	4	1
7	1	3	2	3	3
8	1	8	2	3	3
9	2	4	2	3	1
10	2	8	2	3	1
11	1	1	1	4	7
12	6	12	1	4	5
13	3	9	1	4	5
14	1	2	2	2	4
15	1	4	2	2	4
16	0	0	1	1	1

The algorithm was programmed using LINGO 15.0 x64. The Lingo output shows that the files were processed in 20 time units, while 4 extra processors were rented, and the batch process exceeded the SLA by 2 time units, which indicates that penalty cost was imposed. Once the batch process started, the program sets all initialization conditions, which means that ready files subset $I\prime^T$ is empty. At the beginning of each time unit T, the precedence parameters l_{ij}^T for all files are checked to determine which files are ready to be processed. All files having precedence parameter l_{ij}^T = 1 are considered ready and inserted to the ready files subset $I\prime^T$. It is worth mentioning that files 0 and 16 are start and end files with processing time n_i = 0 which means they won't be allocated to any processor. The reason of their existence is to start and end the network for critical path calculation purposes.

The algorithm started at T = 0 with files 1, 2, 3, 4, 6, 9, and 10 ready for processing; therefore, they were inserted into the ready files subset $I\prime^T$. At T = 0 files 4 and 6 were processed by leased processor 2 and 1 respectively because these files have the highest calculated weight $\alpha_i^{T=0}$ and predetermined priority β_i while the rest of ready files were shifted for the next time unit. At T = 1, the values of precedence parameter l_{ij}^T are updated for all files, so the ones that have not been processed or not finished processing still have the value of 1 and are consequently still included in the ready files subset $I\prime^T$ while file 6 which has a processing time n_i of 1 has the value of l_{ij}^T =0 and no longer exist in the subset $I\prime^T$ since it is considered ready. Also, an additional processor V^T was rented and utilized at that time unit because the criteria of renting a new processor was satisfied. It was found that the critical path of the remaining network activities exceeds the SLA, so the program needs to take an action to try to avoid the delay. The decision of renting a new processor is made since the cost of renting a new processor TH was found to be less than the penalty cost TCp at that time unit and also since there are ready files for the next time unit that exceeds the total number of available processor. During T = 1 file 4 was processed by leased processors 1 and 2, as well as by the additionally rented processor 1.

At T = 2 another additional processor was rented based on the above-explained mechanism. File 4 continued to be processed by leased processors 1 and rented processors 1 and 2 since it has a multiprocessing of e_i = 3. Also, file 2 was processed by leased processor 2. At T = 3 an additional third processor was rented and file 1 was processed by leased processors 1 and 2 and rented processor 3 due to its multiprocessing criteria. File 4 was processed by rented processors 1 and 2 and by that it is considered ready. At T = 4 the forth additional processor was rented and used to process file 1 along with rented processors 1 and 3 while rented processor 2 and leased processor 1 were used to process file 3. File 5 was processed by leased processor 2. T = 5 had the same files allocations as T = 4. It is noted that the program did not rent any more extra processor starting from T = 5 onwards which means it utilized 4 out of the 5 processors available for renting and that is based on the renting mechanism. The same steps were executed on all files until the end of processing at T = 19 when all files were processed.

The batch process cost calculation was based on using Equation (46) by using the input values listed earlier in this section and the allocation results from Lingo output; Table 2 demonstrates the detailed costs. Also, Table 2 clarifies the cost of allocating files to leased processor and that includes hardware and software fixed costs as well as software variable cost. Similarly, rented processors allocation cost which includes hardware and software fixed costs as well as software variable cost is shown. Then the opportunity costs associated with each processor type is calculated. Penalty cost is determined at the end of the batch process and total cost is found by summing all costs for each time unit. In Table 2, column (1) represents the time unit T, column (2) shows the total number of existing leased processors K, column (3) identifies how many leased processors are actually being acquired at each time unit T, column (4) calculates the leased processors variable cost Csv while the fixed software Csf and hardware Ch costs are calculated at the end because they are not related to time. Leased processors opportunity cost is determined in column (5) as per Equation (27). For rented processors, column (6) shows the number of additionally rented processors V^T at that time unit T, column (7) represents the number of rented processors actually being acquired at each time unit T. In column (8), and based on model assumption 14 which states that rented processors are paid for from the time unit T they are rented onwards, rented processors total allocation cost is calculated using all types of costs (extra fixed hardware cost Ceh, extra fixed software cost $Cesf$ and extra variable software cost $Cesv$). It is worth mentioning that in case of an additional processor being rented but not utilized due to unavailability of ready files, the total allocation cost will equal fixed hardware cost Ceh plus fixed software cost $Cesf$ while the variable software cost $Cesv$ will not exist since the processor is not being utilized. Rented processors opportunity cost is found in column (9) using fixed hardware cost Ceh plus fixed software cost $Cesf$. Finally, column (10) sums all the above costs for each time unit T.

At the end of Table 2 leased fixed costs are added, they represent fixed hardware cost Ch plus fixed software cost Csf for each leased processor k. Also as mentioned above penalty cost is calculated based on number time units the processing is delayed beyond the SLA. Since leased processors fixed hardware cost Ch and fixed software cost Csf are calculated per unit time by dividing them by BW, remaining opportunity cost for basic processor exists in case the batch process time END is less than batch window BW. It represents the opportunity cost of the leased processors for the time units between the end of batch process END and BW.

From Table 2, we can see that from T = 0 until T = 17, the basic allocation cost was showing the utilization of both leased processors, which explains the zero value for opportunity cost of leased processors during the same period. However, at T = 18 and 19 one leased processor was utilized and that ended up in variable allocation cost for one processor and opportunity cost for the other. It can be also noticed that from T = 0 up to T = 10, every rented processor was utilized which ended in zero opportunity cost. After T = 10 some rented processors were not utilized due to unavailability of ready files such as at T = 11 where 3 out of 4 rented processors were utilized. Also at T = 12, 13, 16, 17, 18, and 19 none of the rented processors were utilized due to the unavailability of ready files.

Table 2. DBP cost summary.

	Leased Processors				Rented Processors				(10) Total Cost/Time Period $
(1) *T*	(2) No. of P	(3) No. of Acquired P	(4) Allocation Variable cost $	(5) Oppo. Cost $	(6) No. of P	(7) No. of Acquired P	(8) Total Allocation Cost $	(9) Oppo. Cost $	
0	2	2	4.00	0.00	0	0	0.00	0.00	4.00
1	2	2	4.00	0.00	1	1	8.75	0.00	12.75
2	2	2	4.00	0.00	2	2	17.50	0.00	21.50
3	2	2	4.00	0.00	3	3	26.25	0.00	30.25
4	2	2	4.00	0.00	4	4	35.00	0.00	39.00
5	2	2	4.00	0.00	4	4	35.00	0.00	39.00
6	2	2	4.00	0.00	4	4	35.00	0.00	39.00
7	2	2	4.00	0.00	4	4	35.00	0.00	39.00
8	2	2	4.00	0.00	4	4	35.00	0.00	39.00
9	2	2	4.00	0.00	4	4	35.00	0.00	39.00
10	2	2	4.00	0.00	4	4	35.00	0.00	39.00
11	2	2	4.00	0.00	4	3	32.50	6.25	42.75
12	2	2	4.00	0.00	4	0	25.00	25.00	54.00
13	2	1	2.00	5.00	4	0	25.00	25.00	57.00
14	2	2	4.00	0.00	4	4	35.00	0.00	39.00
15	2	2	4.00	0.00	4	4	35.00	0.00	39.00
16	2	2	4.00	0.00	4	0	25.00	25.00	54.00
17	2	2	4.00	0.00	4	0	25.00	25.00	54.00
18	2	1	2.00	5.00	4	0	25.00	25.00	57.00
19	2	1	2.00	5.00	4	0	25.00	25.00	57.00
					Total dynamic cost $ for all periods				**795.25**
					Penalty cost $				**400.00**
					Leased processors fixed costs $				**220.00**
					Remaining opportunity cost for Leased processors $				**20.00**
					Batch Process Total Cost $				**1435.25**

The above illustrative example shows the effectiveness of the developed algorithm in allocating files to processors. The algorithm managed to allocate highly prioritized and weighted files before the ones with lower priority and weight. Also, the algorithm will advise renting the necessary number of extra processors to accomplish the batch process goal while trying to minimizing cost. In the illustrated example, the program rented 4 extra processors to achieve minimum real batch process time, which is 20 time units. Although that exceeds the SLA specified time of 18 time units, it is the minimum possible execution time for this network due to network logic and predecessors' relations.

The illustrative example shows that the batch processing is performed using a set of assumptions and constraints under which the problem makes the best decision at that time unit. Decisions are made dynamically based on the current status and previous decisions. This decision process ascertains that the best decision is taken at each iteration. We do not define the global network (of all feasible assignments of jobs to servers) to perform a direct optimization on it, we rather generate the subnetwork of feasible assignments at each iteration (Step 3 of the algorithm). This sequence of optimum decision-making ensures that the solution at the end is global. Not being optimal would mean that a better solution exists at some stage in the optimization process, which would contradict stage 3 as built.

5. Sensitivity Analysis

The whole research was motivated by working with a company in the field, therefore, whatever assumptions and constraints applied to the algorithm are based on practice. Given the initial results obtained from the illustrative example, they were promising and could be easily extended to cover other networks.

Sensitivity analysis was performed in two parts. The first part was conducted on the illustrative example network by changing different parameters. In part two, the algorithm performance was tested using networks with varying sizes and complexities.

5.1. Parameters Variation Analysis

Different parameters were tested and the summary of results total cost and process time are shown in Figures 4 and 5, respectively.

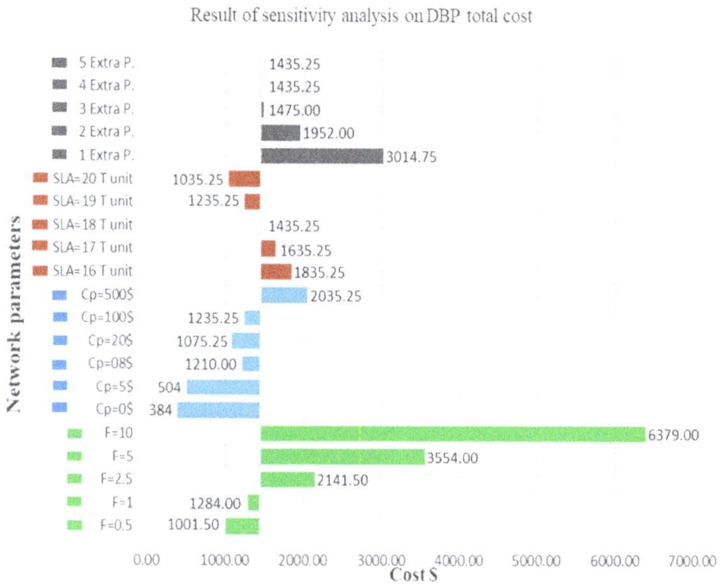

Figure 4. Result of sensitivity analysis on DBP total cost.

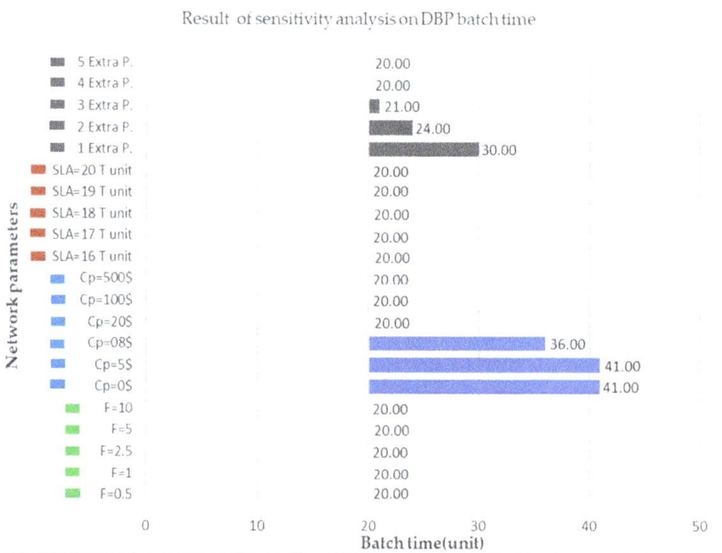

Figure 5. Result of sensitivity analysis on DBP batch time.

5.1.1. Varying Number of Processors Available to Rent

In the case of having four processors available for rent to be used in the batch process, the results were the same as the case of five available processors since the same number of processors were actually rented as in the illustrative example results shown earlier. However, having three available processors to rent resulted in a longer batch process time and higher total cost in addition to that, the SLA was exceeded by more time units. Having two processors available for rent resulted in more delay in batch process time, increased the total cost, and the SLA was exceeded by 6 time units. The batch process had the highest delay and total cost in the last case of having only one available processor to rent. The previous results shows that the algorithm is renting additional processors only when needed in order to perform the batch process with minimum execution time and total cost.

5.1.2. Changing SLA Value

Different values for the SLA were tested. The results show the lower the SLA value, the higher the penalty cost will be or the need to rent additional processors to avoid delay and the opposite in case of higher SLA. The values tested are for SLA = 16, 17, 19, and 20. It is recommended that, when deciding on the SLA time between the client and the service provider, both sides study the data batch network carefully to decide on the right SLA terms that serve both sides and achieve the goal of the batch process.

5.1.3. Varying Penalty Cost per Time Unit

Different penalty cost values were assumed and the algorithm was tested accordingly. The results showed that the lowest batch process cost is obviously obtained when the penalty cost is set to zero. In this case, there will not be any trade-off between cost of renting an additional processor and any other cost; however, the program needed more time to run since the completion time to process doubled. In the case of the penalty, cost equals to $5 same results were obtained as in the case of zero penalty cost. Three extra processors instead of four were used with a penalty cost equal to 8 and the total batch process time was higher; however, the total cost is less. In cases of penalty cost of $20 and $100 per time unit, the same number of extra processors were rented as of the case of penalty cost per unit time = $200 but with a less total bath cost. Increasing the penalty cost further to $500 will not affect the way files are allocated to servers since the program will not be able to squeeze the batch time more even if the trade-off between renting more extra processors and penalty cost goes in favor of utilizing another rented processor simply because of the network′s activity relations. In other words, due to precedence constraints jobs are processed only when they are available. Therefore, even if more resources are available, the duration will not be reduced since the resources will not be utilized; i.e., paying more money for resources may not reduce the completion time.

5.1.4. Changing the Processor Rental Costs

When increasing the renting cost of an additional processor to 2.5 times the leased processor cost, the program rented the same number of processors to finish the batch process because the penalty cost is still higher relatively. It only ended up increasing the total batch cost, while the same number of additional processors were utilized. Increasing the processors renting cost to 5 times the leased processor cost did not stop the program from renting additional processors to finish the batch process because the penalty cost is still relatively higher. However, the total batch cost increased while the same number of additional processors were utilized. To prove the efficiency of the algorithm, the case of equal costs for leased and rented processors was tested, the algorithm rented only what it needed from available additional processors to finish the batch process. Finally, in the case of setting costs ratio to 0.5, the total price went lower but the files-to-processors allocation stayed the same.

The above findings and analysis prove that when the algorithm reaches the optimum solution, it does not utilize any unnecessary resources since it is part of the objective function to minimize all types of costs while trying to meet SLA deadline and satisfy all priorities and constraints.

5.2. Jobs Network Size Analysis

In the second part of the sensitivity analysis, the developed algorithm was tested by varying the number of jobs and the network complexity. Different network sizes and relationship complexities were generated using a random network generator RanGen2 software [46]. Several data for different network sizes of 15, 25, 50, and 100 jobs were generated. Each network size was also generated based on precedence complexity measure by an indicator of complexity "I2 index" which is a measure of the closeness of a network to a serial or parallel network based on the number of progressive levels. If I2 = 0 then the network activities are all in parallel, meaning no relation between them, while if I2 = 1 then the network activities are all in series [47]. The average program run time for the complete DCSDBP Algorithm for each network is shown in Table 3. The results demonstrate that the algorithm is efficient since the program run time is relatively low and acceptable.

Table 3. Run times for variant network sizes with different complexities.

No. of Network Activities	Complexity Index I2	Run Time (s)
15	0.2	2
	0.5	3
	0.8	3
25	0.2	5
	0.5	2
	0.8	4
50	0.2	11
	0.5	13
	0.8	14
100	0.2	33
	0.5	34
	0.8	34

6. Conclusions

The financial data supply chain is of huge importance to the banking sector. It impacts financial institutes' performance and customer service. Therefore, it is of great necessity to manage the scheduling of the financial data supply chain. The main tool utilized in the financial data supply chain is data batch processing. Batch scheduling and processing are extremely important because they are widely used in service industries to track tasks and data continuously. However, there is a lack of an efficient scheduling solution for data batch scheduling which creates a major issue for the financial sector. The goal of this work is to develop an iterative Dynamic cost scheduling for DBP (DCSDBP) algorithm that includes all aspects of DBP. Different types of costs associated with the batch process were taken into consideration to develop the iterative scheduling algorithm. While the algorithm worked towards minimizing these costs, it aimed at the same time to allocate files based on their weight and priority without violating network predecessors' relations. Also, the algorithm tries to satisfy the time limit specified in the SLA. The developed algorithm proved its effectiveness in allocating data files to available resources while satisfying priority and predecessors constraints in addition to maintaining the minimum possible cost, keeping in mind the SLA time limit. After coding the developed algorithm using Lingo, a number of networks were used to test it. It was concluded from the results that it is more effective to include all types of costs along with priority, weight, predecessor, and time factors, which led to a more effective allocation and a lower total batch process cost. It can also be seen from the results that renting more processors does not necessarily mean that the batch process will be performed in a shorter time because network logic relations or 'predecessors' relations' govern the process's total time. The decision of whether or not to rent a new processor and when to do so is very important since it will affect the whole batch process in terms of file allocations to processors and total processing cost and time. Our research has positive implications on the performance and customer service of financial institutes and banks that choose to adopt it. It optimizes the scheduling of the data batch process which reflects on a more efficient and reliable financial data supply chain and through better management. The algorithm was developed under certain assumptions; while we tried to generalize it to cover batch processing, there are some limitations that could be addressed in future researches. For instance, it was assumed that resources costs are the same for leased processors, this could be generalized to assume different costs or even different costs as a future research direction. Also, additional research could be done on cases where renting additional processors has varying costs. Future researchers might also work on developing the additional processors renting mechanism to allow more than one processor to be rented for each time unit in case that serves the total completion time and maintains a low cost. In addition, one of our basic assumptions is that processors reservation is not allowed, which can be researched further to test the case where processor reservation is allowed and how it can be implemented; in addition to its impact on the different aspects of the batch process such as total process time, total cost and basic and extra processor utilization.

Author Contributions: A.A.S.: conceptualization, methodology, software programming, validation, and writing the original draft. A.S. and M.N.: conceptualization, methodology, and finalizing the manuscript. All authors have read and agreed to the published version of the manuscript.

Funding: The authors received no specific funding for this work.

Institutional Review Board Statement: Not applicable.

Informed Consent Statement: Not applicable. This article does not contain any studies with human participants or animals performed by any of the authors.

Data Availability Statement: The data presented in this study are available on request from the corresponding author.

Conflicts of Interest: The authors have no conflict of interest to declare.

References

1. Jensen, C.T. Smarter Banking, Horizontal Integration, and Scalability. 2010. Available online: http://www.redbooks.ibm.com/redpapers/pdfs/redp4625.pdf (accessed on 15 June 2021).
2. Chang, Y.-C.; Chang, K.-H.; Chang, T.-K. Applied column generation-based approach to solve supply chain scheduling problems. *Int. J. Prod. Res.* **2013**, *51*, 4070–4086. [CrossRef]
3. Bullynck, M. What Is an Operating System? A Historical Investigation (1954–1964). In *Reflections on Programming Systems: Historical and Philosophical Aspects*; Philosophical Studies Series 2542–8349; Springer International Publishing: Cham, Switzerland, 2018; pp. 49–79.
4. Microsoft-Corporation. Batch Applications—The Hidden Asset. 2006. Available online: http://download.microsoft.com/download/4/1/d/41d2745f-031c-40d7-86ea-4cb3e9a84070/Batch%20The%20Hidden%20Asset.pdf (accessed on 15 June 2021).
5. Antani, S. Batch Processing with WebSphere Compute Grid: Delivering Business Value to the Enterprise. 2010. Available online: http://www.redbooks.ibm.com/redpapers/pdfs/redp4566.pdf (accessed on 16 June 2021).
6. Barker, M.; Rawtani, J. *Practical Batch Process Management*; Elsevier: Burlington, VT, USA, 2005.
7. Matyac, E. Financial Supply Chain Management. *Str. Financ.* **2015**, *96*, 62–63.
8. Fahy, M.; Feller, J.; Finnegan, P.; Murphy, C. Co-operatively re-engineering a financial services information supply chain: A case study. *Can. J. Adm. Sci.* **2009**, *26*, 125–135. [CrossRef]
9. Mbaka, A.; Namada, J. Integrated financial management information system and supply chain effectiveness. *Am. J. Ind. Bus. Manag.* **2019**, *9*, 204–232. [CrossRef]
10. Page, A.J.; Keane, T.M.; Naughton, T.J. Multi-heuristic dynamic task allocation using genetic algorithms in a heterogeneous distributed system. *J. Parallel Distrib. Comput.* **2010**, *70*, 758–766. [CrossRef] [PubMed]
11. Méndez, C.A.; Cerdá, J.; Grossmann, I.E.; Harjunkoski, I.; Fahl, M. State-of-the-art review of optimization methods for short-term scheduling of batch processes. *Comput. Chem. Eng.* **2006**, *30*, 913–946. [CrossRef]
12. Osman, M.S.; Ndiaye, M.; Shamayleh, A. Dynamic scheduling for batch data processing in parallel systems. In Proceedings of the 3rd International Conference on Operations Research and Enterprise Systems-Volume 1: ICORES, Angers, France, 6–8 March 2014; pp. 221–225.

13. Al Sadawi, A.; Shamayleh, A.; Ndiaye, M. Cost Minimization in Data Batch Processing. In Proceedings of the 6th International Conference on Industrial Engineering and Operations Management, Kuala Lumpur, Malaysia, 8–10 March 2016.
14. Lim, S.; Cho, S.-B. *Intelligent OS Process Scheduling Using Fuzzy Inference with User Models*; Springe: Berlin/Heidelberg, Germany, 2007; pp. 725–734.
15. Xhafa, F.; Abraham, A. Computational models and heuristic methods for Grid scheduling problems. *Future Gener. Comput. Syst.* **2010**, *26*, 608–621. [CrossRef]
16. Aida, K. Effect of Job Size Characteristics on Job Scheduling Performance. In *Lecture Notes in Computer Science*; Springe Science & Business Media: Berlin/Heidelberg, Germany, 2000; pp. 1–17.
17. Stoica, I.; Abdel-Wahab, H.; Pothen, A. A microeconomic scheduler for parallel computers. In Proceedings of the Workshop on Job Scheduling Strategies for Parallel Processing, Santa Barbara, CA, USA, 25 April 1995; pp. 200–218.
18. Stoica, I.; Pothen, A. A robust and flexible microeconomic scheduler for parallel computers. In Proceedings of the 3rd International Conference on High Performance Computing (HiPC), Trivandrum, India, 19–22 December 1996; pp. 406–412.
19. Islam, M.; Khanna, G.; Sadayappan, P. *Revenue Maximization in Market-Based Parallel Job Schedulers*; Technical Report; Ohio State University: Columbus, OH, USA, 2008; pp. 1–13.
20. Damodaran, P.; Vélez-Gallego, M.C. A simulated annealing algorithm to minimize makespan of parallel batch processing machines with unequal job ready times. *Expert Syst. Appl.* **2012**, *39*, 1451–1458. [CrossRef]
21. Mehta, M.; Soloviev, V.; DeWitt, D.J. Batch scheduling in parallel database systems. In Proceedings of the IEEE 9th International Conference on Data Engineering, Vienna, Austria, 19–23 April 1993; pp. 400–410.
22. Grigoriev, A.; Sviridenko, M.; Uetz, M. Unrelated Parallel Machine Scheduling with Resource Dependent Processing Times. In Proceedings of the Integer Programming and Combinatorial Optimization: 11th International IPCO Conference, Berlin, Germany, 8–10 June 2005; pp. 182–195.
23. Bouganim, L.; Fabret, F.; Mohan, C.; Valduriez, P. Dynamic query scheduling in data integration systems. In Proceedings of the 16th International Conference on Data Engineering, San Diego, CA, USA, 28 February–3 March 2000; pp. 425–434.
24. Ngubiri, J.; van Vliet, M. A metric of fairness for parallel job schedulers. *Concurr. Comput. Pract. Exp.* **2009**, *21*, 1525–1546. [CrossRef]
25. Arpaci-Dusseau, A.; Culler, D. Extending Proportional-Share Scheduling to a Network of Workstations. In Proceedings of the International Conference on Parallel and Distributed Processing Techniques and Applications, Las Vegas, NV, USA, 30 June–3 July 1997.
26. Ferguson, D.; Nikolaou, C.; Sairamesh, J.; Yemini, Y. *Economic models for allocating resources in computer systems. Market-Based Control: A Paradigm for Distributed Resource Allocation*; World Scientific: Singapore, 1996; pp. 156–183.
27. Kuwabara, K.; Ishida, T.; Nishibe, Y.; Suda, T. An Equilibratory Market-Based Approach for Distributed Resource Allocation And Its Applications To Communication Network Control. In *Market-Based Control: A Paradigm for Distributed Resource Allocation*; World Scientific: Singapore, 1996; pp. 53–73.
28. Chun, B.N.; Culler, D.E. A Malleable-Job System for Timeshared Parallel Machines. In Proceedings of the 2nd IEEE/ACM International Symposium on Cluster Computing and the Grid, Washington, DC, USA, 21–24 May 2002; p. 30.
29. Sairamesh, J.; Ferguson, D.F.; Yemini, Y. An approach to pricing, optimal allocation and quality of service provisioning in high-speed packet networks. In Proceedings of the INFOCOM'95, Boston, MA, USA, 2–6 April 1995; pp. 1111–1119.
30. Yeo, C.S.; Buyya, R. A taxonomy of market-based resource management systems for utility-driven cluster computing. *Softw. Pract. Exp.* **2006**, *36*, 1381–1419. [CrossRef]
31. Islam, M.; Balaji, P.; Sabin, G.; Sadayappan, P. Analyzing and Minimizing the Impact of Opportunity Cost in QoS-aware Job Scheduling. In Proceedings of the 2007 International Conference on Parallel Processing (ICPP 2007), Xi'an, China, 10–14 September 2007; p. 42.
32. Mutz, A.; Wolski, R. Sc-International Conference for High Performance Computing. Efficient auction-based grid reservations using dynamic programming. In *2008 SC-International Conference for High Performance Computing, Networking, Storage and Analysis*; IEEE: Piscataway, NJ, USA, 2008; pp. 1–8.
33. Mutz, A.; Wolski, R.; Brevik, J. Eliciting honest value information in a batch-queue environment. In *2007 8th IEEE/ACM International Conference on Grid Computing*; IEEE: Piscataway, NJ, USA, 2007; pp. 291–297.
34. Lavanya, M.; Shanthi, B.; Saravanan, S. Multi objective task scheduling algorithm based on sla and processing time suitable for cloud environment. *Comput. Commun.* **2020**, *151*, 183–195. [CrossRef]
35. Muter, İ. Exact algorithms to minimize makespan on single and parallel batch processing machines. *Eur. J. Oper. Res.* **2020**, *285*, 470–483. [CrossRef]
36. Jia, Z.; Yan, J.; Leung, J.Y.; Li, K.; Chen, H. Ant colony optimization algorithm for scheduling jobs with fuzzy processing time on parallel batch machines with different capacities. *Appl. Soft Comput.* **2019**, *75*, 548–561. [CrossRef]
37. Li, S. Parallel batch scheduling with inclusive processing set restrictions and non-identical capacities to minimize makespan. *Eur. J. Oper. Res.* **2017**, *260*, 12–20. [CrossRef]
38. Josephson, J.; Ramesh, R. A novel algorithm for real time task scheduling in multiprocessor environment. *Clust. Comput.* **2019**, *22*, 13761–13771. [CrossRef]
39. Ying, K.-C.; Lin, S.-W.; Cheng, C.-Y.; He, C.-D. Iterated reference greedy algorithm for solving distributed no-idle permutation flowshop scheduling problems. *Comput. Ind. Eng.* **2017**, *110*, 413–423. [CrossRef]

40. Li, M.; Lei, D. An imperialist competitive algorithm with feedback for energy-efficient flexible job shop scheduling with transportation and sequence-dependent setup times. *Eng. Appl. Artifi. Intell.* **2021**, *103*, 104307. [CrossRef]
41. Lei, D.; Yuan, Y.; Cai, J.; Bai, D. An imperialist competitive algorithm with memory for distributed unrelated parallel machines scheduling. *Int. J. Prod. Res.* **2020**, *58*, 597–614. [CrossRef]
42. Rahman, H.F.; Janardhanan, M.N.; Poon Chuen, L.; Ponnambalam, S.G. Flowshop scheduling with sequence dependent setup times and batch delivery in supply chain. *Comput. Ind. Eng.* **2021**, *158*, 107378. [CrossRef]
43. Luo, S. Dynamic scheduling for flexible job shop with new job insertions by deep reinforcement learning. *Appl. Soft Comput. J.* **2020**, *91*, 106208. [CrossRef]
44. Yun, Y.; Hwang, E.J.; Kim, Y.H. Adaptive genetic algorithm for energy-efficient task scheduling on asymmetric multiprocessor system-on-chip. *Microprocess. Microsyst.* **2019**, *66*, 19–30. [CrossRef]
45. Saraswati, D.; Sari, D.K.; Kurniadi, S.P. Minimizing total tardiness in parallel machines with simulated annealing using python. *Int. J. Adv. Sci. Technol.* **2019**, *29*, 645–654.
46. Vanhoucke, M.; Coelho, J.; Debels, D.; Maenhout, B.; Tavares, L.V. An evaluation of the adequacy of project network generators with systematically sampled networks. *Eur. J. Oper. Res.* **2008**, *187*, 511. [CrossRef]
47. Higgins, J.P.T.; Thompson, S.G.; Deeks, J.J.; Altman, D.G. Measuring inconsistency in meta-analyses. *BMJ* **2003**, *327*, 557. [CrossRef]

algorithms

MDPI

Article

Parallel Hybrid Particle Swarm Algorithm for Workshop Scheduling Based on Spark

Tianhua Zheng, Jiabin Wang * and Yuxiang Cai

College of Engineering, Huaqiao University, Quanzhou 362000, China; 19014084012@stu.hqu.edu.cn (T.Z.); 19014084001@stu.hqu.edu.cn (Y.C.)

* Correspondence: fatwang@hqu.edu.cn

Abstract: In hybrid mixed-flow workshop scheduling, there are problems such as mass production, mass manufacturing, mass assembly and mass synthesis of products. In order to solve these problems, combined with the Spark platform, a hybrid particle swarm algorithm that will be parallelized is proposed. Compared with the existing intelligent algorithms, the parallel hybrid particle swarm algorithm is more conducive to the realization of the global optimal solution. In the loader manufacturing workshop, the optimization goal is to minimize the maximum completion time and a parallelized hybrid particle swarm algorithm is used. The results show that in the case of relatively large batches, the parallel hybrid particle swarm algorithm can effectively obtain the scheduling plan and avoid falling into the local optimal solution. Compared with algorithm serialization, algorithm parallelization improves algorithm efficiency by 2–4 times. The larger the batches, the more obvious the algorithm parallelization improves computational efficiency.

Keywords: hybrid mixed-flow workshop; hybrid particle swarm algorithm; algorithm parallelization; computational efficiency

Citation: Zheng, T.; Wang, J.; Cai, Y. Parallel Hybrid Particle Swarm Algorithm for Workshop Scheduling Based on Spark. *Algorithms* **2021**, *14*, 262. https://doi.org/10.3390/a14090262

Academic Editor: Frank Werner

Received: 7 August 2021
Accepted: 23 August 2021
Published: 30 August 2021

1. Introduction

The traditional shop scheduling model takes single shop scheduling as the goal, but, in actual discrete manufacturing [1], the job shop and the flow shop are closely connected. The production process includes parts processing, component assembly and product assembly. In this production environment, optimizing one of the workshops leads to a mismatch between the progress of parts processing and subsequent component-assembly and final assembly workshops, resulting in a large amount of inventory and prolonging the product cycle, affecting the production process. Therefore, in the face of the problem of hybrid mixed-flow workshop scheduling, it is necessary to establish integrated scheduling of multiple workshops from the perspective of overall optimization.

The current solutions to the hybrid workshop scheduling problem include accurate calculations for low-complexity and small-scale problems [2–4] and heuristic algorithms. Due to accurate calculation, the calculation time increases exponentially with the complexity of the workshop scheduling problem and the application value is limited. For heuristic algorithms, it performs well on today's workshop scheduling problems, so heuristic algorithms are widely used today. Smutnicki [5] proposed an approximation algorithm based on tabu search, with the goal of minimizing processing time and studying a mixed flow shop with a limited intermediate buffer area. Wang et al. [6] proposed a multi-objective genetic algorithm to study the integrated scheduling problem of flow shop with buffer. Seidgar et al. [7] considered the coordination trade-off model of maximum process time and average completion time and used intelligent algorithms to solve and study the optimization of two-stage flow-shop scheduling with assembly tasks. Na et al. [8] proposed an evolutionary algorithm using three-segment coding to study the production planning and scheduling of mixed-flow products in flexible workshops with processing tasks and assembly tasks. Zhang et al. [9] used an optimized genetic algorithm to solve the problems of minimum total completion time and long equipment idle time for single-piece and small-batch hybrid workshop scheduling. Teymourian [10] faced the problem of assembly job mixed-flow shop scheduling, to the artificial immune algorithm they added the ant colony algorithm to change the antibody to avoid falling into the local minimum and obtain a better scheduling plan. Lou et al. [11] proposed an immune cloning algorithm to solve the problem when studying the optimization problem of hybrid workshop scheduling and achieved an effective solution. Hu et al. [12] proposed a genetic algorithm for multi population parallel and population screening and updating in a phased convergence manner to study the hybrid mixed-flow workshop scheduling problem. Li et al. [13] investigated hybrid mixed-flow workshop scheduling by proposing a hybrid genetic algorithm with the goal of minimizing cache area inventory. Lu et al. [14] proposed the game particle swarm optimization algorithm to study the hybrid mixed-flow workshop scheduling with the goal of parts shop uniformity and minimum inventory. Wang [15] proposed an immune genetic algorithm to study hybrid mixed-flow workshop scheduling with the objective of minimizing the maximum completion time. Tang et al. [16] proposed an improved immune genetic algorithm that introduced a multi-agent negotiation mechanism and simulated annealing algorithm to study the mixed scheduling problem of job shop and flow shop.

Intelligent algorithms are widely used in solving actual complex engineering problems. Nejah et al. [17] introduced the advantages and disadvantages of different intelligent algorithms in 3D indoor deployment problems and evaluated the performance of different intelligent algorithms on 3D indoor deployment problems. Mnasri et al. [18] introduced the application and analysis of existing hybrid intelligent algorithms on the deployment of sensor nodes in wireless sensor networks. The particle swarm optimization algorithm (PSO) stands out among many intelligent algorithms for its advantages, such as high solution accuracy and fast convergence speed. Zhao et al. [19] proposed an improved particle swarm algorithm with decreasing disturbance index on the multi-objective job shop scheduling problem. Mansour et al. [20] faced the problem of shop scheduling with congestion constraints and proposed a combination of a local search algorithm based on probabilistic perturbation and a particle swarm algorithm. Experiments show that the improved algorithm can quickly obtain the best solution; Jamrus et al. [21] proposed a hybrid genetic particle swarm optimization algorithm for flexible job shop scheduling. Experiments show that the proposed algorithm has high solution quality and good practicability. The particle swarm optimization algorithm has a wide range of applications in solving practical problems. Therefore, this paper also uses an improved particle swarm algorithm to solve the problem.

Spark [22,23] is a memory-based distributed computing framework. Comparing the Spark and Hadoop platforms, Hadoop is suitable for offline batch processing of files, but is not suitable for iterative operations. When Spark deals with iterative problems, it does not need to store the results of the iterations to disk, which makes up for the inefficiency of Hadoop Mapreduce that reads operations from the disk every time it deals with iterative problems. When programming Spark in parallel, the input data are decomposed into multiple batch processing fragments, the data are converted into RDD (resilient distributed datasets) and the data are encapsulated in RDD. Through the parallel operation of RDD, the parallel operation of data processing is realized [24]. The basic idea of realizing the parallel particle swarm algorithm is to convert the particle swarm to RDD and initialize it to multiple small populations of the same size. After parallel processing of these small populations, a feasible solution is finally obtained [25,26]. According to the idea of parallelization, a parallel hybrid particle swarm optimization algorithm is proposed for the mixed-flow hybrid workshop scheduling problem.

The existing intelligent algorithm adopts three-stage coding [13,15] to solve the hybrid mixed-flow workshop scheduling problem, which is only applicable to the case of a small batch. Nowadays, the scale and complexity of workshop scheduling are constantly increasing. In the case of relatively large batches, it is easy to fall into the problem of local optimization using its existing three-stage coding intelligent algorithm. Therefore, in the case of a large batch, three-stage coding is not used in the problem of hybrid mixed-flow workshop scheduling. Each workshop is coded independently for independent scheduling. The independent scheduling optimization of the workshop leads to a too long running time of the algorithm. Therefore, the algorithm is improved by combining Spark to realize the parallelization of the algorithm and reduce the running time of the algorithm. In this paper, a hybrid mixed-flow workshop scheduling model is established. In the case of a large batch, a hybrid particle swarm optimization parallelization algorithm based on Spark is proposed to avoid the algorithm falling into local optimization and the workshop scheduling scheme can be obtained effectively and quickly. It has important theoretical significance and application value to solve the problem of hybrid mixed-flow workshop scheduling.

2. Problem Description and Modeling

The hybrid mixed-flow workshop is composed of three parts: the first part is the parts-processing workshop, which is produced in batches; the second part is the flow shop of the component-assembly workshop, which is assembled in units; the third part is the flow shop for the final assembly of the product, which is assembled in units, as shown in Figure 1 below.

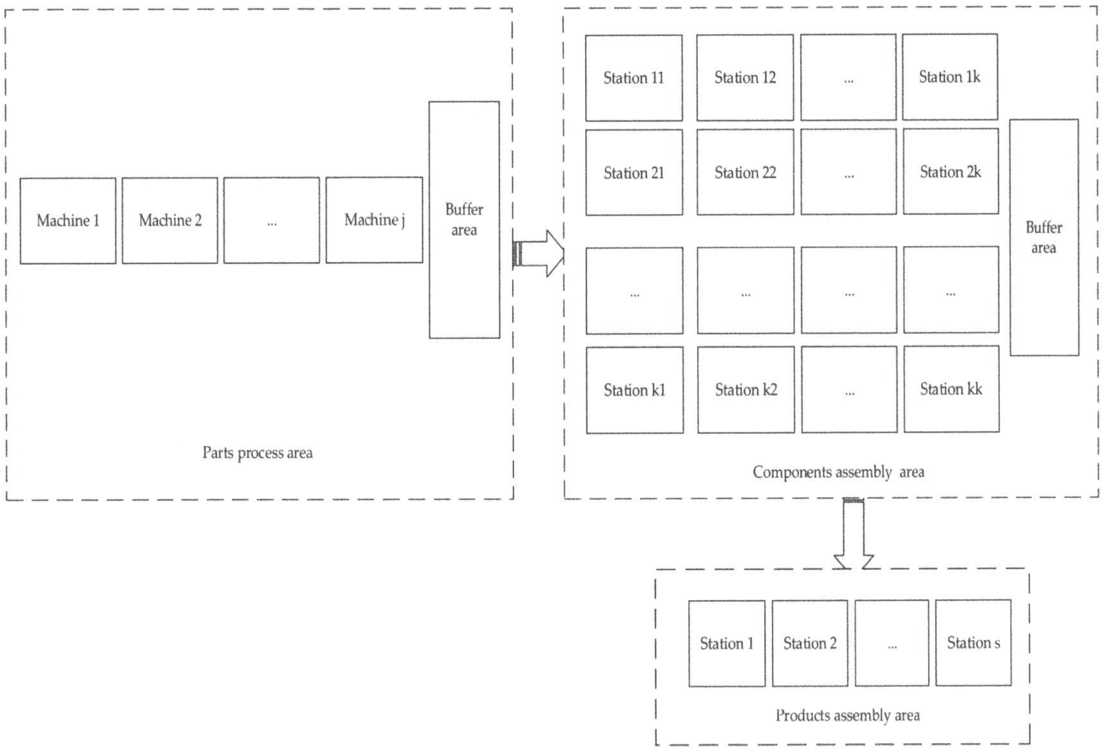

Figure 1. Hybrid mixed-flow workshop.

The parts-processing workshop consists of j machines, processing i parts; the component-assembly workshop is composed of k assembly stations, producing x components; the product-assembly workshop consists of s assembly stations to produce y products. For the convenience of research, the following assumptions are given [13]:

(1) At the beginning, all equipment and assembly stations are ready to perform production tasks at any time.

(2) Different types of parts can be produced in the workshop and the sequence, processing machine and time in the production process of the parts are known.
(3) The assembly time of different types of parts and products at the stations on the assembly line is known.
(4) The process time of the same type of products, components and parts on the machine and the workstation is the same.
(5) In the job shop, only the processes of the same part have process constraints and there are no process constraints between different parts.
(6) The process time of the process includes the preparation time and transportation time of the process.
(7) The parts-process workshop processes a batch of parts for the components-assembly workshop and the product-assembly workshop; or the parts-assembly workshop processes certain parts for the assembly station of the product-assembly workshop. Moreover, if the assembly station does not need more, then these parts or components are temporarily stored in the buffer zone. Ignore the delivery time.

The objective function is to minimize the maximum completion time and the model is as follows:

$$G = \min(E_{i,j} + E_{x,k} + E_{y,s}) \tag{1}$$

In Equation (1), $E_{i,j}$ represents the maximum completion time when all parts i are processed on j machines in the parts-processing workshop; $E_{x,k}$ represents the maximum completion time of all components in the assembly shop x in k stations; $E_{y,s}$ represents the maximum completion time for all products y in the product-assembly workshop to complete assembly at s workstations.

In the actual production process, the parts-processing workshop must meet the process constraints and equipment constraints. Parts are processed in corresponding machines and processes in accordance with process constraints and equipment constraints. In the assembly process, the component-assembly workshop and the product-assembly workshop, in accordance with the process and station constraints, operate at the corresponding assembly position and complete the pre-process before proceeding to the next process operation. The completion time of the workpiece at the station on the assembly line should meet the sum of the completion time of the previous product at this station and the maximum completion time of the workpiece at the previous station and the processing time at the current station. The constraints are as follows.

Parts-processing workshop:

$$\text{Equipment constraints}: \ E_{i,j} - t_{i,j} + r \times c_{i,h,j} \geq E_{i,h} \tag{2}$$

$$\text{Process constraints}: \ E_{g,i} - t_{i,g} + r \times d_{i,g,j} \geq t_{g,i} \tag{3}$$

$$\lim r -> +\infty$$

Component-assembly workshop and product-assembly workshop:

$$\text{Station constraint}: \ E_{x,k} - t_{x,k} + r(1 - c'_{x,h,k}) \geq E_{x,h} \tag{4}$$

$$\text{Process constraints}: \ E_{g,k} - E_{x,k} + r(1 - d'_{x,g,k}) \geq t_{g,k} \tag{5}$$

$$\text{TIme constraint}: \ E_{x,k} = t_{x,k} + \max(E_{x-1,k}, E_{x,k-1}) \tag{6}$$

$$\lim r -> +\infty$$

In Equations (2) and (3), the value of $c_{i,h,j}$ is 1 and 0; 0 means that the device M_h is placed in front of M_j to process N_i and 1 means other. The value of $d_{i,g,j}$ also has two values of 0 and 1; 0 means that the workpiece N_i is placed in front of the N_g workpiece and is processed by the M_j equipment and 1 means others. $E_{i,j}$ is the time when the part N_i is completed on the machine M_j; $t_{i,j}$ is the time required to process the part N_i on the machine M_j. In Equations (4)–(6), the values of $c'_{i,h,j}$ are 0 and 1; 1 means that the workstation h is placed in front of k to assemble the workpiece x, 0 means other. The values of $d'_{i,g,j}$ are 0 and 1; 1 means that the workpiece x is placed before g and works on workstation k and 0 means others.

At present, the intelligent algorithm deals with the hybrid mixed-flow workshop scheduling model. The algorithm uses three-level coding [15] for unified scheduling and solving. However, as the batches of parts and assembly components and products become larger and larger, this kind of coding can easily fall into a local optimal situation. Therefore, in order to solve this problem, each workshop is independently coded. Independently optimize scheduling for each workshop. This process increases the complexity of the algorithm and increases the running time. Therefore, the proposed algorithm is parallelized to reduce the running time of the algorithm and improve the efficiency of the algorithm.

3. Parallelized Hybrid Particle Swarm Algorithm Based on Spark

3.1. Parallel Hybrid Particle Swarm Algorithm

The particle swarm algorithm is a simulation of bird predation. In the process of solving, the solution of each particle corresponds to the position of the particle. The particle swarm algorithm has two attributes, speed and position. Speed represents the speed of movement and position represents the direction of movement.

The shop scheduling problem is a discrete optimization problem, the solution space is in different continuous domains. Because the traditional particle swarm algorithm particles fall into update stagnation and fall into the local optimal situation, combine the genetic algorithm and particle swarm algorithm to solve the shortcomings of traditional particle swarm algorithm and construct a parallelized hybrid particle swarm algorithm. The algorithm flow is as shown in Figure 2.

The pseudo code of the Algorithm 1 is as follows.

Algorithm 1. Hybrid Particle Swarm Algorithm

```
*Initialization*/
Generate N random workpiece sequences in each workshop according to the number of input products; solve the objective function value k after the crossover operation, according to Equations (2)–(6); max_iter is the maximum number of iterations; i corresponds to each particle population; ii corresponds to the number of iterations.
Set initial values for: max_ iter, N; i, ii
Initialize and solve the particle swarm's own optimal m and global optimal value n according to the default order of the workpiece;
for ii in rang(max_iter):
  /*The particles and the global optimal particles are cross-operated*/
  for i in rang(N):
Cross operation between each particle and the global optimal particle;
     Update N;
     Solve the objective function after crossover: k = fitness(N);
Output the optimal new_n value of the most global particle swarm; its own optimal value new_m
    /*Update m, n*/
     If new_n < n then n = new_n; If new_m < m then m = new_m;
end for
  /*The particle and its own optimal history particle perform cross operation*/
  for i in rang(N):
     Each particle crosses with its own optimal history particle
     Update N;
     Solve the objective function after crossover: k = fitness(N);
     Output the optimal new_n value of the most global particle swarm; its own optimal value new_m
    /*Update m, n*/
```

```
        If new_n < n then n = new_n; If new_m < m then m = new_m;
      end for
    /*Single-site mutation for each particle swarm */
    for i in rang(N):
        Random single-site mutations for each particle swarm;
        Update N;
        Calculate the objective function value after mutation: k = fitness(N);
        Output the optimal new_n value of the most global particle swarm; its own optimal
  value new_m
      /*Update m, n*/
        If new_n < n then n = new_n; If new_m < m then m = new_m;
    end for
  end for
  /*Output*/
  Output the global optimal k and corresponding N workpiece production sequencing
```

Figure 2. The main process of parallelized hybrid particle swarm optimization.

3.2. Detailed Design of the Algorithm

3.2.1. Coding Scheme Design

The research problem is mixed mixed-flow workshop scheduling, in which there are job workshops and flow workshops and the coding methods in genetic coding are compared. The three workshops are designed with a unified coding. After the coding design is completed, the workshops are independently optimized and dispatched. First, determine the minimum production ratio of the number of products produced according to actual needs. According to the minimum production ratio, determine the minimum production ratio for the product-assembly workshop, component-assembly workshop and parts-processing workshop, then perform independent coding. In the workshop, letters and numbers are used to represent products, components and parts. The same letters represent the same products, components and parts. If we need to put into production, the P, Q and R products are 2, 1 and 2; the number of required components X and Y is 2 and 3; the parts required for parts processing A, B and C are 2, 1 and 2. Then, the coding method in the product-assembly workshop can be (P1, P2, Q1, R1, R2); the coding of the component-assembly workshop is (X1, X2, Y1, Y2, Y3); the coding of the part processing workshop is (A1, A2, A3, B1, C1, C2, C3).

3.2.2. Crossover and Mutation

Enter the number of artifacts to generate N (total number of particles) random artifact sequences. After crossover and mutation with the global optimal value and its own optimal value, respectively, filter and update the one that can produce a better target value particle. In this step, the crossover and mutation operations can be regarded as random walk operations on the permutation group of the workpieces arranged in order. The mutation is a single-step walk of exchange and the crossover can be a walk formed by a combination of multiple basic exchanges. This step is similar to the speed update in the classic PSO. Whether to perform a walk is only True or False in this algorithm. This step simulates the weighting factor [27] in the classic PSO. Crossing with the local (self) and global optimal values, respectively, simulates the two velocity terms in the classic PSO. Both the mutation and crossover operations have a certain degree of randomness, which ensures that a single particle can jump out of the local optimal solution possibility.

3.2.3. Parallelization of Hybrid Particle Swarm Algorithm

Pyspark is a tool of Spark and a library of sparkAPI written in python provided by Spark. Parallelization is achieved through Pyspark. First, the PSO coding is converted into a parallel RDD, then the process of solving the objective function is applied to all the particles through the Map operation provided by Spark. The time for each particle to be transformed into the objective function is summarized to obtain the optimal result.

4. Instance Verification

4.1. Examples of Mixed Mixed-Flow Workshop Scheduling

Now, we take the loader manufacturing workshop as an example [15] to verify the model and algorithm. The production system is composed of the parts-processing workshop, component-assembly workshop and product-assembly workshop. The four products produced are Q1, Q2, Q3, and Q4. The corresponding parts and component demand matrix of the products are shown in Table 1, below.

The parts-processing workshop mainly produces eight kinds of self-made parts. The set of parts is {A, B, C, D, E, F, G, H} and the set of machines in the workshop is {M_1, M_2, $\cdots$, M_{10}}. The parts in batches are processed on the machine. The processing time and process sequence are shown in Table 2 below and the time unit is s.

Table 1. Product demand matrix.

Parts	Q1	Q2	Q3	Q4	X	Y
A	1	1	/	/	/	/
B	/	/	1	1	/	/
C	1	1	/	/	/	/
D	/	/	1	1	/	/
E	1	1	/	/	/	/
F	/	/	1	1	/	/
G	/	/	/	/	1	/
H	/	/	/	/	/	1
Component X	1	1	/	/	/	/
Component Y	/	/	1	/	/	/

Note: "/" means that the product has no relationship with the required parts.

Table 2. Parts-processing time and process sequence.

	Parts							
Machine	**A**	**B**	**C**	**D**	**E**	**F**	**G**	**H**
M_1	300.1	375.1	0	0	0	0	0	0
M_2	375.2	450.2	0	0	0	0	0	0
M_3	375.3	450.3	0	0	0	0	0	0
M_4	0	0	450.1	450.1	0	0	450.1	525.1
M_5	0	0	0	0	450.1	525.1	375.2	450.2
M_6	0	0	525.2	525.2	0	0	0	0
M_7	0	0	0	0	525.2	450.2	0	0
M_8	0	0	375.3	375.3	375.3	375.3	0	0
M_9	0	0	0	0	0	0	600.3	600.3
M_{10}	0	0	375.4	375.4	600.4	600.4	0	0

The component-assembly workshop is mainly responsible for the assembly of components X and Y. The assembly time and steps are shown in Table 3 below and the unit is s.

Table 3. Component-assembly process and time.

Process	Component X	Component Y
1	147	126
2	126	147
3	126	168
4	105	105
5	157	168
6	126	105
7	168	168
8	147	126
9	147	168

The final assembly line of the product has 33 assembly stations and the corresponding assembly time and procedures for products Q1, Q2, Q3 and Q4 are shown in Table 4 below and the unit is s.

Table 4. Product final assembly process and time.

Process	Q1	Q2	Q3	Q4
1	105	84	91	105
2	140	147	133	126
3	154	161	140	175
4	140	126	140	147
5	133	147	126	140
6	147	154	147	161
7	126	133	133	140
8	147	140	154	147
9	147	133	133	140
10	140	140	133	140
11	140	147	147	154
12	154	161	147	154
13	126	133	133	126
14	147	154	147	161
15	126	133	133	140
16	140	147	140	133
17	147	154	140	147
18	140	147	147	140
19	140	133	140	133
20	154	161	147	161
21	140	133	140	168
22	168	161	161	168
23	161	161	154	147
24	168	175	161	168
25	161	168	161	168
26	140	147	147	147
27	126	133	140	133
28	126	126	126	119
29	154	154	147	140
30	161	154	154	161
31	161	147	168	161
32	140	133	126	133
33	161	168	161	161

During the planning period, the tasks for the production of products Q1, Q2, Q3 and Q4 are divided into 320 units, 160 units, 320 units and 320 units. The minimum production ratio is 2:1:2:2. According to the known conditions, it can be known that the required parts X and Y are divided into 480 and 640 and the minimum production ratio is 3:4. The required parts A–H are 480, 640, 480, 640, 480, 640, 480 and 640, respectively, and the minimum production ratio is 3:4:3:4:3:4:3:4. Calculate according to the parallelized particle swarm algorithm, set the size of the population to 20 and the number of iterations to 300.

It runs in a 64-bit stand-alone Windows 10 operating system, 32 G running memory, 10 cores and 20 threads. In Spark's Local mode, parallel computing of algorithms is realized. In the case of local[N] mode, the optimal plans for the assembly scheduling of parts, components and products are obtained, respectively, {E1, G1, F1, D1, G2, D2, F2, B1, F3, C1, F4, A1, H1, A2, E2, C2, B2, A3, D3, H2, H3, G3, B3, D4, H4, B4, C3, E3}; {X1, X2, Y1, Y2, Y3, Y4, X3}; {Q3, Q1, Q1, Q3, Q2, Q4, Q4}; the total completion time is 15,508 s. Using the immune genetic algorithm IA [15], the total completion time is 15,679 s. Using the PSO algorithm, the total completion time is 15,660 s. Figure 3 shows the evolution curve of this algorithm.

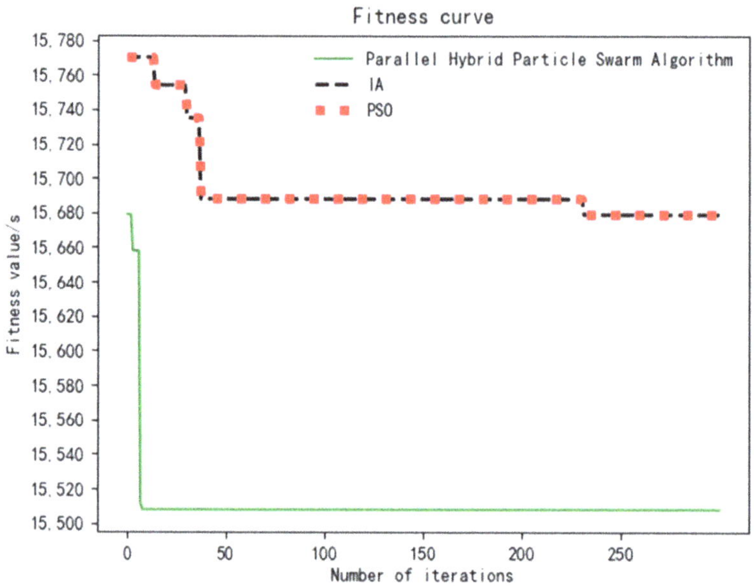

Figure 3. Algorithm evolution curve.

In this paper, the parallel hybrid particle swarm optimization (PHPSO), IA and PSO algorithms are set to the same number of iterations of 50. C_{best} is the optimal value of the operation, A_{ver} is the average value of the operation and the relative deviation of the value dev [28]. Among them, dev1 is the comparison between PHPSO and IA and dev2 is the comparison between PHPSO and PSO. If dev is positive, the solution obtained by the compared algorithm is better. If dev is negative, the solution obtained by PHPSO is better. Table 5 shows algorithm comparison.

Table 5. Algorithm comparison.

PHPSO		IA		PSO			
C_{best}(/s)	A_{ver}(/s)	C_{best}(/s)	A_{ver}(/s)	C_{best}(/s)	A_{ver}(/s)	dev_1(%)	dev_2(%)
15,508	15,526.92	15,688	15,734.38	15,660	15,682.4	−1.16	−0.98

It can be seen from Table 5, that PHPSO finds the optimal value within 50 iterations of running time and the IA and PSO algorithms cannot find the optimal solution, indicating that the PHPSO algorithm has a good ability to find the optimal solution. The average value obtained by PHPSO in 50 iterations is smaller, indicating that the algorithm has a strong global search ability, avoiding the limitation of the algorithm that is easy to fall into the local optimum and the algorithm has strong convergence.

The parallel hybrid particle swarm optimization algorithm is compared with immune genetic algorithm IA and PSO. A stand for IA or PSO algorithms. The comparison results of the largest completion time of parts-, components- and product-assembly workshops are shown in Table 6. The deviation obtained by the hybrid particle swarm algorithm solution and the IA solution is

$$Dev = [(A - C_{PHPSO})/C_{PHPSO}] \times 100\% \tag{7}$$

Table 6. Comparison of results.

Algorithm	Workshop	Processing Time/s	Dev/%
PHPSO	Parts	7500	0
	Component	2247	0
	Product	5761	0
IA	Parts	7650	2
	Component	2247	0
	Product	5782	0.36
PSO	Parts	7575	1
	Component	2247	0
	Product	5838	1.34

From Table 6, we can see that the PHPSO algorithm used in this article has a better solution than the GA algorithm and the PSO algorithm in the parts workshop and product-assembly workshop. Through the analysis of the results, the parallelized hybrid particle swarm optimization algorithm can achieve overall optimization.

4.2. Computing Performance

To test the parallelization performance of the hybrid particle swarm algorithm, set the population to 20 and the number of iterations to 40. Compare the running time of algorithm serialization and algorithm parallelization. The tested data are as follows: when the number of products is 7, the ratio of products is [2:1:2:2]; when the number of products is 10, the ratio of products is [2:3:2:3]; when the number of products is 14, the ratio of products is [3:4:5:2]. Compared with the running time of algorithm parallelization and algorithm serialization, the computing speed is greatly improved by 2–4 times. As the number of products input increases, the speed increases more obviously, reflecting the advantage of the Spark platform in processing a large amount of data. The running time of the algorithm is shown in Figure 4 below.

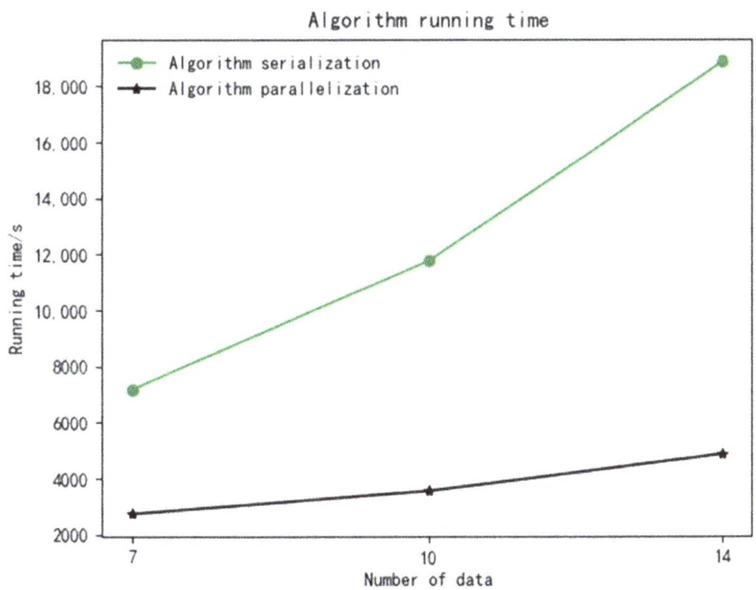

Figure 4. Algorithm running time.

4.3. Results Discussion

In the case of a large batch in the hybrid mixed-flow workshop scheduling problem, the algorithm in this paper can effectively solve the job shop scheduling problem and avoid the algorithm falling into local optimization. Combined with the Spark platform, the parallel design of the algorithm is realized. Compared with the serial operation of the algorithm, the parallel design of the algorithm improves the efficiency of the algorithm. When the bulk becomes larger, the demand data are also more complex and the enhancement of the efficiency of the algorithm is also more obvious, in line with the advantages of the Spark platform for big data processing. This paper also has limitations. Because this paper is a single objective optimization, there are many influencing factors in the actual job shop scheduling, such as inventory cost, so the next research should apply the proposed algorithm to the job shop scheduling of multi-objective optimization.

5. Conclusions

In this paper, a parallel hybrid particle swarm optimization algorithm is proposed for hybrid mixed-flow workshop scheduling problem. The Spark platform is combined with intelligent algorithms to solve the problem of workshop scheduling in high-volume situations. This can provide some reference for solving large-scale data processing in workshop scheduling.

In the future, it is necessary to apply the parallel hybrid particle swarm algorithm to the multi-objective shop scheduling problem. Consider combining the intelligent algorithm for solving multi-objectives with the algorithm in this paper to improve it, so that it can be applied to the problem of multi-objective workshop scheduling.

Author Contributions: Conceptualization, T.Z.; methodology, T.Z.; software, Y.C.; validation, T.Z.; formal analysis, T.Z.; investigation, Y.C.; data curation, J.W.; writing—original draft preparation, T.Z.; writing—review and editing, J.W. All authors have read and agreed to the published version of the manuscript.

Funding: This research received no external funding.

Conflicts of Interest: The authors declare no conflict of interest.

References

1. Lefkowitz, I.; Schoeffler, J.D. Multilevel control structures for three discrete manufacturing processes. *IFAC Proc. Vol.* **1972**, *5*, 96–103. [CrossRef]
2. Djellab, H.; Djellab, K. Preemptive hybrid flowshop scheduling problem of interval orders. *Eur. J. Oper. Res.* **2002**, *137*, 37–49. [CrossRef]
3. Bolat, A.; Al-Harkan, I.; Al-Harbi, B. Flow-shop scheduling for three serial stations with the last two duplicate. *Comput. Oper. Res.* **2005**, *32*, 647–667. [CrossRef]
4. Guirchoun, S.; Martineau, P.; Billaut, J.C. Total completion time minimization in a computer system with a server and two parallel processors. *Comput. Oper. Res.* **2005**, *32*, 599–611. [CrossRef]
5. Smutnicki, C. A two-machine permutation flow shop scheduling problem with buffers. *Oper.-Res.-Spektrum* **1998**, *20*, 229–235. [CrossRef]
6. Wang, B.; Rao, Y.; Shao, X.; Xu, C. A MOGA-based Algorithm for Sequencing a Mixed-model Fabrication/Assembly System. *Zhongguo Jixie Gongcheng/China Mech. Eng.* **2009**, *20*, 1434–1438. [CrossRef]
7. Seidgar, H.; Kiani, M.; Abedi, M.; Fazlollahtabar, H. An efficient imperialist competitive algorithm for scheduling in the two-stage assembly flow shop problem. *Int. J. Prod. Res.* **2014**, *52*, 1240–1256. [CrossRef]
8. Na, H.; Park, J. Multi-level job scheduling in a flexible job shop environment. *Int. J. Prod. Res.* **2014**, *52*, 3877–3887. [CrossRef]
9. Zhang, H.; Wu, Y.; Software, S.O. Single piece and small batch mixed-shop scheduling algorithm. *China Sci. Pap.* **2015**, *10*, 962–966.
10. Komaki, G.M.; Teymourian, E.; Kayvanfar, V. Minimising makespan in the two-stage assembly hybrid flow shop scheduling problem using artificial immune systems. *Int. J. Prod. Res.* **2016**, *54*, 963–983. [CrossRef]
11. Lou, G.; Cai, Z. Improved hybrid immune clonal selection genetic algorithm and its application in hybrid shop scheduling. *Clust. Comput.* **2018**, *22*, 3419–3429. [CrossRef]
12. Hu, H.; Lu, J.; Li, Y. Study of mixed-model hybrid shop fuzzy scheduling problem based on multi-populations parallel genetic algorithm. *J. Zhejiang Univ. Technol.* **2012**, *40*, 554–558. [CrossRef]

13. Li, X.; Lu, J.; Chai, G.; Tang, H.; Jiang, L. Hybrid Genetic Algorithm for Mixed-model Hybrid-shop Scheduling Problem. *Zhongguo Jixie Gongcheng/China Mech. Eng.* **2012**, *23*, 935–940. [CrossRef]
14. Lu, J.; Hu, H.; Dong, Q. Game theory and particle swarm optimization for mixed-model hybrid-shop scheduling problem. *J. Zhejiang Univ. Technol.* **2015**, *43*, 398–404.
15. Wang, M. Research on Multi-level Hybrid Workshop Integrated Scheduling Based on Immune Genetic Algorithm. Master's Thesis, Lanzhou University of Technology, Lanzhou, China, 2020.
16. Tang, H.; Ding, B.; Li, X.; Lu, J. Improved immune genetic algorithm for mixed-model scheduling problem. *China Mech. Eng.* **2014**, *25*, 1189. [CrossRef]
17. Nasri, N.; Mnasri, S.; Val, T. 3D node deployment strategies prediction in wireless sensors network. *Int. J. Electron.* **2020**, *107*, 808–838. [CrossRef]
18. Mnasri, S.; Nasri, N.; Val, T. The Deployment in the Wireless Sensor Networks: Methodologies, Recent Works and Applications. In Proceedings of the International Conference on Performance Evaluation and Modeling in Wired and Wireless Networks (PEMWN 2014), Sousse, Tunisia, 4–7 November 2014.
19. Zhao, F.; Tang, J.; Wang, J.; Jonrinaldi, N.A. An improved particle swarm optimization with decline disturbance index (DDPSO) for multi-objective job-shop scheduling problem. *Comput. Oper. Res.* **2014**, *45*, 38–50. [CrossRef]
20. Mansour, E.; Bassem, J.; Patrick, S. Combinatorial particle swarm optimization for solving blocking flowshop scheduling problem. *J. Comput. Des. Eng.* **2016**, *3*, 295–311. [CrossRef]
21. Jamrus, T.; Chien, C.F.; Gen, M.; Sethanan, K. Hybrid particle swarm optimization combined with genetic operators for flexible job-shop scheduling under uncertain processing time for semiconductor manufacturing. *IEEE Trans. Semicond. Manuf.* **2017**, *31*, 32–41. [CrossRef]
22. Zaharia, M.; Chowdhury, M.; Franklin, M.J.; Shenker, S.; Stoica, I. Spark: Cluster computing with working sets. *HotCloud* **2010**, *10*, 95.
23. Dongfei, S.O.N.G.; Hua, X.U. Research and Parallelization of DBSCAN Algorithm. *Comput. Eng. Appl.* **2018**, *54*, 52–56.
24. Qiu, R. The Parallel Design and Application of the CURE Algorithm Based on Spark Platform. Master's Thesis, South China University of Technology, Guangzhou, China, 2014.
25. Li, F. Parallel Programming of Particle Swarm Optimization Algorithm Based on Spark and Its Application in Reservoir Scheduling. Master's Thesis, Xi'an University of Technology, Xi'an, China, 2017.
26. Peng, A.; Peng, Y.; Zhou, H. Multi-core parallel computation for deriving joint operating rule curves in multi-reservoir system under the condition of inter-basin water transfer. *J. Hydraul. Eng. China* **2014**, *45*, 1284–1292. [CrossRef]
27. Shi, Y. A Modified Particle Swarm Optimizer. In Proceedings of the 1998 IEEE International Conference on Evolutionary Computation Proceedings, Anchorage, AK, USA, 4–9 May 1998.
28. Gu, X.; Huang, M.; Liang, X. An improved genetic algorithm with adaptive variable neighborhood search for FJSP. *Algorithms* **2019**, *12*, 243. [CrossRef]

algorithms

MDPI

Article

A Practical Staff Scheduling Strategy Considering Various Types of Employment in the Construction Industry

Chan Hee Park and Young Dae Ko *

Department of Hotel and Tourism Management, College of Hospitality and Tourism, Sejong University, 209 Neungdong-ro, Seoul 05006, Korea
* Correspondence: youngdae.ko@sejong.ac.kr; Tel.: +82-10-4725-3480

Abstract: The Korean government implemented a 52-h workweek policy for employees' welfare. Consequently, companies face workforce availability reduction with the same number of employees. That is, labor-dependent companies suffer from workforce shortage. To handle the workforce shortage, they increase irregular employees who are paid relatively less. However, the problem of 'no-show', due to the stochastic characteristics of irregular employee's absence, happens. Therefore, this study aims to propose a staff scheduling strategy considering irregular employee absence and a new labor policy by using linear programming. By deriving a deterministic staff schedule through system parameters derived from the features and rules of an actual company in the numerical experiment, the practicality and applicability of the developed mathematical model are proven. Furthermore, through sensitivity analysis and simulation considering the stochastic characteristics of absences, various proactive cases are provided. Through the proactive cases, the influence of the change of the average percent of irregular employees' absences on the total labor costs and staff schedules and the expected number who would not come to work could be given when assuming the application in practice. This finding can help decision-makers prepare precautious measures, such as assigning extra employees in case of an irregular employee's absence.

Keywords: construction industry; irregular employees; staff scheduling; mathematical model; business level strategies; decision-making; organizational effectiveness

Citation: Park, C.H.; Ko, Y.D. A Practical Staff Scheduling Strategy Considering Various Types of Employment in the Construction Industry. *Algorithms* **2022**, *15*, 321. https://doi.org/10.3390/a15090321

Academic Editors: Francisco Saldanha da Gama and Frank Werner

Received: 21 July 2022
Accepted: 6 September 2022
Published: 9 September 2022

1. Introduction

The construction industry plays a significant role in economic growth [1]. Korea has also developed its economy along with the growth of the construction industry [2]. However, as presented in Figure 1, based on the 2020 Construction Policy Review by the Construction Policy Institute of Korea, the Korean construction industry has not contributed to economic growth since 2017. Moreover, the construction industry has hindered economic growth since 2018 due to problems such as workforce shortage and reduction in investment. According to the Ministry of Employment and Labor, the safety problem and low wage levels are the main reasons companies cannot employ new employees on construction sites. As for the safety problem, about 50 percent of occupational accidents that lead to death takes place in the construction industry. Regarding the wage level, employees in the construction industry are paid 26.1 percent lower than employees in the manufacturing industry. Even compared to the average rate of all industries, it is 15 percent lower [3]. For those reasons, workforce shortage happens in the construction industry in Korea. According to [4], the number of lacking employees on construction sites will increase to 96 thousand in 2024 from 83 thousand in 2020.

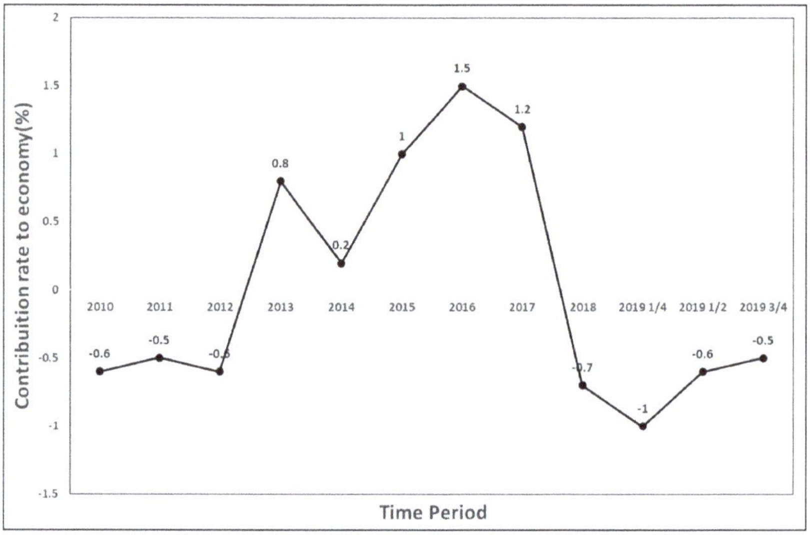

Figure 1. Contribution of the construction industry to the economic growth.

To solve the above problems, the government made the policy of the 52-h workweek and expanded hygiene facilities to improve the workplace environment. The 52-h workweek policy is a workhour limit for the employee's welfare. Due to this policy, each employee works 8 to 12 h a day and they cannot work more than 52 h a week. As a result, the company that finishes jobs by employing a small number of people and making them work for more than 52 h a week faces a crisis. That is, when a company needs to work for 70 h, it is more beneficial for them to make one employee work more by paying the extra cost to him/her than employ two employees and make each work 35 h. Moreover, they face workforce availability reduction to the same number of employees compared to before the change of the labor policy. Because of this situation, it is more important to consider human resource management to save labor costs and yield companies' performances [5].

About 50 percent are irregular employees out of the total workforce according to the statistics data from the Korean bank. The reason the percent of irregular employees is high is that many people do not want to be employed in the construction industry due to the possible dangers that can lead to death or disability [6]. In addition, if they employ regular employees, they need to keep paying for them even when they do not have work because of the difficulty of firing them. Due to this, construction companies suffer from workforce shortages, which is regarded as one of the most serious problems in all industries [7]. Moreover, companies want to employ irregular employees, including foreign employees, from an outsourcing company to reduce costs due to an increase in the labor cost [8]. According to [9], foreign employees account for 19.5 percent of the whole workforce size in the construction industry. In addition, it is expected that irregular foreign employees continue to increase. The government presented that about 57 thousand is the proper number of foreign employees in 2019. However, the number of foreign employees was about 210 thousand in the same year [10]. That is, the Korean construction industry faces a situation that has no choice but to employ a greater number of irregular foreign employees.

Several countries already use irregular employees to deal with the workforce shortage. For instance, Malaysia has already been using the irregular foreign workforce actively to manage the workforce shortage problem [11]. Furthermore, a portion of temporary jobs is increasing in the UK labor market [12]. Employing irregular foreign employees can be a realistic way to respond to the workforce shortage. However, it is important to know and understand the Korean way of using irregular employees. Most irregular employees are used in the way of getting paid daily. It is thought that this feature of the way of using irregular employees would be different from other countries that normally contract irregular employees and use them during the contracted period. However, because of the way of using irregular employees, irregular employees do not have loyalty, thus they also have low responsibility for working. In addition, they could have different irregular employees every day because they are normally contracted daily. Thus, they have difficulty keeping track of irregular employees and giving them penalties even when they make trouble due to a daily contract. These issues make it difficult for companies to conduct human resource management efficiently.

This paper considers the actual situation of the construction industry in Korea, such as the workforce shortage due to an increase in labor costs and workforce availability reduction by the change of the labor policy. The main thing considered in the paper is 'no-show', which is a real problem of the actual company that employed irregular employees to deal with the workforce shortage problem. Despite the no-show of irregular employees, it is difficult for the company to control irregular employees, since the authority of giving penalties normally belongs to their outsourcing company in Korea. Nevertheless, the reason a company uses irregular employees is because of lower labor costs than local regular employees. Therefore, the company needs to respond to the unexpected situation that irregular employees suddenly do not come to work. To achieve this, this research uses linear programming to derive a deterministic staff schedule considering the average percent of irregular employee absences. This can be one of the proactive measures to respond to the stochastic characteristics of an irregular employee's absence. Moreover, the simulation of a deterministic staff schedule is conducted to figure out what expectedly happens when assuming the application to a company in practice. Consequently, the performance of how well a staff schedule works is evaluated, and how many irregular employees do not come to work is expected. These can play a role as basic data that help managers decide on a staff schedule.

2. Literature Review

The method suggested in this research is to minimize the total labor cost of a construction company by deriving a deterministic staff schedule. Human resource is crucial in many operations that are heavily labor-oriented. In addition, it is typically one of the most expensive resources of a company [13,14]. That means that human resources are regarded as one of the most important factors to manage in every business. Edie [15] conducted the first research on a quantitative approach to a solution for staff scheduling problems. After this study, a variety of research was conducted in many different industries. Van den Bergh et al. [16] defined three main staff scheduling parts, namely shift scheduling, days off scheduling, and tour scheduling. Shift scheduling involves scheduling across a daily planning horizon, and one worker has just one shift a day. Days off scheduling is about the schedule of the day off for each worker. Tour scheduling is a combination of shift scheduling and days-off scheduling. Moreover, Ganguly and Nandi [17] revealed that staff scheduling is important to meet demands. In this paper, forecasting models, such as Analysis of Variance (ANOVA) and Auto Regressive Integrated Moving Average (ARIMA) were utilized. The demands derived from forecasting models were used for the mathematical model as input parameters to derive an optimal solution for staff scheduling. Furthermore, Maenhout and Vanhoucke [18] suggested a staffing and shift scheduling approach for nurses in the hospital. In this paper, the mathematical model was suggested for a new integrative nurse staff scheduling while considering the impact of several personnel policies on staffing level decisions to obtain an allocation of nurses. Ásgeirsson [19] conducted research on staff scheduling by using metaheuristic algorithms to consider the requests of employees. As a result, fair and feasible schedules were generated for staff scheduling. To summarize, various studies have proved that staff scheduling is beneficial for a company with a shifting policy to minimize labor costs.

The construction industry is interested in scheduling research to assign employees well. Memon and Zin [20] reported the status of resource-driven scheduling implementation in the Malaysian construction industry. It was revealed that about 60% of construction companies used scheduling to meet the construction project deadline under the limits of resource availability. Even though there are several constraints against using staff scheduling, such as high cost, and lack of understanding for scheduling, the importance of scheduling was proved in that many tried to have scheduling. Al-Rawi and Mukherjee [21] focused on a constructive method to solve labor scheduling problems encountered in a construction company. The linear programming technique was used to suggest estimated labor costs for a week and the conditions of part-time labor in each shift. Consequently, the organization could produce a new schedule each week while minimizing labor costs and maximizing labor preferences. Between a diversity of businesses, the hospitality industry is similar to the construction industry in terms of the labor-dependency. Rocha et al. [22] performed research on the optimization of staff schedules for a hotel in Turkey. They handled the problem through operation research (OR). As a result, they reduced the labor costs and the number of employees to finish their work during the same period. Kaya and Dağdeviren [23] studied the optimal allocation of employees to jobs while minimizing total daily labor costs. It proposed a Pareto multistage decision-based genetic algorithm (P-mdGA). As a result, this method helped managers of hotels in need of automatic support to effectively allocate hotel staff to jobs. Azadeh et al. [24] proved that airline crew assignment to flights can minimize total cost. A particle swarm optimization (PSO) algorithm with a local search heuristic was applied to derive a solution for crew scheduling. Consequently, the proposed hybrid PSO algorithm helped assign crew members to the flight while minimizing the total cost.

Not only labor costs but also the welfare of employees, such as workplace environment improvement and policy, have a huge influence on the construction industry. Much research regarding welfare for employees has been conducted in many different industries. Asensio-Cuesta et al. [25] developed the models for job rotation schedules as an aspect of welfare for staff, such as assignments to various jobs considering their skills and knowledge. A multi-criteria genetic algorithm is employed to provide a solution for both workers and management. Therefore, the model prevented reducing fatigue and increased job satisfaction and morale while giving a solution to job rotation scheduling. Ruiz-Torres et al. [26] performed research on scheduling problems considering worker satisfaction to contribute to enlargement in the field of staff scheduling. Metrics of job preference and desirable job variety were used for job satisfaction in scheduling problems. As a result, this paper generated an optimal solution for staff scheduling, considering the job satisfaction of employees. Furthermore, Stolletz and Brunner [27] studied an optimal shift scheduling solution for physicians in hospitals while considering preference, labor agreement, and fairness. In this paper, all constraints were modeled within the linear program (LP). As a result, this model provided a solution that takes fairness between physicians' shifts into consideration to minimize the paid-out hours under the restrictions given by the labor agreement. Shuib and Kamarudin [28] proposed a Binary Integer Goal Programming (BGP) model and a mathematical model to determine an optimal staff schedule at the power station. In addition, this research identified the main criteria and conditions for the BGP model. Consequently, the suggested method generated an optimal staff scheduling solution considering employees' day-off preferences by using MATLAB while focusing on three processes, which were demand modeling, shift scheduling, and day-off scheduling.

To improve the practicality, the uncertainty of irregular employees should be reflected when developing a staff scheduling strategy. Several studies considered the uncertainty of irregular employees. Research on workforce scheduling that considers the unpredictable employee's absence was conducted to guarantee sufficient coverage in medical facilities. Becker et al. [29] proposed integer programming that considers assigning ex-post duties. This paper proved the practicality of the developed models by applying them to local medical facilities in practice. As a result, staff scheduling complexity was reduced. Ingels and Maenhout [30] stated that many organizations make staff schedules under a deterministic operating environment. However, the stochastic environment, such as employee absence, occurs. To manage this uncertainty, this paper proposed a proactive approach to respond to schedule disruptions. By comparing a diversity of the proactive strategies, a proposed preemptive programming approach in this paper was assessed. Steenweg et al. [31] mentioned that short-term uncertainty in the workforce causes gaps between the planned and real shift schedule. Therefore, the unpredictable absence of employees should be considered when deciding on shift scheduling. This paper suggested a framework that can assign heterogeneously skilled employees to jobs optimally to respond to sudden absence. For this framework, the workforce availability was modeled by the stochastic simulation. As a result, the practicality of the framework that can provide efficient shift scheduling was proved by applying it to the actual cases.

This paper also considers the uncertainty of employees, especially irregular employee absence in the construction industry. Many studies about staff scheduling that handle the uncertain nature of employees suggested stochastic modeling. In addition, other studies proposed the strategies for assignment of skilled employees to shift to fill in the absence. However, this paper develops a mathematical model that derives a deterministic staff schedule by considering the average percent of irregular employees' absences. This is because the expected average percent of irregular employees' absences could be different from the actual average percent of their absences in practice. That is, even a staff schedule derived from the stochastic modeling cannot ensure that all irregular employees follow a staff schedule because it is performed only with reliance on the probability of absence. Therefore, this paper focuses on providing various proactive cases by deriving a deterministic staff schedule and conducting a simulation about it to evaluate performance. Consequently, the simulation helps a company expect how many irregular employees would not come to work when applying a deterministic staff schedule to a company. However, this cannot also guarantee that all irregular employees follow a staff schedule well because the possibility of their absences still exists. However, deriving a deterministic staff schedule and simulating it can contribute to providing a systematic procedure to manage the sudden absences of irregular employees. Therefore, this procedure can help managers prepare the precautious measures to rapidly respond to irregular employee absence.

3. Mathematical Formulation

3.1. Problem Description

Companies in the construction industry suffer from workforce shortage problems due to the 52-h workweek policy and a no-show by irregular employees. Before the explanation of the problem description in detail, irregular employees that are often shown in this paper are defined as foreign and local irregular employees who do not belong to a company and are paid daily. They are not part-time workers. Under the 52-h workweek policy, each employee can work 8 to 12 h a day and cannot exceed to work 52 h a week. In addition, if they work more than 8 h a day, it is regarded as overtime work. Along with the government policy, irregular employee absence worsens the workforce shortage. According to the managers of the construction company considered in this paper, the average percent of irregular employee absence is from 20% to 30% per day. As a result, this company often faces workforce availability reduction. To consider this uncertainty of irregular employee absence, the mathematical model introduces the average percent of irregular employee absence to derive a conservative and deterministic staff schedule that assumes they normally do not come to work according to their absence percent. However, the percent of irregular employees' absences is not constant in the real world. It is always stochastic. Thus, this paper performs the simulation of a derived staff schedule to consider the stochastic situation of irregular employees' absences. Furthermore, by changing the average percent of irregular employee absence, the change in total labor cost and staff schedules are examined depending on the percent of irregular employee absence more closely through sensitivity. Additionally, there are two types of jobs. There are four workplaces, namely the first floor, the second floor, open storage, and the office. Moreover, this company always needs more than 45 employees and more than 18 employees during the daytime and nighttime per day. To sum up, by conducting several numerical experiments in this paper, it is expected to provide proactive cases for a staff schedule considering the stochastic characteristics of irregular employee absence under the new labor policy in Korea.

3.2. Notation

3.2.1. Known Parameters

This paper derives a conservative and deterministic solution for a staff schedule that can minimize the total labor cost considering the new labor policy and the average percent of irregular employee absence. The following notations in Table 1 are composed of elements regarding the construction industry and the company's rules.

Table 1. Known parameters.

Variables	Meaning
I	Set for employees, including regular and irregular workers, $i \in I$
Pt	Set for irregular employees, such as foreign workers and sub-contractors, $pt \in Pt$
Ep	Set for regular employees, $ep \in Ep$
M	Set for managers, $m \in M$
P	Set for workplaces, $p \in P$
F	Set for floors excluding any other workplaces, $f \in F$
J	Set for jobs, $j \in J$
D	Set for days, $d \in D$
N	Set for weeks, $n \in N$
W_n	Set for days of the nth week
D_{sun}	Set for Sundays
D_{work}	Set for workdays
$cost_{id}$	Cost for regular employees i on day d (USD/day)
$hours_{i,d}$	Workhour for regular employees i on day d (hour)
$partcost_{pt,d}$	Cost for irregular employees pt on day (USD/day)
$parthours_{pt,d}$	Workhour for irregular employees pt on day d (hour)
$overcost_{i,d}$	Overtime work cost for irregular employees i on day d (USD/day)
$overhours_{i,d}$	Overtime workhour for irregular employees i on day d (hour)
min_d	Minimum number of needed workers on day d during daytime
$overmin_d$	Minimum number of needed workers on day d during nighttime
A_d	The average percent of irregular employees' absences on day d

3.2.2. Decision Variables

The decision variables in Table 2 for this mathematical model show the allocation of the employee to a specific workplace on a certain day.

Table 2. Decision Variables.

Variables	Meaning
$X_{i,j,p,d}$:	It becomes 1, if regular employee i is assigned to job j at workplace p on day d, otherwise 0
$Y_{i,j,p,d}$	It becomes 1, if irregular employee i is assigned to job j at workplace p on day d, otherwise 0
$R_{i,j,p,d}$	It becomes 1, if irregular employee i is assigned to job j at workplace p on day d after considering absence, otherwise 0
$O_{i,j,p,d}$	It becomes 1, if regular employee i is assigned to job j at workplace p on day d during nighttime, otherwise 0

3.3. Mathematical Model

Equation (1) is an objective function that minimizes the total labor cost. It consists of the sum of regular employees' total labor costs, the sum of irregular employees' total labor costs, and the sum of total overtime work costs:

$$\sum_{i\in I}\sum_{j\in J}\sum_{p\in P}\sum_{d\in D} Cost_{id}\times X_{ijpd}+\sum_{i\in Pt}\sum_{j\in J}\sum_{p\in P}\sum_{d\in D} Partcost_{id}\times R_{ijpd}+ \sum_{i\in I}\sum_{j\in J}\sum_{p\in P}\sum_{d\in D} Overcost_{id}\times O_{ijpd} \quad (1)$$

3.3.1. Constraints for Staff Scheduling during Daytime

Equations (2) and (3) represent the relationship between decision variables $R_{i,j,p,d}$ and $Y_{i,j,p,d}$. The actual number of irregular employees is decided by Equation (2) which multiplies the number of irregular workers following the schedules without absence by A_d. Equation (3) determines value of decision variable $R_{i,j,p,d}$. $R_{i,j,p,d}$ can be 1 when decision variable $Y_{i,j,p,d}$ is 1:

$$\sum_{i\in Pt}\sum_{j\in J}\sum_{p\in P} R_{ijpd}\le \sum_{i\in Pt}\sum_{j\in J}\sum_{p\in P} A_d * Y_{ijpd}, \forall d\in D_{work} \quad (2)$$

$$2*\sum_{j\in J}\sum_{p\in P} R_{ijpd}\le \sum_{j\in J}\sum_{p\in P} Y_{ijpd}+1, \forall d\in D_{work}, \forall i\in Pt \quad (3)$$

Equations (4) and (5) mean that each regular employee and irregular employee cannot exceed coming to work five days a week due to the 52-h workweek policy. Equations (6) and (7) ensure that all employees must work between 40 and 52 h a week due to the 52-h workweek policy:

$$\sum_{j\in J}\sum_{p\in P}\sum_{d\in W_n} X_{ijpd}\le 5, \forall i\in I, \forall n\in N \quad (4)$$

$$\sum_{j\in J}\sum_{p\in P}\sum_{d\in W_n} Y_{ijpd}\le 5, \forall i\in Pt, \forall n\in N \quad (5)$$

$$\sum_{j\in J}\sum_{p\in P}\sum_{d\in W_n} Parthours_{id}\times Y_{ijpd}\ge 40, \forall i\in Pt, \forall n\in N \sum_{j\in J}\sum_{p\in P}\sum_{d\in W_n} Parthours_{id}\times Y_{ijpd}\le 52, \forall i\in Pt, \forall n\in N \quad (6)$$

$$\sum_{j\in J}\sum_{p\in P}\sum_{d\in W_n} hours_{id}\times X_{ijpd}+\sum_{j\in J}\sum_{p\in P}\sum_{d\in W_n} Overhours_{id}\times O_{ijpd}\ge 40, \forall i\in I, \forall n\in N$$
$$\sum_{j\in J}\sum_{p\in P}\sum_{d\in W_n} hours_{id}\times X_{ijpd}+\sum_{j\in J}\sum_{p\in P}\sum_{d\in W_n} Overhours_{id}\times O_{ijpd}\le 52, \forall i\in I, \forall n\in N \quad (7)$$

Equations (8) and (9) determine the allocation of the employee to the workplace and job. Each employee should be assigned to a workplace to perform just only one job. Equation (10) shows that all employees have a day off on Sunday. Equation (11) indicates that the number of employees who come to work is more than the minimum number of employees that a company needs a day:

$$\sum_{j\in J}\sum_{p\in P} X_{ijpd}\le 1, \forall i\in I, \forall d\in D_{work} \quad (8)$$

$$\sum_{j\in J}\sum_{p\in P} Y_{ijpd}\le 1, \forall i\in Pt, \forall d\in D_{work} \quad (9)$$

$$\sum_{i\in I}\sum_{p\in P}\sum_{j\in J} X_{ijpd}+\sum_{i\in Pt}\sum_{p\in P}\sum_{j\in J} Y_{ijpd}+\sum_{i\in I}\sum_{p\in P}\sum_{j\in J} O_{ijpd}=0, \forall d\in D_{sun} \quad (10)$$

$$\sum_{i\in I}\sum_{j\in J}\sum_{p\in P} X_{ijpd}+\sum_{i\in Pt}\sum_{j\in J}\sum_{p\in P} R_{ijpd}\ge Min_d, \forall d\in D_{work} \quad (11)$$

Equations (12)~(14) determine the allocation for the workplace on the first floor and second floor. Equation (12) means that the necessary number of workers, including regular and irregular workers, is more than 15 on each floor at least per day. Equation (13) is about the assignment of a manager for supervision and one manager should work on each floor. Equation (14) means two workers doing Job 2 must be on one of two floors at least:

$$\sum_{i\in I}\sum_{j\in J} X_{ijpd}+\sum_{i\in Pt}\sum_{j\in J} R_{ijpd}\ge 15, \forall p\in F, \forall d\in D_{work} \quad (12)$$

$$\sum_{i\in M}\sum_{j\in J} X_{ijpd}\ge 1, \forall d\in D_{work}, \forall p\in F \quad (13)$$

$$\sum_{i \in I} \sum_{p \in F} X_{i2pd} = 2, \forall d \in D_{work} \tag{14}$$

Equations (15) and (16) determine the allocation to open storage. Equation (15) represents that more than two employees are needed for open storage. Equation (16) means that open storage does not need managers:

$$\sum_{i \in Ep} X_{i13d} + \sum_{i \in Pt} R_{i13d} \geq 2, \forall d \in D_{work} \tag{15}$$

$$\sum_{i \in M} \sum_{j \in J} X_{ij3d} = 0, \forall d \in D_{work} \tag{16}$$

Equations (17)~(19) are about the allocation to the office. Equation (17) shows that more than one manager should be assigned to the office. Equation (18) means that any other regular employees, besides managers, cannot work in the office. Equation (19) indicates that when managers are assigned to Job 2, they cannot work in the office and should work on one of the first and second floors at least:

$$\sum_{i \in M} \sum_{j \in J} X_{ij4d} \geq 1, \forall d \in D_{work} \tag{17}$$

$$\sum_{i \in Ep} \sum_{j \in J} X_{ij4d} = 0, \forall d \in D_{work} \tag{18}$$

$$\sum_{i \in I} X_{i24d} = 0, \forall d \in D_{work} \tag{19}$$

Equations (20) and (21) are related to the allocation of irregular employees. Equation (20) means that irregular employees cannot perform Job 2. Equation (21) shows that irregular employees also cannot work in the office. Equation (22) represents how many managers must work during the daytime:

$$\sum_{i \in Pt} \sum_{p \in F} R_{i2pd} = 0, \forall d \in D_{work} \tag{20}$$

$$\sum_{i \in Pt} \sum_{j \in J} R_{ij4d} = 0, \forall d \in D_{work} \tag{21}$$

$$\sum_{i \in M} \sum_{j \in J} \sum_{p \in P} X_{ijpd} = \sum_{i \in M} \sum_{j \in J} X_{ij1d} + X_{ij2d} + X_{ij4d}, \forall d \in D_{work} \tag{22}$$

3.3.2. Constraints for Staff Scheduling during Nighttime

Equations (23)~(32) are to determine the allocation of overtime work. Overtime work can be performed by only regular employees according to the rules of this company. In addition, only three types of first floor, second floor, and open storage are considered for the allocation. Equation (23) decides whether employees can work at nighttime or not. It is determined by the condition that only employees who perform daytime work can perform overtime work. Equation (24) represents that employees can work less than three times a week at night, owing to the 52-h workweek policy:

$$2 * \sum_{j \in J} \sum_{p \in P} O_{ijpd} \leq \sum_{j \in J} \sum_{p \in P} X_{ijpd} + 1, \forall i \in I, \forall d \in D_{work} \tag{23}$$

$$\sum_{j \in J} \sum_{p \in P} \sum_{d \in W_n} O_{ijpd} \leq 3, \forall i \in I, \forall n \in N \tag{24}$$

Equation (25) is about how many employees are needed for overtime work. Equation (26) refers to the allocation of each employee to jobs at nighttime. Equations (27) and (28) determine the allocation for the first floor and second floor. Equation (27) shows more than eight employees are needed for each floor. Equation (28) means that only one employee is assigned to the first floor or second floor to perform Job 2:

$$\sum_{i \in I} \sum_{j \in J} \sum_{p \in P} O_{ijpd} \geq overmin_d, \forall d \in D_{work} \tag{25}$$

$$\sum_{j \in J} \sum_{p \in P} O_{ijpd} \leq 1, \forall i \in I, \forall d \in D_{work} \tag{26}$$

$$\sum_{i\in I}\sum_{j\in J} O_{ijpd} \geq 8, \forall p \in F, \forall d \in D_{work} \tag{27}$$

$$\sum_{i\in I}\sum_{p\in F} O_{i2pd} = 1, \forall d \in D_{work} \tag{28}$$

Equations (29) and (30) determine the allocation at open storage. Equation (29) indicates that more than one employee should be assigned to open storage. Equation (30) shows that managers cannot be assigned at open storage. Equation (31) means that more than one manager must work at night after working in the daytime. Equation (32) means that no one is assigned to the office during overtime work:

$$\sum_{i\in E_p} O_{i13d} \geq 1, \forall d \in D_{work} \tag{29}$$

$$\sum_{i\in M}\sum_{j\in J} O_{ij3d} = 0, \forall d \in D_{work} \tag{30}$$

$$\sum_{i\in M}\sum_{j\in J}\sum_{p\in P} O_{ijpd} \geq 1, \forall d \in D_{work} \tag{31}$$

$$\sum_{i\in I}\sum_{j\in J} O_{ij4d} = 0, \forall d \in D_{work} \tag{32}$$

4. Solution Process

Linear programming used as a method in this paper can be solved by the simplex method. The simplex method can be utilized to solve linear programming [32]. The simplex method is based on forming the inverse of the basic matrix and updating the inverse [33]. That is, it is the repetition of searching for feasible solutions, calculating the value of the objective function, and comparing the derived value and the optimal value until finding the optimal solution. The process of the simplex is shown in Figure 2. First of all, all equations should be converted into standard equation form after inserting slack variables and create an initial simplex table. After this, find the entering variables. When solving the maximization problem, the variable with the largest absolute value of the coefficient becomes the entering variable. The next thing is to find leaving variable. To achieve this, the ration between entering variable and solution should be calculated. At this time, the variable with the lowest ration value becomes the leaving variable. After deciding on entering variable and leaving variable, the intersection point of the entering variable and leaving variable becomes the pivot element and all values of the row in the simplex table with the pivot element should be divided by the pivot element. The rest of the rows should be updated by using the new pivot row made previously. Lastly, if there is no new leaving variable, iterations terminate. If not, go back to the step of finding the entering variable. Various computer packages based on the simplex method were already developed. A developed mathematical model in the paper is also solved by one of the packages. The package used in the paper is CPLEX, which is the mathematical optimization software package. The version is 20.1.0. The darker parts in Figure 2 are processed by CPLEX.

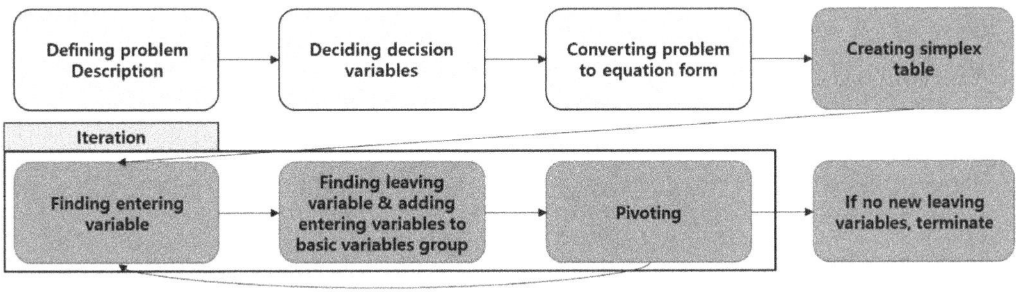

Figure 2. Solution process of the simplex method.

5. Numerical Experiment

5.1. Parameters Setting

The company has 40 regular employees, consisting of 36 normal regular workers and 4 managers. Furthermore, they have 22 irregular employees. The minimum necessary number of employees is at least 45 during the daytime. In addition, the number of workplaces is four spaces, namely the first floor, second floor, open storage, and the office. Other known parameters are set and presented in Table 3, except for known parameters regarding costs. The daily labor cost of each employee for both daytime and overtime is presented in Tables 4 and 5. The known parameters to create an optimal schedule for the numerical experiment are in Table 3.

Table 3. System parameters.

Parameters	Value	Parameters	Value
$hours_{i,d}$	8	min_d	45
$parthours_{pt,d}$	8	$overmin_d$	18
$overhours_{i,d}$	4	A_d	0.8

Table 4. Costs for all employees during daytime (unit: USD/day).

	Manager	Regular Employee	Irregular Employee
Weekday	USD 140	USD 120	USD 110
Weekend	USD 210	USD 180	USD 165

Table 5. Costs for all regular employees during nighttime (unit: USD/day).

	Manager	Regular Employee
Weekday	USD 105	USD 90
Weekend	USD 105	USD 90

The cost for all employees is in Table 4. Each employee is paid daily according to company policy. Regular employees are paid more than irregular employees. Managers are paid about USD 20 more than normal regular employees. The reason for the different levels in paycheck between weekdays and weekends is because of the implementation of a 52-h workweek policy that regards Saturday as an overtime workday. Table 5 represents the paycheck for regular employees at nighttime. The reason the company uses only regular employees at night is because of the rules of the company considered in the paper. They want to allow regular employees to earn money in the middle of a situation where most work is gradually conducted by irregular employees due to the high labor cost of regular employees.

5.2. Result

5.2.1. Before Applying a Mathematical Model

This company did not have a staff schedule before. Due to this, they suffered from inefficient management of human resources. A staff schedule in Figure 3 is made based on the record of employee working patterns. Before the explanation of Figure 3, how to see a staff schedule is explained. In Figure 3, the row number means employees and the column number represents days. The numbers that are the darkest gray in row number stand for managers. The number in each cell indicates the assigned workplace and the cells with the diagonal pattern are Job 2, and without the diagonal pattern are Job 1. When it comes to jobs, Job 1 means normal work and Job 2 is equipment supervisor who takes responsibility for everything regarding equipment. If looking at Figure 3, more employees sometimes came to work than the number of employees a company needs, and fewer employees sometimes came to work than the number of employees a company needs. An example of the former one is Day 3, and the latter is Day 1. Especially, when looking at Day 24, placing enough workforce on the second floor failed. Originally, more than 15 employees should be assigned on each floor during the daytime. However, only 12 employees were assigned that day. This directly shows inefficient human resource management. Moreover, about 46.6 employees came to work on average, which means it was a bigger number than the daily number of employees (45) that a company needs. This causes larger labor costs than when 45 employees come to work, on average.

5.2.2. After Applying a Mathematical Model

Unlike a staff schedule before applying a mathematical model, a derived staff schedule is more efficient. As shown in Figure 4, all constraints regarding work in the daytime are satisfied. For example, 45 employees are scheduled to work if looking at Day 1. In addition, job assignments are met as well. Continuing looking at Day 1, more than 15 employees are assigned on each floor and two of the employees conduct Job 2 as equipment supervisors. Furthermore, more than one manager is assigned on each floor to supervise other regular and irregular employees as well. Moreover, over two of the employees work at open storage and a manager works in an office. That is, the failure of employees' assignments caused by a manager's random employee assignment does not happen. Other days, as well as Day 1 meet all constraints for job assignments. Along with this, the 52-h workweek policy is well applied in the mathematical model as the result shows. There are no employees who come to work for more than five days a week. All employees have a day off on Sunday.

Furthermore, the purpose of the developed mathematical model is to minimize the total labor cost of regular and irregular employees. This means that the result in the numerical experiment is for a company that has a priority of saving the total labor cost. Therefore, if looking at the result in Figure 4, as many irregular employees as possible are scheduled on each workday even though the average percent of irregular employee absence is considered. It is more advantageous for a company to minimize the total labor costs by using as many irregular employees as possible out of 22 irregular employees due to relatively low labor costs. However, it is seen that as many irregular employees as possible are not used. This is because there are rules on conducting jobs for a company and there are jobs that can be conducted by regular employees. A company allocates overtime work by assigning only regular employees to jobs for consideration for regular employees as well. To conduct overtime work, regular employees should work during the daytime. Thus, the result in Figure 4 is derived, even though a company has enough irregular employees that can cover more jobs.

Index for employees	Days for working 1	2	3	4	5	6	7	8	9	10	11	12	13	14	15	16	17	18	19	20	21	22	23	24	25	26	27	28
1	1	2	1	1		2		2	2	1	4	4			1	2	1	4	1			1	1	2	2	4		
2	1	1	4	4	1			1	2	4	1		2		4	2	1		1	1		2	2		4	1	1	
3	4	2	1	2	1			4	1	2	2	1			1	4	4	2		2		4	1	4	2	2		
4	2	4	2		4	4			4	2	2	1	4			1	1	4	4	4		1	4	1	1		4	
5	2	1		2	2	2		2	3	1	1	3			1	2	1	2	3			1	1	4		2	2	
6		1	1	3	2			1	2		2	1	2		2	2	3	1	1			1	2	1	2		2	
7	3	2	2		1	1		2		2	1	2	1			1	2	2	3	1		2	1	2	1		2	
8		1	2	1	1	1		2	1	1	2	1	2		1	1	2	2	1			2	2	2	1	1	1	
9	2		2	3	1	1		2	1	2	1	2			2	2	1	2	1			3	2	1	2		2	
10	1		3	1	1	2		3	1	2	1	2	1		3	1	1	1	2			1	2		2	2	1	
11	1		1	1	1	2		2	2	1	3		3		1		2	2	2	3		2	1	1	3		2	
12	2	2	1		1	2		2	1	1	1	2			1	2		1	1	2			1	2	1	1	3	
13	2	1	1		1	3		2	2	1	2		1		2		1	1	2	2		2	3		1	2	1	
14		2	3	2	2	2		1	1	2		1	1		2	1	2		1	3		2		1	1	2	1	
15	1	2	1	1	2			2		1	1	2	2		2	2	3	2		1		1	2		2	3	1	
16	1	2	1	3		1		2	1	2	2		1		1	3	1		1	2		2	2	1	1		2	
17	1	2		2	1	2			2	3	2	1	2			2	1	2	2	1		1		2	1	2	1	
18		2	2	1	2	1		1	2	1		2	1		1	2		1	2	2		2	1		1	1	2	
19	1	2	2	1	2			1	1		2	1	3		2	1	2		1	1			1	1	2	2	2	
20	3	2	2		2	1		1	1	2	1	2			1	1		2	1	2		2		1	2	2	1	
21	2		1	1	1	2		1	2	1		1	1			2	1	3	1	2		2	1	3		1	2	
22		1	1	2		2		3		2	2		2		2	1	1		2	1		1	2	1		1	2	
23			2	1	1	2		2	1	2		2	1		2	2		2	1	1			2	2	1	1	2	
24	1	3	3	1		2				1	2		1		1		2	1	1	2		1		1	2	2	1	
25	2		1	1	1	2		3	1		2	1	2		2	3			2	1		2	1		2	1	2	
26	1	1		2	2	1		1	2	1		2	1		2	1		2	3	2		1		1	1	2	1	
27	2	2	1	2		1		1	2	1		3				1	2	1	2	2		2	2		2	1	2	
28	1	2	1	1	1				2	3	1	2	2		1		1	2	1	1			3	1	1	2	1	
29	2	1	1		2	3		1		2	2	1	1		1	2		2	1	1		3	2	2	1		3	
30	2	1	2	1	1			2	1	2	1	2				2	1	3	2	1		1	2	1	2		3	
31	2	1	2		2	1		2	3	2		1	2		3	1	2		2	2		2	2	1	1		1	
32	2	1	1	1		2		1		1	1	1	1			1	2	1	1	2			1	3	1	1	2	
33	2	1	2		1	2		1	1	2		1	1		2		2	1	1	2		1	1	2		2	1	
34		1	2	2		1		1	1	2	1	2	2		1	1		2	2	1		3	2	1	2		2	
35	2	1	1	1	1			1	2	1	2		1		2	2		3	1	1		2	1		2	1	1	
36	1	2	1	1	1			1	1	2	1	1			2		2	1	2	1		2	2	1	1		2	
37	2	1	2	1		2		2		2	3	2	1		1	2	2		1	2		1		1	3	1	2	
38	1		1	2	2	1		3	2	1		2	1			2	1	1	2	3		2	1	2		2	2	
39	2		1	2	1	2		1	2	1	2	1			1	1		2	2	2		2	2		1	2	1	
40	2		2	1	2	2			2	2	2	1	2			1	1	1	2	1		1	2		1	3	2	
41	1		1	1		2		2	1	2	1		2		1		3	1	2			1		1	2		1	
42	1	2			1	1				1	1		3			2	1		1	2			2	1		1	2	
43		1	2		2			2	2		1		2		2	1			2			1	2		1	2		
44	2			2	1	1		1		2	2	2			1	3		2		2		2		1	2	2		
45				1	3	1		2		1		1	2		2			1	3	1			2		1	1	1	
46	1	1	2			1			3	3		1	1			1	2		2	2			1	1		2	1	
47	2			2	3				2		2		3		3	1	2	1				1	2			1		
48		2	1	1		2		1		1		1	1		1	2			1	2		3		1	2		1	
49		1	1		2	1		1	1	1	2				2			1	1				1		1	2	2	
50	2	2		1					1	2			1		1		1		1			2	2		1		1	
51		1	1	3		1		1		1	1	3	1		1	1		2		1		2		1	1	1		
52			1	1	2					2		2	1			2			2	1			1			2	2	
53		2		1	1	1		1	1		1		2			2		1		1			3	1	1	1		
54	1		1	1		2			1	2	2	2	3		3		2		1			1	1				2	
55		1	2		1	3				2		1	1			1		1	2			2	3	1	1			
56	1	2	1					2			2		1		1	1	2		2			1		2		1	1	
57		2	1	2	2			1		1	2	2				2		1	1			2	2	1			2	
58		1	2	1		2			2	1	1		1		1		1			2		2			1	2		
59	2		1	1		1				2		3	2				1	2					3	2		1	2	
60	1	1	1	2					1	3		2	1		1		2	3		1		1		2	2			
61		2	1			2				2		1	1				1		2				1	1		1	2	
62			2	2	1	1		2	1		1	2			1		3		1	1		2	1	3	2	2		

Positions of employees	Types of Jobs	Workplaces			
Manager	Job 1	1	1st Floor	3	Open storage
Regular workers	Job 2	2	2nd Floor	4	Office
Irregular workers					

Figure 3. A staff schedule before applying a mathematical model.

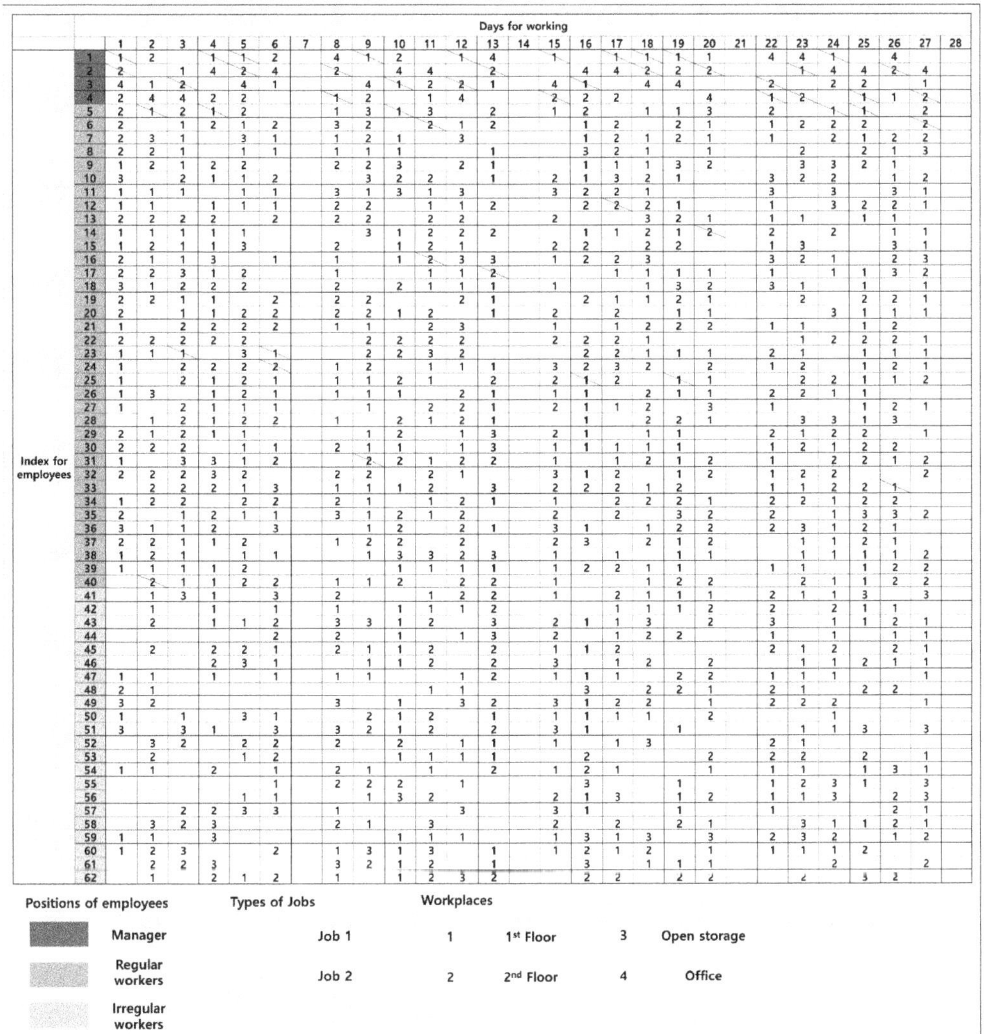

Figure 4. Optimal staff schedule during daytime.

Comparing a staff schedule before and after applying a mathematical model, the following things can be found. First, there is a difference in the number of employees who come to work per day on average. Consequently, about 1.6 employees come to work less than before after applying a mathematical model every day. Second, a developed mathematical model prevents situations where employees come to work more or less than the number of employees a company needs a day. This can aid in the improvement of human resource management. Third, a company can save total labor costs even though the company has the same number of employees as before. It was USD 143,525 before applying a mathematical model and it is USD 138,335 after applying a mathematical model. That is, a company can save a total labor cost of USD 5190. Lastly, the different employee work pattern is found due to consideration of the change in labor policy. Some employees came to work more than 6 days a week before applying a developed model. However, it is constrained by a mathematical model at the moment because a company should follow the change of labor policy, which is each employee should work less than 5 days a week.

The number of days regular employees come to work is constrained after applying a mathematical model due to the change in labor policy and high labor costs. Some regular employees come to work 4 days a week. This could be shown not to allow them to work more. However, it indirectly proved that a company that did not efficiently manage human resources has several employees more than the number they need to have. This can be an opportunity to rethink and optimize the number of employees a company needs to possess.

According to Figure 5, the rules relating to overtime work are also well-considered. First, nobody is assigned to the office. Second, only one manager is assigned to supervise regular employees on one of the two floors. For instance, one manager of four managers is assigned on the first floor to play the role of supervisor during overtime work if looking at Day 1. Third, an employee who performs as equipment supervisor is assigned to one of two floors. Lastly, one employee is also allocated to open storage at least. To sum up, a staff schedule at daytime and nighttime that satisfies constraints is derived considering the total labor cost.

5.3. Evaluation of a Derived Staff Schedule

This paper provides a conservative and deterministic staff schedule by using a mathematical model that considers the average percent of irregular employees' absences, which is an uncertain characteristic. Even though irregular employee absence is stochastic, the reason this paper derives a deterministic staff schedule is that it is impossible to predict if irregular employees come to work or do not come to work perfectly only based on the probability of each irregular employee's absence. That is, even the result derived from the stochastic model cannot guarantee that each irregular employee follows a staff schedule without absences. However, the reason to perform the simulation after deriving a deterministic staff schedule is that it is meaningful in that it can give the result that can help managers respond to the irregular employee's absence. Figure 6 is the result of the simulation. Row numbers from 41 to 62 mean irregular employees and column numbers mean days of work. In addition, O means that irregular employees come to work, and X means that irregular employees do not come to work. The result shows whether each irregular employee follows their schedule when considering each employee's absence percent.

If looking at Table 6 below, the actual percent of each irregular employee's absence is different from the expected percent of each employee's absence. In other words, even though the average percent of an irregular employee's absence is considered as the stochastic characteristic through the simulation, it cannot ensure that managers have a staff schedule that can predict the absences of irregular employees perfectly. Furthermore, as shown in Figure 6, the lacking number of irregular employees can be confirmed. If managers prepare a conservative measure, they will assign more irregular employees on the days when some irregular employees are expected to not come to work. However, preparing additional irregular employees makes extra labor costs for a construction company. Nevertheless, it is more important to finish work by assigning extra irregular employees within due time. Saving labor costs is the next thing to do. Moreover, according to the days of absence shown in Table 6, the number of days when each irregular employee does not come to work can be confirmed. For example, the 44th irregular employee does not come to work 7 days out of 13 days. This irregular employee has an actual percent of absence of 53.8%. It is 23.8% higher than an expected percent of absence of 30%. This type of employee is the main cause to make a company fail to follow a staff schedule and assign enough workforce to jobs. This finding can be an opportunity to help a manager rethink the recruitment of other irregular employees. To sum up, the reason this paper derives a conservative and deterministic staff schedule and performs the simulation about it is that it can contribute to presenting the systematic procedure for irregular employee absence. This procedure could aid managers in preparing precautious measures for a staff schedule while considering the stochastic characteristics of irregular employee absence.

		Days for working																											
		1	2	3	4	5	6	7	8	9	10	11	12	13	14	15	16	17	18	19	20	21	22	23	24	25	26	27	28
	1						1						2	2					1		2				2		1		
	2			1	2						1	2																	
	3	2														2				1			1			1			
	4		1			1			2	1							1	2						1				1	
	5		1	1	2				1	2				2			1		1	1			2		1	2			
	6	2				3	2		1				2	1			3			2	1		2		2			2	
	7	2	1				2			1	2						2	1		2			2				1	2	
	8	3				2	2			1	2			1				2	1		2					2	2	1	
	9	2		1		2				2	1		1				2		2		2				3	1	1		
	10	1			1		3			2	1	2				2			1	1				1	2		1		
	11		2	2			2				1					1		1	2				2		2		3		
	12	1	2		3				3				2	2				1	2	2					1		2	2	
	13		2		1		1		2			3							2	1			2				2		
	14		2		2	2				3	1	1					2	1		3			2		1			1	
	15		3	2		2			1		2	2				3	2		1				1					3	
	16		1	3			2		1			3		2		1			1				1		1		1		
	17			1	1	2						2	2	1					2	2	1				1		1	2	
	18		1		2				2			1		2		2					1			2		2			
	19	1			1		1		2	2				1			1	2		1				2		1		1	
Index for regular employees	20	1		1	1				2		2			1				3		1	2					2	2	1	
	21			3	1	1			1	1		1						1	1		1		3	2		1			
	22	2	2	1							1		1				2	3	2					1	2		2		
	23	1		1						2		2	3					2	2		2			1		1		2	
	24	1				1	1		1			1	2			1			2		1			2			2	1	
	25			1	2		2		1		2			3			1				3					2	1	2	
	26	1			1		2			1			1	2		1	1				2		1	3					
	27	1				1	3					1	2	1		1	2	2					2			2		2	
	28		1		1		1		1		2		3				2				1			2		1	1		
	29		1		1	1					1		1			2	2			1				1	1			1	
	30	2		2		2			2	2			1			2	1			2			1	1	1				
	31	2				1	1				2		1	2		2		1					2		1			3	
	32	2	2						2	2		2					2	2		2			1	2					
	33					3				1		1		2		2		2		1				2	2	2			
	34			2		1				2		2	1			1		1		2			1	1		2			
	35				2	1	2				1	1	1			1		2			2				1		2	1	
	36		2	2			1			3	2			2		1				2	1		2	1		2			
	37		2	2	2				2		3		2				1		3		1			2	2	1			
	38		1			2	1			1	2	2				2				3	2			2		3	2		
	39	2		2	2							1	2	1			1	1	1				1				3		
	40		2	2		2			2	1				1		1			1		2				2	1		2	

Positions of employees: Manager; Regular workers

Types of Jobs: Job 1; Job 2

Workplaces: 1 1st Floor; 2 2nd Floor; 3 Open storage

Figure 5. Optimal schedule of regular employees during overtime.

			Day for working																											
		Percent of absence	1	2	3	4	5	6	7	8	9	10	11	12	13	14	15	16	17	18	19	20	21	22	23	24	25	26	27	28
	41	20%		O	O	O		O		O			O	O	O		O		O	O	O	O		O	O	O	O		O	
	42	20%		O		O		O		O		O	O	O	O				O	O	X	O		O		X	O	O		
	43	15%		O		O	O	O		O	O	O	O		X		O	O	O	O		O		O		O	O	O	O	
	44	30%						X		X		O		X	O		O		X	O	X			O		X		O	X	
	45	25%		O		O	O	O		X	O	O	O		O		O	O	X					O	O	O		O	X	
	46	20%				O	O	X			O	O	O		O		O		X	O		O			O	X	O	O	O	
	47	20%	O	O		O		O		X	O			O	O		O	O	O		O	O		O	O	O			X	
	48	30%	O	X									X	X				O		O	X	X		O	O		O	O		
	49	15%	O	O						O		O		O	O		O	O	O	O		O		O	O	O			O	
	50	20%	O		O		O	O			O	O	O		X		O	O	O	O		O				O				
Index for irregular employees	51	20%	O		O	O		O		X	O	X	O		O		O	O			O				O	O	O		X	
	52	20%		O	O		O	O		O		O		O	O		O		O	O				O	O					
	53	10%		O			O	O				O	O	O	O			O				O		O	O		O		O	
	54	10%	O	O		O		O		O	O		O		O		O	O	O			O		O	O		O	O	O	
	55	25%						O		X	O	X		O				O			O			O	O	O	O		X	
	56	15%					O	O			O	O	O				O	O	O		O	O		O	O	O		O	O	
	57	25%			O	O	O	O		O				O			O	O			O			O				O	O	
	58	10%		O	O	O				O	O		O				O		X		O	O			O	O	O	O	O	
	59	20%	O	O		O						X	O	O			O	O	O	O		O		O	O	O		O	O	
	60	20%	O	O	O			O		O	O	O	O		O		O	O	X	O		O		O	O	O	O			
	61	25%		O	O	O				O	O	X	O		X			O		O	O	X				O			O	
	62	15%		O		O	O	O		O		O	O	O	O			O	O		X	O			O		O	O		
		No. of lacking employees	0	1	0	0	0	2		5	0	4	1	2	3		0	0	5	0	4	2		0	0	3	0	0	5	

Figure 6. Result of simulation for evaluation of a staff schedule.

Table 6. Information on each irregular employee's work and absence.

Index of Irregular Employees	Expected Percent of Absence	No. of Scheduled Workdays	No. of Absence Days	Days of Absence	Actual Percent of Absence
41	20%	18	0	-	0%
42	20%	16	2	19, 24	12.5%
43	15%	19	1	13	5.3%
44	30%	13	7	6, 8, 12, 17, 19, 24, 27	53.8%
45	25%	17	3	8, 17, 27	17.6%
46	20%	16	3	6, 17, 24	18.6%
47	20%	17	2	8, 27	11.8%
48	30%	12	5	2, 11, 12 19, 20	41.7%
49	15%	15	0	-	0%
50	20%	14	1	13	7.1%
51	20%	16	3	8, 10, 27	18.6%
52	20%	13	0	-	0%
53	10%	13	0	-	0%
54	10%	17	0	-	0%
55	25%	12	3	8, 10, 27	25%
56	15%	15	0	-	0%
57	25%	12	0	-	0%
58	10%	15	1	17	6.7%
59	20%	16	1	11	6.3%
60	20%	18	1	17	5.6%
61	25%	14	3	10, 13, 20	21.4%
62	15%	16	1	19	6.3%

5.4. Sensitivity Analysis

In this mathematical model, the average percent of irregular employee absence is one of the major factors that change the result of the total labor cost and staff schedules. However, the irregular employee absence is unpredictable due to its inherently uncertain nature. Therefore, to observe the change in the total labor cost and staff schedules, the average percent of an irregular employee's absence is examined with a variety of values. The average percent of an irregular employee's absence is set at 100%, 95%, 90%, 85%, 80%, 75%, 70%, 65% and under 60%. By performing sensitivity analysis with these values above, many significant meanings are discovered. As represented in Table 7, total labor costs, the average percent of regular employee attendance, and the average percent of irregular employee attendance differ depending on the average percent of irregular employee's absence. The average percent of regular employee attendance tends to be increased if the average percent of irregular employee absences is decreased. In other words, this is the situation where more regular employees come to work to replace low-paid irregular employees who are absent. This causes a rise in total labor cost because regular employees are paid more than irregular employees. However, 40 regular employees cannot cover all irregular employees who do not come to work when the average percent of irregular employee absence is under 60% as presented in Table 7. Thus, it is necessary that the company either take measures to prevent the average percent of irregular employee absence from becoming too low, or to increase the number of regular employees to derive a staff schedule that can satisfy the necessary workload.

Table 7. Changes in the percent of regular and irregular employees and total cost.

Attendance Rate of Irregular Employees	The Average Percent of Working Regular Employees	The Average Percent of Working Irregular Employees	Total Cost (USD)
100%	63.5%	36.5%	176,860
95%	64.6%	35.4%	177,035
90%	66%	34%	177,205
85%	67.7%	32.3%	177,405
80%	69.1%	30.9%	177,575
75%	70.8%	29.2%	177,770
70%	72.1%	27.9%	177,945
65%	73.8%	26.2%	178,190
Under 60%		Infeasible	

The number of irregular employees expected to come to work, and the number of irregular employees coming to work are different depending on the average percent of irregular employee absence every month in Figure 7. This is because of the influence of the condition that the minimum necessary number of regular employees should come to work to guarantee stability for completing the workload. For this reason, the difference between the number of irregular employees expected to come to work, and the number of irregular employees coming to work is inclined to reduce when the average percent of irregular employee absence is decreased due to an increase in the number of regular employees who cover irregular employees. It implies that gradually decreasing the number of irregular employees while coming up with ideas to encourage them not to be absent is better to keep up stability and reinforce the job efficiency when the necessary number of regular employees is fixed. As a result, given the stability of staff schedules, it is thought that reasonable schedules could be made when the average percent of irregular employee absence is 75%, although the total cost increases a little compared to 80%.

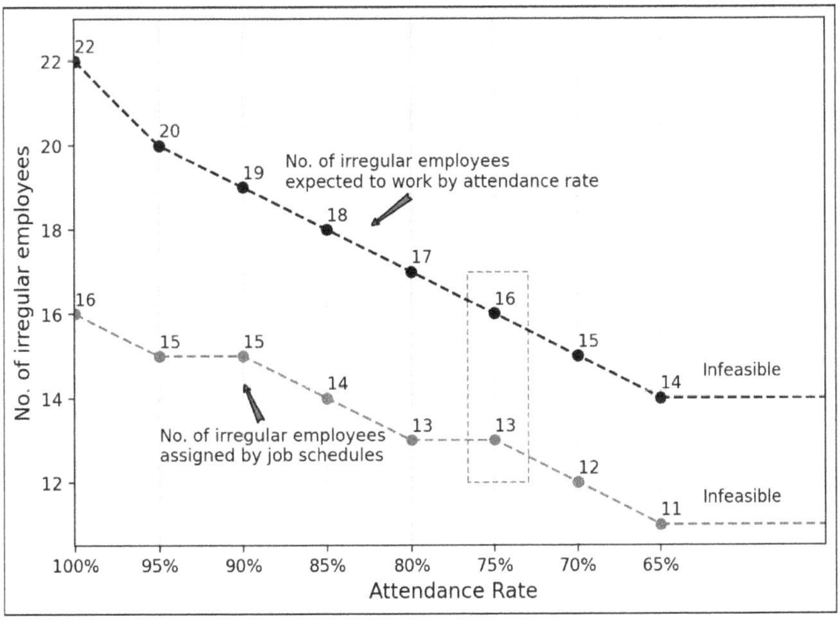

Figure 7. The difference between an expected number and the assigned number of irregular employees depending on attendance rate (the percent of irregular employees' absences).

As mentioned ahead, the average percent of regular employee attendance is increased as the average percent of irregular employee absence is decreased. This results in increasing stability in performing the job. On the other hand, the total labor cost keeps moving up, since the cost of regular employees is normally higher than the cost of irregular employees. In other words, labor costs can be decreased by increasing the number of irregular employees, and the stability of staff schedules can be increased by decreasing the number of irregular employees. Therefore, it is important to make staff schedules considering factors such as labor costs and stability of staff schedules after taking the conditions and situations of a construction company without being biased as one factor. Thus, this research is expected to help a manager with decision-making for a staff schedule by providing various proactive cases depending on the change of the average percent of irregular employee absence through sensitivity analysis in the numerical experiment.

6. Conclusions

6.1. Contributions

This study proposes a staff scheduling strategy to minimize total labor costs considering the actual features of the Korean construction industry, such as an increase in labor costs and the change in labor policy. The contributions of this paper are as follows. First, this paper suggests a mathematical model that can save the total labor cost and aid the management of human resources. As shown in the numerical experiment, a mathematical model decreases the unnecessary number of employees from about 46.6 to 45 a day on average. This can allow a company to have an opportunity to save labor costs and rethink and optimize the number of employees they should have. Second, the practicality to apply the developed mathematical model to other industries is proven. This study considers an actual construction company suffering from the problem of no-show, derived from the situation that the company increases irregular employees to handle workforce shortage due to the rise of labor costs and a new labor policy in Korea. Through the numerical experiment with system parameters derived from human resources, types of jobs, workplaces, and the rules of work of a company, the applicability of the developed mathematical model to a company is proved in practice. Therefore, this paper would help conduct research on staff scheduling for the actual company as one of the basic references. Third, the change in labor policy is considered when developing a mathematical model. The optimal solution for staff scheduling by using this mathematical model is derived in the situation of workforce availability reduction compared to the same number of employees due to the influence of changed labor policy. In other words, this paper could play a role as a guide for staff scheduling that must consider the change of labor policy in the future in Korea. Lastly, this paper assists the manager of a company with decision-making for staff schedules by providing various proactive cases while considering the sudden absence of employees. Despite the difficulty in considering unpredictable employee absence due to the inherently uncertain nature of irregular employees, additional numerical experiments, which are the simulation and sensitivity analysis, are performed in the paper. The result of the simulation predicts what expectedly happens when assuming the application of a deterministic staff schedule in practice. In particular, the predictive information on how many irregular employees would not come to work is given. It is impossible to guarantee that they would follow staff schedules perfectly in the real world. Nevertheless, the reason to perform the simulation is to allow managers to have a systematic procedure to respond to the absence of irregular employees, not to provide a staff schedule that makes all irregular employees follow the staff schedule. Moreover, through this sensitivity analysis with the change of the average percent of absence, this paper observes the influence of irregular employee absence on the change of the value of the objective function and staff schedule. Through the additional numerical experiments, various proactive cases are provided by considering the absence of irregular employees. This can help managers prepare the precautious measures to respond to the stochastic irregular employee's absence. Thus, it is expected to contribute to helping the manager with decision-making for staff schedules.

6.2. Future Research

This paper could be expanded to further staff scheduling research that considers shifts. This paper does not consider shifts due to no shifts in the construction industry in general. However, many studies about staff scheduling consider shifts. Thus, if the developed mathematical model in this paper is improved considering the characteristics of shifts, it is expected that the developed mathematical model could be applied to relatively more and various industries. Furthermore, many objective functions can be considered to gain an optimal solution for staff scheduling. The current objective function is to minimize labor costs. This means that this staff scheduling strategy considers a company more than employees, despite considering the policy called the 52-h workweek policy. However, it seems necessary to create the objective function for a mathematical model that considers employees as well as the company in the future, because employees' satisfaction with job assignments plays a crucial role in an organization's success [34]. Moreover, research on figuring out the factors that influence the sincerity of irregular employees is needed in terms of their welfare. Conducting this research can help make a proper working environment. In conclusion, various factors regarding both company and employees in various ways should be considered to derive a good solution when staff scheduling problems are handled.

Author Contributions: Conceptualization, Y.D.K.; methodology, C.H.P.; software, C.H.P.; validation, Y.D.K., C.H.P.; formal analysis, C.H.P.; investigation, C.H.P.; resources, Y.D.K.; data curation, C.H.P.; writing—original draft preparation, C.H.P.; writing—review and editing, Y.D.K.; visualization, C.H.P.; supervision, Y.D.K.; project administration, Y.D.K. All authors have read and agreed to the published version of the manuscript.

Funding: This research received no external funding.

Institutional Review Board Statement: Not applicable.

Informed Consent Statement: Not applicable.

Data Availability Statement: Not applicable.

Conflicts of Interest: The authors declare no conflict of interest.

References

1. Naoum, S.G. Factors influencing labor productivity on construction sites. *Int. J. Product. Perform. Manag.* **2016**, *65*, 401–421. [CrossRef]
2. Choi, D.S.; Le, H.; Lee, Y.D. The relationship between Korean construction industry and GDP in economic development process. *Korean J. Constr. Eng. Manag.* **2013**, *14*, 70–77.
3. Ministry of Employment and Labor. Available online: http://www.moel.go.kr/policy/policyinfo/young/bbsView.do;jsessionid=eCpFT7AfMl1DRaodwQO5ZP7oPDyz3nX1h1E3aRaK8USeBAL84QS8f1LxSw9EZH5W.moel_was_outside_servlet_www1?bbs_seq=20200300901 (accessed on 12 July 2022).
4. Ministry of Employment and Labor. Available online: http://www.moel.go.kr/policy/policydata/view.do?bbs_seq=20191200830 (accessed on 12 July 2022).
5. Ho, H.; Kuvaas, B. Human resource management systems, employee well-being, and firm performance from the mutual gains and critical perspectives: The well-being paradox. *Hum. Resour. Manag.* **2020**, *59*, 235–253. [CrossRef]
6. Kang, S.Y.; Min, S.; Won, D.; Kang, Y.J.; Kim, S. Suggestion of an improved evaluation method of construction companies' industrial accident prevention activities in south korea. *Int. J. Environ. Res. Public Health* **2021**, *18*, 8442. [CrossRef] [PubMed]
7. Kim, S.; Chang, S.; Castro-Lacouture, D. Dynamic modeling for analyzing impacts of skilled labor shortage on construction project management. *J. Manag. Eng.* **2018**, *36*, 04019035. [CrossRef]
8. Korkmaz, S.; Park, D.J. Comparison of safety perception between foreign and local workers in the construction industry in Republic of Korea. *Saf. Health Work* **2018**, *9*, 53–58. [CrossRef]
9. Newsis. Available online: https://mobile.newsis.com/view.html?ar_id=NISX20181211_0000499414#_enliple (accessed on 11 July 2022).
10. Construction & Economy Research Institute of Korea. Available online: http://www.cerik.re.kr/report/issue/detail/2060 (accessed on 12 July 2022).
11. Hamid, A.R.A.; Singh, B.S.B.J.; Mazlan, M.S. The construction labour shortage in Johor Bahru, Malaysia. *Int. J. Eng. Res. Technol.* **2013**, *2*, 508–512.
12. Ward, K.; Grimshaw, D.; Rubery, J.; Beynon, H. Dilemmas in the management of temporary work agency staff. *Hum. Resour. Manag. J.* **2001**, *11*, 3–21. [CrossRef]

13. Cheah, C.Y.; Chew, D.A. Dynamics of strategic management in the Chinese construction industry. *Manag. Decis.* **2005**, *43*, 551–567. [CrossRef]
14. Becker, T. A decomposition heuristic for rotational workforce scheduling. *J. Sched.* **2020**, *23*, 539–554. [CrossRef]
15. Edie, L.C. Traffic delays at toll booths. *J. Oper. Res. Soc.* **1954**, *2*, 107–138. [CrossRef]
16. Van den Bergh, J.; Beliën, J.; De Bruecker, P.; Demeulemeester, E.; De Boeck, L. Personnel scheduling: A literature review. *Eur. J. Oper. Res.* **2013**, *226*, 367–385. [CrossRef]
17. Ganguly, A.; Nandi, S. Using statistical forecasting to optimize staff scheduling in healthcare organizations. *J. Health Manag.* **2016**, *18*, 172–181. [CrossRef]
18. Maenhout, B.; Vanhoucke, M. An integrated nurse staffing and scheduling analysis for longer-term nursing staff allocation problems. *Omega* **2013**, *41*, 485–499. [CrossRef]
19. Ásgeirsson, E.I. Bridging the gap between self-schedules and feasible schedules in staff scheduling. *Ann. Oper. Res.* **2014**, *218*, 51–58. [CrossRef]
20. Memon, A.H.; Zin, R.M. Resource-driven scheduling implementation in Malaysian construction industry. *Int. J. Sustain. Constr. Eng. Technol.* **2010**, *1*, 77–90.
21. Al-Rawi, O.Y.M.; Mukherjee, T. Application of linear programming in optimizing labour scheduling. *J. Math. Financ.* **2019**, *9*, 272–285. [CrossRef]
22. Rocha, M.; Oliveira, J.F.; Carravilla, M.A. Cyclic staff scheduling: Optimization models for some real-life problems. *J. Sched.* **2013**, *16*, 231–242. [CrossRef]
23. Kaya, B.Y.; Dağdeviren, M. A Human Resources Management Application for Hospitality Management in Turkey. *Int. J. Bus. Manag. Stud.* **2018**, *10*, 39–50.
24. Azadeh, A.; Farahani, M.H.; Eivazy, H.; Nazari-Shirkouhi, S.; Asadipour, G. A hybrid meta-heuristic algorithm for optimization of crew scheduling. *Appl. Soft Comput.* **2013**, *13*, 158–164. [CrossRef]
25. Asensio-Cuesta, S.; Diego-Mas, J.A.; Canós-Darós, L.; Andrés-Romano, C. A genetic algorithm for the design of job rotation schedules considering ergonomic and competence criteria. *Int. J. Adv. Manuf. Technol.* **2012**, *60*, 1161–1174. [CrossRef]
26. Ruiz-Torres, A.J.; Ablanedo-Rosas, J.H.; Mukhopadhyay, S.; Paletta, G. Scheduling workers: A multi-criteria model considering their satisfaction. *Comput. Ind. Eng.* **2019**, *128*, 747–754. [CrossRef]
27. Stolletz, R.; Brunner, J.O. Fair optimization of fortnightly physician schedules with flexible shifts. *Eur. J. Oper. Res.* **2012**, *219*, 622–629. [CrossRef]
28. Shuib, A.; Kamarudin, F.I. Solving shift scheduling problem with days-off preference for power station workers using binary integer goal programming model. *Ann. Oper. Res.* **2019**, *272*, 355–372. [CrossRef]
29. Becker, T.; Steenweg, P.M.; Werners, B. Cyclic shift scheduling with on-call duties for emergency medical services. *Health Care Manag. Sci.* **2019**, *22*, 676–690. [CrossRef] [PubMed]
30. Ingels, J.; Maenhout, B. Employee substitutability as a tool to improve the robustness in personnel scheduling. *OR Spectr.* **2017**, *39*, 623–658. [CrossRef]
31. Steenweg, P.M.; Schacht, M.; Werners, B. Evaluating shift patterns considering heterogeneous skills and uncertain workforce availability. *J. Decis. Syst.* **2021**, *30*, 27–49. [CrossRef]
32. Nash, J.C. The (Dantzig) simplex method for linear programming. *Comput. Sci. Eng.* **2000**, *2*, 29–31. [CrossRef]
33. Bartels, R.H.; Golub, G.H. The simplex method of linear programming using LU decomposition. *Commun. ACM* **1969**, *12*, 266–268. [CrossRef]
34. Lorber, M.; Skela Savič, B. Job satisfaction of nurses and identifying factors of job satisfaction in Slovenian Hospitals. *Croat. Med. J.* **2012**, *53*, 263–270. [CrossRef]

algorithms

MDPI

Article

A Static Assignment Algorithm of Uniform Jobs to Workers in a User-PC Computing System Using Simultaneous Linear Equations

Xudong Zhou [1], Nobuo Funabiki [1,*], Hein Htet [1], Ariel Kamoyedji [1], Irin Tri Anggraini [1], Yuanzhi Huo [1] and Yan Watequlis Syaifudin [2]

1 Graduate School of Natural Science and Technology, Okayama University, Okayama 700-8530, Japan
2 Information Technology Department, State Polytechnic of Malang, Malang 65141, Indonesia
* Correspondence: funabiki@okayama-u.ac.jp

Abstract: Currently, the *User-PC computingsystem (UPC)* has been studied as a low-cost and high-performance distributed computing platform. It uses idling resources of personal computers (PCs) in a group. The job-worker assignment for minimizing *makespan* is critical to determine the performance of the UPC system. Some applications need to execute a lot of *uniform jobs* that use the identical program but with slightly different data, where they take the similar CPU time on a PC. Then, the total CPU time of a worker is almost linear to the number of assigned jobs. In this paper, we propose a *static assignment algorithm* of *uniform jobs* to workers in the UPC system, using *simultaneous linear equations* to find the *lower bound* on *makespan*, where every worker requires the same CPU time to complete the assigned jobs. For the evaluations of the proposal, we consider the uniform jobs in three applications. In *OpenPose*, the CNN-based *keypoint* estimation program runs with various images of human bodies. In *OpenFOAM*, the physics simulation program runs with various parameter sets. In *code testing*, two open-source programs run with various source codes from students for the *Android programming learning assistance system (APLAS)*. Using the proposal, we assigned the jobs to six workers in the testbed UPC system and measured the CPU time. The results show that *makespan* was reduced by 10% on average, which confirms the effectiveness of the proposal.

Keywords: UPC; distributed computing platform; uniform job; static assignment; linear equations

Citation: Zhou, X.; Funabiki, N.; Htet, H.; Kamoyedji, A.; Anggraini, I.T.; Huo, Y.; Syaifudin, Y.W. A Static Assignment Algorithm of Uniform Jobs to Workers in a User-PC Computing System Using Simultaneous Linear Equations. *Algorithms* **2022**, *15*, 369. https://doi.org/10.3390/a15100369

Academic Editor: Frank Werner

Received: 28 August 2022
Accepted: 4 October 2022
Published: 7 October 2022

1. Introduction

Currently, the *User-PC computing (UPC)* system has been studied as a low-cost and high-performance distributed computing platform [1]. The UPC system uses idling resources of personal computers (PCs) in a group to handle a number of various computing jobs from users. Then, the proper assignment of incoming jobs to workers is very important to effectively deal with them by using computational resources properly. As a result, the job assignment algorithm is critical to achieve the minimization for *makespan* to complete all the demanded jobs in the UPC system.

Previously, we proposed the algorithm of assigning *non-uniform jobs* to workers in the UPC system [2]. In *non-uniform jobs*, the programs are much different from each other, including the developed programming languages, the number of threads, and the requiring data. The execution time for each *non-uniform job* is highly different from the others. The previous algorithm can find the job-worker assignment through two stages sequentially, of which are heuristic due to the nature of the *NP-hardness* and cannot guarantee the optimality of the solution.

Some applications need to execute a lot of *uniform jobs* that use the identical program but with slightly different data/files, where they take a similar CPU time on a PC. The applications include deep learning (machine learning), physics simulations, software testing, computer network simulations, mathematical modeling, and mechanics modeling.

These jobs have the common feature of a similar CPU time when they run on a specific PC. The *uniform jobs* often need a long CPU time. For example, in physics or network simulations, it can take several days to run one job. Nevertheless, it will be necessary to find the best result of all the input data by repeating them to slightly change some parameter values for the program and running them. This work can be common in research activities using computer simulations.

In this paper, we propose a *static assignment algorithm* of *uniform jobs* to workers in the UPC system, using *simultaneous linear equations* to find the *lower bound* on *makespan*, where every worker requires the same CPU time to complete the assigned jobs. The *simultaneous linear equations* describe the equality of the estimated CPU time among the workers, and the equality of the total number of assigned jobs to workers with the number of given jobs. The estimated CPU time considers simultaneous executions of multiple jobs on one worker by using its multiple cores. Since solutions of *simultaneous linear equations* become real numbers in general, the integer number of jobs assigned to each worker is introduced to them in a greedy way.

For evaluations of the proposal, we consider *uniform jobs* in the three applications for the UPC system, namely, *OpenPose* [3], *OpenFOAM* [4], and *code testing* [5,6]. For *OpenPose*, the CNN-based program runs with 41 images of human bodies. For *OpenFOAM*, the physics simulation program runs with 32 parameter sets. For *unit testing*, the open-source programs run with 578 source codes that were submitted from students to the server in the *Android programming learning assistance system (APLAS)*. These jobs were applied to the proposed algorithm and were assigned to six workers in the testbed UPC system by following the results. Then, the CPU time was measured by running them. For comparisons, two simple algorithms were also implemented where the jobs were applied, and the CPU time was measured. The evaluation results show that the difference between the longest CPU time and the shortest one among the six workers became 92 s, and *makespan* of the UPC system was reduced by 10% on average from the results by comparative algorithms. Thus, the effectiveness of the proposal was confirmed.

The proposed algorithm limits the application to the jobs where the CPU time is nearly equal to a worker. This limitation can simplify the job scheduling algorithm to only considering the number of jobs assigned to each worker, while neglecting the differences between individual jobs. Fortunately, it is possible to alleviate this limitation to a certain degree by considering the granularity of the CPU time on a worker. The CPU time of a job that is applicable to the proposal is often proportional to the number of iteration steps before the termination, or to the number of elements in the computational model. For example, in computer network simulations, the number of iteration steps need to be selected with the unit time before simulations, where the CPU time is usually proportional to it. By considering a multiple of a constant number of iteration steps, such as 100, the CPU time can be estimated even if the number of iteration steps is widely changed with this granularity. In future works, we will study this extension of the proposed algorithm to increase its applicable applications.

The rest of this paper is organized as follows: Section 2 discusses related works. Section 3 reviews the UPC system, *OpenPose*, *OpenFOAM*, and *code testing* in *APLAS*. Section 4 presents the *static assignment algorithm* of *uniform jobs* to workers in the UPC system. Section 5 evaluates the proposal through experiments. Section 6 extends the proposal to multiple job-type assignments. Finally, Section 7 concludes this paper with future works.

2. Related Works in the Literature

In this section, we discuss some related works in the literature.

In [7], Lin proposed several linear programming models and algorithms for identical jobs (*uniform jobs*) on parallel uniform machines for individual minimizations of several different performance measures. The proposed linear programming models provide structured insights of the studied problems and provide an easy way to tackle the scheduling problems.

In [8], Mallek et al. addressed the problem of scheduling identical jobs (*uniform jobs*) on a set of parallel uniform machines. The jobs are subjected to conflicting constraints modeled by an undirected graph G, in which adjacent jobs are not allowed to be processed on the same machine. The minimization of the maximum *makespan* in the schedule is known to be *NP-hard*. To solve the general case of this problem, they proposed mixed-integer linear programming formulations alongside lower bounds and heuristic approaches.

In [9], Bansal et al. proposed the two-stage *Efficient Refinery Scheduling Algorithm (ERSA)* for distributed computing systems. In the first stage, it assigns a task according to the min–max heuristic. In the second stage, it improves the scheduling by using the refinery scheduling heuristic that balances the loads across the machines and reduces *makespan*.

In [10], Murugesan et al. proposed a multi-source task scheduler to map the tasks to the distributed resources in a cloud. The scheduler has three phases: the task aggregation, the task selection, and the task sequencing. By using the ILP formulation, this scheduler minimizes *makespan* while satisfying the budget allotted by the cloud user based on the divisible load theory.

In [11], Garg et al. proposed the *adaptive workflow scheduling (AWS)* for grid computing using the dynamic resources based on the rescheduling method. The AWS has three stages of the initial static scheduling, the resource monitoring, and the rescheduling, to minimize *makespan* using the directed acyclic graph workflow model for grid computing. It deals with the heterogeneous dynamic grid environment, where the availability of computing nodes and link bandwidths are inevitable due to existences of loads.

In [12], Gawali et al. proposed the two-stage *Standard Deviation-Based Modified Cuckoo Optimization Algorithm (SDMCOA)* for the scheduling of distributed computing systems. In the first stage, it calculates the sample initial population among all the available number of task populations. In the second stage, the modified COA immigrates and lays the tasks.

In [13], Bittencourt et al. reviewed existing scheduling problems in cloud computing and distributed systems. The emergence of distributed systems brought new challenges on scheduling in computer systems, including clusters, grids, and clouds. They defined a taxonomy for task scheduling in cloud computing, namely, pre-cloud schedulers and cloud schedulers, and classified existing scheduling algorithms in the taxonomy. They introduced future directions for scheduling research in cloud computing.

In [14], Attiya et al. presented a modified *Harris hawks optimization (HHO)* algorithm based on the *simulated annealing (SA)* for scheduling the jobs in a cloud environment. In this approach, SA is employed as a local search algorithm to improve the convergence rate and the solution quality generated by the standard HHO algorithm. HHO is a novel population-based, nature-inspired optimization paradigm proposed by Heidari et al. [15]. The main inspiration of HHO is the cooperative behavior and the chasing style of Harris' hawks in nature. In the HHO model, several hawks explore prey, respectively, and simultaneously after attacking the target from different directions to surprise it.

In [16], Al-Maytami et al. presented a novel scheduling algorithm using *Directed Acyclic Graph (DAG)* based on the *Prediction of Tasks Computation Time algorithm (PTCT)* to estimate the preeminent scheduling algorithm for prominent cloud data. The proposed algorithm provides a significant improvement with respect to *makespan* and reduces the computational complexity via employing *Principal Components Analysis (PCA)* and reducing the *Expected-Time-to-Compute (ETC)* matrix.

In [17], Panda et al. proposed an *energy-efficient task scheduling algorithm (ETSA)* to address the demerits associated with the task consolidation and scheduling. The proposed algorithm *ETSA* takes into account the completion time and the total utilization of a task on the resources, and follows a normalization procedure to make a scheduling decision. The *ETSA* provides an elegant trade-off between energy efficiency and *makespan*, more so than the existing algorithms.

3. Reviews of UPC System and Three Applications

In this section, we review the *User-PC computing system (UPC)* system and the three applications in this paper.

3.1. UPC System

First, we review the *UPC* system. The UPC system can provide computational powers efficiently for members in a group, such as engineers in a company or students in a laboratory, by using idling computing resources of their PCs. To allow various application programs to run on different PC environments, the UPC system adopts *Docker*. *Docker* is a popular software tool that has been designed to create, deploy, and execute various application programs on various platforms by packaging the necessary dependencies of the application [18].

Figure 1 shows the overview of the UPC system. The UPC system adopts the *master-worker model*. Users submit computing jobs to the *UPC master* through the *UPC web server*. After synchronizations of the jobs, the *UPC master* assigns the submitted jobs to the appropriate *UPC workers*. Each worker computes its assigned jobs and returns the results to the master upon completion. Users can access the results at the web browser.

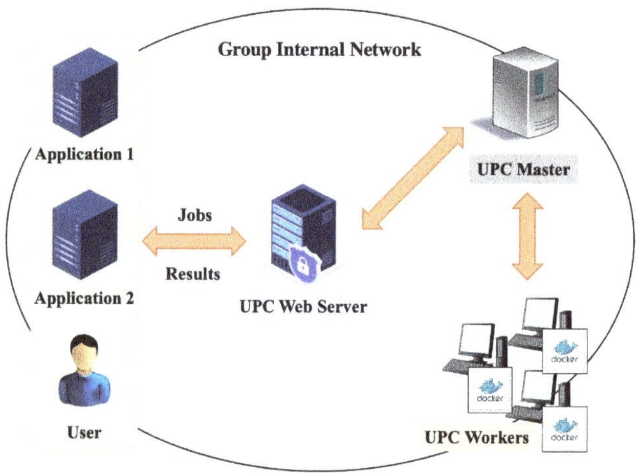

Figure 1. Overview of UPC system.

For further details, the usage flow of the UPC system will be described:

1. Job reception: A user submits jobs from the web browser and requests to compute them in the UPC system.
2. Worker assignment: The UPC master selects an appropriate active worker to compute each job using a job-worker assignment algorithm.
3. Docker image generation: The UPC master generates the *Docker image* to execute the job on the assigned worker.
4. Docker image transmission: The master sends the *Docker image* to the assigned worker.
5. Job execution: The worker generates the *Docker container* from the image and executes the job there.
6. Result transmission: The worker returns the result to the master upon completion.
7. Result response: The master shows the computing results of the jobs to the user through the web server.

3.2. OpenPose

Next, we review *OpenPose*. It has been developed by researchers at Carnegie Mellon University and is an popular open-source software for real-time human pose estimation [3].

It extracts the feature points, called *keypoints*, of the human body in the given image using *Convolutional Neural Network (CNN)*. The *keypoints* represent the important joints in a human body, the contours of eyes, lips in the face, fingertips, and joints in the hands and feet. Using the *keypoints*, the shapes of a body, face, hands, and feet can be described. Since it has been developed based on CNN, the CPU time is very long when computed on a conventional PC.

OpenPose is used in our group for developing the *exercise and performance learning assistant system (EPLAS)* to assist practicing exercises or learning performances by themselves at home [19]. *EPLAS* offers video content of *Yoga* poses by instructors whose performances should be followed by users. During the practice, it automatically takes photos of important scenes of the user. Then, it extracts the keypoints of the human body using *OpenPose* to rate the poses in the photos by comparing the coordinates of them between the user and the instructor.

3.3. OpenFOAM

Then, we review *OpenFOAM*. It is an open-source software for the *computational fluid dynamics (CFD)* simulations and has been developed primarily by *OpenCFD Ltd.* (Bracknell, UK) It has an extensive range of features to solve anything from complex fluid flows involving chemical reactions, turbulence, and heat transfer, to acoustics, solid mechanics, and electromagnetics [4]. Furthermore, the optimal parameter selection is critical for the high accuracy of the results, and it needs a lot of iterations of selecting parameters in *OpenFOAM* and running it with the parameter values. We applied the *parameter optimization method* for *OpenFOAM* [20]; it needs to run *OpenFOAM* with a lot of different parameters.

Meanwhile, it is also applied for developing the *air conditioning guidance system* [21] in our research. The estimation or prediction of the distributions of the temperature or humidity inside a room using this simulation model is necessary to properly control the air conditioner. By estimating the room environment changes under various actions, it will be possible to decide when the air conditioner is turned on or off. Even the timing to open or close windows in the room can be selected. To estimate or predict the distributions in a room together with sensors, the CFD simulation using *OpenFOAM* has been investigated. Then, the optimization of the parameters in *OpenFOAM* is critical in order to fit the simulation results well with the corresponding measured ones.

3.4. Code Testing

Finally, we review the *code testing* in the *Android programming learning assistance system (APLAS)*. *APLAS* has been developed in our group as the automatic and self-learning system for Android programming using *Java* and *XML* [5,6]. The *code testing* is the process to validate a source code by running the corresponding *test code* on a testing framework. To confirm the validity of the answer source code from a student in satisfying the required specifications in the assignment, *APLAS* implements the *code testing* function using *JUnit* for unit testing of *Java* codes [22] and *Robolectric* for integration testing with *XML* codes [23,24]. *APLAS* needs to run the *code testing* function with a lot of different source codes from many students, which usually takes a long time.

In *ALPAS*, *Java* codes can be directly tested on *JUnit*. However, the Android-specific components, such as the *Layout*, the *Activity*, the *Event Listener*, and the *Project Resources* that will be described in *XML*, cannot be directly tested on *JUnit*. The building tool *Gradle* is used to build and integrate them as *Java* classes. Then, *Robolectric* is used to generate *Java* objects—called *shadow objects*—for them, so that they can be tested on *JUnit*.

4. Proposal of Static Uniform Job Assignment Algorithm

In this section, we present the static *uniform job* assignment algorithm to workers in the UPC system.

4.1. Objective

To design the algorithm, it is observed that when the *makespan* of every worker becomes equal, the objective of the problem on the *makespan* minimization can be achieved. Otherwise, the maximum *makespan* can be reduced by moving some jobs at the bottleneck worker which determines this maximum *makespan* to other workers, if the number of assigned jobs to any worker can take a real number. Only when every worker has the same *makespan*, the maximum *makespan* cannot be reduced.

$$minimize\{max(m_w^t)\} \ for \ t \in T, w \in W \tag{1}$$

The minimization of the maximum *makespan* among all the workers is given as the objective of the problem, where *makespan* m_w^t at worker w for type t is given by the summation of the CPU time for preparation and execution.

4.2. Simultaneous Linear Equations

In this paper, the following *simultaneous linear equations* have been derived to find the optimal job-worker assignment, such that the estimated CPU time required to complete the assigned jobs becomes equal among all the workers. The solutions of the *simultaneous linear equations* will be the *lower bound* on *makespan*. Since the solutions become real numbers in general, the integer number of assigned jobs to each worker should be introduced to them.

$$\begin{aligned} C_i^t + \frac{R_{i,D_i}^t}{D_i} \times x_i^t = C_j^t + \frac{R_{j,D_j}^t}{D_j} \times x_j^t \\ for \ i \neq j, i \in W, j \in W, t \in T. \end{aligned} \tag{2}$$

To satisfy the objective of the equal CPU time among the workers, $R_{w,D_w}^t / D_w$ gives the best CPU time to solve one job at worker w by running D_w jobs.

4.3. Problem Formulation

To present the static *uniform jobs* assignment algorithm to workers in the UPC system, the problem to be solved is formulated here.

4.3.1. Variables

The following variables are defined for the problem to be solved:

- t: Particular job type;
- w: Particular worker;
- x_w^t: # of the assigned jobs to worker w for type t;
- m_w^t: *Makespan* at worker w to complete all the assigned jobs for type t;
- d_w: # of running jobs in parallel using multi-threads at worker w.

4.3.2. Constants

The following constants are given as the inputs to this problem:

- T: Set of job types;
- W: Set of workers;
- N^t: Total # of jobs for type t;
- D_w: # of jobs for the best throughput at worker w for any type;
- C_w^t: CPU time at worker w to prepare job executions for type t;
- $R_{w,d}^t$: CPU time at worker w to execute d jobs for type t in parallel.

Here, D_w represents the number of simultaneously running jobs for job type t at worker w, which maximizes the number of completed jobs per unit time. This is constant for any job type in each application, because it depends on the common program in the application for every job type.

C^t_w represents the CPU time required to initiate the execution of the program at worker w. For example, in the *code testing* application, it represents the CPU time to initiate the *Gradle Wrapper* daemon and generate *shadow objects* that are necessary to run the *code testing function*.

$R^t_{w,d}$ can be measured using any worker by running jobs for job type t while increasing the number of running jobs in parallel from 1 until D_w.

4.3.3. Constraints

The following two constraints must be satisfied in the problem:

- The total number of the assigned jobs to workers must be equal to N^t for any type t.

$$\sum_{w \in W} x^t_w = N^t \ (t \in T) \tag{3}$$

- Any worker cannot run d jobs in parallel when d is larger than the D_w (let d_w for worker w) due to the PC specifications.

$$d_w \leq D_w \tag{4}$$

4.4. Conditions for Uniform Job Assignment

For the *uniform job* assignment to workers in the UPC system, the following conditions are assumed:

- Several job types may exist for *uniform jobs* in each application, where different job types may need the different CPU time, memory size, and number of CPU cores due to the differences in data;
- Each job is fully executed on one worker until it is completed;
- Each worker may have different performance specifications from the others;
- Each worker may have a different number of running jobs in parallel, using multi-threads for the best throughput;
- The CPU time to run the certain number of jobs in parallel is given for each worker and job type.

4.5. Static Uniform Job Assignment Algorithm

Here, we note that the CPU time may be different depending on the number of running jobs in parallel in each worker that has multiple cores. To reduce the CPU time by increasing the job completion throughput, D_w jobs of type t should run at worker w as much as possible, since it will give the best throughput. Based on this observation, we present the three-step static *uniform job* assignment algorithm. Figure 2 shows the flowchart of the proposal.

4.5.1. First Step

By solving the *simultaneous linear equations* composed of (2) and (3), the optimal number of assigned jobs of type t to worker w, $\hat{x^t_w}$, is obtained, assuming that any real value is acceptable for it.

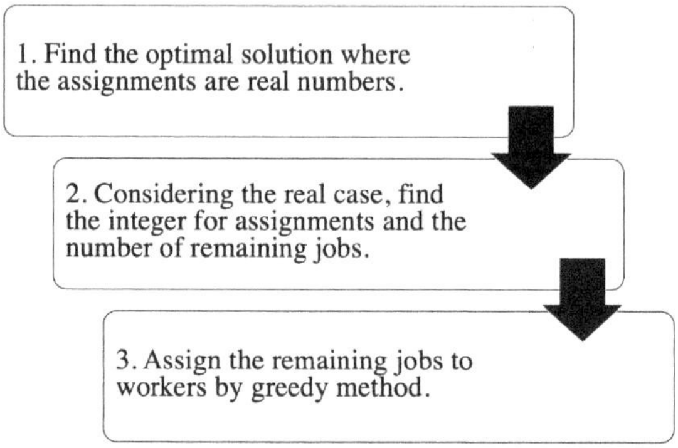

Figure 2. Flowchart of the proposal.

4.5.2. Second Step

The solution in the first step becomes feasible only when $\hat{x^t_w}$ is a multiple of D_w for type t. Unfortunately, $\hat{x^t_w}$ does not satisfy the condition, in general. Therefore, in the second step, as the closest integer number to satisfy the condition, the following $\tilde{x^t_w}$ jobs will be assigned to the worker (worker w), where $\lfloor y \rfloor$ gives the largest integer equal to or smaller than y:

$$\tilde{x^t_w} = \lfloor \frac{\hat{x^t_w}}{D_w} \rfloor \times D_w \tag{5}$$

Then, the number of the remaining jobs (let r^t for type t) is calculated by:

$$r^t = N^t - \sum_{w \in W} \tilde{x^t_w} \tag{6}$$

Besides, the estimated *makespan* for each worker (let em^t_w for worker w and job type t) after the job assignment is calculated by:

$$em^t_w = C^t_w + R^t_{w,D_w} \times \frac{\tilde{x^t_w}}{D_w} \tag{7}$$

Therefore, after completing the procedures for all the job types, the estimated *makespan* for each worker is calculated by:

$$EM_w = \sum_{t \in T} em^t_w \tag{8}$$

As the objective of the algorithm, the maximum estimated *makespan* among the workers is calculated by:

$$EM = \{max(EM_w)\} \; for \; w \in W \tag{9}$$

4.5.3. Third Step

In the third step, the remaining jobs (r_t) in the second step will be assigned to workers in a greedy way, such that the increase in the maximum estimated *makespan* EM is minimized. It is noted that the remaining jobs may exist for any job type. Here, to utilize the parallel job computation using multiple threads on multiple cores for each worker as much as possible, the simultaneous assignment of multiple jobs to one worker is always considered.

1. Find the worker whose $\hat{EM_w}$ is smallest among the workers (let worker w).

$$\hat{EM_w} = EM_w + R^t_{w,D_w} \tag{10}$$

2. Assign Δx^t_w jobs to worker w.

$$\Delta x^t_w = \begin{cases} D_w, & r_t > D_w \\ r_t, & r_t \leq D_w \end{cases} \quad (11)$$

3. Update the number of the remaining jobs (r_t), and the number of assigned jobs and *makespan* of the worker w by:

$$\begin{aligned} x^t_w &= x^t_w + \Delta x^t_w, \\ EM_w &= EM_w + R^t_{w,\Delta x^t_w}, \\ r_t &= r_t - \Delta x^t_w \end{aligned} \quad (12)$$

4. If the number of the remaining jobs becomes zero ($r_t = 0$), terminate the procedure.
5. Go to 1.

5. Evaluation

In this section, we evaluate the proposal through extensive experiments which are running jobs in three applications on the testbed UPC system.

5.1. Testbed UPC System

Table 1 shows the PC specifications in the testbed UPC system. One master and six workers are used here.

Table 1. PC specifications.

PC	# of Cores	CPU Model	Clock Rate	Memory Size
master	4	Core i5	3.20 GHz	8 GB
PC1	4	Core i3	1.70 GHz	2 GB
PC2	4	Core i5	2.60 GHz	2 GB
PC3	4	Core i5	2.60 GHz	2 GB
PC4	8	Core i7	3.40 GHz	4 GB
PC5	16	Core i9	3.60 GHz	8 GB
PC6	20	Core i9	3.70 GHz	8 GB

5.2. Jobs

Table 2 shows the specifications of the jobs for the eight job types in our experiments. For the *code testing* application in *APLAS*, six job types are prepared, where each job type represents one assignment to students in *APLAS*. These job types run the same programs of *JUnit* and *Robolectric*, but accept many different data of answer source codes and test codes. For the other applications, only one job type is considered.

Table 2. Job specifications.

Job Type	# of Jobs	Ave. Job Size (KB)	Ave. LOC	Ave. Peak Mem. Use (GB)
BassixAppX1	97	548	1288	1.80
BassixAppX2	125	623	1499	1.82
ColorGame	114	177	1834	1.94
SoccerMatch	88	381	2632	2.39
AnimalTour	71	31,048	4625	4.21
MyLibrary	83	409	4850	2.51
OpenPose	41	62	N/A	2.69
OpenFOAM	32	27	N/A	0.035
total/ave.	651	4159	N/A	2.17

5.3. CPU Time

Table 3 shows the constant CPU time required to start running the jobs on each worker for each of the six job types. Tables 4–6 show the increasing CPU time when the number of jobs is increased by one until the number for the best throughput for each type.

Through preliminary experiments, we found the number of simultaneously running jobs for the highest throughput for each worker. For *code testing* in *APLAS*, *PC1*, *PC2*, and *PC3* can run only one job in parallel due to the low specifications. This number is two for *PC4*, five for *PC5*, and six for *PC6*. For *OpenPose*, any worker can only execute one job because it uses a lot of threads to compute CNN. For *OpenFOAM*, for each worker, the CPU time is constant at any number of simultaneously running jobs until it reaches the number of cores in the worker.

Table 3. Constant CPU time to start jobs (s).

Job Type	PC1	PC2	PC3	PC4	PC5	PC6
BassixAppX1	9	6	6	5	4	4
BassixAppX2	9	6	6	5	4	4
ColorGame	9	6	6	5	4	4
SoccerMatch	10	6	6	6	5	4
AnimalTour	18	16	16	13	9	8
MyLibrary	11	7	7	6	5	4
OpenPose	10	9	9	8	7	7
OpenFOAM	5	5	5	4	3	3

Table 4. Increasing CPU time at *PC1*∼*PC4* (s).

Job Type	PC1	PC2	PC3	PC4: 1 Job	PC4: 2 Jobs
BassixAppX1	58	37	37	25	32
BassixAppX2	38	24	24	15	21
ColorGame	60	35	35	25	31
SoccerMatch	128	71	71	46	56
AnimalTour	301	58	58	37	46
MyLibrary	119	43	43	27	34
OpenPose	70	35	35	26	N/A
OpenFOAM	415	206	206	170	170

Table 5. Increasing CPU time at *PC5* (s).

Job Type	1 Job	2 Jobs	3 Jobs	4 Jobs	5 Jobs
BassixAppX1	18	21	25	27	31
BassixAppX2	11	13	16	19	22
ColorGame	16	19	22	26	30
SoccerMatch	31	37	43	55	62
AnimalTour	25	29	50	67	79
MyLibrary	17	20	32	41	47
OpenPose	22	N/A	N/A	N/A	N/A
OpenFOAM	128	128	128	128	128

Table 6. Increasing CPU time at *PC6* (s).

Job Type	1 Job	2 Jobs	3 Jobs	4 Jobs	5 Jobs	6 Jobs
BassixAppX1	16	17	20	23	27	31
BassixAppX2	9	10	12	15	18	21
ColorGame	15	17	19	22	24	28
SoccerMatch	27	31	36	44	54	61
AnimalTour	23	26	30	35	38	44
MyLibrary	16	18	21	27	33	39
OpenPose	21	N/A	N/A	N/A	N/A	N/A
OpenFOAM	106	106	106	106	106	106

5.4. Comparative Algorithms

For performance comparisons, we implemented two simple algorithms to assign *non-uniform jobs* to workers.

The first one is the *First-Come-First-Serve (FCFS)* algorithm. It assigns each job to the first available worker, starting from the worker with the highest specification until the one with the lowest. It limits the worker to executing only one job at a time.

The second is the *best throughput-based FCFS (T-FCFS)* algorithm. The difference between T-FCFS and *FCFS* is that each worker may execute multiple jobs simultaneously until the best throughput.

5.5. Total Makespan Results

Table 7 compares the maximum *makespan* results for each job type when the testbed UPC system runs the jobs by following the assignments found by the algorithms. Furthermore, it shows the *lower bound (LB)* on the maximum *makespan* found at *First Step* of the proposed algorithm for the reference of them.

Table 7. Maximum *makespan* results (s).

Job Type	FCFS	T-FCFS	Proposal	LB
BassixAppX1	536	268	221	203.04
BassixAppX2	470	235	184	178.67
ColorGame	621	276	233	224.04
SoccerMatch	828	414	370	356.03
AnimalTour	666	319	289	262.82
MyLibrary	520	260	238	227.07
OpenPose	272	272	220	209.97
OpenFOAM	1044	131	131	81.55
Total	4957	2175	1886	1743.19

The results indicate that for any job type, the maximum *makespan* result by the proposal is better than the results by the two compared algorithms and is close to the lower bound. Thus, the effectiveness of the proposal is confirmed. It is noted that the results by *FCFS* are far larger than the ones by the others because FCFS does not consider simultaneous multiple job executions for a worker.

5.6. Individual Makespan Results

For reference, Tables 8–10 show *makespan* or the total CPU time of each worker and the largest CPU time difference between the workers and the three algorithms. For *OpenFOAM*, no job was assigned to *PC1–PC4*, because all of the 32 jobs can be executed simultaneously at *PC5* and *PC6*. The largest CPU time difference by the proposal is smaller than the ones by the others, except for *ColorGame*, *SoccerMatch*, *AnimalTour*, and *MyLibrary*, where in Table 4, the increasing CPU time of *PC1* is much larger than other workers, and the far smaller number of jobs was assigned. Therefore, the proposal can balance well the job assignments among the workers.

Table 8. FCFS *makespan* detail (s).

Job Type	PC1	PC2	PC3	PC4	PC5	PC6	Diff.
BassixAppX1	536	516	516	510	506	500	36
BassixAppX2	470	450	450	440	435	442	35
ColorGame	621	574	574	570	560	570	61
SoccerMatch	828	770	770	780	792	775	58
AnimalTour	638	666	666	650	612	620	54
MyLibrary	520	500	500	462	462	480	58
OpenPose	240	264	264	272	261	252	32
OpenFOAM	840	844	844	1044	917	981	204

Table 9. T-FCFS *makespan* detail (s).

Job Type	PC1	PC2	PC3	PC4	PC5	PC6	Diff.
BassixAppX1	268	215	215	222	210	241	58
BassixAppX2	235	210	210	208	208	214	27
ColorGame	276	246	246	252	258	256	30
SoccerMatch	414	385	385	372	377	390	42
AnimalTour	319	296	296	295	298	312	24
MyLibrary	260	250	250	240	260	246	20
OpenPose	240	264	264	272	261	252	32
OpenFOAM	0	0	0	0	131	109	131

Table 10. Proposal *makespan* detail (s).

Job Type	PC1	PC2	PC3	PC4	PC5	PC6	Diff.
BassixAppX1	183	191	191	197	190	221	38
BassixAppX2	161	174	174	173	180	184	23
ColorGame	189	216	216	222	233	228	44
SoccerMatch	266	361	361	342	358	370	104
AnimalTour	0	248	248	289	246	272	289
MyLibrary	130	222	222	210	234	238	108
OpenPose	220	219	219	216	205	196	24
OpenFOAM	0	0	0	0	131	109	131

5.7. Discussions

The results in Table 7 show improvements of maximum *makespan* results by the proposed algorithm if compared with *T-FCFS*. However, some differences can be observed against the *lower bound*.

The current algorithm can find the assignment of some remaining jobs to workers, and assign an integer number of jobs to any worker in a greedy way, after the real number solutions are obtained by solving the *simultaneous linear equations*. A greedy method is usually difficult to give a near-optimum solution, since it only considers the local optimality under the current assignment.

To improve the solution quality, a local search method using iterations has often been adopted for solving combinatorial optimization problems, including this study. Therefore, we will study the use of a local search method for the remaining job assignment in the proposed algorithm.

6. Extension to Multiple Job Types Assignment

In this section, we extend the proposed algorithm to the case when jobs for multiple job types are assigned together.

6.1. Algorithm Extension

In *First Step* of the proposed algorithm, the linear equations are modified in this extension to consider the CPU time to complete all the jobs for the plural job types assigned to each worker:

$$\sum_{t \in T} (C_i^t + \frac{R_{i,D_i}^t}{D_i} \times x_i^t) = \sum_{t \in T} (C_j^t + \frac{R_{j,D_j}^t}{D_j} \times x_j^t) \quad \text{for } i \neq j, i \in W, j \in W. \tag{13}$$

The number of variables to be solved is $|W||T|$, where $|W|$ represents the number of workers and $|T|$ represents the number of job types, respectively. Thus, $|W||T|$ linear equations are necessary to solve them. In the original algorithm, for each job type, $(|W| - 1)$ linear equations are derived for the CPU time equality and one equation is for the job number. Thus, $|W||T|$ equations can be introduced.

However, in this extension, the total number of linear equations for the CPU time equality is reduced to $(|W| - 1)$ because all the job types need to be considered together here.

Therefore, to solve the linear equations uniquely, the following $(|W|-1)(|T|-1)$ linear equations will be introduced by considering the total CPU time for $(|T|-1)$ job types together for $(|T|-1)$ combinations of $(|T|-1)$ job types, in addition to the total CPU time for $|T|$ job types together in (13):

$$\sum_{t \in T-\{u\}} (C_i^t + \frac{R_{i,D_i}^t}{D_i} \times x_i^t) = \sum_{t \in T-\{u\}} (C_j^t + \frac{R_{j,D_j}^t}{D_j} \times x_j^t) \quad (14)$$
$$for\ i \neq j, i \in W, j \in W, u \in T.$$

where $T-\{u\}$ represents the set of the job types in T except for job type u.

The $(|T|-1)$ combinations of $(|T|-1)$ job types are selected by excluding the combination where the following estimated total CPU time to execute all the jobs in the remaining job types on *PC6* is smallest:

$$\sum_{t \in T-\{u\}} (C_6^t + \frac{R_{6,D_6}^t}{D_6} \times N^t) \quad (15)$$

Then, in *Second Step* and *Third Step*, the estimated *makespan* for each worker and the maximum estimated *makespan* among the workers are modified to consider all the given job types together.

6.2. Total Makespan Results

Table 11 shows the maximum *makespan* results when the testbed UPC system runs the jobs by following the assignments by the extended algorithm. When compared with the result by the original algorithm, it is reduced by 5%, and becomes closer to the *lower bound*. The difference between our result and the lower bound is very small. Thus, this extension is effective when plural job types are requested at the UPC system together.

Table 11. Maximum *makespan* results (s) by proposal.

Original	Extended	LB
1886	1799	1743.19

6.3. Discussions

The result in Table 11 confirms some reduction in the total *makespan* result by the extended algorithm. However, there is still a difference when compared to the *lower bound*. Thus, it is necessary to further improve the algorithm.

One idea for this improvement in the extended algorithm will not be to limit the exclusion of one job type combination—where the estimated total CPU time to execute all jobs in the remaining job types on *PC6* is the smallest—and to generate the linear equations for the CPU time equality. Instead, every combination will be excluded one by one to obtain the result for each combination exclusion. Then, the best one will be selected among them.

7. Conclusions

This paper proposed the static *uniform job* assignment algorithm to workers in the UPC system. The *simultaneous linear equations* have been derived to find the optimal assignment of minimizing the maximum *makespan* among the workers, where the CPU time to complete the assigned jobs becomes equal among all the workers.

For an evaluation, the 651 *uniform jobs* in three applications, *OpenPose*, *OpenFOAM*, and *code testing* in *APLAS*, were considered to run on six workers in the testbed UPC system, and the *makespan* was compared with the results by two simple algorithms and the lower bounds. The comparisons confirmed the effectiveness of the proposal.

The novelty of the proposal is that with a very simple formula, it is able to provide the near-optimal solutions to *NP-complete* problems in the *User-PC computing (UPC) system*, a typical distributed system. The current algorithm limits the jobs whereby the computing time for a worker is nearly equal. This limitation can simplify our approach of considering the simple assignment of the number of jobs for each worker without considering the differences among individual jobs.

Fortunately, it is possible to alleviate this limitation by considering the granularity of the CPU time for a worker. The CPU time of a job in suitable applications to the proposal is often proportional to the number of iteration steps before the termination or the number of elements in the model. By considering a multiple of a constant number of iteration steps, the CPU time can be estimated even if the number of iteration steps is widely changed with this granularity; this finding will be in future studies.

In future studies, we will also improve the algorithm for remaining job assignments and simultaneous job assignments of multiple job types, and we will study the combination of *uniform jobs* and *non-uniform jobs* in the job-worker assignment algorithm for the UPC system.

Author Contributions: Conceptualization, N.F.; Data curation, X.Z. and H.H.; Resources, H.H., A.K., I.T.A., Y.H. and Y.W.S.; Software, X.Z.; Supervision, N.F.; Writing–original draft, X.Z.; Writing–review & editing, N.F. All authors have read and agreed to the published version of the manuscript.

Funding: This research received no external funding.

Data Availability Statement: Not applicable.

Conflicts of Interest: The authors declare no conflict of interest.

Abbreviations

The following abbreviations are used in this paper:

UPC	User-PC Computing System
PC	Personal Computer
APLAS	Android Programming Learning Assistance System
CNN	Convolutional Neural Network
CFD	Computational Fluid Dynamics
XML	Extensible Markup Language
CPU	Central Processing Unit
ERSA	Efficient Refinery Scheduling Algorithm
ILP	Integer Linear Programming
AWS	Adaptive Workflow Scheduling
COA	Cuckoo Optimization Algorithm
SDMCOA	Standard Deviation-Based Modified Cuckoo Optimization Algorithm
HHO	Harris Hawks optimization
PTCT	Prediction of Tasks Computation Time algorithm
PCA	Principal Components Analysis
ETC	Expected Time to Compute
ETSA	Energy-Efficient Task Scheduling Algorithm
SA	Simulated Annealing
AC	Air Conditioners
LOC	Lines Of Codes
FCFS	First Come First Serve
T-FCFS	Best Throughput-Based FCFS
LB	Lower Bound

References

1. Htet, H.; Funabiki, N.; Kamoyedji, A.; Kuribayashi, M.; Akhter, F.; Kao, W.-C. An implementation of user-PC computing system using Docker container. *Int. J. Future Comput. Commun.* **2020**, *9*, 66–73.
2. Kamoyedji, A.; Funabiki, N.; Htet, H.; Kuribayashi, M. A proposal of job-worker assignment algorithm considering CPU core utilization for user-PC computing system. *Int. J. Future Comput. Commun.* **2022**, *11*, 40–46. [CrossRef]

3. OpenPose 1.7.0. Available online: Cmu-perceptual-computing-lab.github.io/openpose/web/html/doc/index.html (accessed on 15 August 2022).
4. OpenFOAM. Available online: ww.openfoam.com (accessed on 15 August 2022).
5. Syaifudin, Y.W.; Funabiki, N.; Kuribayashi, M.; Kao, W.-C. A proposal of Android programming learning assistant system with implementation of basic application learning. *Int. J. Web Inf. Syst.* **2019**, *16*, 115–135. [CrossRef]
6. Syaifudin, Y.W.; Funabiki, N.; Mentari, M.; Dien, H.E.; Mu'aasyiqiin, I.; Kuribayashi, M.; Kao, W.-C. A web-based online platform of distribution, collection, and validation for assignments in Android programming learning assistance system. *Eng. Lett.* **2021**, *29*, 1178–1193.
7. Lin, Y. Fast LP models and algorithms for identical jobs on uniform parallel machines. *Appl. Math. Model.* **2013**, *37*, 3436–3448. [CrossRef]
8. Mallek, A.; Bendraouche, M.; Boudhar, M. Scheduling identical jobs on uniform machines with a conflict graph. *Comput. Oper. Res.* **2019**, *111*, 357–366. [CrossRef]
9. Bansal, S.; Hota, C. Efficient refinery scheduling heuristic in heterogeneous computing systems. *J. Adv. Inform. Technol.* **2011**, *2*, 159–164. [CrossRef]
10. Murugesan, G.; Chellappan, C. Multi-source task scheduling in grid computing environment using linear programming. *Int. J. Comput. Sci. Eng.* **2014**, *9*, 80–85. [CrossRef]
11. Garg, R.; Singh, A. Adaptive workflow scheduling in grid computing based on dynamic resource availability. *Eng. Sci. Technol.* **2015**, *18*, 256–269. [CrossRef]
12. Gawali, M.B.; Shinde, S.K. Standard deviation based modified Cuckoo optimization algorithm for task scheduling to efficient resource allocation in cloud computing. *J. Adv. Inform. Technol.* **2017**, *8*, 210–218. [CrossRef]
13. Bittencourt, L.F.; Goldman, A.; Madeira, E.R.M.; da Fonseca, N.L.S.; Sakellariou, R. Scheduling in distributed systems: A cloud computing perspective. *Comput. Sci. Rev.* **2018**, *30*, 31–54. [CrossRef]
14. Attiya, I.; Elaziz, M.A.; Xiong, S. Job scheduling in cloud computing using a modified Harris Hawks optimization and simulated annealing algorithm. *Comput. Intelli. Neuro.* **2020**, *2020*, 3504642. [CrossRef] [PubMed]
15. Heidari, A.A.; Mirjalili, S.; Faris, H.; Aljarah, I.; Mafarja, M.; Chen, H. Harris Hawks optimization: Algorithm and applications. *Future Gen. Comput. Syst.* **2019**, *97*, 849–872. [CrossRef]
16. Al-Maytami, B.A.; Hussain, P.F.A.; Baker, T.; Liatsis, P. A Task Scheduling Algorithm With Improved Makespan Based on Prediction of Tasks Computation Time algorithm for Cloud Computing. *IEEE Access* **2019**, *7*, 160916–160926. [CrossRef]
17. Panda, S.K.; Jana, P.K. An energy-efficient task scheduling algorithm for heterogeneous cloud computing systems. *Clust. Comput.* **2019**, *22*, 509–527. [CrossRef]
18. Mouat, A. *Using Docker: Developing and Deploying Software with Containers*, 1st ed.; O'Reilly Media, Inc.: Sebastopol, CA, USA, 2015.
19. Anggraini, I.T.; Basuki, A.; Funabiki, N.; Lu, X.; Fan, C.-P.; Hsu, Y.-C.; Lin, C.-H. A proposal of exercise and performance learning assistant system for self-practice at home. *Adv. Sci. Technol. Eng. Syst. J.* **2020**, *5*, 1196–1203. [CrossRef]
20. Zhao, Y.; Kojima, K.; Huo, Y.-Z.; Funabiki, N. CFD parameter optimization for air-conditioning guidance system using small room experimental model. In Proceedings of the 4th Global Conference on Life Sciences and Technologies, Osaka, Japan, 7–9 March 2022; pp. 252–253.
21. Huda, S.; Funabiki, N.; Kuribayashi, M.; Sudibyo, R.W.; Ishihara, N.; Kao, W.-C. A proposal of air-conditioning guidance system using discomfort index. In *InInternational Conference on Broadband and Wireless Computing, Communication and Applications* ; Springer: Cham, Switzerland, 2020; pp. 154–165.
22. Wahid, M.; Almalaise, A. JUnit framework: An interactive approach for basic unit testing learning in software engineering. In Proceedings of the 3rd International Conference on Engineering Education and Information Technology, Kuala Lumpur, Malaysia, 17–19 May 2011.
23. Robolectric. Available online: www.robolectric.org (accessed on 15 August 2022).
24. Linares-Vásquez, M.; Bernal-Cardenas, C.; Moran, K.; Poshyvanyk, D. How do developers test android applications. In Proceedings of the 2017 IEEE International Conference on Software Maintenance and Evolution, Shanghai, China, 17–22 September 2017.

algorithms

Article

The Assignment Problem and Its Relation to Logistics Problems

Milos Seda

Institute of Automation and Computer Science, Faculty of Mechanical Engineering, Brno University of Technology, Technicka 2896/2, 623 00 Brno, Czech Republic; seda@fme.vutbr.cz

Abstract: The assignment problem is a problem that takes many forms in optimization and graph theory, and by changing some of the constraints or interpreting them differently and adding other constraints, it can be converted to routing, distribution, and scheduling problems. Showing such correlations is one of the aims of this paper. For some of the derived problems having exponential time complexity, the question arises of their solvability for larger instances. Instead of the traditional approach based on the use of approximate or stochastic heuristic methods, we focus here on the direct use of mixed integer programming models in the GAMS environment, which is now capable of solving instances much larger than in the past and does not require complex parameter settings or statistical evaluation of the results as in the case of stochastic heuristics because the computational core of software tools, nested in GAMS, is deterministic in nature. The source codes presented may be an aid because this tool is not yet as well known as the MATLAB Optimisation Toolbox. Benchmarks of the permutation flow shop scheduling problem with the informally derived MIP model and the traveling salesman problem are used to present the limits of the software's applicability.

Keywords: assignment problem; traveling salesman problem; vehicle routing problem; flow shop scheduling problem; GAMS, genetic algorithm

Citation: Seda, M. The Assignment Problem and Its Relation to Logistics Problems. *Algorithms* **2022**, *15*, 377. https://doi.org/10.3390/a15100377

Academic Editor: Frank Werner

Received: 7 September 2022
Accepted: 13 October 2022
Published: 16 October 2022

1. Introduction

The *Assignment Problem* (abbreviated to AP) [1] and its mathematical model is a problem that is the basis of the field of combinatorial optimization [2,3]. The problem in its basic form has been successfully handled by the discovery of Harold Kuhn, who proved that his method [4], derived from the results of the theoretical work of the Hungarian mathematicians Dénes König and Jenö Egerváry and dubbed the *Hungarian method* in their honor, finds a solution in polynomial time $\mathcal{O}(n^3)$ [5] in an efficient implementation.

However, this does not make the assignment problem less interesting because it has many analogs in bipartite graph matching problems of the graph theory [5,6].

The assignment problem is most extensively addressed in [5,7], where we find theoretical foundations for the existence of perfect matching, implementation details for the Hungarian method, and a number of other related problems such as the k-cardinality assignment problem, the semi-assignment problem, the bottleneck assignment problem, the algebraic assignment problem, quadratic assignment problems, and multi-index assignment problems.

These are still variants closely related in meaning to the basic version of the matching problem, although the time complexity may no longer be polynomial, and, in the case of the quadratic matching problem, it is a non-linear problem.

In this paper, however, we focus on similarities of a different kind, namely in the mathematical model, where a completely different relationship to the underlying problem may be found because it allows, often with small modifications, for expressing problems from a different application domain, to switch between linear, mixed integer, and even non-linear problem classes, thus changing its computational complexity and solvability.

Perhaps the most well-known combinatorial optimization problem, the Travelling Salesman Problem [8], is a slight modification of this, with the Vehicle Routing Problem [9]

also stemming from this. On the other hand, from the assignment problem, with other modifications, we can easily move to logistic distribution operations [10], agricultural applications [11], set covering problems [12] with many interesting applications in telecommunications [13], and scheduling problems [14].

Concerning two selected problems of exponential complexity, the Travelling Salesman Problem (TSP) and the Permutation Flow Shop Scheduling Problem (PFSSP) [15], we will also deal with their solvability. We have very good experience in solving sets covering problems of $\mathcal{O}(2^n)$ complexity [13] using GAMS (General Algebraic Modelling System), where it is possible to find the optimal solution in the available time even for instances with matrices of hundreds of rows and thousands of columns, and it has also proven itself in solving the problem of finding the Steiner minimum tree in networks, which also has exponential time complexity.

Since the two problems mentioned above are permutational in nature with the factorial time complexity, they are more challenging than the set covering problems.

For extremely large TSP instances (many hundreds of cities), heuristics must be used, e.g., differential evolution [16], genetic algorithm [17–20], memetic search [21], simulated annealing [22], neural network [23], and improved neighbourhood search algorithms [24,25].

Many stochastic heuristics are inspired by the behaviour of animals in nature, e.g., deer [26], spider monkey [27], hyena [28], wolf [29], cuckoo [30,31], sparrow [32], frog [33], and ant colony [34].

On the other hand, stochastic heuristic methods are not suitable for TSP instances up to 100 cities because they may not find the optimal solution and the convergence time is often unsure, as, e.g., shown in the comparison of different methods in [28].

However, there are also approaches based on deterministic methods such as cutting plane [35], branch and bound [36] and branch and cut [37,38].

According to listings in the GAMS environment, the latter method is in some way incorporated into GAMS and, therefore, it makes sense to explore its limits of applicability. These, together with the GAMS source code, are discussed in detail in Section 6.

Scheduling problems seem far from the assignment problem. But one of them, the PFSSP, shares with the assignment problem a permutational nature in the ordering of jobs, where each job (with its operations) is assigned to exactly one position and each position can contain only one job (with its operations), which corresponds in the assignment problem to the fact that each task is assigned to a single worker and each worker solves only one task. There are additional constraints, and the aim is to minimize the total scheduling time (makespan), but we can still say that the derived PFSSP model is related to the assignment problem.

As in the case of the TSP, heuristic methods are used for large instances of different variants of flow shop scheduling problems, e.g., differential evolution [39], genetic algorithm [40,41], genetic programming [42], memetic algorithm [43], tabu-search [44], harmony search [45], iterated greedy algorithms [46–48], multi-local search [49], hybrid metaheuristics [50,51], reinforcement learning [52], fireworks algorithm [53], and also nature-inspired algorithms, e.g., ant colony optimization [54], firefly particle swarm optimization [55], migrating birds optimization [56] and whale swarm algorithm [57].

However, the exact methods [58,59], linear programming approach [60] and branch and bound [61], are also applicable so we will again focus on the usability of the GAMS tool.

2. The Assignment Problem Model

In most common problem formulation, we have n workers who need to be assigned n tasks in such a way that each worker is assigned a single task and each task is solved by a single worker.

For each worker-task pair, we know the time it takes the worker to complete the task. The task is to find an assignment that minimizes the total time to complete all tasks.

Let c_{ij} denote the time taken by the ith worker for the jth task. The decision variables are binary, $x_{ij} = 1$ if the ith worker is assigned the jth task, $x_{ij} = 0$ in the opposite case. Then, the problem can be formulated as follows:

$$z = \sum_{i=1}^{n} \sum_{j=1}^{n} c_{ij} x_{ij} \rightarrow \min \tag{1}$$

subject to

$$\sum_{i=1}^{n} x_{ij} = 1,\ j = 1, \ldots, n \tag{2}$$

$$\sum_{j=1}^{n} x_{ij} = 1,\ i = 1, \ldots, n \tag{3}$$

$$x_{ij} \in \{0, 1\},\ i = 1, \ldots, n,\ j = 1, \ldots, n \tag{4}$$

Equation (2) ensures that each task is assigned to a single worker, and Equation (3) ensures that each worker is assigned a single task.

The assignment problem can also be viewed as a problem of finding a permutation

$$\begin{pmatrix} 1 & 2 & \ldots & n \\ \pi_1 & \pi_2 & \ldots & \pi_n \end{pmatrix},$$

where ith worker is assigned to task π_i and

$$z = \sum_{i=1}^{n} c_{i\pi_i} \rightarrow \min$$

Since the number of different permutations of n elements is $n!$, it is not possible to find the optimal solution for large instances in the available time by enumerating all possibilities. However, due to the Hungarian method mentioned above, we no longer use this approach.

3. Routing Problems

With a different interpretation of the variables and a possible extension of the constraints, the assignment problem changes into a series of other problems. In this section, we consider two routing problems.

3.1. Travelling Salesman Problem

The *Travelling Salesman Problem* (TSP) [8,62] is mathematically similar to the assignment problem model, differing only in one additional constraint, but the meaning of the decision variables $x_{ij} = 0$ is different. It is formulated as follows: Given n cities and distances among them, the objective is to find a round trip through all cities with a minimum length (alternatively, with a minimum total transportation cost).

Since the starting city 1 is fixed, the number of routes is given by the permutations of cities 2, 3, ..., n, and is therefore equal to $(n-1)!$. If there are no one-way segments anywhere in the transportation between cities, routes in reverse order of cities do not affect the length, and then we can reduce the number of routes to $(n-1)!/2$, but still the time complexity of exploring all routes is $\mathcal{O}(n!)$.

If we denote by c_{ij} the distance between cities i and j (alternatively, the price of transportation between cities i and j), x_{ij} a binary decision variable that takes the value 1 when city j on the route immediately follows city i, otherwise it takes the value 0, δ_i is the order of city i on the route, then the Travelling Salesman Problem can be formulated as follows:

$$z = \sum_{i=1}^{n} \sum_{j=1}^{n} c_{ij} x_{ij} \rightarrow \min \tag{5}$$

subject to

$$\sum_{i=1}^{n} x_{ij} = 1,\ j = 1, \ldots, n \tag{6}$$

$$\sum_{j=1}^{n} x_{ij} = 1,\ i = 1, \ldots, n \tag{7}$$

$$\delta_i - \delta_j + nx_{ij} \leq n - 1,\ i \neq j,\ i = 2, \ldots, n,\ j = 2, \ldots, n \tag{8}$$

$$x_{ij} \in \{0,1\},\ i = 1, \ldots, n,\ j = 1, \ldots, n \tag{9}$$

Constraints (6) and (7) ensure that each city (vertex of the graph) is traversed exactly once (entered and left exactly once); the system of subtour elimination constraints (8), referred to in the English literature by Miller, Tucker, and Zemlin as *MTZ constraints*, prevents the formation of subtours, as we will show below in Theorem 1.

Equation (8) follows from the following reasoning:
(i) If $x_{ij} = 1$, then j is the immediate successor of i, and if $\delta_i = t$, then $\delta_j = t + 1$. Hence, $\delta_i - \delta_j + nx_{ij} = t - (t+1) + n = n - 1$.
(ii) If $x_{ij} = 0$, then $\delta_i - \delta_j + nx_{ij} = \delta_i - \delta_j$ and this difference in the order of the cities in the route for $i \neq j$ can be at most equal to $n - 1$.

From (i) and (ii), a common conclusion $\delta_i - \delta_j + nx_{ij} \leq n - 1$ already follows, which, for all combinations of feasible values of i and j, is expressed by inequality (8).

Without the constraint (8), constraints (6) and (7) are satisfied by splitting the route into several subtours, e.g., for 15 vertices, the two conditions mentioned above are satisfied by the subtours $1 - 3 - 7 - 9 - 12 - 1, 2 - 4 - 10 - 11 - 13 - 15 - 2$ and $5 - 6 - 8 - 14 - 5$.

Theorem 1. (Miller, Tucker, Zemlin) *The variables $x_{ij} \in \{0,1\}$, $i = 1, \ldots, n$, $j = 1, \ldots, n$ satisfying constraints (6) and (7) form a Hamiltonian circle if and only if the subtour elimination constraints (8) are satisfied.*

Proof. Suppose that x_{ij} satisfies the subtour elimination constraints but does not form a Hamiltonian circle. Then x_{ij} due to (6) and (7) form at least two subtours, one containing the initial vertex 1 and another without it. Let S be a subtour that does not contain vertex 1 and let $E(S)$ be the set of edges in S. Summing the conditions over the edges of $E(S)$ we get:

$$\sum_{(i,j)\in E(S)} (\delta_i - \delta_j + nx_{ij}) \leq (n-1)|E(S)|,$$

since the values of δ_i and δ_j eliminate each other in this subtour, we get

$$n|E(S)| \leq (n-1)|E(S)|,$$

which is a contradiction.

Assume now that x_{ij} forms a Hamiltonian circle. If 1 is the initial vertex of this circle, and for each vertex $i \neq 1$, $\delta_i = k$, if i is the kth vertex of the Hamiltonian circle, then it is clear that the conditions (8) are satisfied. □

3.2. Vehicle Routing Problem

A generalization of the Travelling Salesman Problem is the *Vehicle Routing Problem* (VRP) [9,63–66] where a desired quantity of goods needs to be delivered from a central depot to customers by vehicles of a certain capacity.

We are looking for closed routes of individual vehicles that start and end at the depot, each customer is served exactly once by exactly one vehicle, the requirements of all customers are met and the total transport costs are minimal.

Consider the following notation:
n ... number of customers
0 ... depot (start and end of each vehicle's route)

K ... number of (identical) vehicles
$d_j \geq 0$ ... request of the jth customer (for depot $d_0 = 0$)
Q ... vehicle capacity ($KQ \geq \sum_{j=1}^{n} d_j$)
c_{ij} ... the cost of transport from i to j ($c_{ii} = 0$)
x_{ij} ... binary decision variable equal to 1 if j is immediately followed by i on the route, $x_{ij} = 0$ otherwise
δ_i ... the load left in the vehicle after visiting customer i.

$$z = \sum_{i=0}^{n} \sum_{j=0}^{n} c_{ij} x_{ij} \rightarrow \min \tag{10}$$

subject to

$$\sum_{i=0}^{n} x_{ij} = 1,\ j = 1, \ldots, n \tag{11}$$

$$\sum_{j=0}^{n} x_{ij} = 1,\ i = 1, \ldots, n \tag{12}$$

$$\sum_{i=1}^{n} x_{i0} = K \tag{13}$$

$$\sum_{j=1}^{n} x_{0j} = K \tag{14}$$

$$0 \leq \delta_i \leq Q - d_i,\ i = 1, \ldots, n \tag{15}$$

$$\delta_i - \delta_j + Qx_{ij} \leq Q - d_j,\ i \neq j,\ i = 1, \ldots, n,\ j = 1, \ldots, n, \text{ such that } d_i + d_j \leq Q \tag{16}$$

$$x_{ij} \in \{0, 1\},\ i = 0, \ldots, n,\ j = 0, \ldots, n \tag{17}$$

In the model, (11) and (12) ensure that exactly one vehicle arrives at each customer (11) and exactly one vehicle leaves it (12). Equations (13) and (14) ensure that all K vehicles return to the depot (13) and all K vehicles leave the depot (14).

Equation (16) is analogous to the MTZ constraints in the Travelling Salesman Problem preventing the formation of partial circuits and at the same time ensuring that the requirements of customers i and j can be met when traveling from i to j [67].

The Vehicle Routing Problem has many other specific formulations, e.g., there may be a larger number of depots available, and customers are only ready to receive delivery of goods at certain time intervals. For more details, see the sources listed at the beginning of this section.

4. Distribution Problems

Distribution problems have many different formulations, first, we consider the classical Hitchcock's *Transportation/Transshipment Problem* with m suppliers (sources, warehouses) and n customers (consumers), where we assume the transportation of a single type of material (goods) with an objective to minimize the total cost of transporting the material [68].

Assume the following notation:
$a_i,\ i = 1, \ldots, m$ ... capacity (stocks) of suppliers,
$b_j,\ j = 1, \ldots, n$ ... customer requirements,
$c_{ij},\ i = 1, \ldots, m,\ j = 1, \ldots, n$ ... the matrix of rates for the transport of a unit quantity between the ith supplier and the jth customer,
$x_{ij},\ i = 1, \ldots, m,\ j = 1, \ldots, n$ ...the sought quantity transported between the ith supplier and the jth customer.

If total stocks are equal to total requirements, this means:

$$\sum_{i=1}^{m} a_i = \sum_{j=1}^{n} b_j, \tag{18}$$

we are talking about a *balanced distribution problem*, where all stocks are exhausted and all demands are met, and the following mathematical model corresponds to this:

$$z = \sum_{i=1}^{m}\sum_{j=1}^{n} c_{ij}x_{ij} \rightarrow \min \tag{19}$$

subject to

$$\sum_{j=1}^{n} x_{ij} = a_i,\ i = 1, \ldots, m \tag{20}$$

$$\sum_{i=1}^{m} x_{ij} = b_j,\ j = 1, \ldots, n \tag{21}$$

$$x_{ij} \geq 0,\ i = 1, \ldots, m,\ j = 1, \ldots, n \tag{22}$$

Equation (20) corresponds to the stock drawdown, and Equation (21) expresses the fulfillment of requirements.

Obviously, the assignment problem is a special case of the balanced transportation problem, where:

$$m = n$$

$$a_i = 1,\ i = 1, \ldots, m$$

$$b_j = 1,\ j = 1, \ldots, n$$

$$x_{ij} \in \{0, 1\},\ i = 1, \ldots, m,\ j = 1, \ldots, n$$

However, the balanced case is rare in practice, usually, total stocks exceed total requirements, i.e.,

$$\sum_{i=1}^{m} a_i > \sum_{j=1}^{n} b_j \tag{23}$$

In this case, all requirements can be met, but not every stock will be used up. The model then changes as follows:

$$z = \sum_{i=1}^{m}\sum_{j=1}^{n} c_{ij}x_{ij} \rightarrow \min \tag{24}$$

subject to

$$\sum_{j=1}^{n} x_{ij} \leq a_i,\ i = 1, \ldots, m \tag{25}$$

$$\sum_{i=1}^{m} x_{ij} = b_j,\ j = 1, \ldots, n \tag{26}$$

$$x_{ij} \geq 0,\ i = 1, \ldots, m,\ j = 1, \ldots, n \tag{27}$$

In the case of material shortages, the opposite situation may occur, where the total stock is insufficient for the total requirements, i.e.,

$$\sum_{i=1}^{m} a_i < \sum_{j=1}^{n} b_j \tag{28}$$

This means that stocks are used up but not all requirements can be met. The model must then be modified as follows:

$$z = \sum_{i=1}^{m}\sum_{j=1}^{n} c_{ij}x_{ij} \to \min \tag{29}$$

subject to

$$\sum_{j=1}^{n} x_{ij} = a_i,\ i = 1, \ldots, m \tag{30}$$

$$\sum_{i=1}^{m} x_{ij} \leq b_j,\ j = 1, \ldots, n \tag{31}$$

$$x_{ij} \geq 0,\ i = 1, \ldots, m,\ j = 1, \ldots, n \tag{32}$$

4.1. Container Transportation Problem

The Container Transportation Problem is a special case of Hitchcock's transportation problem, where we assume that materials from suppliers to customers are transported only in containers of a certain capacity. Instead of rates per unit of material transported, there are prices per container transported, being fixed even if the container is not completely full.

From the previous three possibilities for the sum of all stocks and the sum of all requirement relations, the case of the stocks being sufficient to meet all the requirements is given here.

Assume that K is the capacity of the container and y_{ij} gives the number of containers needed for the quantity of material x_{ij}. Obviously, y_{ij} must be integers, the last container to reach the quantity x_{ij} need not be full.

Then, the container transportation problem for all requirements met can be formulated as the following model:

$$z = \sum_{i=1}^{m}\sum_{j=1}^{n} c_{ij}y_{ij} \to \min \tag{33}$$

subject to

$$\sum_{j=1}^{n} x_{ij} \leq a_i,\ i = 1, \ldots, m \tag{34}$$

$$\sum_{i=1}^{m} x_{ij} = b_j,\ j = 1, \ldots, n \tag{35}$$

$$x_{ij} \leq K y_{ij},\ i = 1, \ldots, m,\ j = 1, \ldots, n \tag{36}$$

$$y_{ij} \in \mathbb{Z}_+,\ i = 1, \ldots, m,\ j = 1, \ldots, n \tag{37}$$

$$x_{ij} \geq 0,\ i = 1, \ldots, m,\ j = 1, \ldots, n \tag{38}$$

4.2. Allocation Problem

For the transportation problem described in Section 4, it was possible to provide the required quantity by composing partial quantities from different suppliers (from different warehouses) when fulfilling the requirements.

However, in the *Allocation Problem*, it is required that the required quantity is provided from a single location so the mathematical model of the transportation problem has to be modified by [10] to account for this condition. With the same notation used for the symbols, the meaning of the decision variables x_{ij} is now different. They only assume binary values and $x_{ij} = 1$ if the quantity b_j required by the jth customer is sourced from the ith supplier, if not, $x_{ij} = 0$.

If more than one customer receives the required quantity from the same supplier, the sum of their requirements must not exceed the capacity of that supplier (stock).

The model of the allocation problem with these conditions then takes the following form:

$$z = \sum_{i=1}^{m} \sum_{j=1}^{n} c_{ij} x_{ij} \rightarrow \min \tag{39}$$

subject to

$$\sum_{i=1}^{m} x_{ij} = 1,\ j = 1, \ldots, n \tag{40}$$

$$\sum_{j=1}^{n} b_j x_{ij} \leq a_i,\ i = 1, \ldots, m \tag{41}$$

$$x_{ij} \in \{0,1\},\ i = 1, \ldots, m,\ j = 1, \ldots, n \tag{42}$$

4.3. Location Problem

The *Location Problem* is an extension of the allocation problem [12]. For clarity, let us first summarize all the symbols used.

Consider m locations with capacities a_i, $i = 1, \ldots, m$ that can be used to operate warehouses supplying n customers with demands b_j, $j = 1, \ldots, n$. The operation of the warehouse at the ith location requires a cost f_i, $i = 1, \ldots, m$ for the given period. Let c_{ij}, $i = 1, \ldots, m$, $j = 1, \ldots, n$ be the cost of the jth customer being assigned to get the required quantity from the ith location.

The aim is to decide in which locations to operate the warehouses and to find the assignment of customers to the operated warehouses so that the value of the total cost of operating the system is minimal. Like in the allocation problem, we assume that the demands of each consumer must be covered from a single warehouse.

Therefore, the meaning of the binary decision variables x_{ij} is analogous to the allocation problem, $x_{ij} = 1$, if the quantity b_j required by the jth customer is provided from the warehouse at the ith location, if not, $x_{ij} = 0$.

In addition, there are other binary decision variables y_i, $i = 1, \ldots, m$, where $y_i = 1$ means that the warehouse at the ith location will be operated and, if $y_i = 0$, it will not be operated there.

The model of the location problem with these conditions has the following form:

$$z = \sum_{i=1}^{m} \sum_{j=1}^{n} c_{ij} x_{ij} + \sum_{i=1}^{m} f_i y_i \rightarrow \min \tag{43}$$

subject to

$$\sum_{i=1}^{m} x_{ij} = 1,\ j = 1, \ldots, n \tag{44}$$

$$x_{ij} \leq y_i,\ i = 1, \ldots, m,\ j = 1, \ldots, n \tag{45}$$

$$\sum_{j=1}^{n} b_j x_{ij} \leq a_i,\ i = 1, \ldots, m \tag{46}$$

$$x_{ij} \in \{0,1\},\ i = 1, \ldots, m,\ j = 1, \ldots, n \tag{47}$$

$$y_i \in \{0,1\},\ i = 1, \ldots, m \tag{48}$$

As in the allocation problem, the condition (44) means that each customer takes the entire requested quantity from a single location, the condition (46) monitors the non-overstocking of individual locations by customers receiving the requested quantity from the same location.

Let us have a look at condition (45). The left and right sides are binary variables with the inequality satisfied for the combinations $0 \leq 0$, $0 \leq 1$ and $1 \leq 1$, but not for the combination $1 \leq 0$. This ensures that no customer can get anything from a location where the warehouse will not be operated.

It is clear that, for all combinations of indices i and j, (45) represents a system of mn conditions. Expressing this for the values of the indices j, we get:

$$x_{i1} \leq y_i, \; i = 1, \ldots, m$$

$$x_{i2} \leq y_i, \; i = 1, \ldots, m$$

$$\vdots$$

$$x_{in} \leq y_i, \; i = 1, \ldots, m$$

Summing up the previous inequalities, we get:

$$x_{i1} + x_{i2} + \cdots + x_{in} \leq y_i + y_i + \cdots + y_i \; i = 1, \ldots, m,$$

and hence

$$\sum_{j=1}^{n} x_{ij} \leq n y_i, \; i = 1, \ldots, m \tag{49}$$

Equation (49) is equivalent to (45), but is simpler because it represents only m conditions rather than the mn conditions in the original expression (45).

4.4. Capacitated Network Area Coverage

Let us consider two finite sets I and J, where I is the set of service centers $1, 2, \ldots, m$, and J is the set of customer locations $1, 2, \ldots, n$.

Further, $a_{ij} = 1$ means that customer location j is in a reachable distance to service center i, $a_{ij} = 0$ means that it does not satisfy it, and w_i expresses the weights of service centers (since it is the minimization problem, the greater the weights are, the smaller the coefficient must be).

Similarly, $x_i = 1$ means that service centre i is selected, while $x_i = 0$ means that it is not selected.

Finally, c_i, $i \in I$—capacity of service centre i, b_j, $j \in J$—demand of customer location j, $y_{ij} \in \{0, 1\}$—customer from location j is assigned or is not assigned to service centre i.

In [13], we derived the following model for a capacitated network area coverage:

$$z = \sum_{i \in I} w_i x_i \rightarrow \min \tag{50}$$

subject to

$$\forall j \in J : \sum_{i \in I} a_{ij} x_i \geq 1 \tag{51}$$

$$\forall j \in J : \sum_{i \in I} a_{ij} y_{ij} = 1 \tag{52}$$

$$\forall i \in I : \; c_i x_i \geq \sum_{j \in J} a_{ij} y_{ij} b_j \tag{53}$$

$$\forall i \in I : \sum_{j \in J} y_{ij} \leq n x_i \tag{54}$$

$$\forall i \in I : \; x_i \in \{0, 1\} \tag{55}$$

$$(\forall i \in I)(\forall j \in J) : \; y_{ij} \in \{0, 1\}. \tag{56}$$

A necessary precondition for finding a solution is that the sum of all capacities is sufficient to cover all demands, i.e., $\sum_{i=1}^{m} c_i \geq \sum_{j \in J} b_j$, with each customer having a reachable distance to at least one center, i.e., $\forall j \in J : \sum_{i \in I} a_{ij} > 0$.

In [13], we then modified the previous model for the domain of telecommunication signals considering signal interference and its nonlinear version linearized as follows:

$$z = \left(\sum_{i\in I} w_i x_i\right) / \sum_{i\in I} w_i - \left(\sum_{i\in I}\sum_{j\in I} d_{ij} h_{ij}\right) / \left(\sum_{i\in I}\sum_{j\in I} d_{ij}\right) \rightarrow \min \tag{57}$$

subject to

$$(\forall i \in I)(\forall j \in I): \; h_{ij} \leq x_i \tag{58}$$

$$(\forall i \in I)(\forall j \in I): \; h_{ij} \leq x_j \tag{59}$$

$$(\forall i \in I)(\forall j \in I): \; h_{ij} \geq (x_i + x_j - 1) \tag{60}$$

$$(\forall i \in I)(\forall j \in I): \; h_{ij} \in \{0,1\} \tag{61}$$

$$\forall j \in J: \; \sum_{i\in I} a_{ij} x_i \geq 1 \tag{62}$$

$$\forall j \in J: \; \sum_{i\in I} a_{ij} y_{ij} = 1 \tag{63}$$

$$\forall i \in I: \; c_i x_i \geq \sum_{j\in J} a_{ij} y_{ij} b_j \tag{64}$$

$$\forall i \in I: \; \sum_{j\in J} y_{ij} \leq n x_i \tag{65}$$

$$(\forall i \in I)(\forall j \in I)(i \neq j): \; d_{ij} \geq (x_i + x_j - 1) d_{\min} \tag{66}$$

$$\forall i \in I: \; x_i \in \{0,1\} \tag{67}$$

$$(\forall i \in I)(\forall j \in J): \; y_{ij} \in \{0,1\}. \tag{68}$$

Another possible modification of the model is to meet the demand by composing parts of the capacities of several centers, but with a fragmentation not lower than a certain threshold. This new approach will be presented in detail in a separate paper.

4.5. Transportation Problem with Supply from Primary Source

Consider now a transportation network where, in addition to locations with warehouse stocks and customer requirements, there will also be a primary source, which can represent the location of the transported commodity or a global warehouse, and customers can be supplied both from local warehouses and directly from the primary source.

Assume the constraints and denotations from the location problem and two types of transportation equipment, one with a larger capacity k_1 from the primary source to local warehouses and a cost n_1 per 1 km of travel, and the other with a smaller capacity k_2 to customers and a cost n_2 per 1 km. Denoting the distance from the primary source to the ith local storage by e_i, and the distance from the primary source to the jth customer by g_j, we add binary decision variables z_j to indicate whether the jth customer receives the desired quantity directly from the primary source (in the positive case $z_j = 1$, otherwise $z_j = 0$), the model with primary source and transportation technique information has the following form:

$$z = \sum_{j=1}^{n} \frac{b_j}{k_2} g_j n_2 z_j + \sum_{i=1}^{m}\sum_{j=1}^{n} \left(\frac{b_j}{k_1} e_i n_1 + \frac{b_j}{k_2} d_{ij} n_2\right) x_{ij} + \sum_{i=1}^{m} f_i y_i \rightarrow \min \tag{69}$$

subject to

$$z_j + \sum_{i=1}^{m} x_{ij} = 1, \; j = 1, \ldots, n \tag{70}$$

$$\sum_{j=1}^{n} x_{ij} \leq n y_i, \; i = 1, \ldots, m \tag{71}$$

$$\sum_{j=1}^{n} b_j x_{ij} \leq a_i, \; i = 1, \ldots, m \tag{72}$$

$$x_{ij} \in \{0,1\}, \; i = 1, \ldots, m, \; j = 1, \ldots, n \tag{73}$$

$$y_i \in \{0,1\}, \; i = 1, \ldots, m \tag{74}$$

$$z_j \in \{0,1\}, \; j = 1, \ldots, n \tag{75}$$

The fractions in the objective function according to (69) indicate how many times the distance must be traveled for the customer to receive the required quantity. Since the fractions may have non-integer values, they must be rounded up to integers, the corresponding capacity may not be fully used for the last trip. The expression with the first summation in the objective function corresponds to the total cost of moving material from the primary source directly to customers, and the expression with the double summation in the objective function corresponds to the total cost of moving material from the primary source to local warehouses and from there on to the customers.

If, instead of the conditions of the location problem, the simpler conditions of the allocation problem were assumed (i.e., dropping the decision as to whether or not to use a location for storage), the previous model would be simplified, the conditions (71) and (74) would be dropped and y_i would be omitted in the last term of the objective function (i.e., the fixed costs of all locations would be included).

4.6. Crop Problem

In plant production, an important task is to find a method of sowing the land with agricultural crops (cultures) in such a way that, given the expected yield of crops on the land and the profit from the sale of individual crops, the total profit is maximised.

Assume the following notation:
p_i, $i = 1, \ldots, m$ ... grounds,
r_i, $j = 1, \ldots, m$ ... area of grounds (plays the role of available capacities),
k_j, $j = 1, \ldots, n$ ... agricultural crops (cultures),
c_{ij}, $i = 1, \ldots, m$, $j = 1, \ldots, n$ ... profit from 1 ha of ground p_i, sown with culture k_j
x_{ij}, $i = 1, \ldots, m$, $j = 1, \ldots, n$ ...number of hectares of ground p_i sown with crop k_j.

The mathematical model of the Crop Problem is similar to the basic version of the transportation problem with unbalanced capacities (the ground areas may not be fully used), but it lacks a set of constraints corresponding to the fulfillment of the requirements with the difference that the problem being a maximization one. It takes the following form:

$$z = \sum_{i=1}^{m} \sum_{j=1}^{n} c_{ij} x_{ij} \rightarrow \max \tag{76}$$

subject to

$$\sum_{j=1}^{n} x_{ij} \leq r_i, \; i = 1, \ldots, m \tag{77}$$

$$x_{ij} \geq 0, \; i = 1, \ldots, m, \; j = 1, \ldots, n \tag{78}$$

Equation (77) expresses the use of grounds, which corresponds to the drawdown of supplier stocks in the distribution problem.

If we required each crop j to be sown on some minimum area d_j, then the problem would become an example of the maximization version of the *generalized distribution problem* and the model would be modified as follows:

$$z = \sum_{i=1}^{m} \sum_{j=1}^{n} c_{ij} x_{ij} \to \max \tag{79}$$

subject to

$$\sum_{j=1}^{n} x_{ij} \le r_i, \; i = 1, \dots, m \tag{80}$$

$$\sum_{i=1}^{m} x_{ij} \ge d_j, \; j = 1, \dots, n \tag{81}$$

$$x_{ij} \ge 0, \; i = 1, \dots, m, \; j = 1, \dots, n \tag{82}$$

5. Scheduling Problems

Scheduling problems are numerous and varied. They arise in diverse areas such as flexible manufacturing systems, production planning, computer design, logistics, timetabling, communication, etc. [14].

Here we focus on one of them, the Permutation Flow Shop Scheduling Problem (PFSSP), which, like the Assignment problem and the Traveling Salesman Problem, is permutational in nature.

It can be briefly described as follows: There are a set of m machines (processors) and a set of n jobs. Each job comprises a set of m operations which must be done on different machines. All jobs have the same processing operation order when passing through the machines. There are no precedence constraints among operations of different jobs. Operations cannot be interrupted, and each machine can process only one operation at a time. The problem is to find the job sequences on the machines which minimizes the makespan (i.e., the maximum completion times of all operations).

Mathematical Model of PFSSP

Consider three finite sets J, M, O where J is a set of jobs $1, \dots, n$, M is a set of machines $1, \dots, m$, and O is a set of operations $1, \dots, m$.

Denote:

J_i ... the ith job in the permutation of jobs
p_{ik} ... processing time of the job $J_i \in J$ on machine k

$(\forall i \in J)(\forall k \in M): \; v_{ik}$ = waiting time (idle time) on machine k before starting job J_i
$(\forall i \in J)(\forall k \in M): \; w_{ik}$ = waiting time (idle time) of job J_i after finishing processing on machine k while waiting for machine $k+1$ to become available

Define the following decision variables:

$$\forall i, j \in J: \; x_{ij} = \begin{cases} 1, & \text{if job } j \text{ is assigned to the } i\text{th position in the permutation } (J_i = j) \\ 0, & \text{otherwise} \end{cases} \tag{83}$$

Figure 1 illustrates the use of the variables v_{ik} and w_{ik} on an example with 5 jobs and 3 machines.

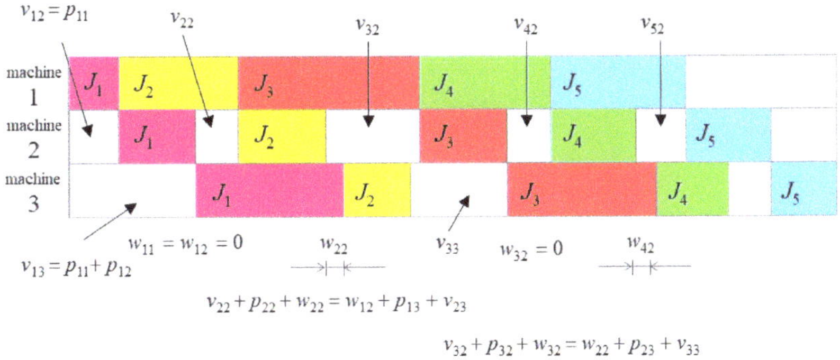

Figure 1. Meaning of the variables v_{ik} and w_{ik}.

From Figure 1, we can draw some more general conclusions:

- The first task in a permutation can always continue the next operation on the next machine without delay because it does not wait for the completion of any other operation.
- It follows from the previous conclusion that waiting times to start the operation of the first task in the permutation on the second and subsequent machines are given by the sum of the durations of the operations of that task on the previous machines.
- Equalities of 3 addition terms in Figure 1 can be generalized into a Gantt chart between all pairs of neighboring machines.
- The duration of the entire schedule (makespan) is given by the sum of the waiting times for the start of operations on the last machine and the duration of these operations.

All verbal conclusions are expressed formally by the following system of equations:

$$\forall i \in J : \sum_{j=1}^{n} x_{ij} = 1 \tag{84}$$

$$\forall j \in J : \sum_{i=1}^{n} x_{ij} = 1 \tag{85}$$

$$\forall k \in M - \{m\} : w_{1k} = 0 \tag{86}$$

$$\forall k \in M - \{1\} : v_{1k} = \sum_{r=1}^{k-1} \sum_{i=1}^{n} p_{ir} x_{1i} \tag{87}$$

$$(\forall i \in J - \{n\})\,(\forall k \in M - \{m\}) :$$

$$v_{i+1,k} + \sum_{j=1}^{n} p_{jk} x_{i+1,j} + w_{i+1,k} = w_{ik} + \sum_{j=1}^{n} p_{j,k+1} x_{ij} + v_{i+1,k+1} \tag{88}$$

$$C_{\max} = \sum_{i=1}^{n} (v_{im} + \sum_{j=1}^{n} p_{jm} x_{ij}) \tag{89}$$

6. Computational Results

From the above problems, we select two, TSP and PFSSP, that are NP-hard in the decision versions [69,70].

To give an idea of the cardinality of the search space of these permutation problems, we present a few factorials as follows:
10! = 3628800 $\approx 3.6 \times 10^6$
20! = 2432902008176640000 $\approx 2.4 \times 10^{18}$
30! = 265252859812191058636308480000000 $\approx 2.6 \times 10^{32}$
40! = 815915283247897734345611269596115894272000000000 $\approx 8.1 \times 10^{47}$
50! $\approx 3 \times 10^{64}$

...
$100! \approx 9.3 \times 10^{157}$

The traditional approaches to such problems are based on computations using heuristic methods [71,72] for large instances such as genetic algorithms, simulated annealing, tabu search, differential evolution [73], firefly algorithm, particle swarm optimization, and ant colony optimization. Then, statistical tests are applied to examine at a certain significance level (e.g., $\alpha = 0.05$), to what extent the mean value of the results obtained by different methods and different settings of their parameters at a larger number of runs is the same or different (and, therefore, one of the methods gives better results). For the *t*-test, we assume that the sets of values have a normal distribution. However, this assumption may be false, and then one of the non-parametric tests, such as the Wilcoxon test, must be used.

Since, given the validity of the No Free Lunch Theorem [74,75], one should not expect a general conclusion that any of the heuristics for each problem instance gives better results than other heuristics.

In this paper, we do not explore heuristics using instead a mixed integer programming model with software tools built as solvers in the GAMS environment [76,77] to find an exact solution by deterministic computation.

Statistical evaluations are, therefore, meaningless here. What can be said, however, is that the power of this software today is considerably greater than it was 20 years ago, when, in our experience, for a problem with a complexity of $\mathcal{O}(20!)$, the system ended up with a runtime error and the message "`insufficient space to update U-factor` ...". The performance of GAMS has been steadily increasing over the years, although the source code of the solvers is not freely available, from [78] it can at least be seen that it includes, among others, CPLEX, GUROBI, Lindo, and the results of the work of academic departments of Princeton University, Stanford University, and Zuse Institute Berlin. Today, GAMS calculates the exact solution for PFSSP with 20 jobs on a laptop with Intel(R) Core(TM) i5-10210U CPU @ 1.60 GHz 2.11 GHz processor, 8 GB operational memory and 64-bit operating system in less than 3 min, as shown in the following subsection.

Of course, with a computer of better technical parameters for the same time limit we get results for larger instances of the problem, but it seems to be better to use a heuristic beyond this boundary, e.g., our GA 'war elimination' modification [79].

Since PFSSP has a more complex model than TSP, we start with it and include its complete GAMS code.

6.1. PFSSP Computational Results

For PFSSP with 10 jobs, 6 machines, processing times from the TABLE section (it corresponds to the first benchmark in Table 1) and the model given by Equations (84)–(89), the program code in GAMS can be, e.g., as follows:

```
* Permutation flow shop scheduling problem
$TITLE permutation flow shop scheduling problem
$OFFSYMXREF
$OFFUELLIST
$OFFUELXREF

OPTION ITERLIM=200,000
* ITERLIM number of iterations
OPTION OPTCR=0.00001
*OPTION OPTCR=0.001
* OPTCR stopping in MIP in case the best solution is within the limits
* 100*OPTCR% of the global~extreme

* section defining indexes
SETS
  I jobs /1*10/
  K machines /1*6/;
```

```
  ALIAS(I,J);
* J - position of the job in the permutation
  ALIAS(K,R);

* input data section
PARAMETERS
  N,M;
  N=CARD(I);
  M=CARD(K);
TABLE P(I,K)
        1    2    3    4    5    6
  1    333  991  996  123  145  234
  2    333  111  663  456  785  532
  3    252  222  222  789  214  586
  4    222  204  114  876  752  532
  5    255  477  123  543  143  142
  6    555  566  456  210  698  573
  7    558  899  789  124  532   12
  8    888  965  876  537  145   14
  9    889  588  543  854  247  527
 10    999  889  210  632  451  856;

*variables section (decision variables and objective function)
VARIABLES
  X(I,J) is 1 if job j is assigned to position i in the permutation, 0, otherwise
  V(I,K) waiting time on machine k before the start of job i in the permutation
  W(I,K) waiting time of job i in the permutation after finishing processing
* on machine k, while machine k+1 becomes free
  Cmax total processing time for all tasks (makespan);
BINARY VARIABLE X;
NONNEGATIVE VARIABLE V;
NONNEGATIVE VARIABLE W;

*section describing the system of (in)equalities
EQUATIONS
  EQ1(I)
  EQ2(J)
  EQ3(K)
  EQ4(K)
  EQ5(I,K)
  OBJFCE(K);
  EQ1(I) .. SUM(J,X(I,J)) =E= 1;
  EQ2(J) .. SUM(I,X(I,J)) =E= 1;
  EQ3(K)$(ORD(K) LE (M-1)) .. W(``1'',K) =E= 0;
  EQ4(K)$(ORD(K) GE 2)
      .. V(``1'',K) =E= SUM((R,I)$(ORD(R) LE (ORD(K)-1)),P(I,R)*X(``1'',I));
  EQ5(I,K)$((ORD(I) LE (N-1)) AND (ORD(K) LE (M-1)))
    .. V(I+1,K)+SUM(J,P(J,K)*X(I+1,J))+W(I+1,K) =E=
       W(I,K)+SUM(J,P(J,K+1)*X(I,J))+V(I+1,K+1);
  OBJFCE(K)$(ORD(K) EQ M) .. Cmax =E= SUM(I,V(I,K)+SUM(J,P(J,K)*X(I,J)));

*description of the model, running the solver, and displaying the results
MODEL FLOWSHOP /ALL/;
SOLVE FLOWSHOP USING MIP MINIMIZING Cmax;
DISPLAY X.L, V.L, W.L, Cmax.L;
```

The ability to compute optimal solutions was checked using standard benchmarks from OR-Library (OR = Operations Research) accessible at Brunel University London [80], originally described in [81]. The computational results are summarised in Table 1. For instances with 30 or more jobs, GAMS does not find the optimal solution in the 1000 s time limit, but only a "close" approximation, which, however, differs by less than 10% even for the last instance 75 × 20, where the optimal value is unknown due to the huge size of the search space and is only estimated by the interval. For such cases, we at least suggest a solution method using the genetic algorithm [82].

Table 1. GAMS computational results (10 × 6 corresponds to 10 jobs and 6 machines, etc.; t-l-e = time limit exceeded).

Benchmark	Result/Optimum/Early End	Time [S]	Iterations
10 × 6	7720/7720/no	0.75	31,535
11 × 5	7038/7038/no	0.13	243
12 × 5	7312/7312/no	0.42	13,095
13 × 4	7166/7166/no	0.20	650
14 × 4	8003/8003/no	0.13	262
20 × 10	1566/1566/no	164.45	2,619,405
30 × 10	2120/2093/t-l-e	1000.02	6,398,821
30 × 15	2692/2513/t-l-e	1000.02	4,886,367
50 × 10	3190/3045/t-l-e	1000.03	3,164,599
75 × 20	5372/in [4890, 4951]/t-l-e	1000.03	2,145,971

To do this, we will need a model that builds an appropriate schedule for the permutation. The genetic algorithm will then select a promising part of the search space of permutations in which a good approximation of the optimum can be found in a reasonable amount of time.

If we have processing times p_{ij} for job i on machine j, and a job permutation $J_1, J_2, \ldots, J_n$, then we can calculate the completion times $C_{J_i,j}$ as follows:

$$C_{J_1,1} = p_{J_1,1} \tag{90}$$

$$\forall i \in J - \{1\} : C_{J_i,1} = C_{J_{i-1},1} + p_{J_i,1} \tag{91}$$

$$\forall k \in M - \{1\} : C_{J_1,k} = C_{J_1,k-1} + p_{J_1,k} \tag{92}$$

$$(\forall i \in J - \{1\})(\forall k \in M - \{1\}) : C_{J_i,k} = \max\{C_{J_{i-1},k}, C_{J_i,k-1}\} + p_{J_i,k} \tag{93}$$

$$C_{\max} = C_{J_n,m} \tag{94}$$

As the genetic algorithms [79] are well known, we only summarise parameter settings and describe only the problem-specific operators in more detail.

The fitness function is inversely proportional to the makespan, the smaller the makespan, the higher the value of the fitness function.

The number of individuals in the population was set to 50 and the number of iterations to $10n^2$. The initial population was generated randomly, and the parents for the crossover operation were determined by binary tournament selection.

As to the *crossover* operation, we cannot use the traditional two-point crossover, because it would lead to infeasible solutions. If we change the middle parts of the parent chromosomes P_1 and P_2 in Figure 2, we will obtain offspring (10,5,2,6,10,4,1,6,3,1) and (5,8,4,7,8,9,2,6,3,1) that correspond to no permutations, because some jobs are duplicated or omitted. We used what is called *crossover in a partially mapped representation* where the genes in the middle part of one chromosome are ordered in its offspring by their occurrence in the second parent chromosome.

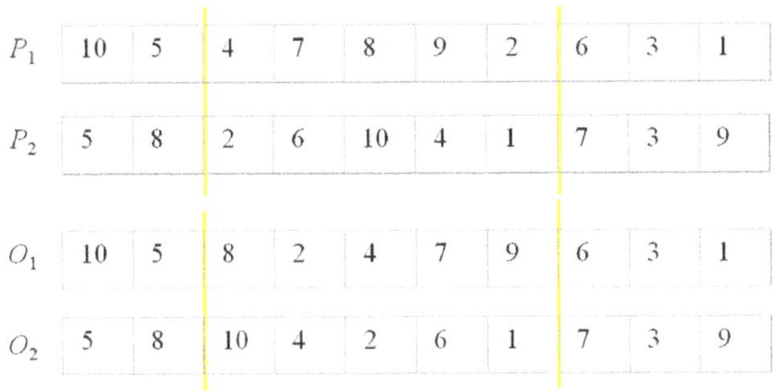

Figure 2. Modified two-point crossover.

From the possible mutation operations, we have selected the *shift mutation*, which removes a value at one position and puts it at another position), see Figure 3.

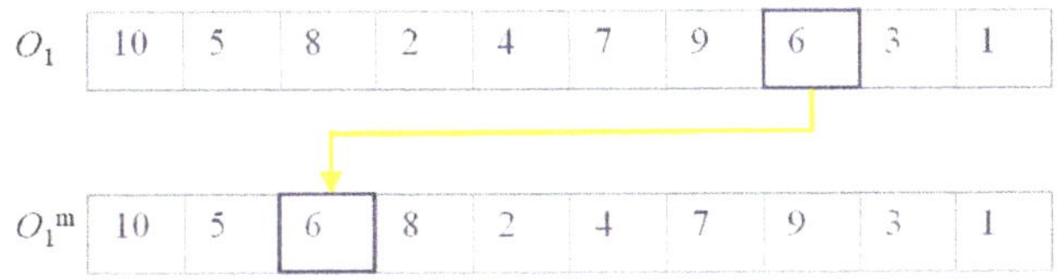

Figure 3. Shift mutation.

The offspring of the parents replaced two randomly selected individuals with below-average fitness function values.

With the above parameter settings, the results for the last 4 instances in Table 1 were obtained as shown in Table 2. The average values from 30 runs are presented here, as well as the best values obtained from them, which for these large instances are better than the values obtained from GAMS when the 1000 s timeout expires. All these results were achieved in less than 10 s because of the small number of iterations of the genetic algorithm.

Table 2. GA computational results—average and the best result from 30 runs, optimum.

Benchmark	Average Result/the Best Result	Optimum
30×10	2126/2099	2093
30×15	2570/2525	2513
50×10	3132/3090	3045
75×20	5261/5203	between 4890 and 4951

6.2. TSP Implementation in GAMS

In describing the source code in GAMS and verifying its computational abilities, we use three benchmarks from the TSPlib library [83] with 24, 52, and 100 cities, or positions in the map given by coordinates.

The following code is written for the `gr24.tsp` benchmark. Since the adjacency matrix is symmetric, only the data of the lower triangular matrix are entered with the remaining data calculated. The EQUATIONS section is a rewrite of the TSP model and its Equations (5)–(8). The x_{ij} binary domain, corresponding to Equation (9), is given by the declaration that precedes this section.

```
$TITLE Travelling Salesman Problem
OPTION ITERLIM=10000000;
OPTION OPTCR=0;

SETS
  I /1*24/;
```

```
  ALIAS (I,J);

PARAMETERS
  N;
  N=CARD(I);

TABLE C(I,J) adjacency matrix
      1   2   3   4   5   6   7   8   9  10  11  12  13  14  15  16  17  18  19  20  21  22  23  24
 1    0
 2  257   0
 3   87 196   0
 4   91 228 158   0
 5  150 112  96 120   0
 6   80 196  88  77  63   0
 7  130 167  59 101  56  25   0
 8  134 154  63 105  34  29  22   0
 9  243 209 286 159 190 216 229 225   0
 10 185  86 124 156  40 124  95  82 207   0
 11 214 223  49 185 123 115  86  90 313 151   0
 12  70 191 121  27  83  47  64  68 173 119 148   0
 13 272 180 315 188 193 245 258 228  29 159 342 209   0
 14 219  83 172 149  79 139 134 112 126  62 199 153  97   0
 15 293  50 232 264 148 232 203 190 248 122 259 227 219 134   0
 16  54 219  92  82 119  31  43  58 238 147  84  53 267 170 255   0
 17 211  74  81 182 105 150 121 108 310  37 160 145 196  99 125 173   0
 18 290 139  98 261 144 176 164 136 389 116 147 224 275 178 154 190  79   0
 19 268  53 138 239 123 207 178 165 367  86 187 202 227 130  68 230  57  86   0
 20 261  43 200 232  98 200 171 131 166  90 227 195 137  69  82 223  90 176  90   0
 21 175 128  76 146  32  76  47  30 222  56 103 109 225 104 164  99  57 112 114 134   0
 22 250  99  89 221 105 189 160 147 349  76 138 184 235 138 114 212  39  40  46 136  96   0
 23 192 228 235 108 119 165 178 154  71 136 262 110  74  96 264 187 182 261 239 165 151 221   0
 24 121 142  99  84  35  29  42  36 220  70 126  55 249 104 178  60  96 175 153 146  47 135 169   0;

SET C2(I,J);
C2(I,J)$(NOT SAMEAS(I,J)) = yes;
C(C2(I,J)) = MAX(C(I,J),C(J,I));

VARIABLES
  X(I,J)
  delta(I)
  Z;
BINARY VARIABLE X(I,J);

EQUATIONS
  EQ1(J)   each city is entered exactly once
  EQ2(I)   each city is left exactly once
  EQ3(I,J) subtour elimination constraints
  EQ4      objective function;
  EQ1(J) .. SUM(I,X(I,J)$(ORD(I) NE ORD(J))) =E= 1;
  EQ2(I) .. SUM(J,X(I,J)$(ORD(I) NE ORD(J))) =E= 1;
  EQ3(I,J)$((ORD(I) GE 2) AND (ORD(J) GE 2) AND (ORD(I) NE ORD(J)))
         .. delta(I)-delta(J)+N*X(I,J) =L= N-1;
  EQ4    .. Z =E= SUM((I,J),C(I,J)*X(I,J));

MODEL TSP/ALL/;
SOLVE TSP USING MIP MINIMIZING Z;
DISPLAY X.L, Z.L;
```

The total length of the route is 1272, the decision variables $x_{i,j}$ have a value of 1 in the following order: $x_{1,16}$, $x_{16,11}$, $x_{11,3}$, $x_{3,7}$, $x_{7,6}$, $x_{6,24}$, $x_{24,8}$, $x_{8,21}$, $x_{21,5}$, $x_{5,10}$, $x_{10,17}$, $x_{17,22}$, $x_{22,18}$, $x_{18,19}$, $x_{19,15}$, $x_{15,2}$, $x_{2,20}$, $x_{20,14}$, $x_{14,13}$, $x_{13,9}$, $x_{9,23}$, $x_{23,4}$, $x_{4,12}$, $x_{12,1}$, and, thus, the circuitous route passes through cities 1, 16, 11, 3, 7, 6, 24, 8, 21, 5, 10, 17, 22, 18, 19, 15, 2, 20, 14, 13, 9, 23, 4, 12, 1, which is in agreement with the published result for the gr24 benchmark. The calculation time was 0.36 s.

The data for the `berlin52.tsp` benchmark are entered differently, namely as a matrix with 52 rows and 2 columns, where the 1st column is the value of the *x*-coordinate and the 2nd column is the value of the *y*-coordinate. The adjacency matrix in this case is obtained by calculating the Euclidean distances between all pairs of positions. This part of the code takes the following form, the rest is the same as in the previous code.

```
SETS
  I /1*52/;
  ALIAS (I,J);

PARAMETERS
  N;
```

```
N=CARD(I);

TABLE XY(I,*)
     1        2
1  565.0    575.0
2   25.0    185.0
3  345.0    750.0
4  945.0    685.0
5  845.0    655.0
6  880.0    660.0
7   25.0    230.0
8  525.0   1000.0
9  580.0   1175.0
10 650.0   1130.0
11 1605.0   620.0
12 1220.0   580.0
13 1465.0   200.0
14 1530.0     5.0
15  845.0   680.0
16  725.0   370.0
17  145.0   665.0
18  415.0   635.0
19  510.0   875.0
20  560.0   365.0
21  300.0   465.0
22  520.0   585.0
23  480.0   415.0
24  835.0   625.0
25  975.0   580.0
26 1215.0   245.0
27 1320.0   315.0
28 1250.0   400.0
29  660.0   180.0
30  410.0   250.0
31  420.0   555.0
32  575.0   665.0
33 1150.0  1160.0
34  700.0   580.0
35  685.0   595.0
36  685.0   610.0
37  770.0   610.0
38  795.0   645.0
39  720.0   635.0
40  760.0   650.0
41  475.0   960.0
42  95.0    260.0
43  875.0   920.0
44  700.0   500.0
45  555.0   815.0
46  830.0   485.0
47 1170.0    65.0
48  830.0   610.0
49  605.0   625.0
50  595.0   360.0
51 1340.0   725.0
52 1740.0   245.0;

PARAMETERS C(I,J);

SET C2(I,J);
C2(I,J)$(NOT SAMEAS(I,J)) = yes;
C(C2(I,J)) = ROUND(SQRT(SQR(XY(I,'1')-XY(J,'1'))+SQR(XY(I,'2')-XY(J,'2'))));
```

The total length of the route is 7542, the calculation time was 1.45 s and the circuitous route passes through positions 1, 49, 32, 45, 19, 41, 8, 9, 10, 43, 33, 51, 11, 52, 14, 13, 47, 26, 27, 28, 12, 25, 4, 6, 15, 5, 24, 48, 38, 37, 40, 39, 36, 35, 34, 44, 46, 16, 29, 50, 20, 23, 30, 2, 7, 42, 21, 17, 3, 18, 31, 22, 1. The optimal route can be seen in Figure 4.

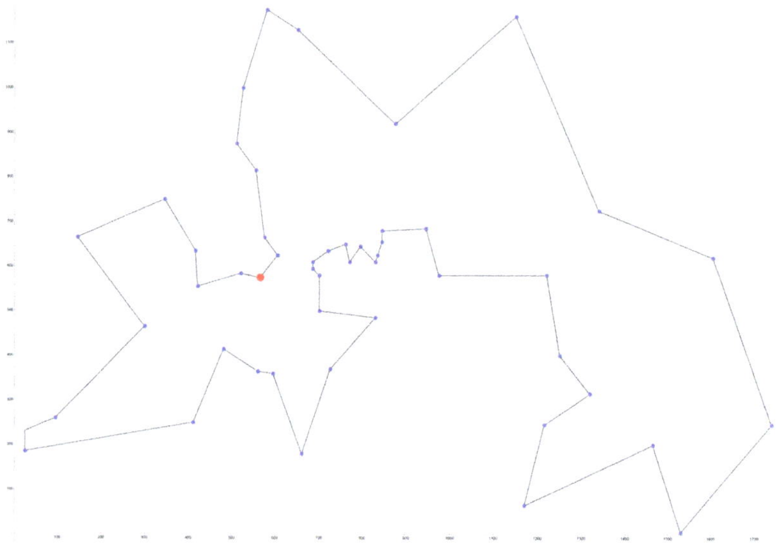

Figure 4. The optimal route for the berlin52.tsp benchmark.

Finally, GAMS for the `kroA100.tsp` benchmark stopped the computation at 1000.02 s by exceeding the time limit, but the intermediate result of the path length 21282 and its traversal through positions 1, 47, 93, 28, 67, 58, 61, 51, 87, 25, 81, 69, 64, 40, 54, 2, 44, 50, 73, 68, 85, 82, 95, 13, 76, 33, 37, 5, 52, 78, 96, 39, 30, 48, 100, 41, 71, 14, 3, 43, 46, 29, 34, 83, 55, 7, 9, 57, 20, 12, 27, 86, 35, 62, 60, 77, 23, 98, 91, 45, 32, 11, 15, 17, 59, 74, 21, 72, 10, 84, 36, 99, 38, 24, 18, 79, 53, 88, 16, 94, 22, 70, 66, 26, 65, 4, 97, 56, 80, 31, 89, 42, 8, 92, 75, 19, 90, 49, 6, 63, 1 corresponds to the known optimal solution for this benchmark. The optimal route is in Figure 5.

Figure 5. The optimal route for the kroA100.tsp benchmark.

For instances with more than 100 positions, it would be necessary to search for an approximation of the optimum using one of the heuristic methods.

One of the first was the use of the so-called *Lin-2-Opt change operator* [8], see Figure 6. Here, two elements are added to the permutation of n cities to visit (into positions 0 and $n+1$), and then the starting city is assigned to those positions to simulate a cyclic tour. Two 'edges' (pairs of neighbouring elements in permutation) are randomly chosen ((p_1, p_2) and

(q_1, q_2) say), the inner elements p_2, q_1 are swapped and the elements between p_2 and q_1 are reversed.

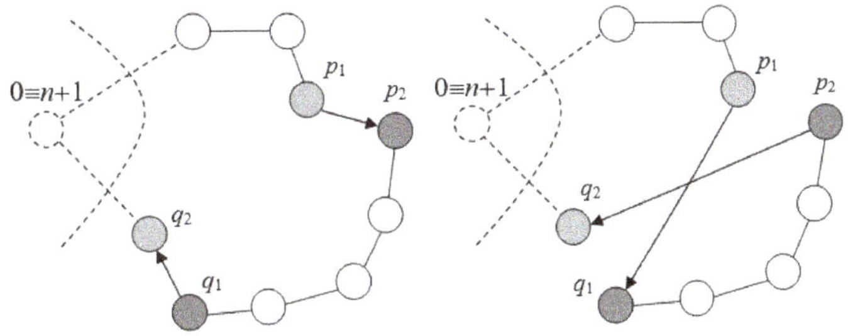

Figure 6. Lin-2-Opt change neighbourhood operation,

Positions 0 and $n+1$ with the fixed value of the starting city can also be used to expand the individuals in the population of the genetic algorithm and then apply the operations presented for the PFSSP.

However, we no longer investigate this for extremely large instances of the TSP problem because heuristics do not guarantee finding an optimal solution, which often is not even known here, and the aim was to find bounds for which we still obtain the precise solution in reasonable time using a 'normal' computer. In the case of GAMS, this bound is an instance with 100 cities.

6.3. Data, Changes in Time, Uncertainty

Data from OR-Library and TSPLIB are related to a specific point in time, in reality they may change over time or may not be completely known.

A more general case of the Travelling Salesman Problem is the *Canadian Traveller Problem* (CTP) [84,85]. Here, the distance matrix may change over time due to the occurrence of events that make some parts of the route inaccessible so that an adaptive strategy must be found. These events are random in nature, which corresponds to the problems of robot navigation in environments where the distribution of obstacles is only discovered as the robot moves through the environment; moreover, the obstacles may move, and thus the locations of potential collisions change dynamically.

In transport tasks, the values of some parameters can change over time, the fuel price is not constant, and the vehicle consumption can only be estimated because it can change according to the traffic situation and the season, which will affect, e.g., the calculation of the objective function (69). Similarly, in the crop problem, we can only estimate crop yields.

In location-based tasks, the problem may arise of adding another center to an existing network of centers to improve the coverage of an area. An example might be an expansion of the existing supermarket network of a chain store. Here it is suggested to use one of the properties of the Voronoi diagram [86,87], a data structure known from computational geometry: Assume a Voronoi diagram with its sites represented by the current centers. The point q is the vertex of the Voronoi diagram if and only if the *largest empty circle* $C(q)$ contains three (or more in a degenerate case) sites on its boundary and none inside. Among these circles, we determine the one with the largest diameter, and its center is then the optimal position for the location of the new center, see Figure 7.

In fact, the calculated position may not be available, the cost of building here may be too high, thus a suitable nearby location must be found, or the center of one of the other empty circles must be chosen in descending order of diameters.

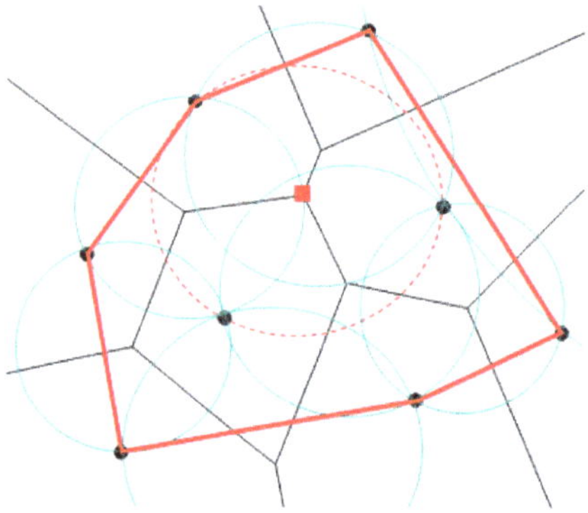

Figure 7. Finding a new location using the largest empty circles.

Another issue is the amount of inventory in logistics operations. The stock changes over time according to demand and needs to be replenished accordingly. We speak about *inventory management* and the resulting sustainability [88–91]. However, demands are stochastic in nature and, in addition, inventory management must take into account the cost of maintaining inventory and losses from premature depletion of inventory for undelivered goods.

In [92], a new mathematical model is derived, the properties of the profit function are proved, and the profitability in a two-channel production system considering carbon emissions and green technology is numerically verified on specific data.

While artificial neural networks (ANN) have very little application in combinatorial optimization, their main use is in cluster analysis, pattern recognition, image processing and prediction, in [93] the authors present an efficient implementation of ANNs in an inventory management model under uncertainty and inflation.

In [94] the unreliability of the supply chain and methods to eliminate this unreliability are explored, and the required mathematical equations are derived and verified by numerical experiments, including sensitivity analysis.

However, all these aspects are beyond the scope of this paper and can be the subject of separate texts as also evidenced by the papers mentioned.

7. Conclusions

This paper studies the assignment problem and its modifications with logistics applications, in routing, distribution, and scheduling tasks. Its first contribution is the correlation of the problem models, which are often distant in nature and time complexity.

It has also shown how the described models can be directly transferred to the GAMS environment. NP-hard Permutation Flow Shop Scheduling Problem (PFSSP) and the Travelling Salesman Problem are used to show that the optimal solution can be determined in the available time of a few minutes for instances with 20 jobs on 10 machines in the case of PFSSP, and for 100 cities in the case of TSP.

Previously, these boundaries were inaccessible with mixed integer programming solvers, but with the new version of GAMS, they have been significantly extended. This of course means first to build the appropriate model (and this is not always a simple matter, as the informal derivation of the PFSSP model in Section 5 showed) and then, for instance, for benchmark libraries (e.g., OR-Library or TSPLIB), to search individually for the appropriate bounds. The findings from PFSSP and TSP are not isolated examples of the successful application of GAMS in solving large instances of optimization versions of NP-complete/NP-hard problems. We have already validated it in [13] in solving the covering problem with matrices of hundreds of thousands of elements, and more recently in solving the Steiner problem in graphs in [95], where first using the terminology of network flows a mixed integer programming model was derived, then modified for GAMS, and finally exact results for a representative class of benchmarks from OR-Library were obtained.

Another goal of this paper was to introduce code generation in GAMS on non-trivial tasks because in the manuals [76,77] we can find only a description of individual elements of this tool, but not the codes of complete task models. In MATLAB, running the computation of an optimization program means writing just a single command (`intlinprog` or `linprog` with the appropriate parameters). Similarly, when solving differential equations, e.g., to calculate the differential equation $y'(x) = 4xy + x^3$ with initial condition $y(4) = 2$, it is enough to enter `dsolve('Dy=4*x*y+x^3','y(4)=2','x')`. In MATHEMATICA, too, to obtain the impulse function of the system described by a differential equation, it is enough to rewrite it in the form of a Laplace transfer and use a single command `InverseLaplaceTransform`. In contrast, the code notation in GAMS is similar to code in programming languages with the definition of constants, the declaration of variables, and the body of the program. Again, there are assignment statements, conditional statements, and loop statements. For example, the binary values of the reachability matrix **A** from the distance matrix **D** and the defined reachable distance threshold D_{max} are determined in GAMS as follows:

```
LOOP(I,
      LOOP(J,
             IF (D(I,J) <= Dmax,
                  A(I,J)=1;
                ELSE
                  A(I,J)=0;
               );
           );
  );
```

The only disadvantage of GAMS is that it has no graphical tools, and the results of the calculations are only in text form. This requires exporting them to a suitable program and postprocessing. In [13] we used MATLAB, here Figures 4 and 5 are generated in the MATHEMATICA environment.

Only where for extremely large instances of problems of exponential complexity we cannot obtain an exact solution using GAMS in a reasonable amount of time (e.g., no more than in tens of minutes), do we use one of the many heuristic methods. Given the No Free Lunch Theorem [74,75], none of them can be recommended as the best in the general case, since finding the optimal solution is not guaranteed and the result is always an approximation of the optimum, so our modification of the genetic algorithm, implemented in Java and described in more detail in [79], can be used without loss of generality.

One-point heuristics (hill climbing, tabu search, simulated annealing) in solving problems where in each iteration the neighborhood operation often generates tens of infeasible solutions and it is necessary to use a repair operator for them (here it concerns the coverage problem), and slow down the computation considerably, so in these cases we prefer, e.g., a genetic algorithm that generates only two new solutions in each iteration.

The model in Section 4.4 is original with another possible modification proposed at the end. Its model has already been built and verified on smaller-scale instances so far and will be investigated in more complex cases.

In future research, we expect to focus on the Quadratic Assignment Problem, the Vehicle Routing Problem and its solvability using GAMS, and applications in agriculture with consideration of data uncertainty using probabilistic models or fuzzy modeling, since yields can only be estimated. Although the Quadratic Assignment Problem has a non-linear objective function with quadratic terms, it can be converted to a mixed integer programming problem using Lawler's linearization [7] and the MIP solver of GAMS can be used again.

Funding: This research received no external funding.

Data Availability Statement: Not applicable.

Conflicts of Interest: The authors declare no conflict of interest.

Abbreviations

The following abbreviations are used in this manuscript:

AP	Assignment Problem
TSP	Travelling Salesman Problem
VRP	Vehicle Routing Problem
PFSSP	Permutation Flow Shop Scheduling Problem
GAMS	General Algebraic Modelling System
GA	Genetic Algorithm
ANN	Artificial Neural Network

References

1. Gass, S.I. *Linear Programming. Methods and Applications*; Dover Books on Computer Science; Courier Corporation: North Chelmsford, MA, USA, 2010.
2. Du, D.Z.; Pardalos, P.M. *Handbook of Combinatorial Optimization. Volume A*; Kluwer Academic Publishers: Dordrecht, The Netherlands, 1999.
3. Du, D.Z.; Pardalos, P.M. *Handbook of Combinatorial Optimization. Volume B*; Springer: Berlin/Heidelberg, Germany, 2005.
4. Kuhn, H.W. The Hungarian Method for the Assignment Problem. *Nav. Res. Logist.* **1955**, *2*, 83–97. [CrossRef]
5. Burkard, R.; Dell'Amico, M.; Martello, S. *Assignment Problems*; Society for Industrial and Applied Mathematics: Philadelphia, PA, USA, 2009.
6. Diestel, R. *Graph Theory*; Springer: Berlin/Heidelberg, Germany, 2005.
7. Burkard, R.E.; Cela, E.; Pardalos, P.M.; Pitsoulis, L.S. *The Quadratic Assignment Problem*; Report; Graz University of Technology: Graz, Austria, 1998; p. 71.
8. Gutin, G.; Punnen, A.P. *The Traveling Salesman Problem and Its Variations*; Springer: Berlin/Heidelberg, Germany, 2007.
9. Nalepa, J. *Smart Delivery Systems. Solving Complex Vehicle Routing Problems*; Elsevier: Amsterdam, The Netherlands, 2020.
10. Ganesh, K.; Malaijaran, R.A.; Mohapatra, S.; Punniyamoorthy, M. *Resource Allocation Problems in Supply Chains*; Emerald Group Publishing Limited: Bingley, UK, 2015.
11. Bohle, C.; Maturana, S.; Vera, J. A Robust Optimization Approach to Wine Grape Harvesting Scheduling. *Eur. J. Oper. Res.* **2010**, *200*, 245–252. [CrossRef]
12. Church, R.L.; Murray, A. *Location Covering Models*; Springer: Berlin/Heidelberg, Germany, 2018.
13. Seda, P.; Seda, M.; Hosek, J. On Mathematical Modelling of Automated Coverage Optimization in Wireless 5G and beyond Deployments. *Appl. Sci.* **2020**, *10*, 8853. [CrossRef]
14. Błażewicz, J.; Ecker, K.H.; Schmidt, G.; Węglarz, J. *Scheduling Computer and Manufacturing Processes*; Springer: Berlin/Heidelberg, Germany, 2013.
15. Rossit, D.; Vásquez, Ó.C.; Tohmé, F.; Frutos, M.; Safe, M. A Combinatorial Analysis of the Permutation and Non-Permutation Flow Shop Scheduling Problems. *Eur. J. Oper. Res.* **2021**, *289*, 841–854. [CrossRef]
16. Ali, I.; Essam, D.; Kasmarik, K. A Novel Design of Differential Evolution for Solving Discrete Traveling Salesman Problems. *Swarm Evol. Comput.* **2020**, *52*, 100607. [CrossRef]
17. Dong, X.; Cai, Y. A Novel Genetic Algorithm for Large Scale Colored Balanced Traveling Salesman Problem. *Future Gener. Comput. Syst.* **2019**, *95*, 727–742. [CrossRef]
18. Placido, A.D.; Archetti, C.; Cerrone, C. A Genetic Algorithm for the Close-Enough Traveling Salesman Problem with Application to Solar Panels Diagnostic Reconnaissance. *Comput. Oper. Res.* **2022**, *145*, 105831. [CrossRef]
19. Zhang, P.; Wang, J.; Tian, Z.; Sun, S.; Li, J.; Yang, J. A Genetic Algorithm with Jumping Gene and Heuristic Operators for Traveling Salesman Problem. *Appl. Soft Comput.* **2022**, *127*, 109339. [CrossRef]
20. Mahrach, M.; Miranda, G.; León, C.; Segredo, E. Comparison between Single and Multi-Objective Evolutionary Algorithms to Solve the Knapsack Problem and the Travelling Salesman Problem. *Mathematics* **2020**, *8*, 2018. [CrossRef]
21. Zhu, Y.; Chen, Y.; Fu, Z.H. Knowledge-Guided Two-Stage Memetic Search for the Pickup and Delivery Traveling Salesman Problem with FIFO Loading. *Knowl.-Based Syst.* **2022**, *242*, 108332. [CrossRef]
22. Larasati, M.R.; Wang, I.L. An Integrated Integer Programming Model with a Simulated Annealing Heuristic for the Carrier Vehicle Traveling Salesman Problem. *Procedia Comput. Sci.* **2022**, *197*, 301–308. [CrossRef]
23. Shi, Y.; Zhang, Y. The Neural Network Methods for Solving Traveling Salesman Problem. *Procedia Comput. Sci.* **2022**, *199*, 681–686. [CrossRef]
24. Karakostas, P.; Sifaleras, A. A Double-Adaptive General Variable Neighborhood Search Algorithm for the Solution of the Traveling Salesman Problem. *Appl. Soft Comput.* **2022**, *121*, 108746. [CrossRef]

25. Schmidt, J.; Irnich, S. New Neighborhoods and an Iterated Local Search Algorithm for the Generalized Traveling Salesman Problem. *EURO J. Comput. Optim.* **2022**, *10*, 100029. [CrossRef]
26. Kanna, S.; Sivakumar, K.; Lingaraj, N. Development of Deer Hunting Linked Earthworm Optimization Algorithm for Solving Large Scale Traveling Salesman Problem. *Knowl.-Based Syst.* **2021**, *227*, 107199. [CrossRef]
27. Akhand, M.; Ayon, S.; Shahriyar, S.; Siddique, N.; Adel, H. Discrete Spider Monkey Optimization for Travelling Salesman Problem. *Appl. Soft Comput.* **2020**, *86*, 105887. [CrossRef]
28. Krishna, M.; Panda, N.; Majhi, S. Solving Traveling Salesman Problem Using Hybridization of Rider Optimization and Spotted Hyena Optimization Algorithm. *Expert Syst. Appl.* **2021**, *183*, 115353. [CrossRef]
29. Panwar, K.; Deep, K. Discrete Grey Wolf Optimizer for Symmetric Travelling Salesman Problem. *Appl. Soft Comput.* **2021**, *105*, 107298. [CrossRef]
30. Reda, M.; Onsy, A.; Elhosseini, M.A.; Haikal, A.Y.; Badawy, M. A Discrete Variant of Cuckoo Search Algorithm to Solve the Travelling Salesman Problem and Path Planning for Autonomous Trolley inside Warehouse. *Knowl.-Based Syst.* **2022**, *252*, 109290. [CrossRef]
31. Zhang, Z.; Yang, J. A Discrete Cuckoo Search Algorithm for Traveling Salesman Problem and Its Application in Cutting Path Optimization. *Comput. Ind. Eng.* **2022**, *169*, 108157. [CrossRef]
32. Zhang, Z.; Han, Y. Discrete Sparrow Search Algorithm for Symmetric Traveling Salesman Problem. *Appl. Soft Comput.* **2022**, *118*, 108469. [CrossRef]
33. Huang, Y.; Shen, X.N.; You, X. A Discrete Shuffled Frog-Leaping Algorithm Based on Heuristic Information for Traveling Salesman Problem. *Appl. Soft Comput.* **2021**, *102*, 107085. [CrossRef]
34. Stodola, P.; Otřísal, P.; Hasilová, K. Adaptive Ant Colony Optimization with Node Clustering Applied to the Travelling Salesman Problem. *Swarm Evol. Comput.* **2022**, *70*, 101056. [CrossRef]
35. Land, A. The Solution of Some 100-City Travelling Salesman Problems. *EURO J. Comput. Optim.* **2021**, *9*, 100017. [CrossRef]
36. Dell'Amico, M.; Montemanni, R.; Novellani, S. Algorithms Based on Branch and Bound for the Flying Sidekick Traveling Salesman Problem. *Omega* **2021**, *104*, 102493. [CrossRef]
37. Pereira, A.; Mateus, G.; Urrutia, S. Valid Inequalities and Branch-and-Cut Algorithm for the Pickup and Delivery Traveling Salesman Problem with Multiple Stacks. *Eur. J. Oper. Res.* **2022**, *300*, 207–220. [CrossRef]
38. Yuan, Y.; Cattaruzza, D.; Ogier, M.; Semet, F. A Branch-and-Cut Algorithm for the Generalized Traveling Salesman Problem with Time Windows. *Eur. J. Oper. Res.* **2020**, *286*, 849–866. [CrossRef]
39. Morais, M.; Ribeiro, M.; da Silva, R.; Mariani, V.; Coelho, L. Discrete Differential Evolution Metaheuristics for Permutation Flow Shop Scheduling Problems. *Comput. Ind. Eng.* **2022**, *166*, 107956. [CrossRef]
40. Qiao, Y.; Wu, N.; He, Y.; Li, Z.; Chen, T. Adaptive Genetic Algorithm for Two-Stage Hybrid Flow-Shop Scheduling with Sequence-Independent Setup Time and No-Interruption Requirement. *Expert Syst. Appl.* **2022**, *208*, 118068. [CrossRef]
41. Wu, X.; Cao, Z. An Improved Multi-Objective Evolutionary Algorithm Based on Decomposition for Solving Re-Entrant Hybrid Flow Shop Scheduling Problem with Batch Processing Machines. *Comput. Ind. Eng.* **2022**, *169*, 108236. [CrossRef]
42. Song, H.B.; Lin, J. A Genetic Programming Hyper-Heuristic for the Distributed Assembly Permutation Flow-Shop Scheduling Problem with Sequence Dependent Setup Times. *Swarm Evol. Comput.* **2021**, *60*, 100807. [CrossRef]
43. Wang, J.J.; Wang, L. A Cooperative Memetic Algorithm with Feedback for the Energy-Aware Distributed Flow-Shops with Flexible Assembly Scheduling. *Comput. Ind. Eng.* **2022**, *168*, 108126. [CrossRef]
44. Harbaoui, H.; Khalfallah, S. Tabu-Search Optimization Approach for No-Wait Hybrid Flow-Shop Scheduling with Dedicated Machines. *Procedia Comput. Sci.* **2020**, *176*, 706–712. [CrossRef]
45. Doush, I.; Al-Betar, M.; Awadallah, M.; Alyasseri, Z.; Makhadmeh, S.; El-Abd, M. Island Neighboring Heuristics Harmony Search Algorithm for Flow Shop Scheduling with Blocking. *Swarm Evol. Comput.* **2022**, *74*, 101127. [CrossRef]
46. Brum, A.; Ruiz, R.; Ritt, M. Automatic Generation of Iterated Greedy Algorithms for the Non-Permutation Flow Shop Scheduling Problem with Total Completion Time Minimization. *Comput. Ind. Eng.* **2022**, *163*, 107843. [CrossRef]
47. Miyata, H.; Nagano, M. An Iterated Greedy Algorithm for Distributed Blocking Flow Shop with Setup Times and Maintenance Operations to Minimize Makespan. *Comput. Ind. Eng.* **2022**, *171*, 108366. [CrossRef]
48. Schulz, S.; Neufeld, J.; Buscher, U. Multi-Objective Iterated Local Search Algorithm for Comprehensive Energy-Aware Hybrid Flow Shop Scheduling. *J. Clean. Prod.* **2019**, *224*, 421–434. [CrossRef]
49. Shao, W.; Shao, Z.; Pi, D. Multi-Local Search-Based General Variable Neighborhood Search for Distributed Flow Shop Scheduling in Heterogeneous Multi-Factories. *Appl. Soft Comput.* **2022**, *125*, 109138. [CrossRef]
50. Pereira, M.; Nagano, M. Hybrid Metaheuristics for the Integrated and Detailed Scheduling of Production and Delivery Operations in No-Wait Flow Shop Systems. *Comput. Ind. Eng.* **2022**, *170*, 108255. [CrossRef]
51. Umam, M.; Mustafid, M.; Suryono, S. A Hybrid Genetic Algorithm and Tabu Search for Minimizing Makespan in Flow Shop Scheduling Problem. *J. King Saud Univ. Comput. Inf. Sci.* **2022**, *in press*. [CrossRef]
52. Brammer, J.; Lutz, B.; Neumann, D. Permutation Flow Shop Scheduling with Multiple Lines and Demand Plans Using Reinforcement Learning. *Eur. J. Oper. Res.* **2022**, *299*, 75–86. [CrossRef]
53. Pang, X.; Xue, H.; Tseng, M.L.; Lim, M.; Liu, K. Hybrid Flow Shop Scheduling Problems Using Improved Fireworks Algorithm for Permutation. *Appl. Sci.* **2020**, *10*, 1174. [CrossRef]

54. Engin, O.; Güçlü, A. A New Hybrid Ant Colony Optimization Algorithm for Solving the No-Wait Flow Shop Scheduling Problems. *Appl. Soft Comput.* **2018**, *72*, 166–176. [CrossRef]
55. Gümüşçü, A.; Kaya, S.; Tenekeci, M.; Karaçizmeli, I.; Aydilek, I. The Impact of Local Search Strategies on Chaotic Hybrid Firefly Particle Swarm Optimization Algorithm in Flow-Shop Scheduling. *J. King Saud Univ. Comput. Inf. Sci.* 2022, *in press*. [CrossRef]
56. Deng, G.; Xu, M.; Zhang, S.; Jiang, T.; Su, Q. Migrating Birds Optimization with a Diversified Mechanism for Blocking Flow Shops to Minimize Idle and Blocking Time. *Appl. Soft Comput.* **2022**, *114*, 107834. [CrossRef]
57. Zhang, C.; Tan, J.; Peng, K.; Gao, L.; Shen, W.; Lian, K. A Discrete Whale Swarm Algorithm for Hybrid Flow-Shop Scheduling Problem with Limited Buffers. *Robot. Comput.-Integr. Manuf.* **2021**, *68*, 102081. [CrossRef]
58. Croce, F.; Salassa, F.; T'Kindt, V. Exact Solution of the Two-Machine Flow Shop Problem with Three Operations. *Comput. Oper. Res.* **2022**, *138*, 105595. [CrossRef]
59. Ho, M.; Hnaien, F.; Dugardin, F. Exact Method to Optimize the Total Electricity Cost in Two-Machine Permutation Flow Shop Scheduling Problem under Time-of-Use Tariff. *Comput. Oper. Res.* **2022**, *144*, 10578. [CrossRef]
60. Oujana, S.; Yalaoui, F.; Amodeo, L. A Linear Programming Approach for Hybrid Flexible Flow Shop with Sequence-Dependent Setup Times to Minimise Total Tardiness. *IFAC PapersOnLine* **2021**, *54-1*, 1162–1167. [CrossRef]
61. Schaller, J.; Valente, J. Branch-and-Bound Algorithms for Minimizing Total Eearliness and Tardiness in a Two-Machine Permutation Flow Shop with Unforced Idle Allowed. *Comput. Oper. Res.* **2019**, *109*, 1–11. [CrossRef]
62. Liu, M.; Li, Y.; Huo, Q.; Li, A.; Zhu, M.; Qu, N.; Chen, L.; Xia, M. A Two-Way Parallel Slime Mold Algorithm by Flow and Distance for the Travelling Salesman Problem. *Appl. Sci.* **2020**, *10*, 6180. [CrossRef]
63. Golden, B.; Raghavan, S.; Wasil, E. *The Vehicle Routing Problem: Latest Advances and New Challenges*; Springer: Berlin/Heidelberg, Germany, 2008.
64. Toth, P.; Vigo, D. *The Vehicle Routing Problem*; Society for Industrial and Applied Mathematics: Philadelphia, PA, USA, 2002.
65. Soto-Mendoza, V.; García-Calvillo, I.; Ruiz-y Ruiz, E.; Pérez-Terrazas, J. Comparison between Single and Multi-Objective Evolutionary Algorithms to Solve the Knapsack Problem and the Travelling Salesman Problem. *Algorithms* **2020**, *13*, 96. [CrossRef]
66. Ochelska-Mierzejewska, J.; Poniszewska-Marańda, A.; Marańda, W. Selected Genetic Algorithms for Vehicle Routing Problem Solving. *Electronics* **2021**, *10*, 3147. [CrossRef]
67. Desrochers, M.; Laporte, G. Improvements and Extensions to the Miller-Tucker-Zemlin Subtour Elimination Constraints. *Oper. Res. Lett.* **1991**, *10*, 27–36. [CrossRef]
68. Stroh, M.B. *A Practical Guide to Transportation and Logistics*; Logistics Network: Burr Ridge, IL, USA, 2006.
69. Garey, M.R.; Johnson, D.S. *Computers and Intractability: A Guide to the Theory of NP-Completeness*, 19th ed.; W.H. Freeman and Company: New York, NY, USA, 1997.
70. Ausiello, G.; Crescenzi, P.; Gambosi, G.; Kann, V.; Marchetti-Spaccamela, A.; Protasi, M. *Complexity and Approximation: Combinatorial Optimization Problems and their Approximability Properties*; Springer: Berlin/Heidelberg, Germany, 1999.
71. Reeves, C.R. *Modern Heuristic Techniques for Combinatorial Problems*; Blackwell Scientific Publications: Oxford, UK, 1993.
72. Michalewicz, Z.; Fogel, D.B. *How to Solve It: Modern Heuristics*; Springer: Berlin/Heidelberg, Germany, 2004.
73. Onwubolu, G.; Davendra, D. *Differential Evolution. A Handbook for Global Permutation-Based Combinatorial Optimization*; Springer: Berlin/Heidelberg, Germany, 2009.
74. Wolpert, D.H.; McReady, W.G. No Free Lunch Theorems for Optimization. *IEEE Trans. Evol. Comput.* **1997**, *1*, 67–82. [CrossRef]
75. Wolpert, D.H.; McReady, W.G. Coevolutionary Free Lunches. *IEEE Trans. Evol. Comput.* **2005**, *9*, 721–735. [CrossRef]
76. Brooke, A.; Kendrick, D.; Meeraus, A. *GAMS Release 2.25. A User's Guide*; The Scientific Press. Boyd & Fraser Publishing Company: Boston, MA, USA, 1992.
77. Rosenthal, R.E. *GAMS—A User's Guide*; GAMS Development Corporation: Washington, DC, USA, 2016.
78. GAMS. Solver Manuals. Report, GAMS Development Corporation. Available online: https://www.gams.com/latest/docs/S_MAIN.html (accessed on 6 September 2022).
79. Seda, P.; Mark, M.; Su, K.W.; Seda, M.; Hosek, J.; Leu, J. The Minimization of Public Facilities With Enhanced Genetic Algorithms Using War Elimination. *IEEE Access* **2019**, *7*, 9395–9405. [CrossRef]
80. Beasley, J.E. OR-Library. Report, Brunel University London. 2018. Available online: http://people.brunel.ac.uk/~mastjjb/jeb/info.html (accessed on 6 September 2022).
81. Beasley, J.E. OR-Library: Distributing Test Problems by Electronic Mail. *J. Oper. Res. Soc.* **1990**, *41*, 1069–1072. [CrossRef]
82. Michalewicz, Z. *Genetic Algorithms + Data Structures = Evolution Programs*; Springer: Berlin/Heidelberg, Germany, 1998.
83. Reinelt, G. *MP-TESTDATA—The TSPLIB Symmetric Traveling Salesman Problem Instances*; Report; Heidelberg University: Heidelberg, Germany, 2013. Available online: http://elib.zib.de/pub/mp-testdata/tsp/tsplib/tsp (accessed on 6 September 2022).
84. Alkaya, A.F.; Yildirim, S.; Aksakalli, V. Heuristics for the Canadian Traveler Problem with Neutralizations. *Comput. Ind. Eng.* **2019**, *159*, 107488. [CrossRef]
85. Liao, C.S.; Huang, Y. The Covering Canadian Traveller Problem. *Theor. Comput. Sci.* **2014**, *530*, 80–88 [CrossRef]
86. Aurenhammer, F. Voronoi Diagrams. A Survey of a Fundamental Geometric Data Structure. *ACM Comput. Surv.* **1991**, *23*, 345–405. [CrossRef]
87. de Berg, M.; Cheong, O.; van Kreveld, M.; Overmars, M. *Computational Geometry: Algorithms and Applications*; Springer: Berlin/Heidelberg, Germany, 2008.

88. Becerra, P.; Mula, J.; Sanchis, R. Green Supply Chain Quantitative Models for Sustainable Inventory Management: A Review. *J. Clean. Prod.* **2021**, *328*, 129544. [CrossRef]
89. Forkan, M.; Rizvi, M.M.; Chowdhury, M.A.M. Multiobjective Reverse Logistics Model for Inventory Management with Eenvironmental Impacts: An Application in Industry. *Intell. Syst. Appl.* **2022**, *14*, 200078.
90. Teerasoponpong, S.; Sopadang, A. Decision Support System for Adaptive Sourcing and Inventory Management in Small- and Medium-Sized Enterprises. *Robot. Comput.-Integr. Manuf.* **2022**, *73*, 102226. [CrossRef]
91. Xiong, X.; Li, Y.; Yang, W.; Shen, H. Data-Driven Robust Dual-Sourcing Inventory Management under Purchase Price and Demand Uncertainties. *Transp. Res. Part E* **2022**, *160*, 102671. [CrossRef]
92. Sarkar, B.; Kar, S.; Basu, K.; Guchhait, R. A Sustainable Managerial Decision-Making Problem for a Substitutable Product in a Dual-Channel under Carbon Tax Policy. *Comput. Ind. Eng.* **2022**, *172*, 108635. [CrossRef]
93. Sarkar, A.; Guchhait, R.; Sarkar, B. Application of the Artificial Neural Network with Multithreading within an Inventory Model under Uncertainty and Inflation. *Int. J. Fuzzy Syst.* **2022**, *24*, 2318–2332. [CrossRef]
94. Guchhait, R.; Sarkar, B. Economic and Environmental Assessment of an Unreliable Supply Chain Management. *RAIRO Oper. Res.* **2021**, *55*, 3153–3170. [CrossRef]
95. Seda, M. Steiner Tree Problem in Graphs and Mixed Integer Linear Programming-Based Approach in GAMS. *WSEAS Trans. Comput.* **2022**, *21*, 257–262. [CrossRef]

algorithms

MDPI

Article

A Hybrid Exact–Local Search Approach for One-Machine Scheduling with Time-Dependent Capacity

Christos Valouxis [1], Christos Gogos [2,*], Angelos Dimitsas [2], Petros Potikas [3] and Anastasios Vittas [2]

[1] Department of Electrical and Computer Engineering, University of Patras, 26500 Patras, Greece
[2] Department of Informatics and Telecommunications, University of Ioannina, 47100 Arta, Greece
[3] Department of Electrical and Computer Engineering, National Technical University of Athens, 15772 Athens, Greece
* Correspondence: cgogos@uoi.gr

Abstract: Machine scheduling is a hard combinatorial problem having many manifestations in real life. Due to the schedule followed, the possibility of installations of machines operating sub-optimally is high. In this work, we examine the problem of a single machine with time-dependent capacity that performs jobs of deterministic durations, while for each job, its due time is known in advance. The objective is to minimize the aggregated tardiness in all tasks. The problem was motivated by the need to schedule charging times of electric vehicles effectively. We formulate an integer programming model that clearly describes the problem and a constraint programming model capable of effectively solving it. Due to the usage of interval variables, global constraints, a powerful constraint programming solver, and a heuristic we have identified, which we call the "due times rule", the constraint programming model can reach excellent solutions. Furthermore, we employ a hybrid approach that exploits three local search improvement procedures in a schema where the constraint programming part of the solver plays a central role. These improvement procedures exhaustively enumerate portions of the search space by exchanging consecutive jobs with a single job of the same duration, moving cost-incurring jobs to earlier times in a consecutive sequence of jobs or even exploiting periods where capacity is not fully utilized to rearrange jobs. On the other hand, subproblems are given to the exact constraint programming solver, allowing freedom of movement only to certain parts of the schedule, either in vertical ribbons of the time axis or in groups of consecutive sequences of jobs. Experiments on publicly available data show that our approach is highly competitive and achieves the new best results in many problem instances.

Keywords: scheduling; constraint programming; heuristics; local search

Citation: Valouxis, C.; Gogos, C.; Dimitsas, A.; Potikas, P.; Vittas, A. A Hybrid Exact–Local Search Approach for One-Machine Scheduling with Time-Dependent Capacity. *Algorithms* **2022**, *15*, 450. https://doi.org/10.3390/a15120450

Academic Editors: Dunhui Xiao and Shuai Li

Received: 25 October 2022
Accepted: 25 November 2022
Published: 29 November 2022

1. Introduction

Scheduling problems are interesting due to their practical usefulness and hardness. Such problems emerge in various domains, including manufacturing, computing, project management, and many others. Since scheduling problems are typically NP-hard, several approaches compete to attain the often unreached optimal solutions. Metaheuristics, heuristics, constraint programming, and mathematical programming often yield excellent results. The latter two are especially sensitive to problem sizes since their exact nature implies that all solutions must be checked or intelligently pruned.

Scheduling is a thoroughly studied subject that is considered a discipline on its own [1]. Scheduling problems are classified using the commonly accepted $(\alpha|\beta|\gamma)$ notation [2], where α refers to the machine environment, β refers to the constraints, and γ refers to the objective function. A valuable asset for appreciating the variety of scheduling problems under the $(\alpha|\beta|\gamma)$ notation can be found at [3].

In this work, we study a variation in the one-machine scheduling with time-dependent capacity problem that Mencia et al. introduced in [4–6]. The problem emerged in the context of scheduling charge times for a fleet of electric vehicles and is an abstraction of the real problem. It is classified as $(1, Cap(t)||\sum t_i)$, meaning that it involves a single machine with capacity that fluctuates through time, with no other constraints, and the objective is minimizing the accumulated tardiness from all jobs. The problem piqued our interest due to its precise definition, the publicly available datasets, and the excellent results that were already published and which we used for comparisons.

We propose a novel way to approach the problem based on a model with an embedded rule (the due times rule) that helps constraint programming solvers reach good solutions fast. We also propose three improvement procedures that are local search routines. We combine the exact and local search parts in our approach to the problem, and we manage to achieve results equal to or better than the best-known results for 91 and 48 cases, respectively, out of 190 public problem instances.

2. Problem Description

A detailed description of the problem exists in [6], so we give a brief description in this section. The problem involves n jobs and one machine with a certain capacity that varies over time. Each job i has a duration P_i and a due date D_i. All jobs are available from the start time ($t = 0$) and consume one unit of the machine's capacity for the period in which the job will eventually be scheduled. Once a job starts, it cannot be preempted and should continue execution until completion. It is imperative that the capacity of the machine is not exceeded at any time. Finally, the objective that should be minimized is the total tardiness of all jobs, which is computed based on the due dates of the jobs. If job i completes execution before its due date, it does not affect the cost. Otherwise, it imposes a cost equal to $c_i - D_i$, where c_i is the completion time that job i assumes in the schedule. The mathematical formulation of the problem is presented in Section 7.

The problem $(1, Cap(t)||\sum t_i)$ is NP-hard, since problems $(1||\sum t_i)$ and $(P||\sum t_i)$ (P denotes a known number of identical machines), which are known to be NP-hard [7], can be reduced to it.

Terminology

In line with the definitions of terms in [6], we use S_i, p_i, d_i, and C_i for the start time, duration, due time, and completion time, respectively, of a job i in a given schedule. Then, T_i is the tardiness of job i which is $max\{0, C_i - d_i\}$.

A concrete example involving 12 jobs and a capacity line that reaches a maximum of four units is presented below. This example is the one used as Example 1 in [5]. Table 1 summarizes information related to it alongside the values associated with an optimal schedule for this problem instance, achieving an optimal cost of 20. The schedule corresponding to the table's third line is presented graphically in Figure 1.

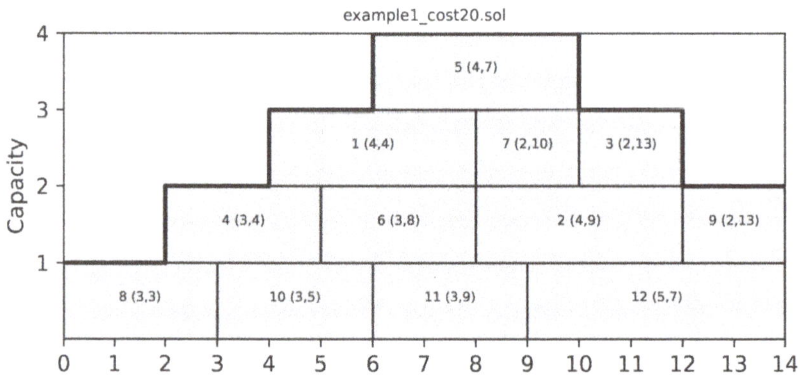

Figure 1. A graphical representation of the schedule in the last line of Table 1.

Table 1. A sample problem instance with 12 jobs. For each job i, the table shows its duration p_i and its due time d_i. Additionally, for a certain schedule, the table shows the start time (S_i), completion time (C_i), and penalty incurred (T_i) for each job i.

i	1	2	3	4	5	6	7	8	9	10	11	12
p_i, d_i	4,4	4,9	2,13	3,4	4,7	3,8	2,10	3,3	2,13	3,5	3,9	5,7
S_i, C_i, T_i	4,8,4	8,12,3	10,12,0	2,5,1	6,10,3	5,8,0	8,10,0	0,3,0	12,14,1	3,6,1	6,9,0	9,14,7

3. Dataset

A dataset consisting of a relatively large number of artificially generated problem instances is publicly available in [8]. The procedure for generating these instances is described in [6], and special care has been taken so that the problems' structures resemble the structure manifested during the process of electric vehicle charging [9]. In total, 190 problem instances exist, as seen in Table 2. The naming of each problem instance is `i<n>_<MC>_<k>`, where `n` is the number of jobs, `MC` is the maximum capacity, and `k` is the sequence number of each problem instance for this `n`, `MC` pair.

Table 2. Problem instances in the dataset. For each pair of a number of jobs and a maximum capacity, 10 individual problem instances exist.

Number of Jobs (n)	Maximum Capacity (MC)
120	3, 5, 7, 10
250	10, 20, 30
500	10, 20, 30
750	10, 20, 30, 50
1000	10, 20, 30, 50, 100

Note that the capacity in all problem instances is a unimodal step function that grows until reaching a peak, then decreases, and finally stabilizes at a positive value.

4. Related Work

Hard combinatorial optimization problems, such as the one-machine scheduling with time-dependent capacity problem, are approached using numerous solving methods [10,11]. The two basic categories of such approaches are the exact ones and the heuristic–metaheuristic ones. In the first category, one can identify mathematical programming (i.e., linear programming, integer programming, and others) [12], constraint programming [13], approaches based on SAT (satisfiability) [14] or SMT (satisfiability modulo theory) solvers [15], and, in general, methods that intelligently examine the complete search space while pruning parts of it during their quest for proven optimal solutions [16]. In the second category, the approaches are numerous, including local search methods [17,18], genetic algorithms [19], genetic programming [20], memetic algorithms [21], differential evolution [22], ant colony optimization [23], particle swarm optimization [24], bees algorithms [25], hyper-heuristics [20], and others.

Heuristically Constructed Schedules

In [6], the authors present the schedule builder algorithm, where jobs are ordered in an arbitrary sequence, and each job is scheduled to start at the earliest possible time. After positioning each job, the capacity of the machine is updated in accordance with the partial schedule. When all jobs are scheduled, the algorithm finishes and returns a feasible schedule. This search space is guaranteed to contain an optimal solution to any problem instance [5]. So, each possible solution can be represented as a sequence of jobs to the schedule builder. Certain metaheuristic algorithms, such as genetic algorithms, may benefit from the idea of representing each possible schedule as a sequence of jobs and searching through the space of all possible permutations.

Here, we present in Algorithm 1 a modification to the schedule builder algorithm that introduces lanes, which are levels formed by the capacity of the problem. So, for example, a problem with a maximum capacity of four has four lanes; the first is always available during the time horizon, and the three others, based on the capacity, have periods of availability and unavailability. Lanes help plot schedules, disambiguate solutions with identical costs, and quickly identify jobs that form sequences of consecutive jobs. In Algorithm 1, we call the function `find_lowest_available_lane` that finds the lowest available lane that can accommodate a job starting at period `t`.

Algorithm 1 Schedule builder using lanes

```
Input: A problem instance P
Output: A feasible schedule S
  demand ← [0,...]
  left ← 0                    ▷ Leftmost time point where capacity is not yet fully utilized
  for all jobs job do
      t ← left
      while True do
          flag = True
          for all capacity[t:t+job.duration], demand[t:t+job.duration] c, d do
              if d > c then
                  flag ← False
                  break
              end if
          end for
          if flag then
              lane = find_lowest_available_lane(job, t)
              S[job.id] ← lane, t
              for all [t:t+job.duration] t′ do
                  demand[t′] ← demand[t′] + 1
                  if demand[t′] = capacity[t′] then
                      left ← t′ + 1
                  end if
              end for
              t ← t + 1
              break
          end if
      end while
  end for
```

5. C-Paths

A fundamental concept that was introduced by Mencia et al. in [4] is the concept of a C-Path. A C-Path is a sequence of consecutive jobs (i.e., in a C-Path, the finish time of each previous job coincides with the start time of the following job) in a schedule. The importance of C-Paths stems from the fact that jobs in each C-Path can easily swap places and keep the schedule feasible. We can consider a graph view of a schedule, where each job is a node and directed edges connect nodes that correspond to consecutive jobs. Then, each path from a source node of the graph (i.e., a node with no incoming edges) to a sink node (i.e., a node with no outgoing edges) is a C-Path. This is demonstrated in Figure 2 for a sample schedule of cost 35 for the toy problem instance shown in Table 1 and its corresponding graph in Figure 3. The list of C-Paths identified in this graph includes the following six: (3,12,4), (3,10,1,6), (3,10,1,2), (7,9,8,5), (7,11,2), and (7,11,6).

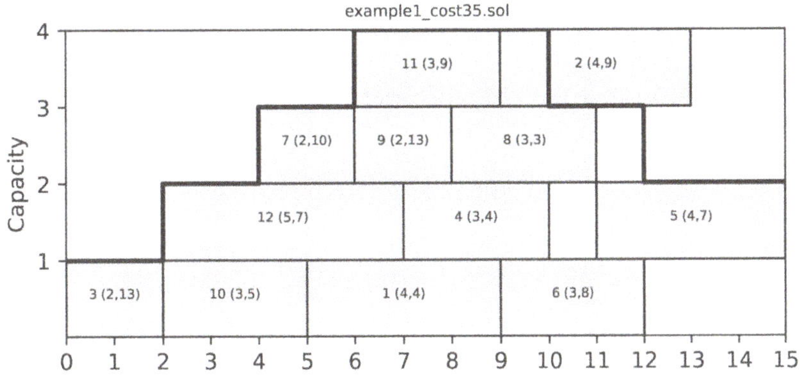

Figure 2. A suboptimal schedule of cost 35 for the toy problem of Table 2. Each job is depicted with a box and annotated with a label of the form $x(y,z)$, where x is the job identification number, y is the duration of the job, and z is its due time.

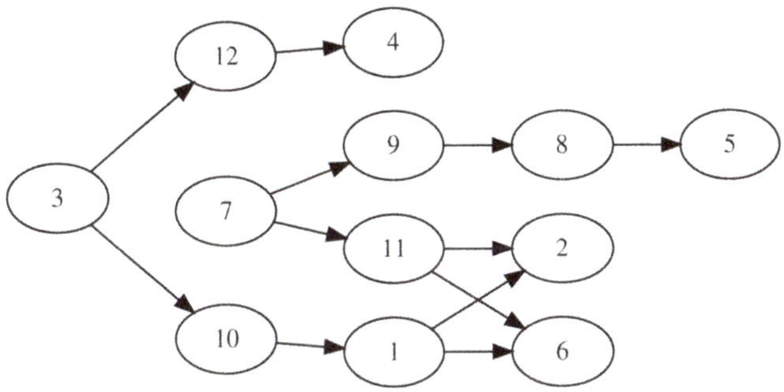

Figure 3. The graph that corresponds to the schedule of Figure 2.

The number of C-Paths might be very large, especially for schedules of big-size problems. This is demonstrated in Table 3, which shows the number of C-Paths for specific schedules of selected problem instances. Note that the number of C-Paths might change dramatically for different schedules of the same problem instance and that larger problem instances might have fewer C-Paths than smaller problem instances for some schedules.

Table 3. Number of C-Paths for schedules of selected problem instances, which can be found in [26].

Problem Instance	Schedule Cost	Number of C-Paths
i120_3_1	848	3
i120_10_1	749	71
i250_10_1	4094	48
i250_30_1	3013	276
i500_10_1	4614	204
i500_30_1	2670	4528
i750_10_1	4409	22,302
i750_50_1	5134	206,022
i1000_10_1	641	903,826
i1000_100_1	71,012	216,694

Fast Computation of C-Paths

Since complete enumeration of all C-Paths is out of the question for problems of large sizes, we opted for a faster method of generating a single C-Path each time it is needed. This method starts by picking a random job, followed by two processes that find the right and the left part of a C-Path, having the selected job as a pivot element. The right-side part of the C-path is formed by choosing the next job that starts at the finish time of the current job. If more than one job exists, one of them is randomly selected and becomes the new current job. This process continues until no more subsequent jobs are found. The left side of the C-Path is formed by setting the initially selected job as the current job once again and finding previous jobs that end at the start time of the current job. Similarly, if more than one exists, one is chosen at random and becomes the new current job. The process ends when no more suitable prior jobs can be found.

6. Due Times Rule

This work contributes to identifying a rule that involves the due times of jobs with equal durations. The rule states that "Jobs with equal duration should be scheduled in the order of their due times". In other words, if two jobs have equal durations, they should swap places if the due time of the job that is scheduled later is sooner than the due time of the job that is scheduled sooner. This rule can be used to strengthen mathematical formulations or as a heuristic for reaching better solutions.

Proof. Suppose that two jobs, i and j, with the same duration, are scheduled such that job i comes first and job j follows. Additionally, suppose that job j has an earlier due time than job i, i.e., $d_j < d_i$. Let t and t' be the finish times of jobs i and j, respectively, and since both jobs have the same duration, $t < t'$ holds. When both jobs have non-negative tardiness values, i.e., $t - d_i \geq 0$ and $t' - d_j \geq 0$, swapping the jobs results again in non-negative tardiness values for both jobs. This holds because the tardiness of job j after the swap will be $t - d_j > t - d_i \geq 0$. Moreover, $t' > t \geq d_i$, so the tardiness of job i after the swap will be $t' - d_i \geq 0$. So, the total tardiness before the swap is $(t - d_i) + (t' - d_j)$, which is equal to the total tardiness after the swap, which is $(t - d_j) + (t' - d_i)$. This situation is depicted in Figure 4a. The top figure shows a possible configuration of two equal-duration jobs that both incur tardiness. It can be easily seen that the total length of the gray bars that represent the tardiness remains the same after swapping jobs i and j.

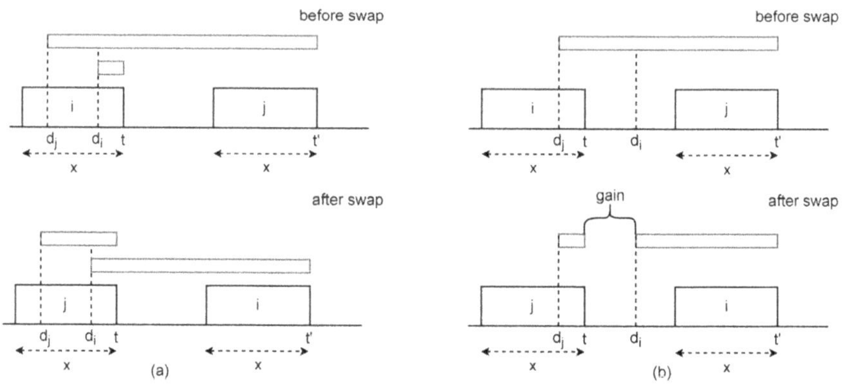

Figure 4. (**a**) Both job i and job j have non-negative tardiness values. (**b**) Job i has no tardiness, but job j incurs tardiness.

The benefit of positioning equal-duration jobs according to their due times occurs when job i completes execution before its due time, and job j incurs some positive value of tardiness. Since job i has no tardiness, the total tardiness of the initial configuration is $t' - d_j$. After the swap, the total tardiness will be $(t - d_j) + (t' - d_i)$. In order to prove that the total tardiness is no greater after the swap, the following inequality must hold: $(t - d_j) + (t' - d_i) \leq t' - d_j$. This inequality leads to the following true proposition: $(t - d_j) + (t' - d_i) \leq t' - d_j \implies t - d_i \leq 0 \implies t \leq d_i$. The last inequality holds since it is the assumption made for this case, i.e., job i has no tardiness. A visual representation of such a situation is depicted in Figure 4b. The upper part of the figure shows the situation where job i is scheduled first, while the lower part of the figure shows the situation after swapping the jobs. Again, the gray bars represent the tardiness of the jobs, and it can be seen that the total tardiness is decreased when the jobs swap places. □

7. Formulation and Implementation

A formulation of the problem that will be used to construct initial solutions to the problem is presented below. Then, the formulation is slightly modified and used for solving problems involving subsets of tasks in an effort to attain better schedules overall.

Let $\mathbb{J}$ be the set of jobs.

Let P_j be the duration of each job $j \in \mathbb{J}$.

Let D_j be the due date of each job $j \in \mathbb{J}$.

Let T be the number of time points. Note that the value of T is not given explicitly by the problem, but such a value can be computed by aggregating the duration of all jobs.

Let $Cap(t)$ be the capacity of the machine at each time point $t \in 0 \ldots T-1$.

We define integer decision variables $s_j \in 0 \ldots T-1-P_j$ that denote the start time of each job $j \in \mathbb{J}$.

Likewise, we define integer decision variables $f_j \in P_j \ldots T-1$ that denote the finish time of each job $j \in \mathbb{J}$.

We also define integer decision variables $z_j \geq 0$ which denote the tardiness of each job $j \in \mathbb{J}$.

Finally, we define binary decision variables x_{jt} and y_{jt}. Each one of the former variables assumes the value 1 if job j starts its execution at time point t, or else it assumes the value 0. Likewise, each y_{jt} variable marks the time point at which job j finishes.

$$min \sum_{j \in \mathbb{J}} z_j \tag{1}$$

$$f_j = s_j + P_j \quad \forall j \in \mathbb{J} \tag{2}$$

$$z_j \geq f_j - D_j \quad \forall j \in \mathbb{J} \tag{3}$$

$$s_j \geq t \cdot x_{jt} \quad \forall j \in \mathbb{J} \quad \forall t \in 0 \ldots T-1 \tag{4}$$

$$s_j \leq t + (M - t) \cdot (1 - x_{jt}) \quad \forall j \in \mathbb{J} \quad \forall t \in 0 \ldots T-1 \tag{5}$$

$$\sum_{t \in 0 \ldots T-1} x_{jt} = 1 \quad \forall j \in \mathbb{J} \tag{6}$$

$$y_{jt+P_j} = x_{jt} \quad \forall j \in \mathbb{J} \quad \forall t \in 0 \ldots T-1-P_j \tag{7}$$

$$\sum_{j \in \mathbb{J}} \sum_{t' \in 0..t} x_{jt'} - \sum_{j \in \mathbb{J}} \sum_{t' \in 0..t} y_{jt'} \leq Cap(t) \quad \forall t \in 0..T-1 \tag{8}$$

A brief explanation of the above model follows.

The aim of the objective function in Equation (1) is to minimize the total tardiness of all jobs.

Equation (2) assigns the proper finish time value to each job given its start time and duration.

Equation (3) assigns tardiness values to the jobs. In particular, when job j finishes before its due time, the right side of the inequality is a negative number, and variable z_j assumes the value 0 since its domain is non-negative integers. When job j finishes after its due time, z_j becomes $f_j - D_j$. This occurs because z_j is included in the minimized objective function and therefore forced to assume the smallest possible non-negative value.

Equations (4) and (5) drive the variables x_{jt} to proper values based on the s_j values. This occurs because, when s_j assumes the value t, x_{jt} becomes 1. It should be noted that M in Equation (5) represents a big value, and $T-1$ can be used for it. For the specific time point t at which a job will be scheduled to begin, the right sides of both equalities will assume the value t. For all other time points besides t, the right sides of the former and the latter equations become 0 and M, respectively.

Equation (6) enforces that only one among all of the x_{jt} variables of each job j will assume the value 1.

Equation (7) dictates the following association rule: for each job j, when x_{jt} becomes 1 or 0, the corresponding y variable of j with the time offset P_j, which is y_{jt+P_j}, will also be 1 or 0, respectively.

Equation (8) guarantees that for each time point, the capacity of the machine will not be violated. The values that the left side of the equation assumes are the numbers of active jobs at each time point t. The first double summation counts the jobs that have started no later than t, while the second double summation counts the jobs that have also finished no later than t. Their difference is obviously the number of active jobs.

Constraint Programming Formulation

The IBM ILOG constraint programming (CP) solver seems to be a good choice for solving scheduling problems involving jobs that occupy intervals of time and consume some types of resources that have time-varying availability [27]. The one-machine scheduling problem can be easily formulated in the IBM ILOG CP solver using one fixed-size interval variable per job (`j`) and the constraint `always_in`, which restricts all of them to assume values that collectively never exceed the maximum available capacity over time. This is possible by using a pulse cumulative function expression that represents the contribution of our fixed interval variables over time. Each job execution requires one capacity unit, which is occupied when the job starts, retained through its execution, and released when the job finishes. In our case, the variable `usage` aggregates all pulse requirements by all jobs. The objective function uses a set of integer variables `z[job.id]` that are stored in a dictionary that has the identifier of each job as keys. Each `z[job.id]` variable assumes the value of the job's tardiness (i.e., the non-negative difference of the job's due time (`job.due_time`) and its finish time (`end_of(j[job.id])`). An additional constraint is added that corresponds to the due times rule mentioned in Section 6. Jobs are grouped by duration, and a list ordered by due times is prepared for each group. Then, for all jobs in the list, the constraint enforces that the order of the jobs must be respected. This means that each job in the list should have an earlier start time than the start time of the job that follows it in the list. The model implementation using the IBM ILOG CP solver's python API is presented below.

```
import docplex.cp.model as cpx

model = cpx.CpoModel()
x_ub = int(problem.ideal_duration() * 1.1)
j = {
    job.id: model.interval_var(
        start=[0, x_ub - job.duration - 1],
        end=[job.duration, x_ub - 1],
        size=job.duration
    )
    for job in problem.jobs
}

z = {
    job.id: model.integer_var(lb=0, ub=x_ub - 1)
    for job in problem.jobs
    }

usage = sum([model.pulse(j[job.id], 1) for job in problem.jobs])

for i in range(problem.nint):
```

```
    model.add(
        model.always_in(
            usage,
            [problem.capacities[i].start, problem.capacities[i].end],
            0,
            problem.capacities[i].capacity,
        )
    )

for job in problem.jobs:
    model.add(z[job.id] >= model.end_of(j[job.id]) - job.due_time)

for k in problem.size_jobs: # iterate over discrete job durations
    jobs_by_due_time = same_duration_jobs[k]
    for i in range(len(jobs_by_due_time)-1):
        j1, j2 = jobs_by_due_time[i][1], jobs_by_due_time[i+1][1]
        model.add(model.start_of(z[j1]) <= model.start_of(z[j2]))

model.minimize(sum([z[job.id] for job in problem.jobs]))
```

The object `problem` is supposed to be an instance of a class that has all relevant information for the problem instance under question (i.e., `jobs` is the list of all jobs, each job besides `id` and `due_time` has also a `duration` property, `nint` is the number of capacity intervals, and `capacities[i].start` and `capacities[i].end` are the start time and end time of the ith capacity step, respectively). Finally, the problem object has the `ideal_duration` method that estimates a tight value for the makespan of the schedule, which is incremented by 10% to accommodate possible gaps that hinder the full exploitation of the available capacity. The "ideal duration" is computed by totaling the durations of all jobs and then filling the area under the capacity line from left to right and from bottom to top with blocks of the size 1×1 until the totaled durations quantity runs out. The rightmost point on the time axis of the filled area becomes the "ideal duration" and is clearly a relaxation of the actual completion time of the optimal solution since each job is decomposed in blocks of the duration one, and no gaps appear in the filled area.

An effort was undertaken to implement the above model using Google's ORTools CP-SAT Solver [28]. This solver has a cumulative constraint that can be used in place of `always_in` to describe the machine's varying capacity. A series of *FixedSizeIntervalVar* variables were used that transformed the pulse of the capacity to a flat line equal to the maximum capacity. Unfortunately, the solver under this specific model implementation could not approximate good results and was finally not used.

8. Local Search Improvement Procedures

We have identified three local search procedures that have the potential to improve the cost of a given schedule. These local search procedures can be considered as "large" moves since they examine a significant number of schedules neighboring the current one.

8.1. Local Search Improve1

The first local search procedure starts by iterating overall jobs. For each job $j1$, each other consecutive job $j2$ is identified, and then each job $j3$ with a duration equal to the aggregated durations of $j1$ and $j2$ is found. Since $j1$ and $j2$ are consecutive, they can be swapped with job $j3$, and the schedule will still remain feasible, as seen in Figure 5. Moreover, the order of the two first jobs does not influence the feasibility. So, two alternatives are tested that compare the imposed penalties before and after the swap, and, if an improvement is found, the swap occurs. The time complexity of this procedure is $\mathcal{O}(|\mathbb{J}|)$ since the maximum number of consecutive jobs for each job is bounded by the maximum capacity, which is a constant number much smaller than the number of jobs.

Moreover, the identification of consecutive jobs and jobs of durations that are equal to the aggregated duration of two other consecutive jobs is performed using Hash Maps that effectively contribute $\mathcal{O}(1)$ to the above complexity. The first one uses times as keys and has a list of jobs starting at these times as values. By using as a key the finish time of a job $j1$, the dictionary returns each job $j2$ that is consecutive to $j1$. The second Hash Map uses the jobs' durations as keys and, as the value for each key x, the list of jobs with the duration x. Note that the second Hash Map is computed only once and remains unchanged through the solution process.

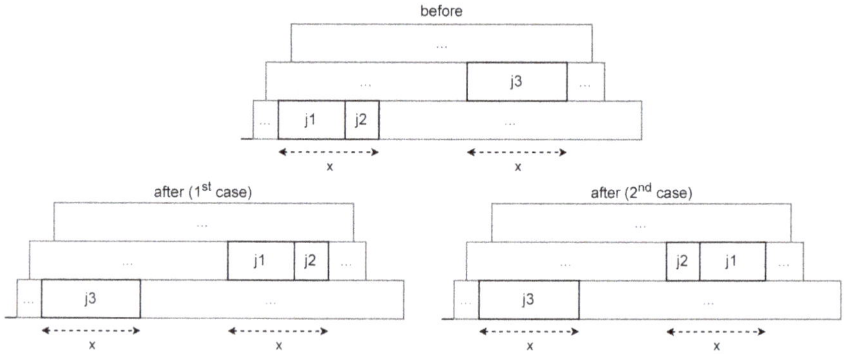

Figure 5. Assuming that job $j3$ has the same duration as the aggregated duration of jobs $j1$ and $j2$, two cases for swapping them become possible. The first one puts $j1$ first and $j2$ second, and the other one puts $j2$ first and $j1$ second.

8.2. Local Search Improve2

The second local search procedure uses C-Paths that are computed as described in Section 5. Each C-Path is traversed from left to right until a job j is found that imposes a cost to the schedule (i.e., has a finish time greater than its due time). The only way that the penalty of a job j can be reduced is by moving it to the left side of the C-Path. So, all jobs that start earlier than job j are examined by swapping places with job j. If the total penalty imposed by job j and a sequence of jobs up to another job k is greater than the penalty after swapping jobs j and k, followed by shifts of jobs in between, then this set of moves occurs. The time complexity of this procedure is $\mathcal{O}(|\mathbb{J}|^2)$. Since each C-Path has a length that is $\mathcal{O}(|\mathbb{J}|)$, and each C-Path is traversed once for identifying jobs with penalties, and then, for each such job, the C-path is again traversed, it follows that the complexity is quadratic. The construction of each C-Path costs $\mathcal{O}(|\mathbb{J}|)$, which is added to the time of the above procedure and gives $\mathcal{O}(|\mathbb{J}|) + \mathcal{O}(|\mathbb{J}|^2)$. Since this occurs for every job, $|\mathbb{J}|$ C-Paths are generated, and this results in a total complexity of $\mathcal{O}(|\mathbb{J}|^3)$ for the second local search procedure. An example of this procedure is depicted in Figure 6.

8.3. Local Search Improve3

The third local search procedure starts by identifying periods where the capacity is not fully used. Given a capacity profile that has the form of a pulse, for each job, the pulse is lowered by one unit for the period during which it is active. This is iterated for all jobs, and, finally, it is possible to exist periods scattered across the horizon that have non-zero capacity remaining. So, jobs with finish times that fall inside these periods (gaps) can possibly be moved to the right, and the schedule should still be feasible. The main idea of this local search procedure is that it allows two jobs of marginally different durations to swap places. This occurs by first identifying two C-Paths with no common jobs that have jobs with finish times falling inside gaps as their rightmost jobs. Given two such C-Paths, each job of them can be swapped with a job of the other C-Path, provided that the slack that the gap provides is adequate for this move. This means that all jobs of a C-Path that are to the right of the smaller of the two swapping jobs should shift to the right, and all jobs of the other C-Path that are to the right of the bigger job should shift to the left, giving the opportunity for further penalty gains. In principle, the number of jobs that might have finish times that fall inside gaps is $\mathcal{O}(|\mathbb{J}|)$, but our experiments showed that, in practice, this number is a small fraction of $|\mathbb{J}|$. Since two C-Paths are involved, and each job of a C-Path has to be checked with each job of the other C-Path, this contributes $\mathcal{O}(|\mathbb{J}|^2)$. Moreover, all possible pairs of jobs that fall in gaps are used as starting points in the construction of the corresponding C-Paths, resulting in another $\mathcal{O}(|\mathbb{J}|^2)$ term. So, the time complexity of the overall procedure is $\mathcal{O}(|\mathbb{J}|^4)$. It should be noted that shifts due to penalty reductions occur rarely, and their amortized contribution to the time complexity is neglected. In practice, the time needed for this move is comparable to the previous one due to the relatively small number of jobs that fall inside gaps. An example of this procedure is depicted in Figure 7.

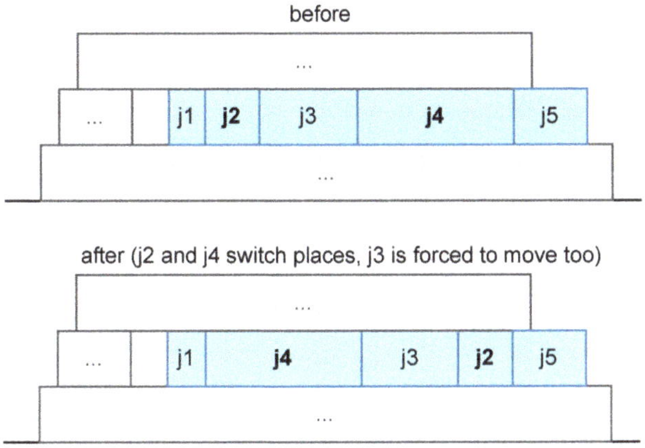

Figure 6. Given a C-Path, this local search procedure swaps two non-consecutive jobs (*j*1 and *j*2) and appropriately shifts the in-between jobs (*j*3) so as to keep the C-Path property for all involved jobs.

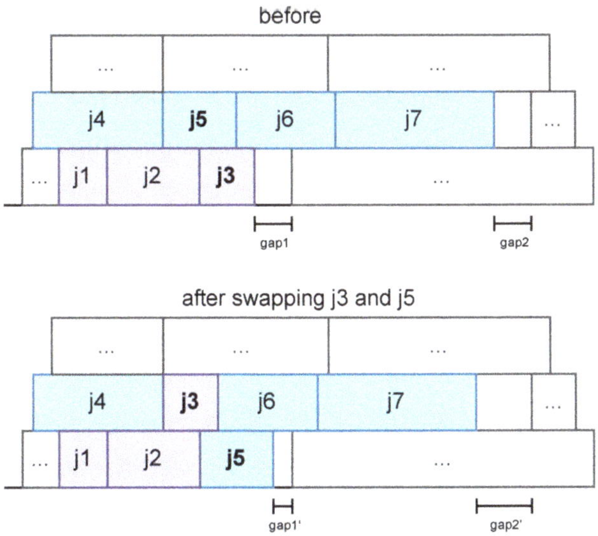

Figure 7. Jobs belonging to two C-Paths swap places to reduce the length or even remove gaps in the schedule.

9. A Multi-Staged Approach

The approach we employed for addressing the problem uses several stages that operate cyclically until the available time runs out.

10. Results

Our experiments were run on a workstation with 32GB of RAM and an Intel Core i7-7700K 4.2GHz CPU (four cores, eight threads) running Windows 10. The constraint programming solver that we used was IBM ILOG CP Optimizer Version 22. The local search procedures, the implementation of the constraint programming model, and the driver program were all implemented in Python. Our results are compared with the results of Mencia et al. in [6], which is a continuation of their previous work in [4,5]. In their most recent work, they present and compare six memetic algorithms termed MA_{SCP}, MA_{iSCP}, MA_{SCP+}, MA_{CB}, MA_{ICP}, and MA_{HYB}. The last one gives the best results out of all others and the previous approaches of the authors, and this is the algorithm with which we compare our approach. MA_{HYB} combines CB and ICP procedures under a memetic algorithm. Both procedures use the concept of a cover. A cover is a disjoint set of C-Paths that covers all jobs. In CB, once a cover is generated, the C-Paths of the cover are examined in isolation for improvements. On the other hand, ICP swaps jobs between C-Paths, again using a cover to select the C-Paths participating in the procedure. In [6], no values for the schedule costs are given, but the relative performances of the six approaches are recorded in tables and graphs instead. So, results about the actual schedule costs of MA_{HYB} and the other approaches that we use in our comparisons hereafter were taken from [8], which the authors cite in their paper.

10.1. CPO vs. CPO+

We call the constraint programming approach, briefly described in [6], CPO (constraint programming optimizer), and our approach described in Section "Constraint Programming Formulation" that exploits the "due rule", CPO+. Results about the performance of CPO were taken from the web repository cited at the end of the previous paragraph.

Table 4 depicts for each problem instance the total tardiness of all jobs for the schedule that CPO and CPO+ produced. It shows that CPO+ manages to find solutions equal to the best-known solutions for 25 out of 190 problem instances, while CPO achieves this for only 2 problem instances (`i120_3_3` and `i120_5_4`). The best values are written in bold. An allotted time of $n/2$ seconds for each problem instance was given for each run, where n is the number of jobs. We used all available cores, which was the default setup for the IBM ILOG CP Optimizer. The results of CPO+ are the best among 10 runs for each problem instance, and random seeds were used to achieve diversity.

Table 4. Best results (total tardiness) from the CPO approach and our CPO+ approach.

Problem Set	CPO										CPO+									
	1	2	3	4	5	6	7	8	9	10	1	2	3	4	5	6	7	8	9	10
i120_3	951	3834	**2410**	1059	3951	3258	730	4095	1690	1326	**867**	**3620**	**2410**	**1019**	**3859**	**3123**	**720**	**4084**	**1663**	**1268**
i120_5	1054	1673	999	**496**	3128	458	550	1227	3486	1245	**1030**	**1538**	**959**	**496**	**3062**	**455**	**519**	**1214**	**3332**	**1151**
i120_7	1201	2768	3798	4206	3220	2786	1712	3306	4694	546	**1133**	**2725**	**3551**	**4083**	**3095**	**2665**	**1655**	**3225**	**4510**	**503**
i120_10	764	1212	1554	935	1612	1157	2530	777	1056	881	**752**	**1129**	**1511**	**887**	**1467**	**1118**	**2464**	**721**	**1006**	**823**
i250_10	4311	552	1480	4871	6921	6563	4857	6108	5453	1405	**4144**	**506**	**1354**	**4755**	**6522**	**6288**	**4604**	**5940**	**5363**	**1320**
i250_20	5905	1974	2971	2774	1343	1786	1644	2408	1730	6632	**5674**	**1899**	**2825**	**2545**	**1097**	**1631**	**1594**	**2202**	**1561**	**6563**
i250_30	3381	3348	5273	5099	4560	5333	3990	803	1808	5600	**3085**	**3114**	**4999**	**4194**	**4304**	**5129**	**3726**	**695**	**1561**	**5418**
i500_10	4791	865	1109	2226	675	6312	3261	4688	497	2227	**4614**	**822**	**963**	**2159**	**610**	**6100**	**2864**	**4472**	**465**	**2130**
i500_20	8212	899	9440	1495	1859	9349	626	3536	6614	6030	**7705**	**790**	**9144**	**1273**	**1799**	**9232**	**525**	**3252**	**6420**	**5886**
i500_30	3064	613	6317	4787	6583	1838	4256	9360	1099	482	**2822**	**501**	**6048**	**4425**	**6114**	**1697**	**3892**	**9051**	**921**	**369**
i750_10	4670	8244	6051	5405	1655	8227	1039	8638	13594	4149	**4460**	**7820**	**5841**	**5110**	**1539**	**7909**	**970**	**8042**	**13,103**	**3906**
i750_20	6100	889	1593	10,151	9927	12,396	5175	11,910	4812	2866	**6046**	**703**	**1320**	**9633**	**9179**	**11,652**	**4875**	**11,414**	**4399**	**2690**
i750_30	5092	6045	3200	3240	733	3028	1243	3281	3118	2256	**4954**	**5314**	**2534**	**3030**	**687**	**2609**	**1114**	**2963**	**2812**	**2089**
i750_50	5989	5766	13,945	2699	11,096	12,590	5748	11,425	5689	6139	**5303**	**5098**	**12,615**	**2433**	**10,190**	**11,998**	**5122**	**10,898**	**5402**	**5242**
i1000_10	712	24,629	1071	15,711	16,299	2188	779	20,902	23,213	4471	**641**	**23,821**	**833**	**15,342**	**15,443**	**2025**	**743**	**20,891**	**22,495**	**4147**
i1000_20	10,379	17,525	20,318	8214	15,211	25,044	10,012	17,482	11,583	11,316	**9470**	**16,355**	**20,265**	**8083**	**14,510**	**24,915**	**9912**	**17,048**	**10,436**	**10,892**
i1000_30	7871	2074	20,964	13,991	4308	13,630	10,763	2713	15,856	20,959	**7054**	**1769**	**18,580**	**12,753**	**3800**	**12,298**	**10,232**	**2239**	**15,631**	**19,138**
i1000_50	3315	16,491	13,047	1520	1630	18,216	21,181	2227	15,473	4682	**2963**	**16,236**	**12,130**	**1239**	**1478**	**17,131**	**20,133**	**2022**	**14,454**	**4199**
i1000_100	**73,637**	**81,104**	28,292	39,057	**76,080**	50,541	47,746	55,973	26,585	17,803	78,963	81,638	**26,446**	**37,719**	77,298	**49,313**	**45,036**	**53,639**	**24,823**	**16,330**

10.2. Hybrid Exact–Local Search

The HELS (hybrid exact–local search) approach is shown using the flowchart in Figure 8. First, the constraint programming solver is employed for the full problem. A period of time of $n/2$ seconds is given for executing this stage. Then, for $3 \times n$ seconds, a loop occurs that includes the three local search procedures, followed by activation of the constraint programming solver again, but this time for subproblems. These subproblems might involve jobs that intersect with vertical ribbons on the time axis or groups of consecutive sequences of jobs (i.e., multiple C-Paths). Note that a reordering of jobs might be needed so that the current solution conforms with the "due rule", else the constraint programming solver might consider the fixed parts of the partial solution to be infeasible. This is denoted by the extra stage "Reorder same duration jobs" after the third local search procedure in Figure 8.

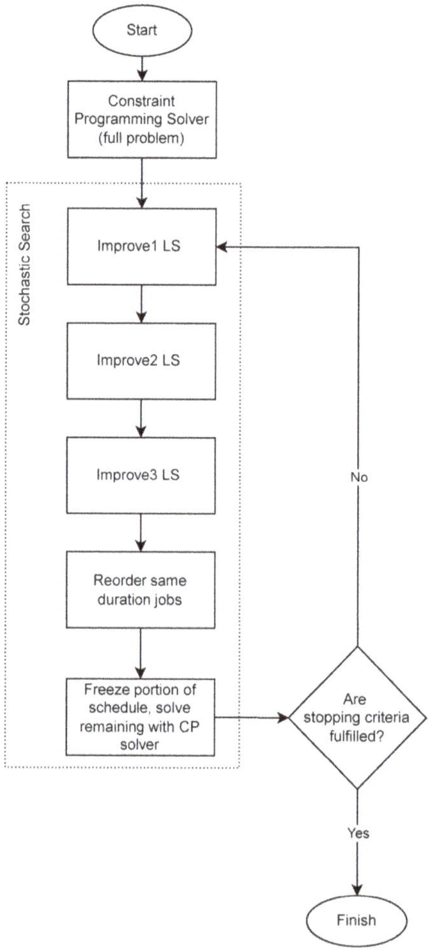

Figure 8. Hybrid Exact–Local Search approach.

Table 5 presents the best results that were achieved by the approach with the best-known results, all of which are provided by MA_{HYB}.

Table 5. Best previously known results (total tardiness) achieved from the MA_{HYB} approach and the results of our HELS approach.

Problem Set	MA_{HYB}										HELS									
	1	2	3	4	5	6	7	8	9	10	1	2	3	4	5	6	7	8	9	10
i120_3	**848**	**3568**	**2410**	**1019**	**3858**	**3120**	**720**	**4084**	**1663**	**1268**	**848**	3570	**2410**	**1019**	**3858**	**3120**	**720**	**4084**	**1663**	**1268**
i120_5	**1030**	**1511**	**959**	**496**	**3061**	**455**	**519**	**1214**	**3223**	**1131**	**1030**	1514	**959**	**496**	**3061**	**455**	**519**	**1214**	3231	**1131**
i120_7	**1120**	**2725**	**3493**	**4021**	**3059**	**2640**	**1655**	**3225**	**4470**	**493**	1121	**2725**	3505	4028	3078	**2640**	**1655**	**3225**	4474	**493**
i120_10	**746**	**1124**	**1442**	**887**	**1447**	**1118**	**2463**	**721**	**977**	**820**	749	1125	1453	**887**	**1447**	**1118**	**2463**	**721**	983	**820**
i250_10	**4094**	**506**	**1349**	**4731**	**6390**	**6280**	**4497**	**5881**	**5321**	**1293**	4103	**506**	**1349**	**4731**	6391	6284	4511	5887	5327	**1293**
i250_20	**5573**	**1882**	**2813**	**2525**	**1054**	**1583**	**1565**	**2190**	**1553**	**6531**	**5573**	1888	**2813**	**2525**	**1054**	1605	1570	**2190**	**1553**	6541
i250_30	**3013**	**3054**	4758	4098	4197	5034	**3641**	**686**	**1502**	5197	**3013**	**3054**	**4753**	**4093**	**4194**	**5019**	**3641**	**686**	**1502**	**5193**
i500_10	**4614**	**822**	**951**	**2102**	**610**	**5981**	**2768**	**4460**	**462**	**1998**	**4614**	**822**	953	2116	**610**	**5981**	2783	**4460**	**462**	2008
i500_20	7649	**790**	**8941**	**1272**	**1719**	9110	**523**	**3180**	**6291**	5661	**7569**	**790**	8970	**1272**	1744	**9097**	**523**	3188	6338	**5659**
i500_30	**2670**	**477**	5975	**4307**	**5869**	**1614**	**3795**	8946	**862**	**352**	**2670**	**477**	**5974**	**4307**	5873	1626	**3795**	**8888**	**862**	**352**
i750_10	4379	**7744**	**5819**	5086	1517	**7895**	952	7996	12,837	**3840**	**4312**	**7744**	5821	**5082**	**1500**	**7895**	**943**	**7962**	**12,814**	**3840**
i750_20	**5891**	**700**	**1314**	9674	**9073**	**11,434**	**4855**	11,353	**4393**	**2632**	5979	**700**	**1314**	**9562**	**9073**	**11,434**	**4855**	**11,284**	**4393**	**2632**
i750_30	**4713**	**5128**	**2364**	2951	**661**	**2577**	**1070**	**2911**	**2700**	**1994**	4767	**5128**	**2364**	**2945**	663	**2577**	**1070**	2912	**2700**	**1994**
i750_50	**5134**	4978	12,601	**2356**	**9840**	**11,483**	**4868**	**10,580**	**5154**	5204	**5134**	**4792**	**12,147**	**2356**	9847	11,500	**4868**	10,583	**5154**	**5028**
i1000_10	**641**	23,729	815	**15,204**	15,393	**2025**	735	20,686	22,358	4028	**641**	**23,521**	**812**	15,206	**15,180**	**2025**	**729**	**20,574**	**22,162**	**3982**
i1000_20	**9440**	16,069	20,168	**7962**	**14,183**	24,693	9816	16,994	**10,290**	**10,781**	**9440**	**15,971**	**19,986**	7975	**14,183**	**24,507**	**9726**	**16,789**	10,301	**10,781**
i1000_30	6902	1687	18,433	**12,399**	3768	**12,090**	9795	**2085**	15,625	18,728	**6780**	**1668**	**18,087**	12,411	**3707**	**12,090**	**9765**	**2085**	**15,528**	**18,483**
i1000_50	**2883**	16,418	**11,613**	**1142**	**1390**	**16,656**	**19,566**	**1886**	**13,740**	**3989**	**2883**	**15,977**	11,618	**1142**	**1390**	16,667	**19,566**	1889	13,747	**3989**
i1000_100	71,034	**75,101**	25,977	**36,374**	67,109	**47,540**	44,545	**52,266**	23,704	15,664	**71,012**	75,181	**25,594**	36,376	**66,419**	47,541	**43,437**	**52,266**	**23,690**	**15,230**

Table 6 consolidates the relative performance of our approach when compared with the best-known results. We can observe that our approach manages to find new best results for 48 of the problem instances. It also equals the best-known results for 91 problem instances. MA_{HYB} achieves better results than our approach for the remaining 51 problem instances. We also compare our solutions with how closely it reaches the previously best-known solution as a percentage value, and we call this the metric "distance%". Negative values mean that our approach sets a new best-known value. We see that the average distance% metric for all problem instances assumes a negative value of −0.1727%, demonstrating its very good performance. This is further supported by Figure 9, which shows for each problem subset consisting of 10 instances, a boxplot of the distance% values. Again, negative values are advantageous for our approach, and the graph clearly shows that our approach achieves excellent results, especially for large problem instances.

Table 6. The HELS approach's performance against the best recorded results.

Best	Equal	Worse	Distance (%)
48	91	51	−0.1727

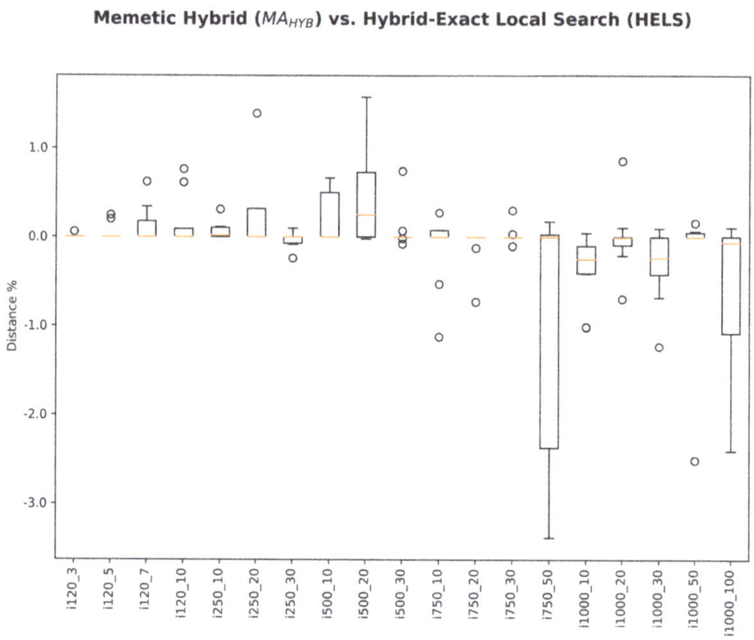

Figure 9. The HELS approach compared with the best-known results derived from the MA_{HYB} approach in [6].

10.3. Discussion

Figure 10 includes three graphs showing the cost of solutions during the allotted execution time. We can see that the costs start from very high values and sharply fall to smaller values, not very far from the final ones. The long tails of the graphs indicate that less time is needed for achieving good quality schedules than the $3.5 \times n$ seconds (n is the number of jobs) that we have used in our experiments. This is further demonstrated by the values of CPO+ and HELS in Tables 4 and 5, with the first ones being close to the second. In particular, for the set of all 190 problem instances, the percentage distance of CPO+ to HELS has a mean equal to 0.077 and a standard deviation equal to 0.069.

Regarding comparing our approach with the one by Mencia et al. [6], we can make a few remarks. First, Mencia et al. do not report in their papers the exact values that their approaches returned; instead, they compare their results to their other less efficient approaches. So, we retrieved the values we use in our comparisons from the site [8] that the authors reference in their paper. Providing exact values alongside solution files that other researchers can download from our repository [26] may attract more interest to the problem. Since the run-time environments used in our case and in Mencia et al.'s case are different, we focus mainly on whether each approach can find the best possible result, given that limited processing power is exploited in both cases. Furthermore, in our case, Figure 10 clearly shows a trend observed in other problem instances: our approach reaches results very close to the final results using only about 1/5 of the allotted execution time.

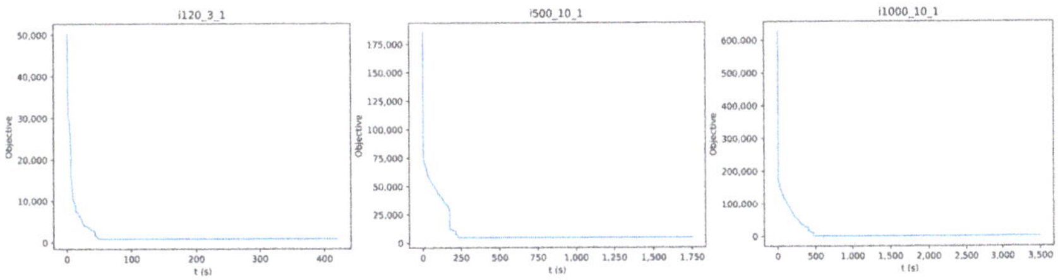

Figure 10. Cost values during the execution time using the HELS approach.

11. Conclusions

In this manuscript, we examined an abstraction of a real-world electrical vehicle charging scheduling problem that comes with a public dataset and high-quality published solutions. This problem involves a number of jobs with given durations and due times that should be scheduled to a single machine with time-dependent capacity, while the objective is the minimization of the aggregated tardiness of all jobs. We proposed some novel ideas, such as the due times rule, local improvement procedures, and problem decompositions. The result was that we managed to achieve better solutions for many problem instances of the already excellent solved dataset. A central component of the proposed approach, which we call the hybrid exact–local search (HELS) approach, is a constraint programming model that utilizes interval variables and global constraints and that is initially called for the full problem and then iteratively for subproblems that stochastically drive the objective to more favorable values. Three improvement procedures are embedded in our HELS approach that perform local searches and succeed in further improving solutions. Our work demonstrates an example of a general tendency. Challenging combinatorial problems increasingly fall into the realm of exact solvers, which are nowadays capable of solving problems of big sizes. If this is not possible for the full problem, hybrid approaches that combine exact solvers over subproblems and approximate solvers can be combined to decompose the problem in a process that results in complete, high-quality solutions.

Author Contributions: Conceptualization, C.G. and C.V.; methodology, C.V.; software, C.G., C.V., and A.D.; validation, C.V., A.D., and P.P.; formal analysis, P.P.; investigation, A.D. and C.G.; resources, A.V.; data curation, A.V.; writing—original draft preparation, A.D. and C.G.; writing—review and editing, C.G., C.V., and A.D.; visualization, A.V.; supervision, C.G. All authors have read and agreed to the published version of the manuscript.

Funding: This research received no external funding.

Data Availability Statement: Problem instances and all solution files using our hybrid exact–local search approach are archived in [26].

Conflicts of Interest: The authors declare no conflict of interest.

References

1. Pinedo, M.L. *Scheduling*; Springer: Berlin/Heidelberg, Germany, 2012; Volume 29.
2. Graham, R.L.; Lawler, E.L.; Lenstra, J.K.; Kan, A.R. Optimization and approximation in deterministic sequencing and scheduling: A survey. In *Annals of Discrete Mathematics*; Elsevier: Amsterdam, The Netherlands, 1979; Volume 5, pp. 287–326.

3. Scheduling Zoo. Available online: http://schedulingzoo.lip6.fr/ (accessed on 21 November 2022).
4. Mencía, C.; Sierra, M.R.; Mencía, R.; Varela, R. Genetic algorithm for scheduling charging times of electric vehicles subject to time dependent power availability. In Proceedings of the International Work-Conference on the Interplay between Natural and Artificial Computation, Corunna, Spain, 19–23 June 2017; Springer: Berlin/Heidelberg, Germany, 2017; pp. 160–169.
5. Mencía, C.; Sierra, M.R.; Mencía, R.; Varela, R. Evolutionary one-machine scheduling in the context of electric vehicles charging. *Integr.-Comput.-Aided Eng.* **2019**, *26*, 49–63. [CrossRef]
6. Mencía, R.; Mencía, C. One-Machine Scheduling with Time-Dependent Capacity via Efficient Memetic Algorithms. *Mathematics* **2021**, *9*, 3030. [CrossRef]
7. Koulamas, C. The single-machine total tardiness scheduling problem: Review and extensions. *Eur. J. Oper. Res.* **2010**, *202*, 1–7. [CrossRef]
8. GitHub Repository for "One Machine Scheduling with Time Dependent Capacity via Efficient Memetic Algorithms" by Mencia R. Available online: https://github.com/raulmencia/One-Machine-Scheduling-with-Time-Dependent-Capacity-via-Efficient-Memetic-Algorithms (accessed on 21 November 2022).
9. Hernández-Arauzo, A.; Puente, J.; Varela, R.; Sedano, J. Electric vehicle charging under power and balance constraints as dynamic scheduling. *Comput. Ind. Eng.* **2015**, *85*, 306–315. [CrossRef]
10. Lenstra, J.K.; Kan, A.R.; Brucker, P. Complexity of machine scheduling problems. In *Annals of Discrete Mathematics*; Elsevier: Amsterdam, The Netherlands, 1977; Volume 1, pp. 343–362.
11. Gupta, S.K.; Kyparisis, J. Single machine scheduling research. *Omega* **1987**, *15*, 207–227. [CrossRef]
12. Gogos, C.; Valouxis, C.; Alefragis, P.; Goulas, G.; Voros, N.; Housos, E. Scheduling independent tasks on heterogeneous processors using heuristics and Column Pricing. *Future Gener. Comput. Syst.* **2016**, *60*, 48–66. [CrossRef]
13. Baptiste, P.; Le Pape, C.; Nuijten, W. *Constraint-Based Scheduling: Applying Constraint Programming to Scheduling Problems*; Springer Science & Business Media: Berlin/Heidelberg, Germany, 2001; Volume 39.
14. Großmann, P.; Hölldobler, S.; Manthey, N.; Nachtigall, K.; Opitz, J.; Steinke, P. Solving periodic event scheduling problems with SAT. In Proceedings of the International Conference on Industrial, Engineering and other Applications of Applied Intelligent Systems, Dalian, China, 9–12 June 2012; Springer: Berlin/Heidelberg, Germany, 2012; pp. 166–175.
15. Ansótegui, C.; Bofill, M.; Palahí, M.; Suy, J.; Villaret, M. Satisfiability modulo theories: An efficient approach for the resource-constrained project scheduling problem. In Proceedings of the Ninth Symposium of Abstraction, Reformulation, and Approximation, Parador de Cardona, Spain, 17–18 July 2011.
16. Brucker, P.; Knust, S.; Schoo, A.; Thiele, O. A branch and bound algorithm for the resource-constrained project scheduling problem. *Eur. J. Oper. Res.* **1998**, *107*, 272–288. [CrossRef]
17. Vaessens, R.J.M.; Aarts, E.H.; Lenstra, J.K. Job shop scheduling by local search. *Informs J. Comput.* **1996**, *8*, 302–317. [CrossRef]
18. Matsuo, H.; Juck Suh, C.; Sullivan, R.S. A controlled search simulated annealing method for the single machine weighted tardiness problem. *Ann. Oper. Res.* **1989**, *21*, 85–108. [CrossRef]
19. Lee, K.M.; Yamakawa, T.; Lee, K.M. A genetic algorithm for general machine scheduling problems. In Proceedings of the 1998 Second International Conference Knowledge-Based Intelligent Electronic Systems, Proceedings KES'98 (Cat. No. 98EX111), Adelaide, Australia, 21–23 April 1998; IEEE: Piscataway, NJ, USA, 1998; Volume 2, pp. 60–66.
20. Gil-Gala, F.J.; Mencía, C.; Sierra, M.R.; Varela, R. Evolving priority rules for on-line scheduling of jobs on a single machine with variable capacity over time. *Appl. Soft Comput.* **2019**, *85*, 105782. [CrossRef]
21. França, P.M.; Mendes, A.; Moscato, P. A memetic algorithm for the total tardiness single machine scheduling problem. *Eur. J. Oper. Res.* **2001**, *132*, 224–242. [CrossRef]
22. Wu, X.; Che, A. A memetic differential evolution algorithm for energy-efficient parallel machine scheduling. *Omega* **2019**, *82*, 155–165. [CrossRef]
23. Merkle, D.; Middendorf, M. Ant colony optimization with global pheromone evaluation for scheduling a single machine. *Appl. Intell.* **2003**, *18*, 105–111. [CrossRef]
24. Lin, T.L.; Horng, S.J.; Kao, T.W.; Chen, Y.H.; Run, R.S.; Chen, R.J.; Lai, J.L.; Kuo, I.H. An efficient job-shop scheduling algorithm based on particle swarm optimization. *Expert Syst. Appl.* **2010**, *37*, 2629–2636. [CrossRef]
25. Yuce, B.; Fruggiero, F.; Packianather, M.S.; Pham, D.T.; Mastrocinque, E.; Lambiase, A.; Fera, M. Hybrid Genetic Bees Algorithm applied to single machine scheduling with earliness and tardiness penalties. *Comput. Ind. Eng.* **2017**, *113*, 842–858. [CrossRef]
26. GitHub Repository for "A Hybrid Exact-Local Search Approach for One-Machine Scheduling with Time-Dependent Capacity" by Gogos C. Available online: https://github.com/chgogos/1MSTDC (accessed on 21 November 2022).
27. Laborie, P.; Rogerie, J.; Shaw, P.; Vilím, P. IBM ILOG CP optimizer for scheduling. *Constraints* **2018**, *23*, 210–250. [CrossRef]
28. Google OR Tools CP-SAT Solver. Available online: https://developers.google.com/optimization/cp/cp_solver (accessed on 21 November 2022).

algorithms

MDPI

Article

Comparison of Single-Lane Roundabout Entry Degree of Saturation Estimations from Analytical and Regression Models

Ana Čudina Ivančev, Maja Ahac *, Saša Ahac and Vesna Dragčević

Faculty of Civil Engineering, University of Zagreb, 10000 Zagreb, Croatia
* Correspondence: maja.ahac@grad.unizg.hr

Abstract: Roundabout design is an iterative process consisting of a preliminary geometry design, geometry performance checks, and the estimation of intersection functionality (based on the results of analytical or regression models). Since both roundabout geometry design procedures and traffic characteristics vary around the world, the discussion on which functionality estimation model is more appropriate is ongoing. This research aims to reduce the uncertainty in decision-making during this final roundabout design stage. Its two objectives were to analyze and compare the results of roundabout performance estimations derived from one analytical and one regression model, and to quantify the model results' susceptibility to changes in roundabout geometric parameters. For this, 60 four-legged single-lane roundabout schemes were created, varying in size and leg alignment. Their geometric parameters resulted from the assumption of their location in a suburban environment and chosen design vehicle swept path analysis. To compare the models' results, the degree of saturation of roundabout entries was calculated based on presumed traffic flows. The results showed that the regression model estimates higher functionality and that this difference (both between the two models and regression models applied on different schemes) is more pronounced as the outer radius and angle between the legs increase.

Keywords: suburban roundabout design; swept path analysis; geometric parameters; performance estimation; capacity assessment

Citation: Čudina Ivančev, A.; Ahac, M.; Ahac, S.; Dragčević, V. Comparison of Single-Lane Roundabout Entry Degree of Saturation Estimations from Analytical and Regression Models. *Algorithms* **2023**, *16*, 164. https://doi.org/10.3390/a16030164

Academic Editor: Frank Werner

Received: 15 February 2023
Revised: 14 March 2023
Accepted: 15 March 2023
Published: 18 March 2023

1. Introduction

Roundabouts are intersections with a one-way circulatory roadway around a central island. In most countries, the vehicles entering the roundabout should give right-of-way to vehicles in the circulatory lane. Consequently, roundabout operational functionality is directly dependent on the traffic conditions in the circulating traffic flow and indirectly dependent on the geometric design of the roundabout. According to [1–3], single-lane roundabouts are a very good solution for the following transportation engineering demands: for reduced intersection dimensions; for intersections with five or more legs; when there is even distribution of traffic on the intersection legs; for traffic volumes under 25,000 veh/day; for a decrease in the waiting time at the intersection; as a measure to calm traffic, especially in urban areas; and for lowering levels of traffic noise, emissions of harmful gases, and the risk of accidents (due to the low driving speeds of approaching and circulating traffic, and fewer conflict points than at standard intersections). Additionally, single-lane roundabouts are increasingly popular solutions in suburban areas due to their design that provides an easy transition in road category and type (from a dual to a single roadway, i.e., from rural to the urban environment), and the fact that they do not require the installation, maintenance, and operation of signal lights.

Roundabout design is an iterative process consisting of a (1) preliminary geometry design, (2) geometry performance checks, which include the design vehicle swept path, fastest path, and visibility analysis, and (3) assessments of intersection functionality through capacity analysis. Roundabout geometry is primarily influenced by the design vehicle swept path. The design vehicle is a vehicle identified as the least maneuverable vehicle expected to use the intersection [4]—a vehicle of a certain type and dimensions that characterize a group of vehicles and fully correspond to the legal regulations on vehicle dimensions [5], or international recommendations [6]. Design vehicles are often chosen depending on the position of the intersection in the road network and the composition and category of expected vehicles (trucks in industrial zones, buses in urban and suburban areas, etc.) [7]. After confirming the preliminary design through the geometry performance checks, the iterative design process shifts to capacity analysis, to assure that the roundabout geometry satisfies traffic performance criteria. If the capacity value is too low or too high, the geometry needs to be redesigned and the capacity analysis repeated [8].

Numerous models have been created over years to assist road designers and traffic analysts in the assessments of intersection functionality. These models can be broadly classified into three categories: (1) probabilistic, analytical, gap-acceptance models, (2) deterministic, empirical regression, geometric models, and (3) time-dependent, microsimulation models. The final selection of the most appropriate roundabout design is usually based on the results of the analytical or regression model for entry capacity assessment [9–13].

The analytical models were created based on combining the main postulates of traffic flow theory and field-measured driver behaviors. This approach resulted in an analytic formulation of the relationship between field measurements and theoretical performance parameters [14]. They consider traffic flow composition and conflict between vehicles in the circulatory roadway and vehicles entering the roundabout [15]. Probability theory is used to estimate to what extent the vehicles entering a roundabout will be able to use an acceptable gap between two consecutive vehicles in the circulating traffic stream [9,16]. They do not directly quantify the relationship between the capacity and geometric parameters of the roundabout [11,13].

On the other hand, regression models were generated from extensive traffic data collected at roundabout entries. They have established relationships between capacity and geometric design features through statistical multivariate regression analyses to fit mathematical relationships between measured entry capacity, circulating flow, and other independent variables that have an impact on entry capacity [9,14]. They consider not only the circulating and entering but also the exiting traffic flow. The relationship between entry capacity and circulating flow is linear or exponential, depending on the model [8,11].

Simulation models are based on modeling the movements and interactions of individual vehicles on a network consisting of links and nodes or connectors. Vehicle movements are governed by gap acceptance, car-following, lane-changing, and other models, and are typically calculated for each vehicle at every specified time step [8]. In recent years, vehicle movements along a roundabout have been studied within the master equation formalism for stochastic exclusion processes of many-particle systems, i.e., many-body interactions. The finite dimensions of vehicles introduce a natural "quantization" of space, and developed models simulate the stochastic motion of particles (vehicles) along a roundabout through the (totally) asymmetric exclusion process [17,18].

Although designers and analysts would like to perform estimations as completely and correctly as possible, model performance in predicting roundabout entry capacities is limited [19]. Even today, the discussion between analytical and regression models characterizes the general situation regarding the estimation of entry capacity at roundabouts [9,12]. The main issues address the fact that both roundabout geometric parameters and traffic characteristics (volume, vehicle composition, and driver behavior) vary widely across the world [20]. However, according to [10,21], geometric parameters have a much stronger impact on roundabout entry capacity than geographic location or country of origin, i.e., "regional" non-geometric driver behavior. Additionally, among the different factors influencing entry capacity, only the geometric parameters of roundabouts can be quantified and modified, i.e., entirely manipulated by the designers to improve roundabouts' operational performance [11].

The two objectives of the research presented in this paper are to (1) analyze and compare the results of roundabout performance estimations derived from analytical and regression models, and (2) quantify the model results' susceptibility to changes in roundabout geometric parameters. The investigation will be performed on 60 four-legged single-lane roundabouts schemes, varying in size and leg alignment, designed according to the results of the chosen design vehicle swept path analysis. The roundabout performance estimations will be performed under the assumption that the entering traffic at each leg is distributed in three travel directions through the roundabouts, in equal shares. To compare the results of the analytical and regression models, the roundabout entry degree of saturation will be calculated. This is a dimensionless value used as the intersection efficiency indicator in both models. The results of this research will reduce the uncertainty in decision-making during the final roundabout design stage.

2. Materials and Methods

A list of symbols used in the manuscript is given in Table 1.

Table 1. List of symbols used in the manuscript.

Group	Symbol	Parameter
Geometric parameters	R_o	outer radius (m)
	R_i	central island radius (m)
	u	circulatory roadway width (m)
	j	number of roundabout legs, j = 1, ... , 4
	δ	angle between the roundabout legs (°)
	l	length of the arc between the adjacent roundabout legs (m)
	e_j	entry width (m)
	e_j'	exit width (m)
	R_j	entry radius (m)
	R_{j+1}'	exit radius (m)
	b_j	distance between exiting and entering traffic flows along the center of the circulatory lane (m)
Traffic parameters	i	direction of travel through roundabout, i = 1, ... , 12
	q_i	traffic flow in the direction i (veh/h)
	O_i	traffic flow in passenger car units in the direction i (pcu/h)
	f_T	conversion factor for traffic composition (pcu/veh)
	Q_{Cj}	circulating traffic flow (pcu/h)
	Q_{Sj}	exiting traffic flows at leg j (pcu/h)
	Q_{Ej}	entering traffic flows at leg j (pcu/h)
	BC_j	base entry capacity of the roundabout at leg j (pcu/h)
	f_P	capacity reduction factor for pedestrian and cycling traffic flow at roundabouts (-)
	C_{Ej}	entry capacity at leg j (pcu/h)
	C_{mj}	entry capacity for mixed traffic flow at leg j (veh/h)
	q_{mj}	mixed traffic flow at leg j (veh/h)
	$x_{mj,A}$	degree of saturation of entry at leg j according to analytical model (-)
	$x_{mj,R}$	degree of saturation of entry at leg j according to regression model (-)
	α	factor reflecting the impact of exiting traffic on entry capacity by distance b (-)
	β	factor for adjusting circulating flow depending on the number of circulating lanes (-)
	γ	factor for adjusting entry capacity depending on the number of circulating lanes (-)

The geometric parameters of a roundabout are the outer radius (R_o), the central island radius (R_i), the circulatory roadway width (u), the number of legs (j), the angle between the legs (δ), entry width (e_j), exit width (e_j'), entry radius (R_j), and exit radius (R_{j+1}'). The selected R_o is influenced by the location of the roundabout (urban, suburban, rural), roundabout task (e.g., traffic calming), spatial constraints, and the number of circulatory lanes. In this investigation, the roundabout geometric parameters, design vehicle used for swept path analysis, and traffic flow characteristics were defined based on the following assumptions: (1) the roundabouts were to be situated in a suburban environment and

(2) the roundabouts were to act as single-lane traffic-calming devices along the transition path from the rural to the urban environment.

A plan view of the analyzed 4-legged single-lane roundabouts schemes was created in AutoCAD. The following initial geometric parameters were used (Figure 1a):

- R_o applied in this investigation varied from 13.0 to 20.0 m, with a 0.5 m increment. According to previous research given in [22], these outer radii are commonly used for single-lane roundabouts worldwide. An increment of 0.5 m was chosen to capture the dispersity of the results and to create a sample that is representative, manageable, and easy to present at the same time;
- The roundabout leg alignment was radial, as is standard in the suburban environment [22];
- The axes of legs 1 and 4 intersected at $\delta = 90°$. The axes of legs 1 and 2 intersected at δ ranging from 75° to 90° with 5° increments. This range was defined after considering the condition given in [23], regarding the length of the arc (l) between the adjacent roundabout legs. According to these guidelines, the length of this arc should be longer than 20 m to ensure the efficiency of the roundabout. Namely, a shorter l makes it difficult for drivers to signal the exit of the intersection when turning right due to the very short time to turn on the turn signals;
- There were 15 m long triangular splitter islands designed at each leg with 0.5 m offset from the defined outer edge of the circulatory roadway;
- The initial alignment of 3.25 m wide entry and exit lanes was defined.

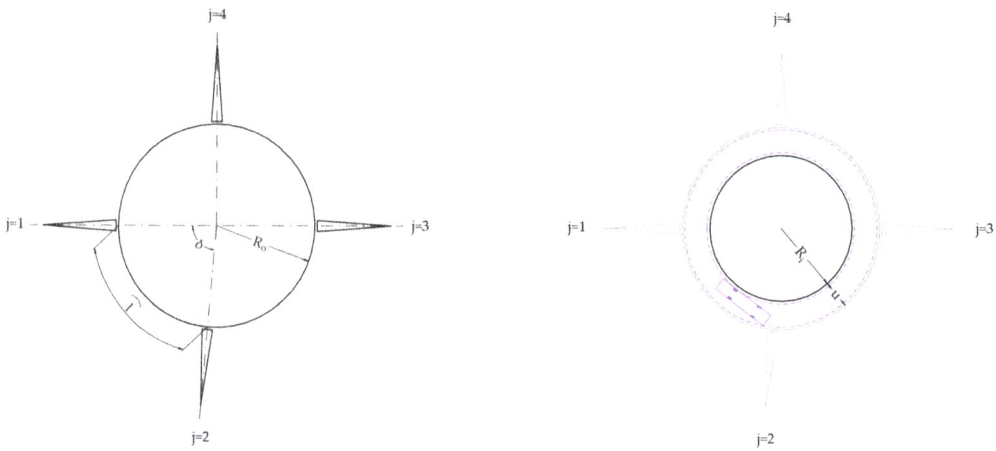

Figure 1. Design of initial geometric parameters: (**a**) the outer radius, legs, and splitter islands; (**b**) the central island radius and the circulatory roadway width defined based on the design vehicle swept path when driving in a full circle.

The geometric parameters R_i, R_j, R_{j+1}', and u resulted from the design vehicle swept path analysis, which was performed in the AutoCAD software add-in Vehicle tracking 2022. The selected design vehicle was a 12 m long bus adopted from the German vehicle library FGSV 2001. The geometric parameters R_i and u (Figure 1b) were defined based on the design vehicle swept path when driving in a full circle [7] while ensuring minimum lateral clearances of 0.5 m [24].

The geometric parameters R_j and R_{j+1}' were defined based on the design vehicle swept path when turning right [24], while ensuring minimum lateral clearances of 0.5 m. Where possible, to achieve wider exits, the roundabout's right roadway edge was designed by considering the condition of $R_{j+1}' \geq R_j + 2$ m (Figure 2a) [25]. Wider roundabout exits are favorable as they enable higher roundabout exit speeds, help minimize the likelihood of congestion and crashes at the exits, provide ease of navigation for long vehicles, and reduce the potential for trailers to track over the outside curb. At roundabouts where it was not possible to design the right roadway edge with radii R_j and R_{j+1}' due to leg alignment, a different procedure was applied. Here, the right roadway edge was designed based on the trajectory of the vehicle's right turn movement and lateral clearances of 0.5 m in cross-section a–a (Figure 2b). The geometric parameters e_j and e_j' were defined as the shortest distance between the intersection point of the drawn line on the edge of the splitter island and the entry line and the right roadway edge on the roundabout entry and exit (Figure 2).

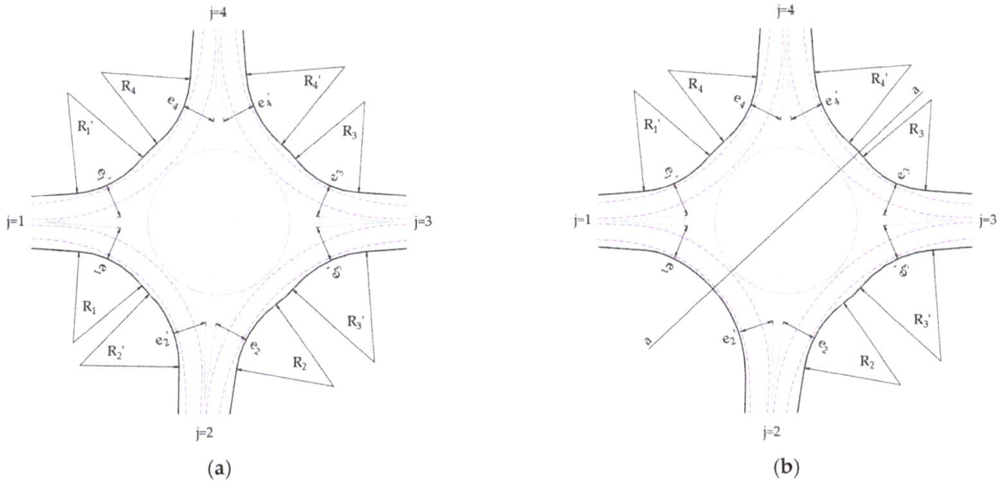

Figure 2. Roadway right edge design based on the trajectory of the vehicle's right-turn movement: (**a**) defined by entry radius and exit radius; (**b**) defined by the trajectory of the design vehicle.

The two observed models for the roundabout entry degree of saturation calculation differ in the utilization of the abovementioned geometric parameters. The analytical HBS 2015 model, given in [26], uses only R_o as an input for calculation. The regression Swiss Bovy model, given in [1], considers the influence of conflicting traffic on the circulatory roadway that is exiting the roundabout at the same leg as the observed entry. The influence of conflicting traffic on the circulatory roadway is defined as the distance between exiting and entering traffic flows along the center of the circulatory lane (b_j) [8], i.e., it considers the joint influence of geometric parameters R_o, R_i, and δ.

Parameter b_j was defined through the following procedure. First, the lines from the center of the outer radius R_o to the center of the radii R_j and R_j' were drawn (Figure 3a). At roundabouts where it was not possible to design the right roadway edge with radii R_j and R_{j+1}', the line from the center of the outer radius R_o perpendicular to the trajectory of the vehicle's right turn movement was drawn (Figure 3b). Then, a circle of radius R_o—$u/2$ was constructed from the R_o center. Traffic stream conflicting points, exiting point (C) and entering point (C′), were defined as intersections of these entities. The distance between exiting and entering traffic streams along the center of the circulatory lane, i.e., the length of the circular arc between conflicting points b_j, was then measured.

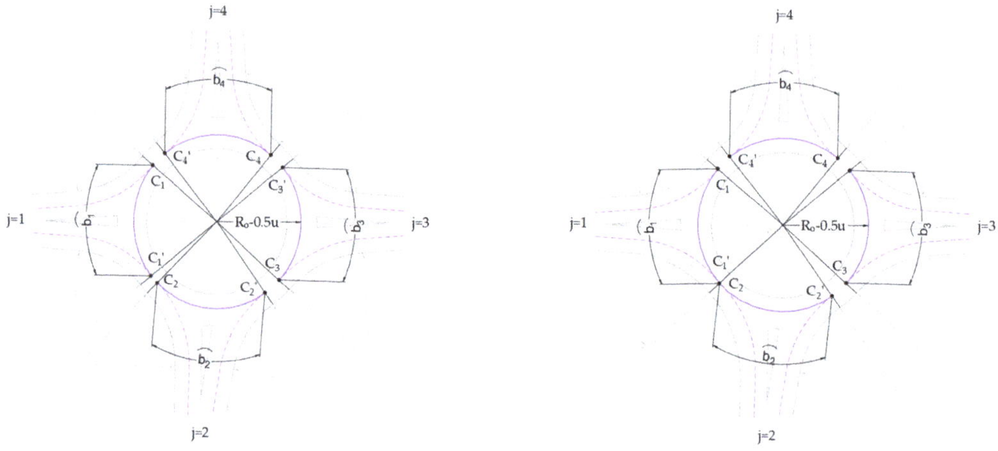

(**a**) (**b**)

Figure 3. Defining the distance b along the center of the circulatory lane, for roadway right edge design defined by the: (**a**) entry and exit radius; (**b**) design vehicle trajectory.

Once designed, the geometric parameters R_i, u, e_j, e_j', and b_j were systematized according to the R_o and δ. When designing a roundabout according to the previously described procedure, it should be noted that the results depend on the experience and subjective approach of the designer. Therefore, to better present the influence of the chosen R_o and δ on the designed parameters, regression analysis was performed, and best-fit curves with a coefficient of determination larger than 0.99 were created. Second-degree polynomial curves were used to describe R_i and u as a function of R_o, and third-degree polynomial curves were used to describe e_j, e_j', and b_j as a function of R_o for different δ. Additionally, the average difference between b_j (j = 1, 2, and 3) for δ = 90° and b_j (j = 1, 2, and 3) for δ = 85°, 80°, and 75° was calculated.

The entry degree of saturation (x_{mj}) was defined as the ratio of entering traffic flow and entry capacity. According to [14], sustainable values of x_{mj} range from 0.0 to 1.0 (values above 1.0 indicate an excess of entering traffic demand over entry capacity). x_{mj} was calculated for each designed scheme considering the following simplifications and assumptions on traffic flow volume, distribution, and composition:

- Three travel directions through the roundabout were considered at each roundabout entry (j = 1, . . . , 4): right turn, straight passage, and left turn (i = 1, . . . , 12).
- Traffic flow q_i at each entry (j = 1, . . . , 4) in each travel direction (i = 1, . . . , 12) was 150 veh/h, adding up to a total of 1800 veh/h passing through the roundabout (Figure 4a).
- The influence of pedestrian and bicycle traffic on roundabout capacity was not considered.
- The influence of heavy vehicles on the traffic flow quality was considered through the homogenization of traffic flows q_i. Flat-rate conversions of each q_i from vehicles per hour (veh/h) to Q_i in passenger car units per hour (pcu/h) were made by using a conversion factor of f_T = 1.1, prescribed by [26] in case of lacking real data on flow composition:

$$Q_i = f_T \cdot q_i, \tag{1}$$

where Q_i is homogenized traffic flow in the direction i (pcu/h), f_T is conversion factor (set to 1.1), and q_i is traffic flow in the direction i (veh/h).

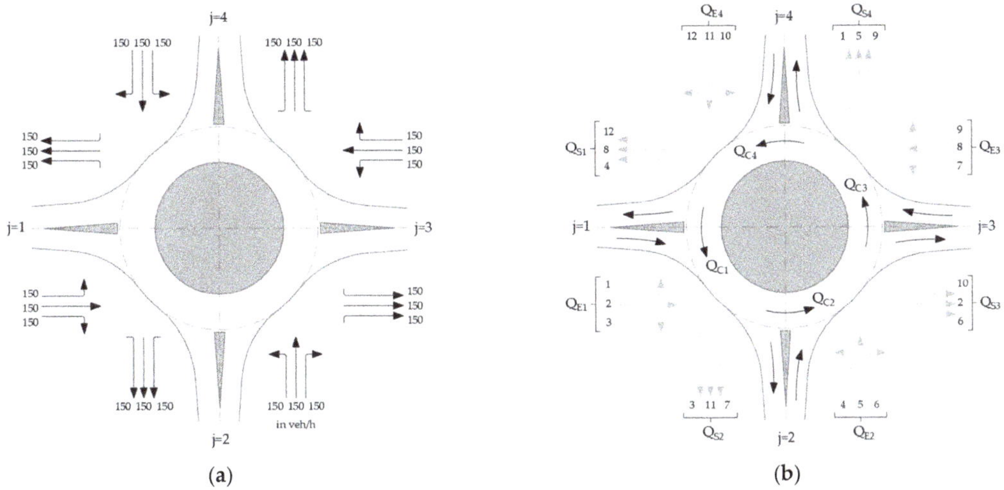

Figure 4. Traffic flows at a four-legged roundabout: (**a**) each entry in each travel direction, in veh/h; (**b**) entering, exiting, and circulating the roundabout.

The same procedure for determining the entering, exiting, and circulating traffic flows given in [26] was used for both the analytical and regression models. Based on assumed traffic conditions, 12 entering and exiting traffic flows Q_i for each travel direction (i = 1, ..., 12) were calculated. Then, the entering traffic flows Q_{Ej}, exiting traffic flows Q_{Sj}, and the circulating traffic flow Q_{Cj} (traffic flow in the circulatory roadway, i.e., the main flow, which has priority over the ones entering the circulatory roadway) were calculated for each leg (j = 1, ..., 4) according to Figure 4b and Table 2.

Table 2. Calculation of entering, exiting, and circulating traffic flow.

Leg j	Q_{Ej} (pcu/h)	Q_{Sj} (pcu/h)	Q_{Cj} (pcu/h)
1	$Q_{E1} = Q_1 + Q_2 + Q_3$	$Q_{S1} = Q_4 + Q_8 + Q_{12}$	$Q_{C1} = Q_7 + Q_{10} + Q_{11}$
2	$Q_{E2} = Q_4 + Q_5 + Q_6$	$Q_{S2} = Q_3 + Q_7 + Q_{11}$	$Q_{C2} = Q_1 + Q_2 + Q_{10}$
3	$Q_{E3} = Q_7 + Q_8 + Q_9$	$Q_{S3} = Q_2 + Q_6 + Q_{10}$	$Q_{C3} = Q_1 + Q_4 + Q_5$
4	$Q_{E4} = Q_{10} + Q_{11} + Q_{12}$	$Q_{S4} = Q_1 + Q_5 + Q_9$	$Q_{C4} = Q_4 + Q_7 + Q_8$

Once the circulating, entering, and exiting traffic flows were established, the x_{mj} was calculated through the following analytical and regression model procedures.

In the analytical model, the circulating flow Q_{Cj} was used as an input variable for determining the base capacity of the approach BC_j. BC_j values for the roundabout with one circulatory lane and the outer radius of roundabout R_o were determined from the chart in Figure 5 [26]. As the chart gave data only for roundabouts with outer radii R_o of 13.5, 15, 17.5, and 20 m, for other investigated R_o values, BC_j was defined through interpolation.

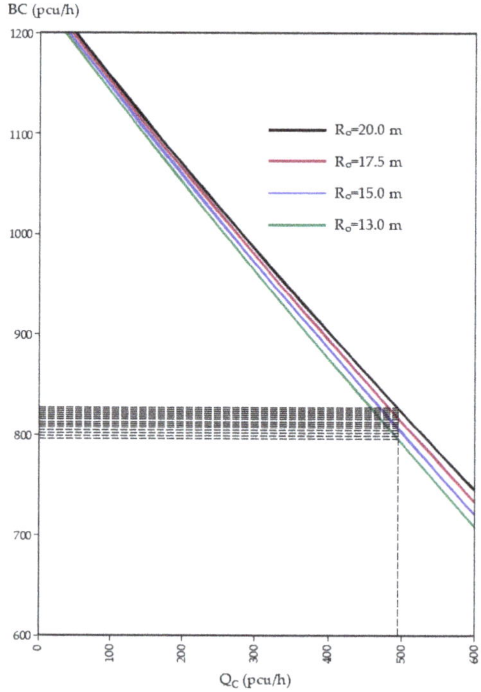

Figure 5. Base capacity at single-lane roundabouts as a function of outer radius.

Roundabout entry capacity C_{Ej} was calculated as

$$C_{Ej} = BC_j \cdot f_p, \tag{2}$$

where C_{Ej} is roundabout entry capacity considering the impact of pedestrian crossings (pcu/h), BC_j is the base entry capacity of the roundabout according to Figure 5 (pcu/h), and f_p is the capacity reduction factor for pedestrian and cycling traffic flow at roundabouts. In this investigation, the influence of pedestrian and bicycle traffic on entering traffic flow was neglected and the f_p factor was set to 1.0. The value of entry capacity C_{Ej} was, therefore, equal to base capacity BC_j.

To determine the degree of saturation x_{mj}, it was necessary to back-calculate the entry capacity values C_{Ej} from passenger car units to vehicles per hour. The entry capacity C_{mj} for the mixed traffic flow was then calculated as

$$C_{mj} = \frac{C_{Ej}}{f_T}, \tag{3}$$

where C_{mj} is the entry capacity for mixed flow (veh/h), C_{Ej} is the entry capacity (pcu/h), and f_T is the conversion factor for traffic composition set to 1.1 because of the absence of real data on flow composition.

Mixed traffic flow q_{mj} in vehicles per hour was then calculated on each leg's entry by summing up the three traffic flows q_i with different directions of travel (right turn, straight passage, and left turn). $x_{mj,A}$ was calculated as the ratio of entering mixed traffic flow q_{mj} in vehicles per hour and entry capacity C_{mj} in vehicles per hour:

$$x_{mj,A} = \frac{q_{mj}}{C_{mj}}, \tag{4}$$

where $x_{mj,A}$ is the entry degree of saturation according to the analytical model, q_{mj} is mixed traffic flow on legs' entry (veh/h), and C_{mj} is entry capacity (veh/h).

In the regression model, entry capacity C_{Ej} in passenger car units per hour was defined as [1]

$$C_{Ej} = \frac{1}{\gamma}\left[1500 - \frac{8}{9}\cdot\left(\beta\cdot Q_{Cj}+\alpha\cdot Q_{Sj}\right)\right], \tag{5}$$

where C_{Ej} is entry capacity (pcu/h), Q_{Cj} is circulating traffic flow in front of the leg being considered (pcu/h), Q_{Sj} is exiting traffic flow on the same leg as the entry (pcu/h), α is a factor reflecting the impact of exiting traffic on entry capacity by distance b_j, β is a factor for adjusting circulating flow depending on the number of circulatory lanes, and γ is a factor for adjusting entry capacity depending on the number of circulatory lanes.

Conflict factor α was determined from the chart in Figure 6 for measured distance b_j and middle curve. The factors β and γ were set to 1.0, as single-lane circulatory roadways were investigated [1].

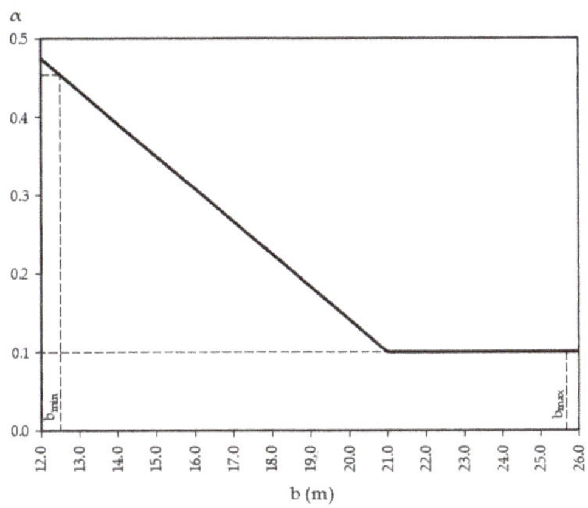

Figure 6. Conflict factor reflecting the impact of exiting traffic on entry capacity by the distance between exiting and entering traffic streams along the center of the circulatory lane.

The degree of saturation of entry was defined as

$$x_{mj,R} = \frac{\gamma\cdot Q_{Ej}}{C_{Ej}}, \tag{6}$$

where $x_{mj,R}$ is the entry degree of saturation according to the regression model, γ is a factor for adjusting entry capacity depending on the number of circulatory lanes (set to 1.0), Q_{Ej} is entering traffic flow (pcu/h), and C_{Ej} is entry capacity (pcu/h).

To present the influence of R_o and δ on calculated x_{mj}, regression analysis was performed, and best-fit curves for x_{mj} values were created. Second-degree polynomial curves with a coefficient of determination larger than 0.99 were used to visualize the trend.

To further quantify the impact of the application of different models in the roundabout design process, the reversed calculation of traffic flow at each leg was performed according to the regression model methodology. The calculation was based on the condition that the intersection enables the same level of saturation as previously defined by the analytical model (i.e., for the previously determined values of $x_{mj,A}$). With this reversed calculation, the potential traffic flow volume in veh/h was determined for each roundabout, summarized, and compared with the input total flow rate of 1800 veh/h.

3. Results

The results of the roundabout geometric design showed that to simultaneously fulfill two roundabout design conditions (regarding preferred arc length and the roundabout's right roadway edge design, Table 3) values of R_o for different δ should be (1) $R_o \geq 13.5$ m for $\delta = 85°$, (2) $R_o \geq 16.5$ m for $\delta = 80°$, and (3) $R_o \geq 19.0$ m for $\delta = 75°$.

Table 3. Overview of two roundabout design conditions' fulfillment (marked with +): Condition 1 ($l \geq 20$ m)/Condition 2 ($R_{j+1} \geq R_j + 2$ m).

R_o (m)	13.0	13.5	14.0	14.5	15.0	15.5	16.0	16.5	17.0	17.5	18.0	18.5	19.0	19.5	20.0
$\delta = 90°$	+/+	+/+	+/+	+/+	+/+	+/+	+/+	+/+	+/+	+/+	+/+	+/+	+/+	+/+	+/+
$\delta = 85°$	−/+	+/+	+/+	+/+	+/+	+/+	+/+	+/+	+/+	+/+	+/+	+/+	+/+	+/+	+/+
$\delta = 80°$	−/−	−/−	−/−	+/−	+/−	+/−	+/−	+/+	+/+	+/+	+/+	+/+	+/+	+/+	+/+
$\delta = 75°$	−/−	−/−	−/−	−/−	−/−	+/−	+/−	+/−	+/−	+/−	+/−	+/−	+/+	+/+	+/+

Considering the fulfillment of the abovementioned conditions (Table 3), designing a roundabout with a $\delta \leq 75°$ is not recommended. However, the roundabout design that does not consider these two design conditions could be applied in the suburban environment because of the spatial limitations. Therefore, calculations of the x_{mj} were performed for all 60 designed roundabouts, based on the calculated traffic flow volumes shown in Figure 7.

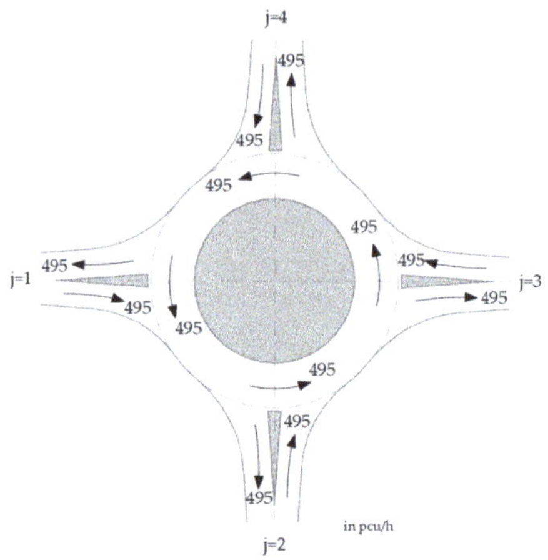

Figure 7. Calculated values of entering, exiting, and circulating traffic flow in pcu/h.

The resulting values of the geometric parameters of the 60 designed roundabouts schemes are shown with their best-fit curves in Figures 8, 9a, 10, 11 and 12a.

As shown in Figure 8, R_i, e_j, e_j', and b_j were proportional to R_o, and u values were inversely proportional. The change in e_1 was (1) proportional to δ, (2) identical for $\delta = 90$ and 85°, (3) identical for $\delta = 80$ and 75° at $R_o = 13.0$ m, and (4) identical for $\delta = 90$, 85, and 80° at $R_o \geq 19.0$ m. The change in e_2 was inversely proportional to δ at $R_o \geq 14.0$ m. The change in e_2' and e_3' at $R_o \geq 16.0$ m showed an uneven trend for different δ. As expected, δ did not affect the entrance and exit widths e_3, e_4, e_1', and e_4'.

As shown in Figures 9a, 10, 11 and 12a, the trend of b_j increasing for different δ corresponded to those of e_j and e_j'. Thus, the change in b_1 (1) was proportional to δ and (2) was identical for $\delta = 90$ and 85°. The change in b_2 was inversely proportional to δ at $R_o \geq 14.0$ m. δ had a negligible effect on the values of b_3 at $R_o < 16$ m. The change in δ had no effect on the values of b_4. Extreme values of b_j were observed for $\delta = 75°$ and $R_o = 13.0$ m ($b_1 = 12.5$ m) at leg 1, and $R_o = 20.0$ m ($b_2 = 25.7$ m) at leg 2.

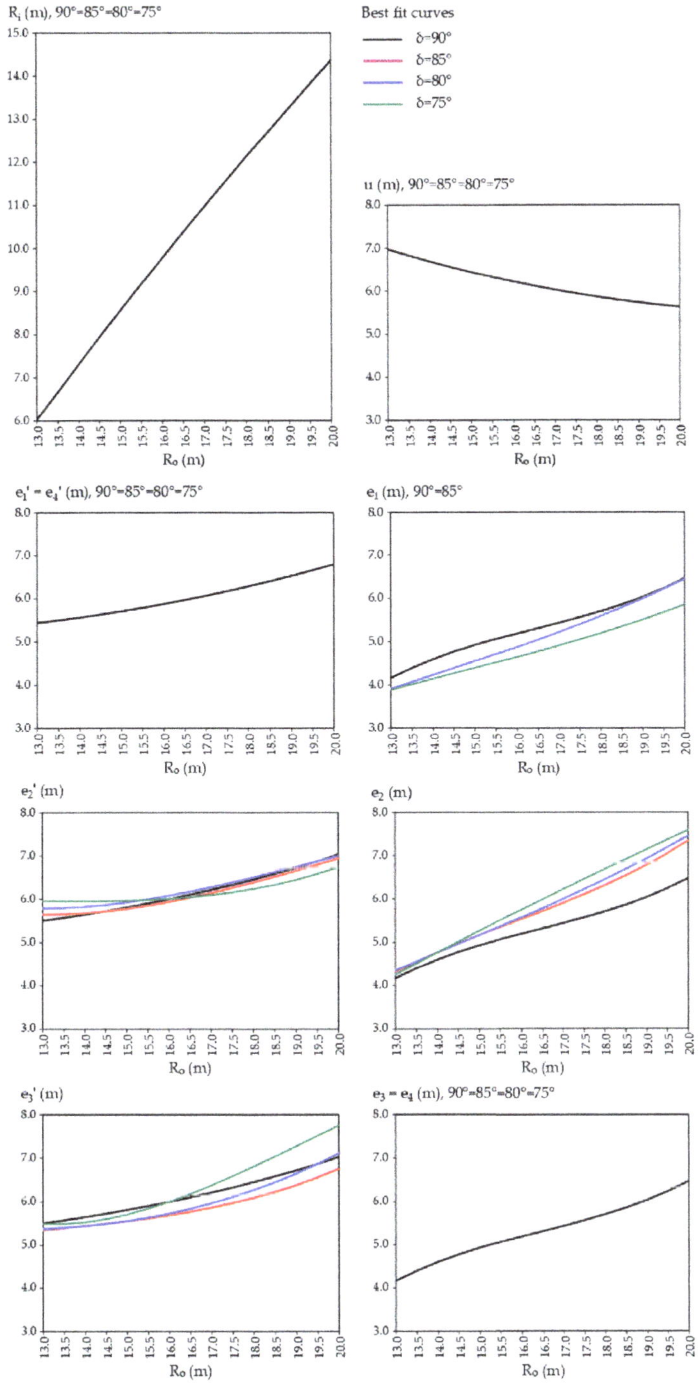

Figure 8. Geometric parameters R_i, e_j, e_j', and u as a function of R_o for different δ.

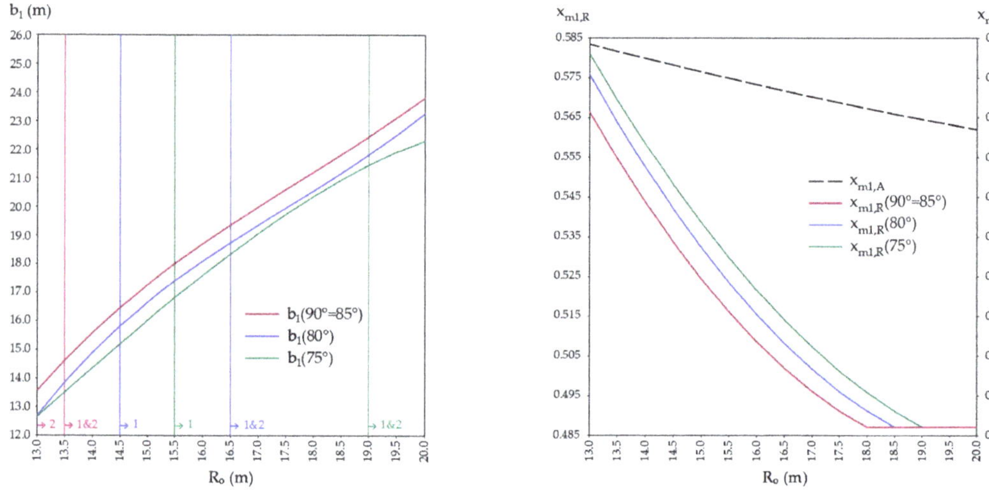

(a) (b)

Figure 9. Investigated parameters at leg 1 as a function of R_o for different δ, considering the application of design conditions 1 and 2: (**a**) geometric parameter b_1; (**b**) traffic parameter x_{m1}.

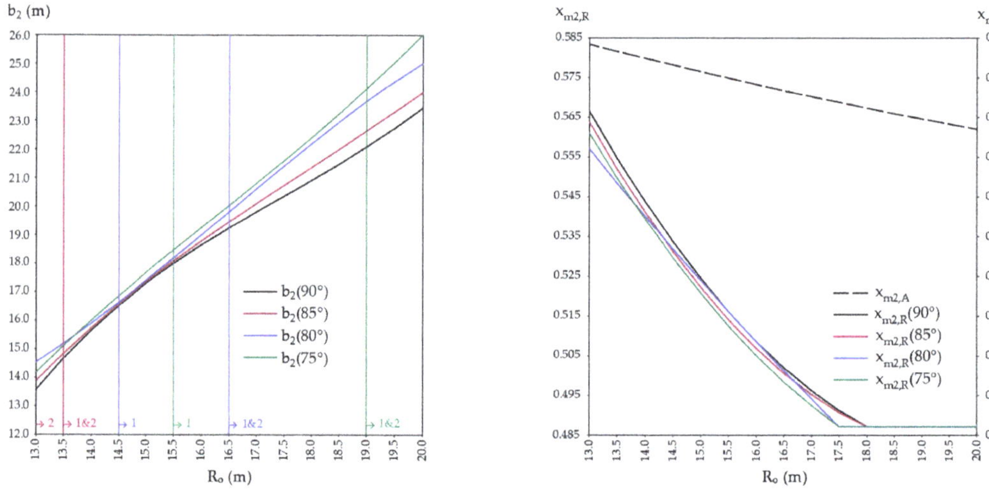

(a) (b)

Figure 10. Investigated parameters at leg 2 as a function of R_o for different δ, considering the application of design conditions 1 and 2: (**a**) geometric parameter b_2; (**b**) traffic parameter x_{m2}.

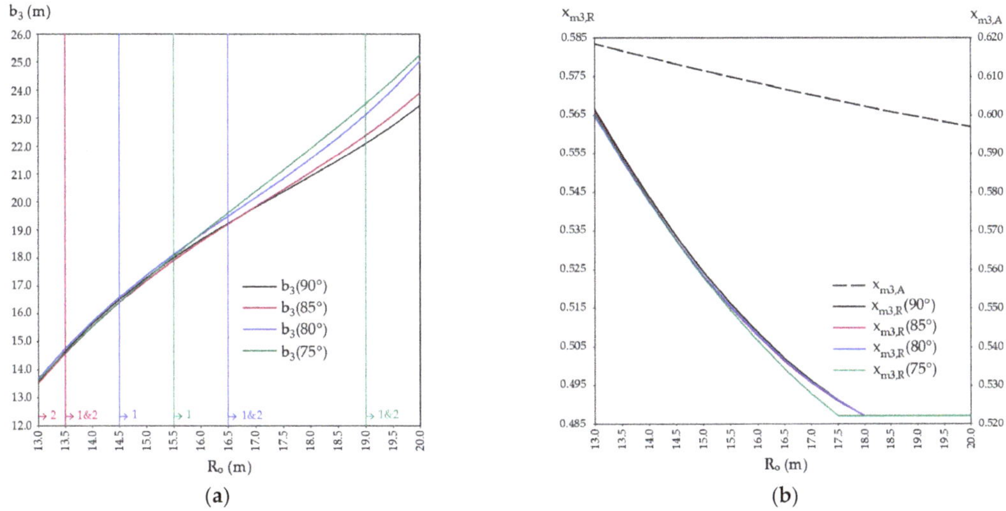

Figure 11. Investigated parameters at leg 3 as a function of R_o for different δ, considering the application of design conditions 1 and 2: (**a**) geometric parameter b_3; (**b**) traffic parameter x_{m3}.

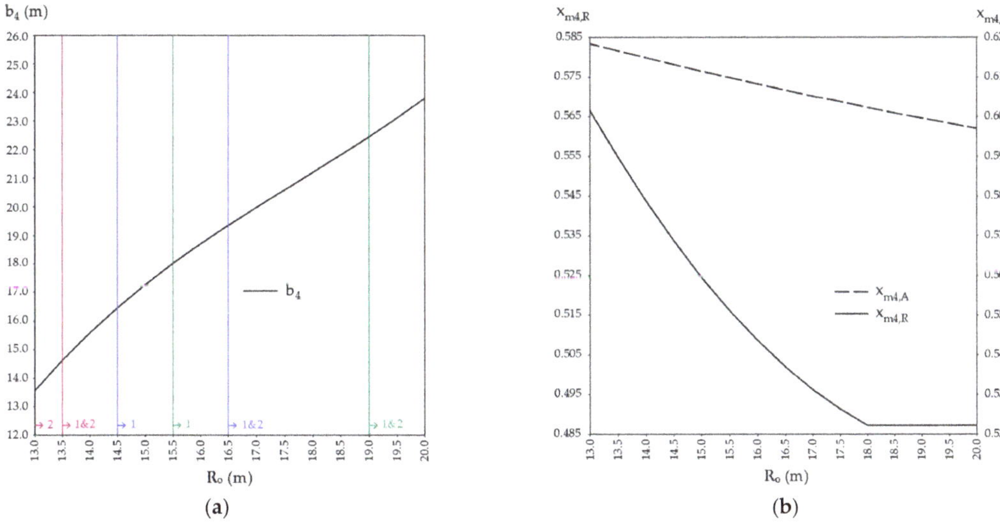

Figure 12. Investigated parameters at leg 4 as a function of R_o for different δ, considering the application of design conditions 1 and 2: (**a**) geometric parameter b_4; (**b**) traffic parameter x_{m4}.

The results of the calculation of the entry degree of saturation with dependence on the R_o of roundabouts and δ according to the analytical model ($x_{mj,A}$) and regression model ($x_{mj,R}$) showed that x_{mj} values were inversely proportional to R_o. $x_{mj,R}$ values followed the observed trend of b_j for all analyzed δ at each roundabout leg (Figures 9b, 10, 11 and 12b). For $R_o \leq 16.5$ m, an established trend showed a more rapid decrease in b_j and, consequently, in $x_{mj,R}$. On the other hand, for $R_o \geq 19.0$ m, it can be stated that the differences in the right roadway edge design, regardless of δ, do not affect $x_{mj,R}$. The values of $x_{mj,A}$ decreased at a lower and uniform rate as R_o increased. $x_{mj,A}$ values were higher than $x_{mj,R}$ by, on average, 16%. The average difference between $x_{mj,A}$ and $x_{mj,R}$ varied between 0.088 and 0.100. These extreme differences were observed for $\delta = 75°$, at leg 1 and leg 2, respectively. At each leg, the average observed difference between the calculated $x_{mj,R}$ for $\delta = 90°$ and $x_{mj,R}$ for the other δ values amounted to (1) 0.3% at leg 2 for δ = 85°, (2) 1.1% at leg 1, and 0.4% at leg 2 for δ = 80°, (3) 1.7% at leg 1, 0.5% at leg 2, and 0.2% at leg 3 for δ = 75°.

Figure 13 shows the average difference between b_1, b_2, and b_3 for δ = 90° and b_1, b_2, and b_3 for δ = 85°, 80°, and 75°, respectively. The change in these differences in b_j values is linear. As expected, b_1 shortened as δ decreased. The opposite is true for b_2 and b_3. The main reason for this is the design of the right roadway edge based on the design vehicle swept path analysis. Namely, on the roundabout exit at legs 2 and 3, the body of the design vehicle swept a wider surface than on the roundabout entry at leg 1, and this surface was ever wider as δ decreased. Therefore, the designed exit radii R_2' and R_3' were significantly larger than the recommended ones and, consequently, the distances b_2 and b_3 were inversely proportional to δ.

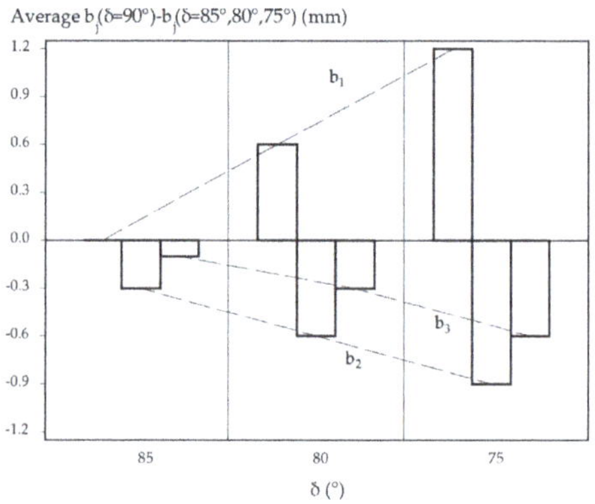

Figure 13. The average difference between b_1, b_2, and b_3 for δ = 90° and b_1, b_2, and b_3 for δ = 85°, 80°, and 75°.

The results of the reversed calculation of traffic flow at each leg according to the regression model methodology showed that, at a given roundabout, the application of the regression model gives the same x_{mj} results as the analytical one for 6% to 15% higher traffic flows q_i. The difference in traffic flow values obtained through this calculation is shown as a percentage concerning the initial total value of 1800 veh/h (Figure 14).

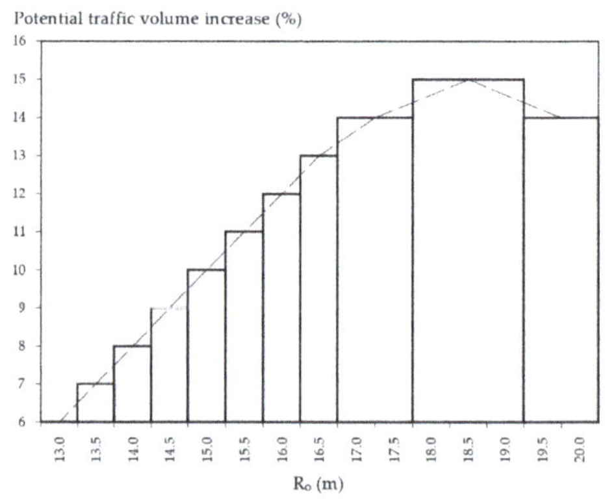

Figure 14. Results of the reversed calculation of traffic flow—the difference in traffic flow values shown as the percentage of the initial 1800 veh/h.

4. Discussion and Conclusions

The iterative process of roundabout design requires shifting between geometry design and capacity analysis, to ensure that chosen roundabout geometry satisfies the desired traffic performance criteria. The quality of traffic flow on the roundabout is indirectly dependent on its geometric parameters, and should be estimated during roundabout design through calculation models or simulations. In this investigation, a comparison of the analytical and empirical models for single-lane roundabout entry degree of saturation estimation was performed on 60 designed four-legged roundabout schemes.

When designing a single-lane roundabout based on the design vehicle swept path analysis, the choice of geometric parameters and the capacity calculation model influences the roundabout performance evaluation results. The observed models differ in the utilization of the geometric parameters: (1) the analytical model uses only the roundabout outer radius as an input for calculation, while (2) the regression model considers the influence of conflicting traffic on the circulatory roadway defined by the distance between exiting and entering traffic flows along the center of the circulatory lane, i.e., it considers the joint influence of roundabout outer radius, the central island radius, and the angle between the roundabout legs.

The results of the geometric and traffic parameters analysis showed that the central island radius and entry capacity are proportional to the outer radius. At the same time, the circulatory roadway width and the entry degree of saturation are inversely proportional to the outer radius. This is in line with the conclusions given in [27], which state that circulatory roadway width significantly influences capacity. As can be seen from our results, the influence of the circulatory roadway width, derived from the design vehicle swept path, on capacity is counterintuitive; narrower circulatory roadways on roundabouts with a larger outer radius enabled higher entry capacity, i.e., lower entry degree of saturation.

According to [11], entry width has a positive correlation with entry capacity. According to [27], the distance between the entry and exit has a greater impact on the entry capacity than the entry radius. The results of our investigation show that an increase in entry width is directly linked with an increase in outer radius value and the design of the right roadway edge derived from the design vehicle swept path, and that it decreases the roundabout entry degree of saturation in the regression model. A larger outer radius in the analytical model results in a lower degree of saturation. A larger outer radius and a greater distance between the conflicting points (dependent not only on radius but also on the width of the circulatory roadway and entry and exit widths) in the regression model result in a lower degree of saturation.

In general, for all the observed combinations of geometric parameters, the regression model results in lower values of roundabout entry degree of saturation. This difference is more pronounced as the outer radius and angle between the roundabout legs increase. This implies that it is possible to justify the chosen roundabout geometric parameters by choosing the capacity analysis model, which will allow higher traffic flow volumes. Namely, the results of the investigation showed that it is possible to increase the traffic flows that could be processed at a given roundabout from 6% to 15% if the regression model is applied instead of the analytical one during roundabout performance evaluation. From the perspective of the time in which the roundabout is expected to satisfy the desired performance criteria and considering that the average annual increase in motor vehicles' number in Europe is 2% (according to the European Automobile Manufacturers' Association), it could be said that the application of the regression model could extend the expected service life of a roundabout by 3 to 7 years.

For further research, the results of this investigation will be compared to and validated by roundabout entry degree of saturation calculations performed with data from field measurements. Additionally, it is planned to reverse-calculate the distance between exiting and entering traffic flows along the center of the circulatory lane for $x_{m,R} = 0.85$, which is defined as the maximum entrance degree of saturation [28]. This will allow the investigation of how this distance affects other roundabout geometric parameters and traffic flows.

The described approach to roundabout capacity model comparison and appropriateness evaluation could be applied to more complex roundabout setups, i.e., to roundabouts with two-lane approaches, two-lane circulatory roadways, different leg numbers and alignments, and the presence of pedestrian and cyclist flow. This investigation could be also conducted for urban areas where spatial and territorial constraints are more stringent, i.e., for roundabouts with minimal outer radii of 6.5 m and with leg alignments defining the minimum distance between exiting and entering traffic flows along the center of the circulatory lane of 9 m.

The investigation presented in this paper has shown that (1) the applied regression model estimates a higher roundabout traffic performance than the analytical one, and (2) this difference (both between the two models and regression models applied on different schemes) is more pronounced as the outer radius and angle between the legs increase. To conclude, the regression model is more suitable for application in suburban roundabout design, i.e., for environments with spatial limitations, and where performance evaluation demands higher traffic flow volumes to be processed through the roundabout. On the other hand, due to its simplicity, the analytical model should be applied in rural areas with more heterogenic and time-variable traffic flows, and for road network planning purposes, preliminary roundabout design, and robust capacity estimations.

Author Contributions: Conceptualization, M.A. and S.A.; methodology, M.A.; formal analysis, A.Č.I. and M.A.; investigation, A.Č.I.; resources, M.A.; data curation, A.Č.I.; writing—original draft preparation, A.Č.I. and M.A.; writing—review and editing, S.A.; visualization, M.A.; supervision, V.D.; project administration, M.A. All authors have read and agreed to the published version of the manuscript.

Funding: This research received no external funding.

Data Availability Statement: Not applicable.

Conflicts of Interest: The authors declare no conflict of interest. The funders had no role in the design of the study; in the collection, analyses, or interpretation of data; in the writing of the manuscript; or in the decision to publish the results.

References

1. Ministry of Transport. *Roundabouts—Application and Design: A Practical Manual*; Ministry of Transport, Public Works and Water Management, Partners for Roads: Amsterdam, The Netherlands, 2009.
2. Alozi, A.R.; Hussein, M. Multi-criteria comparative assessment of unconventional roundabout designs. *Int. J. Transp. Sci. Technol.* **2021**, *11*, 158–173. [CrossRef]
3. *CROW: Eenheid in Rotondes*; CROW Publication no.126; CROW: Ede, The Netherlands, 1998; Available online: https://nmfv.dk/wp-content/uploads/2012/06/RDC_Netherlands.pdf (accessed on 15 March 2023).
4. Ahac, S.; Ahac, M.; Džambas, T.; Dragčević, V. The Design Vehicle Steering Path Construction Based on the Hairpin Bend Geometry-Aplication in Roundabout Design. *Appl. Sci.* **2022**, *12*, 11019. [CrossRef]
5. Regulation on technical conditions of vehicles in road traffic (Official Gazette, no. 85/16, 24/17, 60/20). Available online: https://narodne-novine.nn.hr/clanci/sluzbeni/2016_09_85_1864.html; https://narodne-novine.nn.hr/clanci/sluzbeni/2017_03_24_547.html; https://narodne-novine.nn.hr/clanci/sluzbeni/2020_05_60_1224.html (accessed on 15 March 2023).
6. Directive 96/53/EC and Directive 2002/7/EC. Available online: https://eur-lex.europa.eu/legal-content/EN/TXT/PDF/?uri=CELEX:01996L0053-20150526&from=EN (accessed on 15 March 2023).
7. Građevinski fakultet Sveučilišta u Rijeci. *Smjernice za Projektiranje Kružnih Raskrižja na Državnim Cestama*; Građevinski fakultet Sveučilišta u Rijeci: Rijeka, Croatia, 2014.
8. Yap, Y.H.; Gibson, H.M.; Waterson, B.J. An International Review of Roundabout Capacity Modelling. *Transp. Rev.* **2013**, *33*, 593–616. [CrossRef]
9. Guiffre, O.; Granà, A.; Tumminello, M.L. Exploring the uncertainty in capacity estimation at roundabouts. *Eur. Transp. Res. Rev.* **2017**, *9*, 18. [CrossRef]
10. Johnson, M.T.; Lin, T. Impact of Geometric Factors on the Capacity of Single-Lane Roundabouts. *Transp. Res. Rec. J. Transp. Res. Board* **2018**, *2672*, 10–19. [CrossRef]
11. Zacharia, A.B.; Madhavan, H.; Anjaneyulu, M.V.L.R. Geometric factors influencing entry capacity of roundabouts under heterogeneous traffic conditions. *Arch. Transp.* **2019**, *49*, 87–101. [CrossRef]
12. Pompigna, A.; Guerrieri, M.; Mauro, R. New Extensions and Applications of the Modified Chumanov Model for for Calculating Entry Capacity of Single-Lane Roundabouts. *Sustainability* **2020**, *12*, 6122. [CrossRef]

13. Žura, M. Roundabout Capacity Estimation Model Considering Driver Behaviour on the Exiting and Entry Flows. *Promet – Traffic Transp.* **2022**, *34*, 397–405. [CrossRef]
14. Transportation Research Board, Roundabouts. In *Highway Capacity Manual: A Guide for Multimodal Mobility Analysis*; Transportation Research Board (TRB): Amsterdam, The Netherlands, 2016.
15. Hamim, O.F.; Hadiuzzaman, M.; Hossain, S. Developing empirical model with graphical tool to estimate and predict capacity of rural highway roundabouts. *Int. J. Transp. Sci. Technol.* **2021**, *11*, 726–737. [CrossRef]
16. Batra, V.; Anand, V.; Prakash, V.; Mangal, V.; Kumar, N. A Review of Capacity, Critical Gap and Follow-up Time on an Unsignalised Intersections in Bangalore City. *Int. J. Innov. Sci. Res. Technol.* **2020**, *5*, 912–917.
17. Foulaadvand, M.E.; Maass, P. Phase transitions and optimal transport in stochastic roundabout traffic. *Phys. Rev. E* **2016**, *94*, 012304. [CrossRef] [PubMed]
18. Nava, A.; Giuliano, D.; Papa, A.; Rossi, M. Traffic models and traffic-jam transition in quantum (N+1)-level systems. *SciPost Phys.* **2022**, *Core 5*, 022. [CrossRef]
19. Song, Y.; Hu, X.; Lu, J.; Zhou, X. Analytical approximation and calibration of roundabout capacity: A merging state transition-based modeling approach. *Transportation Res. Part B Methodol.* **2022**, *163*, 232–257. [CrossRef]
20. Anagnostopoulos, A.; Kehagia, F.; Aretoulis, G. Application of Artificial Neural Network for Modelling and Predicting Roundabout Capacity. In Proceedings of the 8th Road Safety & Simulation International Conference, Athens, Greece, 8–10 June 2022.
21. Johnson, M.T.; Hale, D.K. A Case for Geometrically-Based Roundabout Capacity Equation Modeling. In Proceedings of the 5th International Symposium on Highway Geometric Design, Vancouver, BC, Canada, 22–24 June 2015.
22. Ahac, S.; Dragčević, V. Geometric Design of Suburban Roundabouts. *Encyclopedia* **2021**, *1*, 720–743. [CrossRef]
23. *Plangleiche Knoten–Kreisverkehre*; (RVS 03.05.14); Österreichische Forschungsgesellschaft Straße-Schiene-Verkehr (FSV): Wien, Austria, 2010.
24. Ahac, S. Design of Suburban Roundabouts Based on Rules of Vehicle Movement Geometry. Ph.D. Thesis, University of Zagreb, Zagreb, Croatia, April 2014.
25. Rodegerdts, L.; Bansen, J.; Tiesler, C.; Knudsen, J.; Myers, E.; Johnson, M.; Moule, M.; Persaud, B.; Lyon, C.; Hallmark, S.; et al. *NCHRP Report 672: Roundabouts: An Informational Guide*, 2nd ed.; Transportation Research Board: Washington, DC, USA, 2010.
26. Voss, T. HBS 2015 Teil S5 Knotenpunkte ohne Lichtsignalanlage, Germany. 2015.
27. Yap, Y.H.; Gibson, H.M.; Waterson, B.J. Models of Roundabout Lane Capacity. *J. Transp. Eng.* **2015**, *141*, 1–12. [CrossRef]
28. Šurdonja, S.; Deluka-Tibljaš, A.; Babić, S. Optimization of roundabout design elements. *Tech. Gaz.* **2013**, *20*, 533–539.

algorithms

MDPI

Article

A Scheduling Solution for Robotic Arm-Based Batching Systems with Multiple Conveyor Belts †

Kasper Gaj Nielsen [1], Inkyung Sung [2,*], Mohamed El Yafrani [3], Deniz Kenan Kılıç [2] and Peter Nielsen [2]

1 ORTEC Nordic A/S, Stationsparken 25, 2600 Glostrup, Denmark
2 Operations Research Group, Department of Materials and Production, Aalborg University, 9220 Aalborg, Denmark
3 Norlys Energy Trading A/S, Over Bækken 6, 9000 Aalborg, Denmark
* Correspondence: inkyung_sung@mp.aau.dk
† This article is written based on the first author's master thesis for the Mathematics-Economics program of Aalborg University.

Abstract: In this study, we tackle a key scheduling problem in a robotic arm-based food processing system, where multiple conveyors—an infeed conveyor that feeds food items to robotic arms and two tray lane conveyors, on which trays to batch food items are placed—are implemented. The target scheduling problem is to determine what item on an infeed conveyor belt is picked up by which robotic arm at what position, and on which tray the picked up item will be placed. This problem involves critical constraints, such as sequence-dependent processing time and dynamic item and tray positions. Moreover, due to the speed of the infeed conveyor and latency in the information about entering items into the system, this scheduling problem must be solved in near real time. To address these challenges, we propose a scheduling solution that first decomposes the original scheduling problem into sub-problems, where a sub-problem formulated as a goal program schedules robotic arms only for a single tray. The performance of the proposed solution approach is then tested under a simulation environment, and from the experiments, the proposed approach produces acceptable performance.

Keywords: robotic arm-based batching systems; scheduling robotic arms; robotic task-sequencing problem; real-time decision making; give-away minimization

Citation: Nielsen, K.G.; Sung, I.; El Yafrani, M.; Kılıç, D.K.; Nielsen, P. A Scheduling Solution for Robotic Arm-Based Batching Systems with Multiple Conveyor Belts. *Algorithms* **2023**, *16*, 172. https://doi.org/10.3390/a16030172

Academic Editor: Frank Werner

Received: 16 February 2023
Revised: 16 March 2023
Accepted: 16 March 2023
Published: 21 March 2023

1. Introduction

A robotic arm or a machine with a similar feature is an integral part of various autonomous manufacturing and production systems. A robotic arm (or a set of robotic arms) is often placed on or next to a conveyor belt. A conveyor belt brings items to the robotic arm, and the items moving on the conveyor belt are sorted and/or picked by the robotic arm [1]. Figure 1 shows a simplified representation of a robotic arm batching system, where items on a conveyor belt are picked up and put into a tray by a robotic arm.

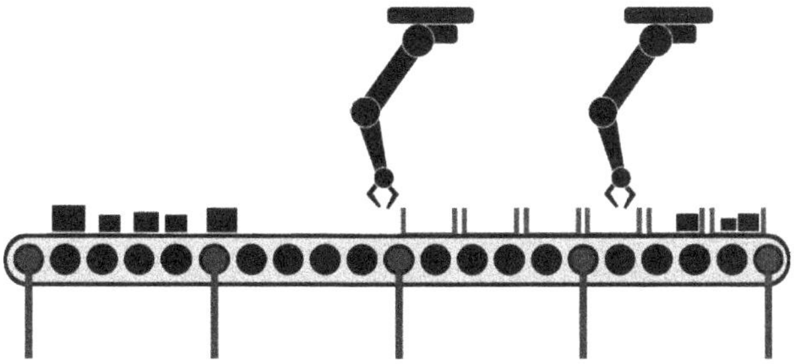

Figure 1. An illustration of a robotic arm batching system.

With a conveyor belt, a robotic arm can significantly improve the throughput of a manufacturing and production system. A robotic arm can also provide flexibility in a system's item flows by transferring an item from one conveyor belt to another. Compared to batching machines that simply push the items out of a conveyor belt, robotic arms also provide more flexibility in the way the items are handled. If the items to carry are heavy or hazardous, the risk of injury to human operators is further minimized by the robotic arm implementation. Moreover, a robotic arm with a conveyor belt has demonstrated its capability to perform tasks that are simple and repetitive. The tasks that should be performed quickly with quality can also be performed successfully by a robotic arm. Picking, placing and sorting tasks are examples of these tasks [2].

The food processing and packaging business are some of the industrial sectors where such advantages of robotic arms with conveyor belts can improve the profits of the business [3]. Imagine a food batching and packaging process where food items of different sizes are grouped into trays of a predetermined standard size or weight. Here, a robotic arm-based system with a sophisticated control mechanism can identify food items moving fast over a conveyor belt and choose the right pieces of food items from a conveyor belt. In this way, the productivity and efficiency of the process can be dramatically improved, and the need for human labor in the process can be minimized [4]. Moreover, a robotic arm-based system is easy to maintain and provides a high level of hygiene and food quality.

It should be noted that the benefits of a robotic arm-based system will not be achieved by simply equipping and implementing the system. An operating system that controls the robotic arm's motion and action is essential for fully exploiting the capability of the robotic arm-based system.

The core of the operating system is to address the scheduling problem involved in a robotic arm-based system operation, which addresses a number of nested decision-making problems. For example, given a target weight of a food package, a robotic arm should determine which item would be picked up and put into which package tray in what order so that the productivity of the system (e.g., the number of food items packed per time unit) is maximized and give-away (additional weights given over a target weight) in a tray is minimized. However, such decision making is complex by its nature and should be made in a very short time to keep the throughput of the system as fast as the speed of a conveyor belt. The relevant decision-making problem contexts and challenges can be found in a container crane scheduling problem, where the interference between cranes and the sequence-dependent container (un)loading time are critical to consider [5], as well as a flow shop scheduling problem with real-time order acceptance [6].

Motivated by the decision-making challenges in a robotic arm-based system and the expected impact of a well-designed scheduling algorithm on the performance of the system, this study addresses a scheduling problem involved in a specific but common robotic arm-based system, where multiple robotic arms operate over a conveyor belt system, in which two types of conveyor belts—an infeed conveyor for food items delivery and a tray lane conveyor for food item trays—are operated. We first identify the key decisions and constraints of the target scheduling problem. A decomposition-based scheduling approach is then proposed to solve the resulting scheduling problem within an available computation time. The performance of the proposed solution approach is finally evaluated in a simulation environment, where items with random weights enter into the robotic arm-based system as a stochastic process.

2. Related Work

2.1. Scheduling Problems for Robotic Arms in Automated Systems

As highlighted in the introduction, robotic arms have been applied to various industrial sectors, including manufacturing and production systems due to their contribution to the overall productivity, reliability, and quality of a target system. A key element for a successful implementation of robotic arms into such systems is to schedule movements of a robotic arm to perform atomic tasks, such as welding, drilling, and spray painting. This scheduling problem is known as the robotic task sequencing problem (RTSP) [7].

Given that a robotic arm has a single configuration to perform a task, the RTSP can be formulated as the traveling salesman problem (TSP) [8]. However, a robotic arm could have multiple configurations especially to avoid collisions during operations and to reduce the duration of the movement, which is known as inverse kinematics solutions. With inverse kinematics, the RTSP can be formulated by the generalized TSP (GTSP), where a location for a task is represented as a bin with multiple nodes, and a travel time between two tasks depends on what nodes in the corresponding bins are visited. Given this setting, a robotic arm should visit all the bins for the target tasks, visiting only a single node within the bins [9]. Please refer to [10,11] for a detailed review on the RTSP.

The extended RTSP can be found in a flexible manufacturing system (FMS), where a robotic arm is often installed to transport items from an input station to multiple workstations and from the workstations to an output station. In this case, not only the robotic arm but also the workstations should be scheduled so that the overall system performance (e.g., workstation utilization and throughput of the system) can be optimized. To address this scheduling complexity, Petri nets are often applied to represent a target system as a discrete-event system [12,13].

The RTSP can also be extended for multiple robotic arms. Here, a goal is to operate robotic arms to move objects to available slots with a minimum total travel distance. The resulting multiple robotic arm scheduling problem can be formulated as a parallel machine scheduling problem for a single-stage production [14]. Note that the multiple robotic arm scheduling problem is in general solved for static task positions; therefore, a solution to the problem is often adjusted by a model predictive control (MPC) planning algorithm that addresses dynamic collision avoidance constraints of the robotic arms [15,16].

2.2. Scheduling Problems for Robotic Arms with Conveyor Belts

Here, we review scheduling problems for robotic arms with conveyor belts especially in food processing systems. Tables 1 and 2 summarize the scheduling problems, batching problems in particular, addressed for a robotic arm-based food processing system in the literature. As comparison criteria, Table 1 considers (1) on what basis the decision was made and (2) the number of conveyor belts, and Table 2 considers (3) the type of conveyor belts, (4) whether there is a buffer between batches, and (5) the characteristics of the robots addressed.

From the literature review shown in the summary tables, it can be highlighted that the existing scheduling mechanisms generally tackle a single decision variable with a single conveyor belt track. On the other hand, our study addresses a robotic arm-based system with multiple conveyor tracks—one track for moving food items and two additional tracks on each side of the food track for trays—which introduces additional decision-making dimensions and constraints to the corresponding robotic arm scheduling problem.

Table 1. Related work for a robotic arm-based batching system.

Study	Target System/Problem	Decision	Tray/Bin Lane Number
[17]	A meat processing system	Batch or trim pieces? (with respect to weights)	1
[18]	A fillet batching operation in a poultry processing plant	Which tray? (with respect to weights)	1
[19]	Batching food items for a specific weight target	Which bin? (with respect to weights)	2

Table 1. *Cont.*

Study	Target System/Problem	Decision	Tray/Bin Lane Number
[20]	Poultry processing plants with batchers	Which tray? (with respect to weights)	1
[21]	Bin covering with a target weight for a poultry processing plant	Which tray? (with respect to weights)	1
[22]	Packing in a conveyor-based automatic sorting system	Which action? - Do {stay, put, pick} - For {current box, buffer}	1
[23]	A robotic arm system with multiple conveyor belts	Which tray? (with respect to weights and conveyor belt track)	2

Table 2. Related work for a robotic arm-based batching system (cont').

Study	Conveyor Belt Type	Buffer	Machine Type
[17]	Two conveyor belts	Yes	Grader (diverter)
[18]	4 track line conveyor belt	Yes	Grader
[19]	1 track line conveyor belt	Yes	Grader
[20]	1 track line conveyor belt	Yes	Batcher (drop)
[21]	1 track line conveyor belt	Yes	Batcher (drop)
[22]	Unidirectional 1 track conveyor belt A circular conveyor for boxes	Yes (for unused product)	Robotic arm
[23]	2 track line conveyor belt	Yes	Robotic arm

2.3. *Solution Algorithms for Scheduling Robotic Arm-Based Batching Systems*

Multiple solution approaches have been proposed to solve and analyze various robotic batching systems. Peeters et al. [18] took a wider view of the system and analyzed the layout of the batching process, determining the size and number of batching machines, the flexibility of different setups, as well as introducing solution approaches. Ásgeirsson [24] proposed an algorithm to be used in an online bin covering problem representing a system that pushes the items into trays instead of picking-and-placing. Furthermore, the authors investigated and proposed algorithms for the semi-online problem. Van Sprang [25] investigated the application of condition-based maintenance strategies. A selection method was proposed to choose the most relevant parts of a machine. Among others, it is based on failure rate and downtime costs and consequences. Raaijmakers [26] analyzed different types of batching machines, modeled the machines mathematically (including an online bin covering variant), and proposed solution strategies for each. Finally, the performance of the batching machines is compared with different types of problem features.

Soft computing methods have been also proposed to tackle robotic batching problems. Hundscheid et al. [21] proposed a hybrid genetic algorithm for a more simple batching machine. The problem is formulated as a *k*-bounded semi-online bin covering problem, which is a frequent model for these types of problems. Hildebrand et al. [23] investigated a deep reinforcement learning approach in the decision process of a robotic batching system and showed promising results.

It should be noted that the robotic arm-based system addressed in Hildebrand et al. [23] has the same system setting as our target system. However, our study tackles the scheduling problem involved in the system by applying a deterministic approach as will be explained in the following sections. The proposed approach has an advantage over the work of Hildebrand et al. [23] in terms of the effort needed to develop and implement a solution approach and the degree of understanding to the solutions derived by the approach.

Based on the reviews presented, we conclude that our target robotic arm scheduling problem with multiple conveyor belts has been rarely addressed in the literature, and the proposed solution approach for the problem is unique from the methodological and implementation perspectives.

3. A Robotic Arm-Based Food Processing System

3.1. Problem Descriptions

The target system of this study is inspired by a completely autonomous robotic arm-based food batching system, which consists of three main components: an infeed conveyor belt, tray lanes next to the infeed conveyor belt and robotic arms. The conveyor belt moves continuously at a fixed speed. It transports food items with different weights arriving from a preceding food production cell. On each side of the conveyor belt, there is a single moving lane and trays, in which food items picked from the conveyor belt are batched in a tray on the lane. The tray lane can both move and stop. When it advances, it moves incrementally and the tray at the end of the lane will be disposed of from the system, being handled by a following package cell. Usually, the advancement will automatically be triggered when the weight of the last tray exceeds a threshold. The third component is the robotic arms. Each one can reach a specific area of the conveyor belts and the tray lanes. Figure 2 illustrates the target robotic arm-based food batching system.

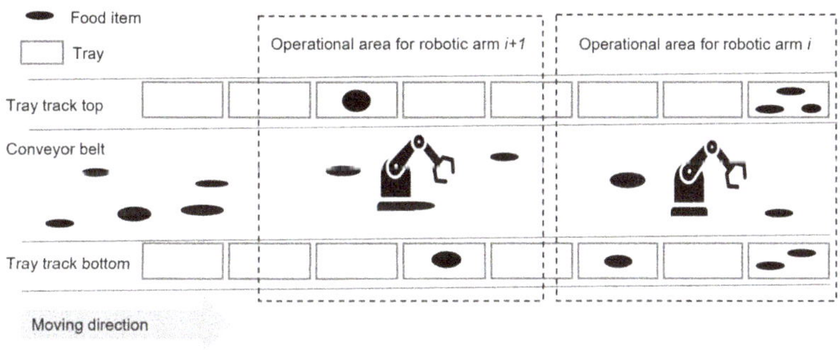

Figure 2. An illustration of a robotic arm batching system.

Given the description of the target robotic arm-based system, the following decision variables can be identified:

- Which robotic arm will pick up an item;
- When and where an item on a conveyor belt will be picked up;
- On which tray on which side of the conveyor belt an item will be placed.

The identified decisions will be made to minimize the give-away of the food items. Give-away is the positive deviation from the target tray weight. Suppose that an order requires trays with target weigh 500 g and the contract will contain a fixed price per tray delivered. If a tray comes to weigh 510 g, then 10 g (or 2%) as a free product is given away.

3.2. The Complexity of the Target Scheduling Problem

Figure 3 shows a simplified flow chart of the basic logic in the robotic batching system with a single robotic arm, a single conveyor lane and a single tray lane. It shows that all the operating parts are mutually interrelated in a highly nested way. Making one decision will affect all the other parts, and they have to be considered in order to ensure feasibility.

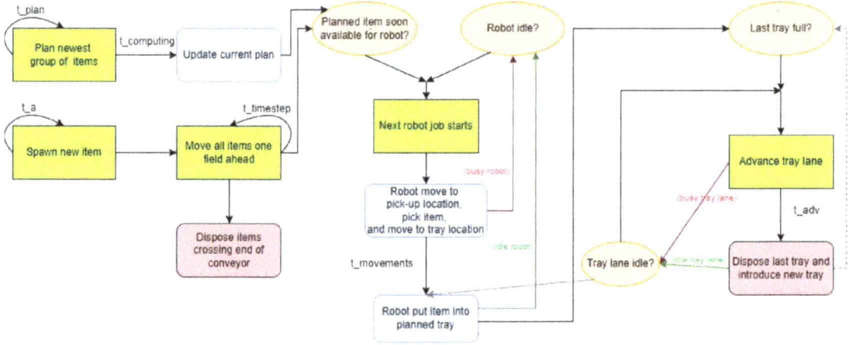

Figure 3. Simplified flow chart of the robotic batching system. *t_plan* is the time between planning newly arrived groups of items (deterministic), *t_computing* is the time to compute the plan (fixed threshold), *t_a* is the arrival times of items (stochastic), *t_timestep* is a single time step, conveyor moves all the time (deterministic), *t_movements* is the time that the robotic arm needs to conduct a task (deterministic), and *t_adv* is the time for the tray lane to advance (deterministic).

Among the interrelationships between the components of the robotic arm-based system and relevant decision variables, the following are highlighted as the key factors that make the target scheduling problem hard to solve:

- The initial position and weight of items are unknown until they enter the conveyor belt;
- The position of an item on a conveyor belt is continuously moving;
- Processing time of a robotic arm depends on (1) the position of an item to pick up and (2) the position of the tray where the robotic arm placed the previous item picked up before the current one;
- A tray track is advanced only when the tray at the end of the track exceeds the target weight, affecting the positions of the entire trays in the system;
- Each robotic arm can handle items in a designated operational area.

4. The Proposed Solution Approach

To the best of our knowledge, no standard optimization model seems to cover the target robotic batching problem of this paper in its entirety. While knapsack variations, such as the bin covering or subset sum problem, can be considered to address the target problem [27,28], the subset sum model does not allow filling past the target, and the bin covering only seeks to fill as many trays as possible without considering the level of overfill, likely resulting in trays with high give-away.

To address the complexity of the target scheduling problem, we propose a decomposition approach that sequentially solves a simplified scheduling problem for a single tray. Specifically, the original problem is decomposed into a series of sub-problems. Each sub-problem is to assign items to multiple robotic arms only for a specific tray, while making the tray reach a target weight. This sub-problem is formulated using a goal programming approach based on the nature of the objective of the scheduling, i.e., to minimize the deviation of a food tray from the target weight of the tray. A series of sub-problems is solved to find schedules for all trays in the system.

In our decomposition approach for the original scheduling problem, a sub-problem for a tray (let us say, A) on a tray track will be solved after solving the sub-problems for the trays placed in the tray track ahead of tray A, based on the dynamics of a conveyor belt. Recall that a tray track will be advanced only when the tray at the end of the track exceeds or meets a target weight, and therefore, it is natural to sequentially solve the sub-problems according to the positions of the corresponding trays so that the dependency between the sub-problems becomes uni-directional and tractable. Under this decomposition scheme, the outcome of a sub-problem solving—what items are scheduled to be picked up and when a tray track will be advanced—will be used to form the following sub-problems.

Finally, once all the sub-problems are solved following the sequence (meaning that all trays are considered for placing the items entered into the robotic arm-based batching system), the same process will begin as a new set of food items enters the system, while keeping the solutions from the previous sub-problem solving. The proposed decomposition-based solution approach is illustrated in Figure 4.

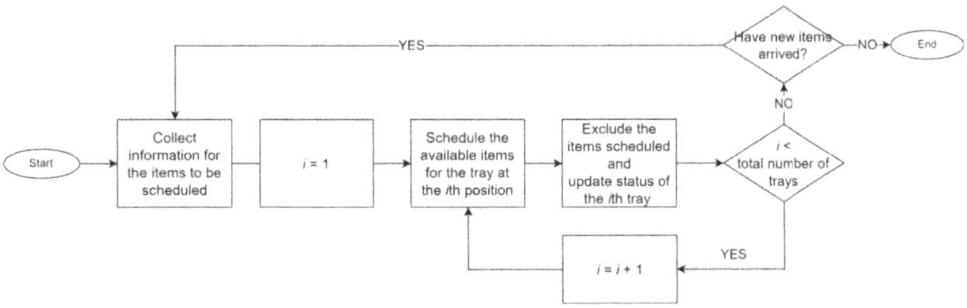

Figure 4. A flow chart of the proposed solution approach.

A Goal Program for a Sub-Problem: Scheduling Robotic Arms Only for a Single Tray

Let us suppose that there are candidate items to be batched by multiple robotic arms into a specific tray on a specific tray lane. These items are included in set V. The weight of item $i \in V$ is denoted by w_i. We also introduce the concept of a field, a specific area of an infeed conveyor belt. For the sake of simplicity, we divide the conveyor belt into a set of the same-sized multiple fields and assume that only a single item can be place on a field at a time. Given this, the arrival time of item i at field f, $AT_{i,f}$ is then calculated based on the speed of the conveyor belt and the spawn time of item i in the system. We also assume that the operational areas (i.e., a set of consecutive fields) of multiple robotic arms are independent and do not overlap. By this assumption, field index $f \in F$ identifies a responsible robotic arm for the field. The set of fields where the robotic arm responsible for field f operates is denoted by OA_f.

It should be noted that the schedules from the previous sub-problems solving are the input to the current sub-problem solving, and these schedules identify the following constraints: when the tray for the current sub-problem should advance, and when the robotic arms are unavailable. Given the constraints and the fact that the processing time of a robotic arm depends on the destination tray where an item will be placed by the robot, the timing for the tray advancement serves as a reference point to compute a robotic arm's processing time. Specifically, we denote the travel time of a robotic arm from field f to the target tray's position after its nth advancement by $\tau_{f \to n}$. Likewise, $\tau_{n \to f}$ denotes the travel time for the opposite movement. Similarly, whether a robotic arm can reach the target tray or not also depends on the tray's advancement and corresponding position. Based on this, we define set Adv_f that includes all the advancement steps, after which a robotic arm working at field f can reach the target tray.

We also compute whether item i will arrive at field f after the nth advancement of the tray, and based on the computation, we create $V_{f,n}$, a set of items that can be handled at field f between the $(n-1)$th and nth tray advancements. Lastly, from the previous sub-problem solutions, we create set $V^-_{i,f}$ and $V^+_{i,f}$, which include the items that are scheduled by the previous sub-problems and should be placed at a predetermined tray before and after item i arrives at field f (i.e., $AT_{i,f}$), respectively.

With the notation, we define the principle decision variable $x_{i,f,n}$ that indicates if item $i \in V$ will be picked up at field $f \in F$ after the nth advancements of the target tray of the sub-problem. Two deviation variables, d^+ and d^-, are also defined to measure the gap between the tray's weight and a target weight.

With the decision variables, the objective function of a sub-problem for the robotic arm scheduling problem that is to minimize the give-away on a tray can be written by

$$\min \quad d^{+} \tag{1}$$

This objective function is then minimized subject to the following constraints. First, we link the primary decision variable to the deviation variables by

$$W_{target} - \sum_{i \in V} \sum_{f \in F} \sum_{n=0}^{N} w_i \cdot x_{i,f,n} = d^{+} - d^{-} \tag{2}$$

where W_{target} is the target weight of the tray. Next, an item can be picked up at most once by a robotic arm, which can be written by

$$\sum_{f \in F} \sum_{n=0}^{N} x_{i,f,n} \leq 1 \quad \forall i \in V. \tag{3}$$

Additionally, in order to pick up item i at field f, a robotic arm for the field should be available. In other words, there should be enough of a time gap for the robotic arm to move from its last position (i.e., the tray where the last previous item is placed on) to field f. This constraint can be written by

$$M + \sum_{n \in Adv_f} \left(AT_{i,f} - M \right) \cdot x_{i,f,n} - \sum_{m \in Adv_g} \sum_{g \in OA_f} \left(AT_{j,g} + \tau_{g \to m} + \tau_{m \to f} \right) \cdot x_{j,g,m} \geq 0, \tag{4}$$

for all $i, j \in \{V | i \neq j\}$ and $f \in F$. $\tau_{g \to m} + \tau_{m \to f}$ is the total time needed for a robotic arm to move item j from field g to the tray's position after the mth advancement and to return to field f to grasp an item.

Next, to schedule item i to be picked up at field f and placed to the tray after the nth advancement (i.e., $x_{i,f,n} = 1$) in the current sub-problem, the following conditions should be met:

- There is enough time for a robotic arm to move to field f after completing all the tasks scheduled to be done before the time when item i arrives at field f;
- Placing item i on the tray after the nth advancement does not delay any following tasks scheduled by upstream sub-problems.

The constraints for these conditions are formulated by

$$M + \sum_{n \in Adv_f} \left(AT_{i,f} - M \right) \cdot x_{i,f,n} - \tau_{j \to a} \geq 0 \quad \forall i \in V, f \in F, j \in V_{i,f}^{-} \tag{5}$$

$$AT_{j,f_j^*} - \sum_{n \in Adv_f} \left(AT_{i,f} + \tau_{f \to n} + \tau_{n \to f_j^*} \right) \cdot x_{i,f,n} \geq 0 \quad \forall i \in V, f \in F, j \in V_{i,f}^{+} \tag{6}$$

where f_j^* is the field where item j is scheduled to be picked up by a previous sub-problem solution.

In addition, an item can be placed in the tray only when the tray lane is not moving. With the set $V_{f,n}$, this constraint can be formulated by

$$x_{i,f,n} \leq 1 \quad \forall i \in V_{f,n}, \ f \in F, \ 0 \leq n \leq N \tag{7}$$

$$x_{i,f,n} = 0 \quad \forall i \in V \setminus V_{f,n}, \ f \in F, \ 0 \leq n \leq N. \tag{8}$$

Lastly, we have binary and positive value constraints for the primary and deviation variables, respectively, which are shown below:

$$x_{i,f,n} \in \{0,1\} \quad \forall i \in V, f \in F, \ 0 \leq n \leq N \tag{9}$$

$$d^+, d^- \geq 0 \tag{10}$$

5. Computational Burden of the Proposed Solution Approach

Recall that a conveyor belt moves fast, feeding items to robotic arms at the same speed. Therefore, considering the fact that it is almost infeasible to know when and how food items enter into a robotic arm-based batching system, solving the robotic arm scheduling problem should be done in (near) real time.

To understand the practical scale of a food processing system and the corresponding computational requirements for the proposed solution approach, we took a field trip to a food processing company in Denmark and conducted interviews with employees of the company. From the activity, we conclude that a schedule for an item should be derived before the item passes the buffer zone that spans from the entry point of the conveyor belt to the entry point of the robotic arms' operational area. The travel time for an item to pass the buffer zone is set as 3.6 s based on the interview. Because items keep entering into a conveyor belt, making it difficult for a scheduling algorithm to fully use the 3.6 s to solve the problem, we assume that only half of the buffer passing time, 1.8 s, is allowed for the scheduling algorithm to solve the scheduling problem. In other words, a series of sub-problems, each of which schedules multiple robotic arms for a specific tray, should be solved within 1.8 s.

To examine the feasibility of the proposed solution approach in the above mentioned context, we develop a simulation model for a food batching system with two robotic arms. The layout of the target food batching system is illustrated in Figure 5a, which is also used to visualize the simulation as shown in Figure 5b. In the figure, the operational area for the robotic arms is colored in green. The buffer zone, consisting of 18 fields, starts from the left side of the conveyor belt, and an item just registered takes 3.6 s to pass the buffer zone. Considering a practical arrival rate of food items at the system, the mean inter-arrival time of items is set as 1.2 s, sampled from exponential distribution. The simulation runs for 30 min in a single replication, and a sub-problem is solved using CPLEX. The experiments are run on a Windows 10 machine with an Intel Core i5-8265U 4-core CPU @ 1.6 GHz with 8 GB RAM.

Figure 6 shows a histogram of the computation time spent to solve a series of the sub-problems for a food item batch (i.e., the items in the first half of the buffer zone). In the chart, 1116 batches are considered. The figure shows that 92% of schedules are derived in less than 1.8 s (the dotted line). The median computational time is 0.66 s with a standard deviation of 0.69.

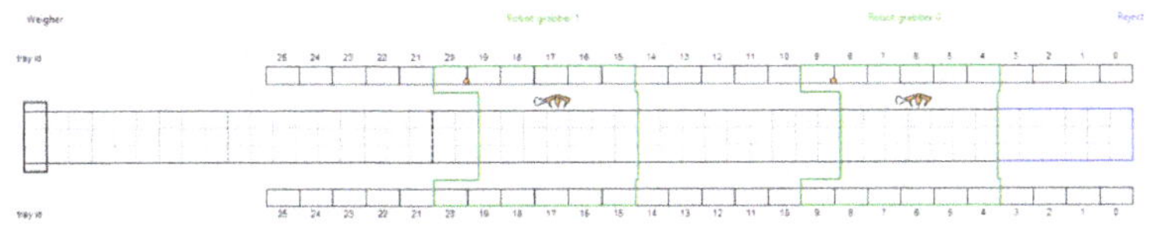

(**a**) A snapshot of the initial status of the simulation model

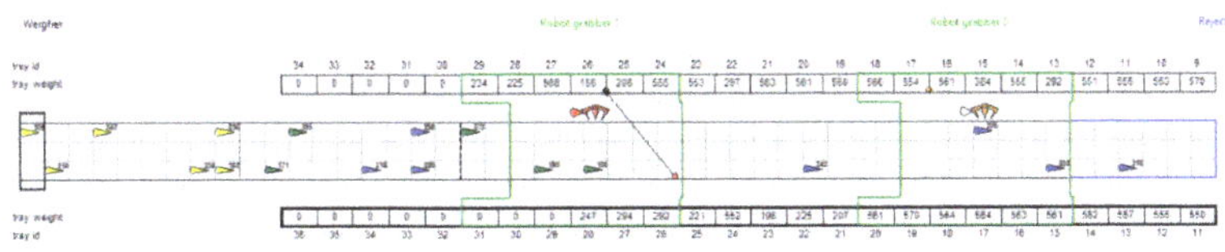

(**b**) A snapshot of a visualized simulation run

Figure 5. A snapshot of the implemented simulation model.

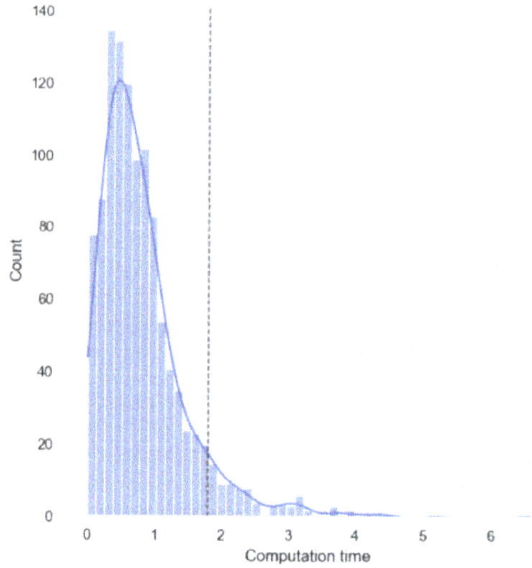

Figure 6. An histogram of the computational budget (second) of the proposed solution.

It should be pointed out that the success rate of 92% is satisfactory, but it tells us that one out of ten scheduling attempts will require more time than allowed, degrading the performance of the robotic arm-based system. A potential approach to tackle this issue is to consider local search heuristics, which are simple but effective for many combinatorial decision-making problems [29].

6. Discussion

6.1. The Objective Function of the Sub-Problem

Note that a tray does not necessarily need to be filled by currently available items. In other words, if there is no item suitable to fill the tray with a target weight, leaving the tray not fully filled would be a good strategy such that items which will arrive later can be considered to fill the tray with the target weight. However, the proposed objective function in the previous section, which is to minimize solely the positive deviation variable, cannot reflect this idea.

As a solution to this issue, one may tune a profit function as a function of a tray's weight in a way that a tray with a room for additional items has a profit if it is likely to find items from the next arrivals that make the tray full with the target weight. For example, if a mean weight of entering items is known as 300 g and it is difficult to find items to fill a tray with a target weight (say 700 g), leaving the tray with 400 g would be beneficial, rather than filling the tray up to 600 g. Figure 7 shows an example of such a profit function.

To test this idea, we tune the profit function as a piecewise linear function based on an arbitrary item weight distribution and reformulate the sub-problem's objective function as a maximization of the profit function. From our experiments, the reformulated problem makes the computation time needed to solve the problem more stable and feasible (meaning that the total computational time needed to solve a series of sub-problems was within 1.8 s in 98% of our test problem instances). Figure 8 shows the histograms of the computational time of the proposed goal program (denoted by GP model) and the reformulated problem (denoted by Hybrid model). The overall give-away level was also lowered by the reformulated problem. However, it is difficult to tune the profit function properly since a distribution of items' weight is hard to know in advance and keeps changing mainly because items are often provided by multiple suppliers. Therefore, we believe the proposed goal programming formulation would be more preferable than the reformulated one in practice.

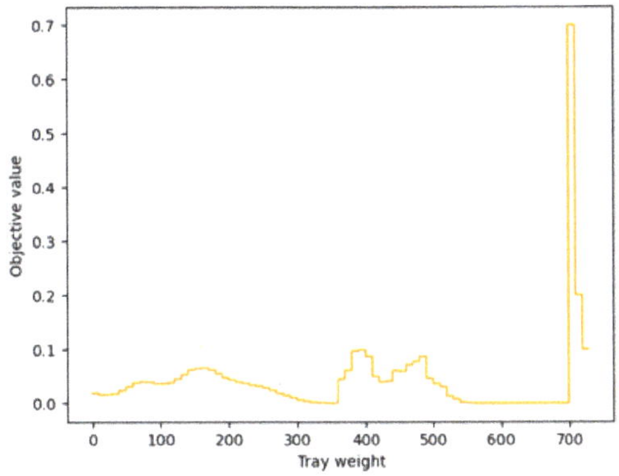

Figure 7. An example of a profit function.

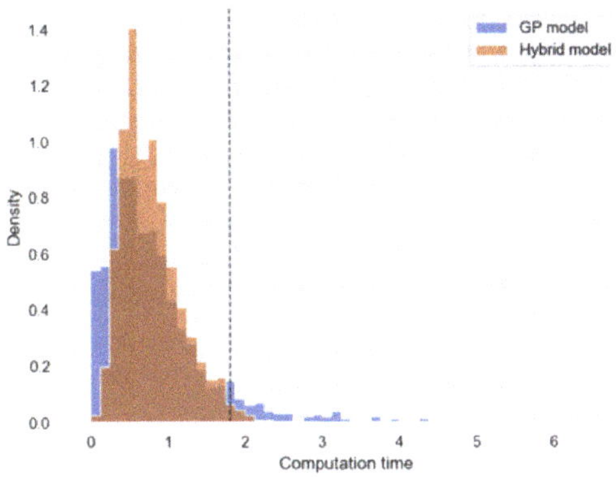

Figure 8. Computation time comparison.

6.2. A Robotic Arm-Based Batching System Configuration

One way to increase the time budget allowed for the scheduling problem solving is to have a long buffer zone or slow down the conveyor belt. Importantly, by this managerial solution, more items can be considered for a single run of a series of sub-problem solving, and thus efficient tray utilization can be achieved. On the other hand, having more items to schedule means a larger scale of scheduling problem solving. Note that the number of decision variables and constraints are exponentially increased as the number of items to schedule increases. Additionally, slowing down a conveyor belt obviously reduces the productivity of the system.

Using the simulation model, we can test the impact of such managerial decisions on the performance level of a robotic arm-based system. As an example, we evaluate the impact of the buffer zone length on the performance of the robotic arm-based batching system and the computational feasibility of the proposed solution approach. With 15 different conveyor belt length settings, keeping the rest of the simulation setting as described in the previous section, we run simulations for this trade-off analysis, and the results are summarized in Figure 9.

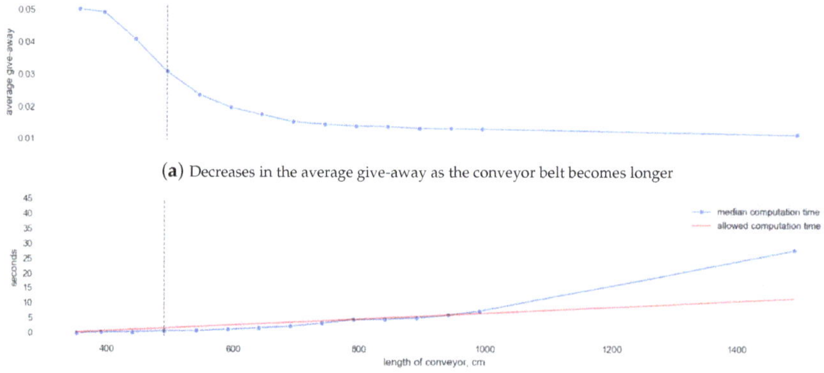

(a) Decreases in the average give-away as the conveyor belt becomes longer

(b) Increases in the computational time (seconds) as the conveyor belt becomes longer

Figure 9. A snapshot of the implemented simulation model.

From the figure, where the current conveyor belt setting is represented by a dotted line, it can be first observed that give-away, the key performance measurement of the target food batching system, is decreased as the buffer zone becomes longer and more items are considered at the moment of the scheduling. On the other hand, one can observe that the computational time for solving the scheduling problem increases as the buffer zone becomes longer and, importantly, this makes the proposed solution approach with a commercial optimization solver no longer feasible.

As observed, it is clear that there is a trade-off between the quality and computational burden of the proposed solution approach. Importantly, this observation implies that the configuration of a robotic arm-based batching system (e.g., the number of robotic arms on a conveyor belt and the length of a buffer zone) should be set carefully, considering not only the physical performance of the system but also the performance of a scheduling solution to the system that actually determines the system performance.

7. Concluding Remarks

The challenge presented in this paper is to schedule robotic arms to fill trays with items with minimal give-away. Compared to similar problems in the literature, our problem has two different conveyor belts, one for food item transition and the other for trays. Importantly, the tray lane conveyor moves only when the last tray of the tracks exceeds the target weight, introducing an additional decision to the robotic arm batching problem. This is a complex but novel problem, especially as it provides a diverse range of research fields through its system structure, allowing for various comparative analyses in terms of the investigated problem, solution approach, and main concern.

To address the target scheduling problem, we proposed a decomposition approach that divides the main robotic arm scheduling problem into smaller sub-problems of each tray. It has computational advantages as it reduces the number of decision-making dimensions, and thus decreases the solution space to search. However, by its nature, a global optimum to the original problem cannot be reached by the proposed solution approach.

We also applied a deterministic solution approach. Instead, a stochastic approach that considers the distribution of incoming items to a conveyor belt can be applied to the problem. In this way, the uncertainties and randomness in a food batching system can be addressed based on knowledge of the system, and thus a more realistic and better solution could be obtained. For this, deep reinforcement learning [23] and other machine learning algorithms can be considered for both batching and food quality and safety [30,31].

Lastly, it is worth noting that other types of conveyor belts in the literature, such as U-shape, loop, and bi-directional [32], together with the corresponding scheduling problems, can be addressed to improve the performance of robotic arm-based batching systems.

Author Contributions: Conceptualization, K.G.N., I.S., M.E.Y. and P.N.; methodology, K.G.N.; software, K.G.N.; validation, K.G.N.; formal analysis, K.G.N. and I.S.; writing—original draft preparation, K.G.N. and I.S.; writing—review and editing, I.S., M.E.Y., D.K.K. and P.N.; visualization, K.G.N.; supervision, I.S., M.E.Y. and P.N. All authors have read and agreed to the published version of the manuscript.

Funding: This research received no external funding.

Institutional Review Board Statement: Not applicable.

Informed Consent Statement: Not applicable.

Data Availability Statement: The data presented in this study are conditionally available upon request to the corresponding author.

Conflicts of Interest: The authors declare no conflict of interest.

References

1. Zhang, Y.; Li, L.; Ripperger, M.; Nicho, J.; Veeraraghavan, M.; Fumagalli, A. Gilbreth: A conveyor-belt based pick-and-sort industrial robotics application. In Proceedings of the 2018 Second IEEE International Conference on Robotic Computing (IRC), Laguna Hills, CA, USA, 31 January–2 February 2018; pp. 17–24.
2. Bogue, R. The role of robots in the food industry: A review. *Ind. Robot. Int. J.* **2009**, *36*, 531–536. [CrossRef]
3. Iqbal, J.; Khan, Z.H.; Khalid, A. Prospects of robotics in food industry. *Food Sci. Technol.* **2017**, *37*, 159–165. [CrossRef]
4. Einarsdóttir, H.; Guðmundsson, B.; Ómarsson, V. Automation in the fish industry. *Anim. Front.* **2022**, *12*, 32–39. [CrossRef] [PubMed]
5. Sung, I.; Nam, H.; Lee, T. Scheduling algorithms for mobile harbor: An extended m-parallel machine problem. *Int. J. Ind. Eng. Theory Appl. Pract.* **2013**, *20*, 211–224.
6. Rahman, H.; Janardhanan, M.; Nielsen, I. Real-time order acceptance and scheduling problems in a flow shop environment using hybrid Ga-PSO algorithm. *IEEE Access* **2019**, *7*, 112742–112755.
7. Suárez-Ruiz, F.; Lembono, T.S.; Pham, Q.C. Robotsp—A fast solution to the robotic task sequencing problem. In Proceedings of the 2018 IEEE International Conference on Robotics and Automation (ICRA), Brisbane, Australia, 21–25 May 2018; pp. 1611–1616.
8. Saha, M.; Roughgarden, T.; Latombe, J.C.; Sánchez-Ante, G. Planning tours of robotic arms among partitioned goals. *Int. J. Robot. Res.* **2006**, *25*, 207–223.
9. Wurll, C.; Henrich, D. Point-to-point and multi-goal path planning for industrial robots. *J. Robot. Syst.* **2001**, *18*, 445–461.
10. Alatartsev, S.; Stellmacher, S.; Ortmeier, F. Robotic task sequencing problem: A survey. *J. Intell. Robot. Syst.* **2015**, *80*, 279–298.
11. Zahorán, L.; Kovács, A. ProSeqqo: A generic solver for process planning and sequencing in industrial robotics. *Robot. Comput.-Integr. Manuf.* **2022**, *78*, 102387.
12. Sutdhiraksa, S.; Zurawski, R. Scheduling robotic assembly tasks using petri nets. In Proceedings of the IEEE International Symposium on Industrial Electronics, Warsaw, Poland, 17 June 1996; pp. 459–465.
13. Nie, W.; Luo, J.; Fu, Y.; Sun, S.; Li, D. Schedule of flexible manufacturing systems based on petri nets and a search with a neural network heuristic function. In Proceedings of the 2020 7th International Conference on Information Science and Control Engineering (ICISCE), Changsha, China, 18–20 December 2020; pp. 1246–1250.
14. Cerda, J.; Henning, G.P.; Grossmann, I.E. A mixed-integer linear programming model for short-term scheduling of single-stage multiproduct batch plants with parallel lines. *Ind. Eng. Chem. Res.* **1997**, *36*, 1695–1707. [CrossRef]
15. Tika, A.; Gafur, N.; Yfantis, V.; Bajcinca, N. Optimal scheduling and model predictive control for trajectory planning of cooperative robot manipulators. *IFAC-PapersOnLine* **2020**, *53*, 9080–9086. [CrossRef]
16. Gafur, N.; Yfantis, V.; Ruskowski, M. Optimal scheduling and non-cooperative distributed model predictive control for multiple robotic manipulators. In Proceedings of the 2021 IEEE/RSJ International Conference on Intelligent Robots and Systems (IROS), Prague, Czech Republic, 27 September–1 October 2021; pp. 390–397.
17. Paape, N.; van Eekelen, J.; Reniers, M. Design of meat processing systems with agent-based production control. *IFAC-PapersOnLine* **2021**, *54*, 1112–1117. [CrossRef]
18. Peeters, K.; Martagan, T.; Adan, I.; Cruysen, P. Control and design of the fillet batching process in a poultry processing plant. In Proceedings of the 2017 Winter Simulation Conference (WSC), Las Vegas, NV, USA, 3–6 December 2017; pp. 3816–3827. [CrossRef]
19. Peeters, K.; Adan, I.J.B.F.; Martagan, T. Throughput control and revenue optimization of a poultry product batcher. *IISE Trans.* **2022**, *54*, 845–857. [CrossRef]
20. Peeters, K.; Adan, J.; Hundscheid, B.; Martagan, T.; Adan, I. Online product allocation in poultry batchers with lookahead. *Comput. Ind. Eng.* **2022**, *165*, 107875. [CrossRef]
21. Hundscheid, B.H.; Peeters, K.; Adan, J.; Martagan, T.; Adan, I.J. A Hybrid Genetic Algorithm for the K-Bounded Semi-Online Bin Covering Problem in Batching Machines. In Proceedings of the 2019 Winter Simulation Conference (WSC), National Harbor, MD, USA, 8–11 December 2019; pp. 2142–2153. [CrossRef]

22. Huang, M.; Wu, J.; Tang, Y.; Shi, L. Optimal Design of a Conveyor-Based Automatic Sorting System. In Proceedings of the 2020 IEEE 16th International Conference on Control & Automation (ICCA), Sapporo, Japan, 6–9 July 2020; pp. 1124–1129. [CrossRef]
23. Hildebrand, M.; Andersen, R.S.; Bøgh, S. Deep Reinforcement Learning for Robot Batching Optimization and Flow Control. *Procedia Manuf.* **2020**, *51*, 1462–1468. [CrossRef]
24. Ásgeirsson, A. On-Line Algorithms for Bin-Covering Problems with Known Item Distributions. Ph.D. Thesis, Georgia Institute of Technology, Atlanta, GA, USA, 2014.
25. Van Sprang, R. Condition Based Maintenance at Marel Poultry. Master's Thesis, Eindhoven University of Technology, Eindhoven, The Netherlands, 2017.
26. Raaijmakers, S. Performance Analysis of Broiler Product Batchers in Poultry Processing Plant. Master's Thesis, Eindhoven University of Technology, Eindhoven, The Netherlands, 2018.
27. Caprara, A.; Kellerer, H.; Pferschy, U. The multiple subset sum problem. *SIAM J. Optim.* **2000**, *11*, 308–319. [CrossRef]
28. Csirik, J.; Johnson, D.S.; Kenyon, C. Better approximation algorithms for bin covering. In Proceedings of the SODA, Washington, DC, USA, 7–9 January 2001; Volume 1, pp. 557–566.
29. El Yafrani, M.; Sung, I.; Krach, B.; Katsilieris, F.; Nielsen, P. Analysis of a local search heuristic for the generalized assignment problem with resource-independent task profits and identical resource capacity. *Eng. Optim.* **2022**, *54*, 1426–1440. [CrossRef]
30. Zhu, L.; Spachos, P. Support vector machine and YOLO for a mobile food grading system. *Internet Things* **2021**, *13*, 100359. [CrossRef]
31. Zhu, L.; Spachos, P.; Pensini, E.; Plataniotis, K.N. Deep learning and machine vision for food processing: A survey. *Curr. Res. Food Sci.* **2021**, *4*, 233–249. [CrossRef] [PubMed]
32. Boysen, N.; Briskorn, D.; Fedtke, S.; Schmickerath, M. Automated sortation conveyors: A survey from an operational research perspective. *Eur. J. Oper. Res.* **2019**, *276*, 796–815. [CrossRef]

algorithms

MDPI

Article

Hybrid Genetic and Spotted Hyena Optimizer for Flow Shop Scheduling Problem

Toufik Mzili [1,*], Ilyass Mzili [2], Mohammed Essaid Riffi [1] and Gaurav Dhiman [3,4,5,6,7,8]

1 Department of Computer Science, Faculty of Science, Chouaib Doukkali University, El Jadida 24000, Morocco
2 Department of Management, Faculty of Economics and Management, Hassan First University, Settat 26000, Morocco; dr.mzili.ilyass@gmail.com
3 Department of Electrical and Computer Engineering, Lebanese American University, Byblos P.O. Box 36, Lebanon
4 Centre for Research and Development, Department of Computer Science and Engineering, Chandigarh University, Gharuan 140413, India
5 Department of Computer Science and Engineering, Graphic Era Deemed to be University, Dehradun 248002, India
6 Division of Research and Development, Lovely Professional University, Punjab 144001, India
7 Chitkara University Institute of Engineering and Technology, Chitkara University, Rajpura 140401, Punjab, India
8 Department of Computer Science, Government Bikram College of Commerce, Patiala 147001, India
* Correspondence: mzili.t@ucd.ac.ma

Abstract: This paper presents a new hybrid algorithm that combines genetic algorithms (GAs) and the optimizing spotted hyena algorithm (SHOA) to solve the production shop scheduling problem. The proposed GA-SHOA algorithm incorporates genetic operators, such as uniform crossover and mutation, into the SHOA algorithm to improve its performance. We evaluated the algorithm on a set of OR library instances and compared it to other state-of-the-art optimization algorithms, including SSO, SCE-OBL, CLS-BFO and ACGA. The experimental results show that the GA-SHOA algorithm consistently finds optimal or near-optimal solutions for all tested instances, outperforming the other algorithms. Our paper contributes to the field in several ways. First, we propose a hybrid algorithm that effectively combines the exploration and exploitation capabilities of SHO and GA, resulting in a balanced and efficient search process for finding near-optimal solutions for the FSSP. Second, we tailor the SHO and GA methods to the specific requirements of the FSSP, including encoding schemes, objective function evaluation and constraint handling, which ensures that the hybrid algorithm is well suited to address the challenges posed by the FSSP. Third, we perform a comprehensive performance evaluation of the proposed hybrid algorithm, demonstrating its effectiveness in terms of solution quality and computational efficiency. Finally, we provide an in-depth analysis of the behavior of the hybrid algorithm, discussing the roles of the SHO and GA components and their interactions during the search process, which can help understand the factors contributing to the success of the algorithm and provide insight into potential improvements or adaptations to other combinatorial optimization problems.

Keywords: flow shop scheduling problem; SHOA; hybrid algorithm; metaheuristics; optimization; spotted hyena optimizer; genetic algorithm; uniform crossover; OR library; computational efficiency

Citation: Mzili, T.; Mzili, I.; Riffi, M.E.; Dhiman, G. Hybrid Genetic and Spotted Hyena Optimizer for Flow Shop Scheduling Problem. *Algorithms* **2023**, *16*, 265. https://doi.org/10.3390/a16060265

Academic Editor: Frank Werner

Received: 21 April 2023
Revised: 15 May 2023
Accepted: 17 May 2023
Published: 25 May 2023

1. Introduction

Combinatorial problems [1] involve finding the optimal arrangement, selection or sequencing of a finite set of elements based on specific constraints and objectives. They are prevalent in various fields, such as mathematics, computer science, engineering, operations research, economics and biology. The importance of solving combinatorial problems stems from their practical applications in decision-making, resource allocation and optimization tasks critical for the efficiency and effectiveness of real-world systems.

Examples of combinatorial problems include the traveling salesman problem [2], which seeks the shortest route for a salesman visiting a set of cities once before returning to the starting point; the knapsack problem, which aims to select items with different weights and values to maximize the total value without exceeding a given weight limit; and the graph coloring problem, which assigns colors to graph vertices so that no two adjacent vertices share the same color. These problems, although seemingly different, share common challenges in terms of computational complexity, as they often require exploring an extensive solution space to identify the optimal solution.

One specific combinatorial problem of significant practical importance is the Flow Shop Scheduling Problem (FSSP) [3]. In this problem, a set of jobs must be processed on a collection of machines in a specific order, with each job consisting of multiple operations executed sequentially. The objective is to find a schedule that minimizes the makespan or the total time required to complete all jobs. Due to the combinatorial nature of this problem, finding an optimal solution becomes increasingly difficult as the number of jobs and machines increases.

Swarm intelligence algorithms [4] have emerged as effective approaches for tackling the optimization of makespan in the FSSP. These algorithms are inspired by the collective behavior of social organisms such as birds, fish, and insects, and their ability to solve complex problems through decentralized and self-organizing processes. Some widely used swarm intelligence algorithms for solving the FSSP include Particle Swarm Optimization (PSO) [5], Ant Colony Optimization (ACO) [6], Whale Swarm Algorithm (WOA) [7] and Rat Swarm Optimization [8].

In the context of the FSSP [9], these algorithms encode potential solutions as particles, ants or bees and iteratively explore the solution space by updating the position or path of these agents based on their own experiences and the collective knowledge of the swarm. The agents collaborate and compete, allowing the swarm to converge towards an optimal or near-optimal solution for the makespan. The effectiveness of swarm intelligence algorithms in solving the FSSP has been demonstrated in various industrial applications, such as manufacturing, transportation and logistics, where efficient job scheduling is critical for reducing production costs, improving resource utilization and enhancing overall performance.

In this article, we propose a novel hybrid algorithm that combines the Spotted Hyena Optimizer (SHO) [10] and Genetic Algorithm (GA) [11] to solve the Flow Shop Scheduling Problem (FSSP). The FSSP is a particular case of the Flow Shop Scheduling Problem (FSSP), in which jobs are processed on a set of machines in a specific order, and all jobs follow the same sequence of operations on the machines. The primary objective is to minimize the makespan, which is the total time required to complete all jobs.

The Spotted Hyena Optimizer (SHO) is a nature-inspired optimization algorithm based on the unique hunting behavior of spotted hyenas. It incorporates four main mechanisms: searching, encircling, attacking and mobbing. These mechanisms help explore the solution space efficiently and exploit the best solutions found during the search process.

The Genetic Algorithm (GA) is a widely-used, population-based optimization method inspired by the principles of natural selection and genetics. It operates on a population of candidate solutions and evolves them over generations using genetic operators, such as selection, crossover and mutation. GAs have been successfully applied to solve numerous combinatorial optimization problems, including the FSSP.

In our hybrid approach, we combine the strengths of both SHO and GA to improve the overall search efficiency and solution quality. The proposed algorithm starts with an initial population generated by the SHO. During the search process, the SHO mechanisms are employed to explore the solution space and to update the hyenas' positions. After a predefined number of iterations, the GA is integrated into the algorithm to further refine the solutions. The GA takes the current hyena positions as an input population and performs selection, crossover and mutation operations to generate offspring. The offspring then replace some of the least fit hyenas in the population, ensuring the best solutions are retained.

This hybridization of SHO and GA capitalizes on the exploration capabilities of the SHO and the exploitation abilities of the GA, resulting in a more robust and efficient algorithm for solving the FSSP. The proposed hybrid method is tested on a set of benchmark instances from the literature, and the results demonstrate its effectiveness in finding near-optimal solutions with competitive computational times. The successful application of the hybrid spotted hyena and genetic algorithm to the FSSP indicates its potential for addressing other complex combinatorial optimization problems in various domains.

The main contributions of this paper can be summarized as follows:

- Development of a Hybrid Algorithm: We propose a new hybrid algorithm that effectively integrates the exploration capabilities of SHO and the exploitation capabilities of GA. This combination ensures a more balanced and efficient search process, allowing the algorithm to find near-optimal solutions for the FSSP.
- Adaptation of SHO and GA to FSSP: We adapt the SHO and GA methods to the specific requirements of FSSP, including encoding schemes, objective function evaluation and constraint handling. This adaptation ensures that the hybrid algorithm is well-suited to address the challenges posed by the FSSP.
- Comprehensive Performance Evaluation: We perform a thorough performance evaluation of the proposed hybrid algorithm using a set of benchmark instances from the literature. The results are compared with those obtained by state-of-the-art algorithms, demonstrating the effectiveness of our hybrid approach in terms of solution quality and computational efficiency.
- Hybrid Algorithm Behavior Analysis: We provide an in-depth analysis of the behavior of the hybrid algorithm, discussing the roles of the SHO and GA components and their interactions during the search process. This analysis helps to understand the factors contributing to the success of the algorithm in solving the FSSP and offers insights into potential improvements or adaptations to other combinatorial optimization problems.

This article is organized into six sections: (1) Introduction, which provides an overview of the combinatorial optimization problem and the motivation for developing the hybrid algorithm; (2) Related Works and Literature Review, where we discuss existing research on swarm intelligence algorithms and their application to the FSSP; (3) Flow Shop Scheduling Problems (FSSP), which offers a detailed description of the FSSP, its challenges and its significance in real-world applications; (4) Methodology, where we present the design and implementation of the proposed hybrid algorithm, combining the Spotted Hyena Optimizer (SHO) and Genetic Algorithm (GA); (5) Experimental Outcomes, where we analyze the performance of the hybrid algorithm using benchmark instances and compare the results with existing state-of-the-art approaches; and finally, (6) Conclusion, where we summarize the main findings of the study, discuss the implications of the results and suggest future research directions in the field of combinatorial optimization.

2. Related Works

In recent years, swarm intelligence has been increasingly applied to solve Flow Shop Scheduling Problems (FSSP) due to its ability to effectively explore and exploit the solution space. The following studies have made significant contributions to this area:

- Tang et al., (2016) [12] proposed an energy-efficient dynamic scheduling approach for a flexible flow shop using an improved particle swarm optimization. The algorithm addresses the dynamic scheduling problem while minimizing energy consumption and makespan.
- C. Zhang et al., (2021) [7] presented a discrete whale swarm algorithm for a hybrid flow-shop scheduling problem with limited buffers, considering practical constraints on buffer area resources and alternative process routes. The algorithm's effectiveness was validated on three groups of instances and a real-world industrial case.
- Li et al., (2022) [13] examined the distributed assembly mixed no-idle permutation flow-shop scheduling problem (DAMNIPFSP) with a focus on minimizing total tardiness. The researchers developed a mixed-integer linear programming model and

proposed a Referenced Iterated Greedy (RIG) algorithm, incorporating novel destruction and reconstruction methods as well as local search methods based on a reference. Experimental results demonstrated the effectiveness of the RIG algorithm, positioning it as a state-of-the-art solution for DAMNIPFSP with the total tardiness criterion.

- Mahmud et al., (2022) [14] introduced a bi-objective integrated supply chain scheduling model and developed two new meta-heuristic algorithms based on multi-objective particle swarm optimization (MOPSO) to solve the strongly NP-hard flexible job shop problem.
- Gümüşçü et al., (2022) [15] investigated the impact of local search strategies on chaotic hybrid firefly particle swarm optimization algorithm in flow-shop scheduling, comparing the results of the solutions obtained using different local search strategies.
- Vali et al., (2022) [16] presented a flexible job shop scheduling problem to optimize patient flow and minimize the total carbon footprint. They developed a metaheuristic optimization algorithm called Chaotic Salp Swarm Algorithm Enhanced with Opposition-based Learning and Sine Cosine (CSSAOS) to solve this NP-hard problem
- Hayat et al., (2023) [17] explored the enhancement of Particle Swarm Optimization (PSO) in tackling Permutation Flow-Shop Scheduling Problems (PFSPs) by hybridizing it with Variable Neighborhood Search (VNS) and Simulated Annealing (SA). The authors compared the performance of the developed hybrid PSO (HPSO) algorithm with 120 distinct Taillard instances, demonstrating its robustness and significantly improved makespan optimization compared to other hybrid metaheuristics.
- Sun et al., (2023) [18] investigated production scheduling technology for knitting workshops utilizing an improved genetic algorithm (IGA) with tabu search. The research, conducted at the Key Laboratory of Modern Textile Machinery & Technology of Zhejiang Province, Zhejiang Sci-Tech University and the School of Automation, Zhejiang Institute of Mechanical & Electrical Engineering aimed to enhance production efficiency and reduce costs. Their proposed IGA demonstrated faster convergence and better search capabilities compared to traditional genetic algorithms, offering valuable insights for advancing intelligent development in knitting production.

Some of the state-of-the-art optimization algorithms for FSSP include GA-SHOA, WD [19], GA [19], IHSA [19], PSO [19], CLS-BFO [20], AGGA [20] and SSO [20]. These algorithms were selected and used for comparison with the hybrid algorithm we propose in this paper. GA-SHOA is a new hybrid algorithm that combines the exploration capabilities of SHOA with the exploitation capabilities of GA to efficiently search the solution space. CLS-BFO is a hybrid algorithm that combines the cuckoo search algorithm (CS) with the Broyden-Fletcher-Goldfarb-Shanno (BFGS) method to solve the FSSP. WD is an algorithm that uses differential evolution (DE) to optimize the FSSP. GA is a well-known metaheuristic algorithm that has been widely used to solve the FSSP. IHSA is a hybrid algorithm that combines the improved harmony search (IHS) algorithm and simulated annealing (SA). PSO is a swarm intelligence algorithm that has been applied to FSSP with promising results. AGGA is another hybrid algorithm that combines the genetic algorithm and the gravitational search algorithm (GSA). SSO is an algorithm that mimics the social behavior of the spotted hyena and has been shown to be effective in solving the FSSP.

Table 1 introduces a comparison of these methods.

Table 1. Comparison of optimization algorithms for the FSSP.

Algorithm	Approach	Operators	Population Size	Selection
GA-SHOA	Hybrid	Uniform Crossover, Mutation	50–100	Roulette Wheel
SSO	Nature-inspired	Randomization, Clustering	20–50	Roulette Wheel
SCE-OB	Evolutionary	Crossover, Mutation	50–200	Rank-based
CLS-BFO	Metaheuristic	Local search, randomization	50–100	Roulette Wheel
ACGA	Hybrid	Adaptive Crossover, Mutation	50–100	Rank-based

3. Flow Shop Scheduling Problems (FSSPs)

Flow Shop Scheduling Problems (FSSPs) is a class of scheduling problems that arise in manufacturing and production systems, where a set of jobs or tasks must be processed through a series of machines in a specific order. FSSPs is a well-studied optimization problem in the field of operations research and has numerous applications in various industries, such as automotive, semiconductor, food processing and textile production, among others.

In a typical flow shop environment, there are multiple machines or workstations, and each job must be processed on every machine in a predetermined sequence. The main objective of the FSSP is to determine the optimal scheduling of jobs on machines to achieve certain performance criteria, such as minimizing makespan, total completion time, total tardiness or a combination of these objectives.

The importance of flow shop scheduling problems lies in their ability to optimize the utilization of resources, reduce production costs and improve overall efficiency in manufacturing systems. Effective flow shop scheduling can lead to:

- Reduced production lead time: By optimizing the job sequence and minimizing the idle time of machines, flow shop scheduling can significantly reduce the total production time.
- Improved resource utilization: Efficient scheduling ensures that machines are utilized optimally, reducing idle time and maximizing production throughput.
- Enhanced customer satisfaction: Timely delivery of products and shorter lead times can increase customer satisfaction and help to maintain a competitive edge in the market.
- Lower inventory costs: By reducing work-in-process inventory and minimizing production time, flow shop scheduling can help lower inventory holding costs.
- Increased competitiveness: Effective flow shop scheduling allows companies to be more agile and responsive to market demands, thus enhancing their competitive position.

Despite its importance, FSSP is a challenging combinatorial optimization problem known to be NP-hard, meaning that finding an optimal solution becomes increasingly difficult as the problem size increases. As a result, researchers have developed various heuristic and metaheuristic algorithms to find near-optimal solutions for the FSSP in a reasonable amount of time, such as particle swarm optimization, genetic algorithms, simulated annealing and ant colony optimization, among others. These methods have been successfully applied to tackle real-world flow shop scheduling problems, resulting in significant improvements in manufacturing efficiency and cost reduction.

The Fob-Shop Scheduling Problem (FSSP) involves assigning a set of n jobs, each consisting of multiple operations, to a set of m machines. The primary objective is to find a schedule that minimizes the makespan (*Cmax*), which is the total completion time of all jobs. A solution can be represented as an n $\times$ m vector of operation sequences that optimizes the completion time.

$$C_{\max} = \max\left(t_{ij} + p_{ij}\right) \quad (1)$$

$$min(C_{nm}+1) \quad (2)$$

where

$$C_{kl} \leq C_{ji} - d_{kl};\ j=1,\ldots,n;\ i=1,\ldots,m;\ kl\ \in\ P_{ji} \quad (3)$$

$$\sum_{ji\epsilon o(t)}^{n} r_{ji} \leq 1;\ i\ \in\ M;\ t\ \geq\ 0 \quad (4)$$

$$C\_ji \geq\ 0;\ j=1,\ldots,n;\ i=1,\ldots,m \quad (5)$$

The constraints are as follows:

- Constraint (2) minimizes the finish time of the operation on machine m + 1 (the makespan).
- Constraint (3) ensures that precedence relationships between operations are maintained.
- Constraint (4) states that each machine can process only one operation at a time.
- Constraint (5) ensures that the finish times are positive.

4. Methodology

The Spotted Hyena Optimizer (SHO) is a metaheuristic, bio-inspired optimization algorithm developed by Dhiman et al. The algorithm is based on the social behaviors of spotted hyenas, which are the largest among the three other hyena species (striped, brown and aardwolf). Spotted hyenas are skillful hunters that typically live and hunt in groups, relying on networks with over 100 members. The SHO algorithm comprises four main steps that emulate the encircling, hunting, attacking and searching behaviors of spotted hyenas (as shown in Figure 1 [10]).

- Encircling prey:

Figure 1. Spotted Hyena Hunting Behavior [10].

The best solution is considered the target prey, and other search agents update their positions based on the obtained best solution. The mathematical model for this behavior is given by:

$$Dh = |B \cdot Pp(x) - P(x)|, \quad (6)$$

$$P(x+1) = Pp(x) - E \cdot Dh\,, \quad (7)$$

- Hunting:

  The hunting strategy of the SHO is defined as follows:

$$Dh = |B \cdot Ph - Pk|, \quad (8)$$

$$Pk = Ph - E \cdot Dh\,, \quad (9)$$

$$Ch = Pk + Pk + 1 + \ldots + Pk + N\,, \tag{10}$$

- Attacking prey:

  The mathematical formulation for attacking prey is given by:

$$P(x+1) = \frac{ch}{N}\,, \tag{11}$$

- Searching for prey:

The search for a suitable solution involves evaluating the E and B vectors. The SHO algorithm can solve various high-dimensional problems with low computational efforts and avoid local optimum issues.

In this study, we will focus on using the encircling behavior to solve the flow shop scheduling problem, and the pseudo-code of the SHO algorithm is provided in Algorithm 1.

Algorithm 1 Spotted Hyena Optimizer (SHO)

```
procedure SHO
  Input: Spotted hyenas population Pi (i = 1, 2, ..., n)
  Output: The optimal search agent
  Initialize parameters h, B, E, and N
  Evaluate the fitness of each search agent
  Ph ← Identify the best search agent
  Ch ← Form a group or cluster of all distant optimal solutions
  while x < MaxIteration do
    for each search agent do
      Update the current agent's position using Equation (10)
    end for
    Update h, B, E, and N
    Ensure search agents stay within the given search space and adjust if necessary
    Compute the fitness of each search agent
    Update Ph if a better solution is found compared to the previous optimal solution
    Modify group Ch based on Ph
    x ← x + 1
  end while
  return Ph
end procedure
```

Alterations to mathematical operators for flow shop problems:

The mathematical operators are redefined to accommodate the flow shop problem as follows:

- $Dh = |B \cdot P\_prey(x) - P(x)|$: The subtraction operation between two rat positions is adapted to a list of swaps to be performed on a job sequence $P(t)$ to obtain the best sequence list Pbest(t).
- $E \cdot Dh$: This operation, involving a real number between [0, 1] and a list of swaps, is redefined to manipulate and decrease the number of swaps generated by the previous equation.
- $P\_prey(x) - E \cdot Dh$: This operation determines the final number of potential swaps to be applied to a job sequence.
- An illustrative example of these modifications is provided below:
- $P\_prey(x)$: 

- $P(x)$: 

- $Dh = |P\_prey(x) - P(x)|$: List of swaps to be performed on a sequence of jobs $P(x)$ to obtain the first sequence list
- $P\_prey(x)$ = [[J5,J1},{J3,J2}]
- $E = 0.5$

- $E \cdot Dh = \frac{1}{2}$ [J5,J1},{J3,J2}] = {J5,J1}
- p_prey (x)- E · Dh = J5 → J3 → J2 → J4 → J1

The Genetic Algorithm (GA) is a popular metaheuristic technique for solving optimization problems, including the Flow Shop Scheduling Problem (FSSP). The Uniform Crossover and Mutation are two genetic operators used within GA that combine parent solutions to create offspring. Here's an example of using a Genetic Algorithm with Uniform Crossover and Mutation to solve the FSSP:

Crossover: Perform the Uniform Crossover on the selected parent individuals to create offspring. In the Uniform Crossover, for each position in the parent's permutation, a random decision is made as to which parent's gene will be inherited by the offspring. For example:

- Parent 1: [1, 2, 3, 4, 5] = J1 → J2 → J3 → J4 → J5
- A random binary mask: [0, 1, 0, 1, 0]
- Parent 2: [5, 4, 3, 2, 1] = J5 → J4 → J3 → J2 → J1
- Offspring 1: [1, 4, 3, 2, 5] = J1 → J4 → J3 → J2 → J5
- Offspring 2: [5, 2, 3, 4, 1] = J5 → J2 → J3 → J4 → J1

Mutation: Apply a mutation operator to each gene of the offspring with a certain probability. The mutation operator randomly changes the value of the gene to another valid value. In the FSSP case, which is a random permutation of two tasks, the mutation operator may swap the positions of two tasks in the offspring's permutation.

For example:

- Offspring 1: [1, 4, 3, 2, 5] = J1 → J4 → J3 → J2 → J5
- Randomly select two genes to mutate 1 and 3 (swap tasks 1 and 3):
- Mutated offspring 1: [1, 4, 2, 2, 5] = J3 → J4 → J1 → J2 → J5

The final algorithm is described as follows in Algorithm 2:

Algorithm 2 Discrete Hybrid Spotted Hyena Optimizer with Uniform Crocgover

procedure HYBRID SHO(2)
  Input: Spotted hyenas population P_i $(i = 1, 2, \ldots, n)$
  Output: The optimal search agent
  Initialize parameters h, B, E, and N
  Evaluate the fitness of each search agent
  $Ph \leftarrow$ Identify the best search agent
  $Ch \leftarrow$ Form a group or cluster of all distant optimal solutions
  while $x < MaxIteration$ **do**
    for each search agent **do**
      Update the current agent's position using Equation (7)
    end for
    Perform Uniform Crossover on selected parent individuals to create offspring
    Apply mutation operators to offspring (inversion)
    Replace some individuals in the population with the newly created offspring
    Update h, B, E, and N
    Ensure search agents stay within the given search space and adjust if necessary
    Compute the fitness of each search agent
    if a better solution is found compared to the previous optimal solution **then**
      Update P_h
    end if
    Modify group C_h based on P_h
    $x \leftarrow x + 1$
  end while
  return P_h
end procedure

5. Experimental Outcomes

The performance of the hybrid GA-SHO algorithm was assessed using over 50 instances from the OR library. The evaluation results are presented in Table 2, which include the instance name ("Instance"), the number of jobs (n) and machines (m) for each instance ("n × m"), the best result achieved by other algorithms ("*BKS*"), the best and worst results obtained through the SHO method ("Best" and "Worst"), the average results ("*Average*") and the average execution time in seconds for 20 runs ("Time"). The "*PDav(%)*" column displays the percentage deviation of the average solution length from the optimal solution length, computed using Equation (12).

$$PDav(\%) = \frac{((Average - BKS) \times 100\%)}{BKS} \quad (12)$$

Table 2. Parameters of Discrete GA-SHO.

Parameter	Value
The population of rat size: N	100
B	A random value between [0, 1]
E	A random value between [0, 1]
Nb iteration	400

The "*PDav(%)*" column emphasizes values of 0.00 in bold when all solutions found in the 20 runs are equal to the length of the best-known solution. If the average of the solutions discovered in all tests is less than the length of the best-known solution, these values are highlighted in bold and blue. This suggests that the GA-SHO algorithm managed to find solutions that either match or surpass the best-known solutions for these instances.

To properly evaluate the effectiveness of the GA-SHO algorithm, it is crucial to compare it with other methods for solving problems.

The comparison is made with the following algorithms: CLS-BFE [20], DEO [19], GA [19], IHSA [19], PSO [19], AGGA [20] and SSO [20].

The initial parameters are described in Table 2.

Figure 2 shows the comparison of the best-obtained results, clearly demonstrating that the GA-SHOA algorithm outperforms other methods (CLS-BFO, IHSA, PSO, DEO, SSO, GA, AGGA) across all instances (REC01 to REC23).

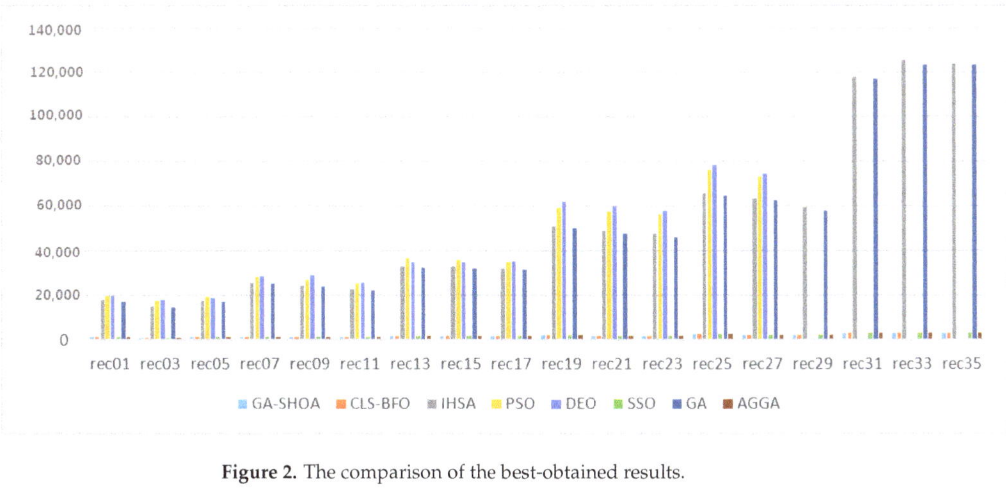

Figure 2. The comparison of the best-obtained results.

Tables 3 and 4 clearly demonstrates that the GA-SHOA algorithm outperforms other methods (CLS-BFO, IHSA, PSO, DEO, SSO, GA, AGGA) across all instances (REC01 to REC23). Here's a more detailed analysis of the data:

- Objective Function Value (Best): For all instances, GA-SHOA consistently attains the most optimal or near-optimal solution. This highlights GA-SHOA's superior ability to find the most optimal or best solutions compared to the other algorithms.
- Standard Deviation (STD): GA-SHOA exhibits notably lower standard deviation values compared to other methods. This suggests that GA-SHOA's results are more reliable and exhibit less variation. A low standard deviation implies that the values are close to the mean or expected value, whereas a high standard deviation implies a wider spread of values. In an optimization context, a lower standard deviation is favorable as it indicates consistent solution quality near the optimal.
- Computation Time: GA-SHOA also outshines other methods in terms of computational efficiency, showcasing faster computation times. For instance, in the case of REC01, GA-SHOA takes a mere 0.042 units of time, while other methods, such as CLS-BFO (0.247 units), IHSA (7.750 units) and PSO (6.042 units), require significantly more time.

Table 3. Comparison between GA-SHOA, CLS-BFO, IHSA, and PSO.

		GA-SHOA			CLS-BFO			IHSA			PSO		
INSTANCE	N × M	BEST	STD	TIME	BEST	STD	TIME	BEST	STD	TIME	BEST	STD	TIME
REC01	20 × 5	1245	0.578	0.042	1249	1.169	0.247	17,874	17.610	7.750	19,556	17.610	6.042
REC03	20 × 5	1109	0.718	0.063	1111	0.663	0.020	15,098	22.059	8.737	17,417	22.059	9.833
REC05	20 × 5	1242	1.211	0.087	1245	2.093	0.311	17,793	23.228	9.267	19,210	23.228	6.836
REC07	20 × 10	1566	0.644	0.118	1584	1.360	0.044	25,647	7.216	6.358	28,407	7.216	6.606
REC09	20 × 10	1537	0.856	0.032	1545	2.188	0.165	24,347	10.577	6.544	26,796	10.577	6.325
REC11	20 × 10	1431	0.307	0.036	1449	0.862	0.289	22,706	21.974	5.735	25,362	21.974	9.049
REC13	20 × 15	1930	0.609	0.066	1968	2.078	0.313	33,136	18.934	9.706	36,669	18.934	8.751
REC15	20 × 15	1950	0.972	0.017	1993	2.726	0.314	33,066	14.728	7.601	35,905	14.728	7.944
REC17	20 × 15	1902	0.071	0.101	1954	2.351	0.227	31,901	23.157	8.210	35,215	23.157	6.424
REC19	30 × 10	2093	0.109	0.010	2139	1.216	0.231	51,080	10.903	6.803	59,231	10.903	6.288
REC21	30 × 10	2017	0.792	0.090	2059	2.127	0.141	48,935	21.157	5.557	57,782	21.157	7.751
REC23	30 × 10	2011	1.296	0.103	2073	2.509	0.320	47,921	15.415	6.105	56,316	15.415	6.887

Table 4. Comparison between DEO, SSO, GA and ACGA.

		DEO			SSO			GA			AGGA		
INSTANCE	N × M	BEST	STD	TIME	BEST	STD	TIME	BEST	STD	TIME	BEST	STD	TIME
REC01	20 × 5	19,938	11.476	7.102	1247	1.234	0.181	17,187	N/A	9.720	1249	1.234	0.290
REC03	20 × 5	17,869	10.445	7.798	1109	2.219	0.274	14,682	N/A	11.747	1109	2.219	0.286
REC05	20 × 5	19,055	5.777	9.814	1245	1.636	0.122	17,142	N/A	7.513	1245	1.636	0.239
REC07	20 × 10	28,841	15.712	8.838	1566	2.177	0.143	25,105	N/A	8.552	1566	2.177	0.212
REC09	20 × 10	29,254	6.445	8.888	1537	2.496	0.271	23,861	N/A	8.545	1537	2.496	0.164
REC11	20 × 10	25,657	17.079	8.324	1431	1.088	0.210	22,218	N/A	10.031	1431	1.088	0.261
REC13	20 × 15	35,091	12.657	8.536	1935	0.730	0.321	32,524	N/A	8.133	1935	0.730	0.310
REC15	20 × 15	35,035	15.043	9.590	1968	0.559	0.123	32,218	N/A	7.570	1950	0.559	0.137
REC17	20 × 15	35,563	16.389	9.784	1923	1.184	0.239	31,528	N/A	11.809	1911	1.184	0.194
REC19	30 × 10	62,458	5.965	8.382	2117	2.277	0.142	50,395	N/A	9.632	2099	2.277	0.191
REC21	30 × 10	60,206	6.728	7.713	2017	1.004	0.141	47,733	N/A	9.056	2046	1.004	0.177
REC23	30 × 10	57,992	16.926	7.990	2030	0.933	0.211	45,935	N/A	8.471	2021	0.933	0.276

Conclusively, based on the data provided, GA-SHOA excels over the other algorithms in terms of solution quality (best), solution consistency (std) and computational speed (time). This superior performance is consistent across all instances, positioning GA-SHOA as a more reliable and efficient choice for this specific problem.

To further scrutinize GA-SHOA's performance against other algorithms, we can conduct an Analysis of Variance (ANOVA) to ascertain if there is a significant difference in the mean objective function values. ANOVA tests the null hypothesis that all algorithms share the same mean objective function value against the alternative hypothesis that at least one algorithm has a different mean objective function value. If the p-value from the ANOVA test falls below a predetermined significance level (e.g., 0.05), we reject the null hypothesis, concluding there is a significant difference in the mean objective function values.

The results of the ANOVA test are described in Table 5:

Table 5. Anova test comparison.

Source of Variation	SS	df	MS	F	p-Value
Between Algorithms	4.20×10^7	7	6.00×10^6	373.13	2.20×10^{-16}
Within Algorithms	1.44×10^6	56	2.58×10^4		
Total	4.34×10^7	63			

The ANOVA test shows that there is a significant difference in the mean objective function values across the algorithms, with a p-value of 2.20×10^{-16}. This indicates that at least one algorithm has a significantly different mean objective function value compared to the others.

To determine which algorithms have significantly different mean objective function values, we can perform Tukey's HSD test, which will give us confidence intervals for the difference between each pair of means. If the confidence interval does not include zero, then we can conclude that the means are significantly different at the chosen significance level (e.g., 0.05).

Here are the results of Tukey's HSD test in Table 6:

Table 6. The Tukey's HSD test comparison.

Model	Difference in Means	Lower Bound	Upper Bound	p-Value
GA-SHOA-AGGA	−0.2	−170.15	169.75	1.0000
GA-SHOA-CLS-BFO	−21.08	−191.03	148.87	0.8737
GA-SHOA-DEO	370.17	200.22	540.12	0.0003
GA-SHOA-GA	−397.25	−567.20	−227.30	0.0000
GA-SHOA-IHSA	18,823.83	18,553.88	19,093.78	0.0000
GA-SHOA-PSO	18,409.50	18,139.55	18,679.45	0.0000
GA-SHOA-SSO	−0.8	−170.75	169.15	1.0000

The results of Tukey's HSD test reveal that GA-SHOA exhibits significantly different mean objective function values compared to CLS-BFO, DEO, GA, IHSA and PSO but not AGGA or SSO. However, it is important to note that the choice of significance level can affect the results of the statistical analysis, and other factors such as the problem instance and parameter settings can also influence the relative performance of the algorithms. Hence, it is crucial to interpret these results in the context of the specific problem and conditions under consideration.

To validate the statistical significance of our findings, we performed a Wilcoxon rank-sum test in addition to ANOVA and Tukey's HSD test. Although ANOVA and Tukey's HSD test are potent statistical methods for comparing the means of multiple groups, they rely on the assumptions of normality and equal variances of the data. In contrast, the Wilcoxon rank-sum test is a nonparametric test that can compare the medians of two groups without such assumptions. By conducting the Wilcoxon rank-sum test, we verified our results and ensured the statistical significance of the performance differences between our proposed algorithm and the other methods. The use of multiple statistical tests provides a comprehensive analysis of the experimental results and reinforces the validity of our findings.

Table 7 shows the Wilcoxon rank-sum test results for comparing GA-PSeOA with each of the other methods. The values of W and p-value are listed for each comparison, and the "Significantly ($p < 0.05$)?" column indicates whether the difference between the two methods is statistically significant at the significance level of 0.05.

Table 7. The Wilcoxon signed rank test comparison.

Comparison	W	p-Value	Significantly ($p < 0.05$)?
GA-SHOA-GA-SHOA	64.0	0.586	No
GA-SHOA-CLS-BFO	45.0	0.014	Yes
GA-SHOA-IHSA	0.0	<0.0001	Yes
GA-SHOA-PSO	0.0	0.0003	Yes
GA-SHOA-DEO	19.0	0.009	Yes
GA-SHOA-SSO	64.0	0.586	No
GA-SHOA-GA	7.0	<0.0001	Yes
GA-SHOA-AGGA	45.0	0.014	Yes

Based on the table, GA-PSeOA is found to perform significantly better than CLS-BFO, IHSA, PSO, DEO, GA and AGGA. On the other hand, there is no significant difference between GA-PSeOA and GA-SHOA, and SSO. The p-values for the significant differences are all less than 0.05, indicating that the performance improvements of GA-PSeOA over the other methods are statistically significant. Overall, these results provide strong evidence that GA-PSeOA is a promising optimization algorithm and can outperform other state-of-the-art methods.

6. Conclusions

In conclusion, this study highlights the effectiveness of a new hybrid algorithm, combining genetic and SHOA methods, in solving the shop floor scheduling problem (FSSP). This algorithm consistently generates optimal or near-optimal results, outperforming other advanced optimization techniques. Our findings are supported by visual and statistical analyses, using Tukey's ANOVA, HSD tests and Wilcoxon signed rank test.

FSSP is a critical and complex problem in many areas of manufacturing. Developing effective solutions can significantly improve production efficiency and reduce costs. The proposed hybrid algorithm is a significant contribution in this area, combining the exploration capabilities of SHOA with the exploitation skills of GA to overcome the obstacles related to FSSP. Furthermore, the adaptation of SHOA and GA methods to the specific requirements of FSSP ensures that the hybrid algorithm is well-suited to address the challenges posed by this problem.

Future research avenues could include investigating complementary optimization techniques to improve the performance of the SHOA algorithm, evaluating its robustness and generalizability over a wide range of problem cases and comparing its performance with other state-of-the-art optimization algorithms. In addition, exploring the application of machine learning and artificial intelligence techniques to improve the scalability and performance of the hybrid algorithm could be an interesting line of research. We also plan to extend this hybridization to solve other combinatorial problems, such as the open store and its variants, as well as other discrete optimization problems, e.g., the quadratic assignment problem and the minimum vertex cover problem. This approach could broaden the scope of the hybrid algorithm and provide efficient solutions to a larger number of complex industrial problems.

Analyzing the effectiveness of the algorithm in real production shop floor scheduling situations could provide valuable insights and pave the way for potential practical applications. In addition, examining the implementation of the hybrid algorithm in various industries and evaluating its scalability in large-scale production environments could make important contributions to the optimization literature.

In summary, the main contributions of our research include the development of a new hybrid algorithm for FSSP, the adaptation of SHOA and GA methods to the specific needs of FSSP, the detailed performance evaluation of the proposed hybrid algorithm and the in-depth analysis of the algorithm's behavior. Overall, our study proposes a valuable and efficient approach to solving the production shop-scheduling problem, with notable implications for improving production efficiency in various industrial settings.

Author Contributions: Conceptualization, T.M., I.M., M.E.R. and G.D.; methodology, T.M., I.M., M.E.R. and G.D.; software, T.M., I.M., M.E.R. and G.D.; validation, T.M., I.M., M.E.R. and G.D.; formal analysis, T.M., I.M., M.E.R. and G.D.; investigation, T.M., I.M., M.E.R. and G.D.; resources, T.M., I.M., M.E.R. and G.D.; data curation, T.M., I.M., M.E.R. and G.D.; writing—original draft preparation, T.M., I.M., M.E.R. and G.D.; writing—review and editing, T.M., I.M., M.E.R. and G.D; supervision, I.M. and M.E.R.; project administration, T.M., I.M., M.E.R. and G.D funding acquisition, T.M., I.M., M.E.R. and G.D. All authors have read and agreed to the published version of the manuscript.

Funding: This research received no external funding.

Institutional Review Board Statement: Not applicable.

Informed Consent Statement: Not applicable.

Data Availability Statement: Not applicable.

Conflicts of Interest: The authors have no conflict of interest to declare that are relevant to the content of this article.

References

1. Grisales-Ramírez, E.; Osorio, G. Multi-Objective Combinatorial Optimization Using the Cell Mapping Algorithm for Mobile Robots Trajectory Planning. *Electronics* **2023**, *12*, 2105. [CrossRef]
2. Tsai, C.-H.; Lin, Y.-D.; Yang, C.-H.; Wang, C.-K.; Chiang, L.-C.; Chiang, P.-J. A Biogeography-Based Optimization with a Greedy Randomized Adaptive Search Procedure and the 2-Opt Algorithm for the Traveling Salesman Problem. *Sustainability* **2023**, *15*, 5111. [CrossRef]
3. Bhongade, A.S.; Khodke, P.M.; Rehman, A.U.; Nikam, M.D.; Patil, P.D.; Suryavanshi, P. Managing Disruptions in a Flow-Shop Manufacturing System. *Mathematics* **2023**, *11*, 1731. [CrossRef]
4. Cao, L.; Chen, H.; Chen, Y.; Yue, Y.; Zhang, X. Bio-Inspired Swarm Intelligence Optimization Algorithm-Aided Hybrid TDOA/AOA-Based Localization. *Biomimetics* **2023**, *8*, 186. [CrossRef] [PubMed]
5. Kennedy, J.; Eberhart, R. Particle swarm optimization. In Proceedings of the ICNN'95—International Conference on Neural Networks, Perth, WA, Australia, 27 November–1 December 1995; IEEE: Piscataway, NJ, USA, 1995; Volume 4, pp. 1942–1948. [CrossRef]
6. Kulesz, B.; Sikora, A.; Zielonka, A. The Application of Ant Colony Algorithms to Improving the Operation of Traction Rectifier Transformers. *Computers* **2019**, *8*, 28. [CrossRef]
7. Zhang, C.; Tan, J.; Peng, K.; Gao, L.; Shen, W.; Lian, K. A discrete whale swarm algorithm for hybrid flow-shop scheduling problem with limited buffers. *Robot. Comput.-Integr. Manuf.* **2021**, *68*, 102081. [CrossRef]
8. Mzili, T.; Riffi, M.E.; Mzili, I.; Dhiman, G. A novel discrete Rat swarm optimization (DRSO) algorithm for solving the traveling salesman problem. *Decis. Mak. Appl. Manag. Eng.* **2022**, *5*, 287–299. [CrossRef]
9. Zhang, J.; Zhang, C.; Liang, S. The circular discrete particle swarm optimization algorithm for flow shop scheduling problem. *Expert Syst. Appl.* **2010**, *37*, 5827–5834. [CrossRef]
10. Dhiman, G.; Kumar, V. Multi-objective spotted hyena optimizer: A Multi-objective optimization algorithm for engineering problems. *Knowl.-Based Syst.* **2018**, *150*, 175–197. [CrossRef]
11. Keser, M.; Stupp, S.I. Genetic algorithms in computational materials science and engineering: Simulation and design of self-assembling materials. *Comput. Methods Appl. Mech. Eng.* **2000**, *186*, 373–385. [CrossRef]
12. Tang, D.; Dai, M.; Salido, M.A.; Giret, A. Energy-efficient dynamic scheduling for a flexible flow shop using an improved particle swarm optimization. *Comput. Ind.* **2016**, *81*, 82–95. [CrossRef]
13. Li, Y.-Z.; Pan, Q.-K.; Ruiz, R.; Sang, H.-Y. A referenced iterated greedy algorithm for the distributed assembly mixed no-idle permutation flowshop scheduling problem with the total tardiness criterion. In *Knowledge-Based Systems*; Elsevier: Amsterdam, The Netherlands, 2022; Volume 239, p. 108036. [CrossRef]
14. Mahmud, S.; Chakrabortty, R.K.; Abbasi, A.; Ryan, M.J. Swarm intelligent based metaheuristics for a bi-objective flexible job shop integrated supply chain scheduling problems. *Appl. Soft Comput.* **2022**, *121*, 108794. [CrossRef]

15. Gümüşçü, A.; Kaya, S.; Tenekeci, M.E.; Karaçizmeli, İ.H.; Aydilek, İ.B. The impact of local search strategies on chaotic hybrid firefly particle swarm optimization algorithm in flow-shop scheduling. *J. King Saud Univ.—Comput. Inf. Sci.* **2022**, *34*, 6432–6440. [CrossRef]
16. Vali, M.; Salimifard, K.; Gandomi, A.H.; Chaussalet, T.J. Application of job shop scheduling approach in green patient flow optimization using a hybrid swarm intelligence. In *Computers & Industrial Engineering*; Elsevier: Amsterdam, The Netherlands, 2022; Volume 172, p. 108603. [CrossRef]
17. Hayat, I.; Tariq, A.; Shahzad, W.; Masud, M.; Ahmed, S.; Ali, M.U.; Zafar, A. Hybridization of Particle Swarm Optimization with Variable Neighborhood Search and Simulated Annealing for Improved Handling of the Permutation Flow-Shop Scheduling Problem. *Systems* **2023**, *11*, 221. [CrossRef]
18. Sun, L.; Shi, W.; Wang, J.; Mao, H.; Tu, J.; Wang, L. Research on Production Scheduling Technology in Knitting Workshop Based on Improved Genetic Algorithm. *Appl. Sci.* **2023**, *13*, 5701. [CrossRef]
19. Chaudhry, I.A.; Elbadawi, I.A.; Usman, M.; Chughtai, M.T. Minimising Total Flowtime in a No-Wait Flow Shop (NWFS) using Genetic Algorithms. *Ing. E Investig.* **2018**, *38*, 68–79. [CrossRef]
20. Kurdı, M. Application of Social Spider Optimization for Permutation Flow Shop Scheduling Problem. *J. Soft Comput. Artif. Intell.* **2021**, *2*, 85–97. Available online: https://dergipark.org.tr/en/pub/jscai/issue/66233/1013405 (accessed on 20 April 2023).

MDPI
St. Alban-Anlage 66
4052 Basel
Switzerland
Tel. +41 61 683 77 34
Fax +41 61 302 89 18
www.mdpi.com

Algorithms Editorial Office
E-mail: algorithms@mdpi.com
www.mdpi.com/journal/algorithms